IN SEARCH OF CHURCHILL

THE CHURCHILL BIOGRAPHY

Volume I: Youth 1874–1900 by Randolph S. Churchill
Volume I: Companion (in two parts)
Volume II: Young Statesman 1900–1914 by Randolph S. Churchill
Volume II: Companion ((in two parts)
Volume III: 1914–1916 by Martin Gilbert
Volume III Companion (in two parts)
Volume IV: 1917–1922 by Martin Gilbert
Volume IV: Companion (in two parts)
Volume V: 1922–1939 by Martin Gilbert
Volume V: Companion 'The Exchequer Years' 1922–1929
Volume V: Companion 'The Wilderness Years' 1929–1935
Volume V: Companion 'The Coming of War' 1936–1939
Volume VI: 'Finest Hour' 1939 – 1941 by Martin Gilbert
Volume VI Companion 'At the Admiralty' 1939–1940
Volume VII 'Road to Victory' 1941–1945 by Martin Gilbert
Volume VIII 'Never Despair' 1945–1965 by Martin Gilbert

OTHER BOOKS BY MARTIN GILBERT

The Appeasers (with Richard Gott)
The European Powers, 1900–1945
The Roots of Appeasement
Atlas of British Charities
Recent History Atlas
American History Atlas
Jewish History Atlas
First World War Atlas
Russian History Atlas
The Arab-Israeli Conflict: Its History in Maps
Sir Horace Rumbold: Portrait of a Diplomat
Churchill: A Photographic Portrait
Jerusalem Illustrated History Atlas
Jerusalem: Rebirth of a City
Exile and Return: The Struggle for Jewish Statehood
Children's Illustrated Bible Atlas
Auschwitz and the Allies
Atlas of the Holocaust
The Jews of Hope: the Plight of Soviet Jewry Today
Shcharansky: Hero of Our Time
The Holocaust: The Jewish Tragedy
Second World War
Churchill: A Life

EDITIONS OF DOCUMENTS

Britain and Germany Between the Wars
Plough My Own Furrow: The Life of Lord Allen of Hurtwood
Servant of India: Diaries of the Viceroy's Private Secretary, 1905–1910

IN SEARCH OF
CHURCHILL

A historian's journey

MARTIN GILBERT

HarperCollins*Publishers*

HarperCollins*Publishers*
77–85 Fulham Palace Road
Hammersmith, London W6 8JB

Published by HarperCollinsPublishers 1994

9 8 7 6 5 4 3 2 1

A catalogue record for this book is
available from the British Library

ISBN 0 00 215356 4

Set in Linotron Janson by
Rowland Phototypesetting Ltd,
Bury St Edmunds, Suffolk

Printed in Great Britain by
HarperCollinsManufacturing Glasgow

CONTENTS

LIST OF ILLUSTRATIONS

LIST OF MAPS

PHOTOGRAPHIC CREDITS

I am grateful to those who, over the years, have lent me photographs or given me permission to use photographs of which they are the copyright holders. For this volume I would like to thank Yusuf Karsh (front cover), United Press International (photograph 1), Paul Maze (5), Mark Cousins (7), Major-General Sir Edmund Hakewill Smith (9), Avis Napier-Clavering (10), John Harvey (12), Sir Desmond Morton (13), Churchill College, Cambridge (140), Maurice Ashley (15), Charles Torr Anderson (16), Ava, Viscountess Waverley (17), *Time Life* (18 and upper back top cover), Press Association (21, 22), Professor William E. Beatty (24), Lady Sargant (25), *Scotsman* (26), Mrs Airlie Madden (27), George Rance (28), Viscount Montgomery of Alamein (29), Viscount Alexander of Tunis (30), Stefan Lorant (31), *Picture Post* (32), and David Gilbert (33, 34, 35, 36, 37 and lower back cover). I have also used two of my own photographs (2, 6).

PREFACE

This book traces some of my travels and discoveries in search of Churchill since 1962. The process of finding out about any historical character can be a surprising one. All biographers who embark on the search find themselves caught up in many adventures and are continually amazed by the diverse ways in which they reach their goal of understanding. In this book I share some of my experiences, in the hope that they may be of interest or amusement, and that something further will emerge from them of the character, struggles and achievements of Churchill himself.

Innumerable people play a part in the quest for a single character. Not a week has gone by since I began my work when I have not written to some individual or archive to seek help on a point of detail. Their responses have seldom failed me. Many people shared their knowledge with me, or helped to elucidate matters that had puzzled me.

Among the objects of my research were several aspects of Churchill's supposed character that have become the focus of considerable speculation or dogma: among them his depressions, his drinking, his love of war, his not infrequent roughness to his staff and secretaries, and the lust for adventure that led to the Dardanelles. There were also topics that people expressed curiosity about, including his sources of secret information during the wilderness years in the 1930s, and his painting. In addition, there were relatively unknown aspects of his character that emerged as I worked: for instance his generosity, his love of nature and his sense of fun.

My own journey began in 1962 when I became a research assistant to Churchill's son Randolph, who had just embarked on his father's biography. After Randolph's death in 1968 I was asked to continue his work and was fortunate to be able to call, as he had done, upon research help. One of my researchers, Susie Sacher stayed on: we were married and worked side by side on every file of the Churchill papers until the eighth volume, *Never Despair*, was completed in 1988. Work on another aspect of the biography begun by Randolph, the Churchill document volumes, continues. The *At The Admiralty* document volume, covering September 1939 to May 1940, was published in 1993.

Among those who helped with comments and advice for this book, or who filled factual gaps large and small, were Jonathan Aitken, Alex Allan, Jean Broome, Grace Hamblin, Sir John Peck, Tom Hartman, Jo Countess of Onslow, Adam Sisman, Edward Thomas and Barbara Twigg.

For several of my Churchill volumes, as also for this book, I was fortunate to be able to enlist the help of Adam O'Riordan, a master grammarian with an eagle eye for error and infelicities, who scrutinized my chapters and saved me from innumerable pitfalls of style and grammar. His death, while this book was being printed, was a great personal sadness.

Having read many hundreds of recollections, I never thought I would write my own. This book owes its origin to the friendship and enthusiasm of Carol O'Brien, then at Collins publishing house, who over several years encouraged me to tell the story of the research trail. More recently, Stuart Proffitt of HarperCollins has been a fount of welcome enthusiasm and wise advice, as has Rebecca Wilson, who guided the book through the press.

The story told in these pages is a personal journey, but it could not have been told without the unstinting help of those of Churchill's contemporaries who, when I approached them, shared with me their recollections, letters, diaries and documents. Many of the stories that I recount derived from the goodwill of those who responded to a stranger to whom they were prepared to entrust their precious memories and materials, for the sake of portraying Winston Churchill. I have acknowledged their help in successive volumes of the biography.

There have been a number of times during the past twenty-five years when different individuals have claimed, in a published memoir or in private conversation, that it was they who had been closest to Churchill, and had known him best, at some particular period. Sometimes these claims were widely publicized on the lecture circuit and on television. But as one former civil servant, who did indeed work closely with Churchill for nearly six years, wrote to me, 'The memory of Winston is nobody's monopoly!' My own search not only bears out this view, but was much enriched by it.

Almost three decades have passed since Churchill's death. During those years many dozens of individuals have engrossed me in hundreds of hours of talk and correspondence, to ensure that many details of his remarkable and versatile life were saved for posterity. Many gems have emerged, in archives and in conversation, during the course of my journey. This book is the story of some of that journey's highlights.

Martin Gilbert
Merton College, Oxford
25 November 1993

I

First Steps

In the summer of 1940 my father, who was then serving with an anti-aircraft gun battery on Hampstead Heath, took advantage of a British Government scheme to send children across the Atlantic to safety. My parents were not well off, and it seemed to them that I would be better cared for there. That July, a month after the fall of France, when the German Army was on the cliffs between Calais and Boulogne, I sailed in the care of an aunt with several hundred other children, to Canada. Our boat, the *Duchess of Bedford*, was in a convoy of fifty ships. In mid-Atlantic, after the destroyer escort had turned back, the convoy was attacked and five ships were sunk by the Germans. The *Duchess of Bedford* sailed on safely, via the iceberg-dotted sea off Labrador, to Quebec. Those icebergs, marvellous for a child to behold, are among my first memories. Shortly afterwards another boat with child evacuees on board, the *City of Benares*, was sunk and seventy-seven children drowned. The scheme was then abandoned.

I was only three years old. Many years later I learned that at the time of the sailing of the *Duchess of Bedford* Churchill had been asked by the organizers of the scheme to give the oldest child a letter to Mackenzie King, the Canadian Prime Minister, thanking him for receiving us. He was so opposed to any children being evacuated to Canada (he saw it as a 'scuttle') that he refused to write the letter, telling the minister concerned: 'I will not send any message through the eldest child, or through the youngest child either.' Thus I missed the chance to hold a Churchill letter in my hands, and to deliver it, though there were, I suppose, several children on board even younger than myself.

I hated Canada, not the country but the separation from my parents, and while the war was still being fought, I returned to

Britain. It was Churchill himself, I later learned, who had noted, in his regular scrutiny of ships in transit and in port, that the ocean liner *Mauretania*, then a troopship, was sailing from New York in the summer of 1944 with several hundred empty berths. He at once suggested that several hundred children be rounded up and brought back. As a result of his intervention I found myself all alone, with an identification tag round my neck, on the night train from Toronto to New York, arriving bewildered in the yawning cavern of Grand Central Station, clutching my brand new Canadian passport ('valid duration war') and standing in a long, slow-moving line by the quayside on a sweltering New York summer afternoon. I did not know, as we later steamed across the Atlantic towards Liverpool, that Churchill had specifically asked the Admiralty to make sure (amidst his many other cares in the immediate aftermath of the Normandy landings) that there were enough lifeboats on board for all the extra children. All that I can recall was a game with the American troops on board, throwing the lifejackets in the air and trying to catch them before they sailed over the side and into the sea.

Liverpool was a shock. I had never seen bombed buildings before: acres of them. As the train left for London, I stood with my eyes glued to the sight of so much destruction. I reached the capital just in time to hear the first V-bombs explode, before being taken by my parents to the safety of North Wales. It was there, on 8 May 1945, that I first heard Churchill speak on the wireless, announcing the victory, though I am ashamed to say that what interested me and my fellow schoolboys at that moment was not the Great Man's speech, but the speech made by George VI: we wanted to hear the King's well-known stutter.

At the end of the war, at the age of nine, I was sent to boarding school in London: my parents did not have enough space for me in their tiny flat. Several of my masters were keen historians. One of them, A.P. White, who had fought in the First World War, would march up and down with a broomstick over his shoulder in place of a rifle, singing the roundhead and cavalier songs of the Civil War. Another, Tommy Fox, encouraged me to find answers to the alleged wonders of communism. One of my first essays for him was a sustained defence of democracy. He also sent me, when I was fifteen, to the Whitestone pond at Hampstead, to challenge the views of the various speakers who then used the pond as an alternative to Hyde Park Corner. On one occasion I answered the anarchist, who was also an atheist, not verbally, but by writing him a five- or six-page poem, setting out what I regarded as the folly of his views. A third master, Alan Palmer, had himself begun to write books on recent history. He made it clear that history was not a 'finished book', a tablet of stone, an immutable science of the known and the understood, but a living and expanding world of discovery. He turned even the dullest corners of diplomatic history into a detective story. It was at his lessons that I decided I wanted to write history.

At school, on 25 October 1951, I celebrated my fifteenth birthday. It was the day Britain went to the polls and Churchill, having been dismissed by the electorate in 1945, was now returned to power at the head of a Conservative peacetime government. He was seventy-six years old, and had first been elected to the House of Commons fifty years earlier.

The election campaign had been a hard-fought one, with repercussions even in the classroom. I had been amazed by the divergence of views among my masters as to Churchill's worth. To some he was a hero against whom no word could be spoken, and whose return as Prime Minister was essential for the nation. To others he was a monster who ought long ago to have been shot, and should now at least be pensioned off, never to return to political life. Of course I had no means of knowing on what these conflicting views were based, or which reflected reality.

In April 1955 I left school. A few days later, and a few days before going into the army, curiosity took me to 10 Downing Street, where I stood on the pavement opposite the front door (the street was open to the public then) and watched with a surprisingly small crowd, mostly journalists and photographers, as Churchill emerged to say goodnight to Queen Elizabeth, his Sovereign, in the reign of whose great-great grandmother he had received his commission in the army. This was Churchill's last official dinner before leaving the stage of history which he had dominated for more than half a century. I remember being struck by how short he was.

A few days after this farewell, of which I had been a teenage witness, Churchill flew to Sicily in search of a place in the sun where he could paint. I went to an army camp in Wiltshire to train as an

3

infantryman. I had hoped to go from school to Oxford, but my college was emphatic that once one had passed the scholarship exam, one must serve one's two years in khaki. My father had hoped that I would follow his footsteps in the jewellery trade, and had even begun to teach me how to turn a small lump of gold into a ring, but it was to university that I wanted to go, and the army was the stepping-stone.

As a conscript, doing my basic infantry training with the Wiltshire Regiment, my curiosity about Churchill grew even stronger when I found among the young soldiers with whom I shared my first barrack-room the same sharp division of opinion that I had found among my masters at school. For some of these seventeen-year-olds he was a hero, for others an ogre.

Chance, or a jackdaw mentality, has preserved a green foolscap notebook in which I wrote down the opinions of those in my first barrack-room, sixteen fellow National Servicemen, most of whom had left school at the age of fifteen. 'The greatest man of the century,' one recruit, a coach-painter in civilian life told me, but after I asked for an example of his greatness he added, 'I have not studied his career.' Another view, equally emphatic, was from a former joiner: 'I detest him. The ordinary man won the war.' This was supplemented from the lumberjack in another bed who told me: 'A warmonger, he supplied the Germans with arms and equipment before 1939. He lined his pockets in 1914–18.'

This last myth, of Churchill's First World War financial dishonesty and speculation, had an ancient origin, but I was only to find out about that many years later.*

From the army I went to Oxford, where the curriculum of 1957 did not lend itself to knowing more about Winston Churchill. During the first year, I and my fellow history undergraduates laboured long hours in the marshes of East Anglia and on the hill ground of Wessex, learning about the departing Romans, and examining the habits and characteristics of the arriving Angles, Saxons, Jutes, Danes, Vikings and Normans. Leaders other than Churchill, kings nicknamed the Unready, the Redhead, the Bold, the Hunchback and the Foolish, were our daily diet. In the second year it was the

---

* I have given an account of this episode in the chapter 'Inkwells of Gold'.

constitutional struggles between Crown and Commonwealth that engaged our attention, with Charles I and Cromwell competing for allegiance, or at least for understanding. Churchill's historical writings about the Civil War and its aftermath did not appear on any reading list. Once, when I mentioned them, I was given the distinct impression by one of my tutors that Churchill was as deplorable a historian as he had been a politician.

In my third year at Oxford we advanced into Churchill's century, reaching the outbreak of the Second World War. Not once did my tutors suggest that Churchill's part in national or international events between 1900 and 1939 had any particular importance, let alone relevance, to my work. A dozen episodes which he had so stamped with his arguments and his personality were described without him. The appeasement debate in which he had taken a leading part was carried on, in my tutorials at least, without him making any contribution. I even did a special project on the British discovery and exploitation of oil in Persia in the first two decades of the century, but my tutor, A.J.P. Taylor, who always enjoyed shocking his pupils with information they had overlooked, made no reference to Churchill's purchase for the government, on the eve of war in 1914, of the majority shareholding of the Anglo-Persian Oil Company. This prescient act secured for the Royal Navy the fuel oil vital for its warships, and made a handsome profit for the Exchequer in addition.

Looking back over his career, this was one of the acts of which Churchill was most proud: in a letter to his wife written in his eighties, he recalled the young civil servant, Richard Hopkins, who had done the hard work of technical preparation for the purchase. I remember how pleased I was to have come across this reference. The occasion was one of Churchill's first meetings with the Greek shipping magnate Aristotle Onassis. 'The conversation turned on politics and Oil,' Churchill told his wife Clementine. 'I reminded him that I had bought the Anglo-Persian for the Admiralty forty or fifty years ago, and made a good profit for the British Government, about 3 or 4 millions! He said he knew all about it. All this reminded me of poor Hopkins – but I think we did it together. I enjoy the credit.'

In 1960 I began graduate work at St Antony's College, Oxford, first on the post-1917 struggle for power in the Ukraine, then on

British rule in India. I have since learned that Churchill had rather a lot to say on both, and had taken a lead in policies and controversies regarding both. Yet neither of my supervisors, both of them deeply versed in their subjects, directed me towards any of his writings, either autobiographical or historical. When, in 1962, Randolph Churchill invited me to join his research team on his father's biography, my knowledge of Churchill was abysmal. It was probably not nil. But it was not very far from nil.

The path to Randolph's door was a strange one. Having written my very first book, *The Appeasers*, and done so with my first pupil, Richard Gott, but before it had been published, I cast about for something to do on my own. I hit upon the idea of editing a book of letters written between 1933 and 1939 by individual English men and women who had visited Nazi Germany during those years: their private letters and diary extracts that would reveal the moods, hopes and fears of the time. I was going to call it *English Eyes on Germany* (I have the draft version with me still).

In search of unpublished material, I asked Lady Diana Cooper, whose husband Duff had resigned from Neville Chamberlain's Government in October 1938 in protest against the Munich Agreement, if she had any private letters that I might look at. She invited me to visit her and was enthusiastic in support of my idea, keen to show just how anguished and far-sighted her Duff had been. As he was one of the 'heroes' of *The Appeasers*, it was not hard for me to agree with her. During our talk she said: 'You really ought to ask Randolph Churchill to help you. He was not only Winston's son. He was a journalist in his own right, he visited Germany several times during the Nazi era, and he was, and is, a lively writer. His letters would be worth publishing.'

Diana Cooper told me that she would write to Randolph, asking him to see me. She did so. Her letter, which he later showed me, read: 'Darling Randy, Here is Martin Gilbert, an interesting researching historian young man, who loves Duff and hates the Coroner. He is full of zeal to set history right. Do see him.' The Coroner in her letter was Neville Chamberlain.

Randolph sent me a letter inviting me to his home in Suffolk. 'I am nearly always here,' he wrote. But I was extremely reluctant to take up his offer to visit him. I had once seen him at the bar of the

Randolph Hotel in Oxford, apparently drunk and certainly loud-mouthed. I had heard stories of his extreme right-wing attitudes, bordering, it was said, on the Fascist. I was busy with my new book, had many other people to see, had begun to find letters in all sorts of unexpected places, and was working my way through the back-numbers of the correspondence columns of various newspapers. Having spent a pleasant afternoon with Arnold Toynbee, in which he recalled his own years in Germany before the war and gave me some letters that he had written at the time to his sister, I saw no particular point in having what might prove to be an unpleasant evening with Randolph Churchill. 'He'll just shout and scream at you,' one friend told me. I had no reason to disagree.

The day came when I succumbed to Randolph's third or fourth telegram asking me when I was going to visit him. It was in March 1962. I travelled by train from Oxford to London, crossed London from Paddington to Liverpool Street, and took the train to Man-ningtree, on the Essex-Suffolk border. It was a journey that I was to make many times, but I shall never forget that first venture into the unknown. I was very nervous and, as the train pulled out of Col-chester, the last station before Manningtree, I wondered if I were doing the right thing. At Manningtree station I was almost the only person to get off.

The train pulled away across the River Stour and into Suffolk. I was alone on the platform. In the station forecourt was a single car, and next to it a dark-suited driver. He greeted me with what seemed a friendly smile, and drove me along narrow lanes. I said nothing and could think of nothing to say. We drove through Constable country, not far from the Mill at Flatford. Reaching the rambling village of East Bergholt we pulled into the drive-way of a large eighteenth-century house. This was Stour, to which I had been bidden. The driver ushered me through the front door and then into a spacious drawing-room.

There was Randolph, in a deep arm chair, out of which he rose slowly: a large, rather cumbersome man, with a somewhat pasty, battered-looking face, ill-fitting trousers which he hitched up even as he was rising from his chair, and the look of an elderly patriarch (he was my age as I write these words). The effect of this slightly alarming appearance was quickly dispelled: he was full of charm, had an engaging twinkle in his eye, and expressed his appreciation that I had made the long journey from Oxford: 'It was kind of you to come.'

There followed a question. Had I bought an *Evening Standard* at Liverpool Street? No, I had not, I replied. He seemed momentarily put out, and I sensed that I had somehow fallen below his expectations, at least on the matter of buying an evening newspaper. Later I learned always to do so, or to risk a serious charge of neglect of duty, stupidity, idleness, or all three. He was a voracious reader, and having been a journalist since the 1930s, had an incredible appetite for news, both domestic and international. He had been a Member of Parliament during the war, and had fought and lost six parliamentary elections. Politics was in his blood. He could never have enough of political gossip: his large black loose-leaved telephone book, which he often used, was a directory of the office and home telephone numbers of all those who ruled Britain, or aspired to do so. Once, angered when his daughter Arabella, who was then in Paris, told him she had not yet received a letter he had sent her a week earlier, he dialled (it was then well after midnight) the home telephone number of the Postmaster-General, and demanded to know why it was taking so long for letters to cross the Channel. I was asked to listen in on the other line, and take notes. The hapless minister, Tony Wedgwood Benn, promised to look into the matter when he got to his Ministry in the morning.

At first glance I was surprised by the opulence of Randolph's house, its plush wallpaper and large rooms. But it was no museum: there were books everywhere, and files, and newspapers galore. After asking about the *Evening Standard*, Randolph turned to the driver who had brought me from the station and said to him: 'Our guest can sleep in Winston's room.' I assumed that this was the room his father used when he visited, not knowing that his father had only visited the house once, some years earlier, and that the 'Winston' in question was Randolph's son, then an undergraduate at Oxford. I was tremendously excited at the idea of sleeping in the Great Man's room, and surprised, when taken up to it, to find how pokey it was.

At dinner that first night I was confronted for the first two courses by three dishes that I had never eaten before, gulls' eggs and hare paté to start with, then Jerusalem artichoke soup. Randolph prided himself on the meals at Stour, telling me that his father had always insisted on 'an important pudding', and had once sent a dessert away with the words 'This pudding has no theme.'

It was a warm evening. After dinner we walked in the garden. Randolph showed me with pride his roses, and again seemed slightly put out, this time at my lack of knowledge of the different varieties of roses and their attributes. He told me that he was much behind with the dead-heading, and I hid my ignorance of what dead-heading meant. In the coming years I was to spend many hours at his behest cutting off the dead roses in order to give the living and future buds a chance to flower. Once, on the eve of the visit of Loelia, Duchess of Westminster, just as her car was drawing up in the driveway, he remembered that the roses had not been dead-headed for some time. These roses included one, 'The Duchess of Westminster', which he wished to show off to Her Grace. I and my fellow researchers were at once sent out to the terrace to get to work, even as Randolph was welcoming the Duchess at the front door.*

Having shown me his rose garden on that first visit, Randolph invited me inside, and began to question me, in a kindly, almost paternal way, about my work as an Oxford graduate. What subject was I working on? What archives did I use? Which dons did I know? Was I a friend of the Regius Professor? I gave my answers, somewhat puzzling him by the fact that I was not a personal friend of the Regius Professor. 'But I have known Hugh for years,' he said, and proceeded to tell me that Hugh Trevor-Roper was exactly the person to help advance my own career, something that he, Randolph, would be all too glad to help with. I was terrified. Later I was to learn how keen Randolph could be to try to use his friendships to help any new boy.

Randolph asked me about the book I was writing and offered to help in any way he could. I was welcome, he said, to consult the

---

* Winston Churchill had been a witness at the duchess's wedding in 1930. Born in St James's Palace, the daughter of Queen Victoria's Private Secretary, she divorced in 1947 and married Sir Martin Lindsay in 1969. Two of her claims to fame in the inter-war years were that she started the fashion of 'bring-a-bottle' parties, and that she once remarked: 'Anybody seen in a bus over the age of thirty has been a failure in life.' She died on 1 November 1993, at the age of ninety-one, a few days before this book went to the printer.

bound volumes of press cuttings of his own journalistic reports from Europe in the 1930s. When I told him that I had just finished a book on the immediate pre-war years he became animated. He spoke with vehemence about the appeasers, whom he described, in a mixture of snarl and hiss, as enemies of Britain. Even worse, he said, his voice getting quite angry and his eyes even angrier, were the French appeasers, whose cowardice had exceeded even that of their British counterparts.

This was an aspect of appeasement that I thought I knew about. My own recent researches into the Munich crisis had shown that the French politicians had initially been willing to challenge Hitler, but had been forced by their British counterparts to adopt a less forceful approach. I said this, and Randolph exploded. How could I possibly know what I was talking about? He had lived through the period. He had known all those involved. He had written about it at the time, as a journalist. He had been a confidant of some of those at the centre of policy-making. French pusillanimity would be a central part of the biography.

I tried to answer back, hoping that facts would buttress my point of view. I told Randolph of a meeting at which Neville Chamberlain had pressed the French leaders not to imagine that Britain would go to war on behalf of Czechoslovakia. Randolph seemed amazed that his assertion was being challenged. But there were no further explosions, only a long-drawn-out set of assertions and counter-assertions. At one moment, when we had reached what seemed to be a sticky impasse, he suddenly cried out, in a voice full of passion: 'What interests me is the truth.' The word 'truth' was spoken with an explosive force that amazed me: it was volcanic in its force, and seemed to come from some very deep well of conviction. I was later to learn that for his father, too, the concept of truth was far from abstract or theoretical: for both father and son, truth was a living, vibrant, highly moral entity, that should always be sought out to the best of one's ability, and without compromise.

As our debate continued, and midnight passed, Randolph refused to give in. 'We have documents to prove that the French were the greater villains,' he said. He then pressed a buzzer, which I heard sounding far off in the house. After a few moments the driver appeared, still in his dark suit. 'Are there any files on the 1930s that my guest and I can see?' Randolph asked. As the driver replied, asking in some detail what it was that Randolph wanted, and showing at the same time a considerable grasp of the appeasement arguments, it began to dawn on me that the driver was not in fact a driver, but one of Randolph's researchers, and a senior one at that. He was in fact Michael Wolff, Randolph's director of research, and a writer on the *Sunday Telegraph*.

Michael, who was to be my ancillary boss for the next few years, left the room, but did not come back with any documents. I was alone with Randolph, and remained alone with him for at least another two hours, though it seemed more like three or four. I too was in due course to learn the trick of leaving an innocent visitor alone with the Boss, to face the music. On that night, luckily for me, the music was not as discordant as it could be. Randolph seemed amused, or at least bemused, at this whipper-snapper answering him back, quoting from documents, not wilting under fire.

After a certain point, certainly after two o'clock, Randolph noticed that I was wilting. He beamed at me with a concerned smile and said, 'It is time to have a little shut-eye before breakfast. Run along, dear boy'; and so I went to bed. The next morning I came down to breakfast. I had been told that Randolph would have his breakfast in bed, as usual, and that after I had eaten I would be taken to the station to return to Oxford. As I was having breakfast, however, Randolph appeared. He was in his dressing-gown and seemed even larger than he had been on the previous evening, but he was all smiles and asked me if we could have a talk. He walked out on to the terrace, his dressing-gown blowing open in the wind, his slippers shuffling on the flagstones. As we walked up and down, he explained that six months earlier he had been asked by his father to write a four-volume biography based on his father's private papers. These papers were even then being brought to Stour, and three researchers were working on them. He wanted a fourth person to help. Would I be willing to join his team? I was quite thrown by this, and asked if I could think it over. He agreed, and said he would wait to hear from me. I was driven to the station and returned to Oxford.

I hesitated. Some of my friends warned me that working for Randolph would be a dead-end. Many new universities beckoned in those years, their history departments calling out for young graduates. To work for Randolph would be to put oneself outside the academic world, to appear to be lacking in seriousness. The very subject of Churchill, let alone Randolph's reputation as a buffoon, would mean an end to all sorts of possibilities. Other friends thought differently. Here was a chance to work on a major archive, to study Churchill's personal and political papers, to get a glimpse of the closed world of a large private collection. I could work there for a year, then return to academic life with enviable knowledge.

The idea of working in an archive was tempting, even if the whole thing might not last more than six months. I was hoping to be elected that summer to a two-year Junior Research Fellowship at Merton College. The chance of going to Stour for a few months would be a bonus, before plunging into graduate work, writing a thesis, obtaining a doctorate, and teaching.

More telegrams came from Randolph, saying that he hoped I would come to work for him. Suddenly I panicked. Was this an absurd thing to do, to move out of the Oxford cocoon to which I had for so long aspired and in which I was just beginning to flourish? I went to see the Warden of St Antony's, Bill Deakin, who had been Winston Churchill's literary assistant from 1936 to 1940 and again from 1945 to 1955. Bill knew Randolph well and encouraged me to try. The whole thing could not possibly last more than six months, he said, a year at the most. But it would be an experience. Through Churchill's life I would get to know a great deal about recent history. Working with Randolph, for however short a period, would provide me with a lifetime of anecdotes.

I wrote to Randolph, accepting his offer.

II

'The Beast of Bergholt'

My employment with Randolph was to begin in October 1962. Merton College, which had just elected me to a Junior Research Fellowship, agreed that I could also spend time working with Randolph at Stour. My friends, and I, assumed that my engagement would be of short duration. I was still there four and a half years later. I started work under the watchful eye of Michael Wolff, who bore the brunt of responsibilty for the whole enterprise: the other researchers and the secretaries of what Randolph called the 'book office'.

Much has been made of Randolph's irascibility and worse: in these pages I hope a fair picture will emerge of a man who made many enemies by his often violent conduct, but who could be kind, considerate and generous. On my first working day at Stour, which was also my twenty-sixth birthday, he somewhat shyly handed me a gift: a copy of his book *Fifteen Famous English Homes*, inscribed 'Martin Gilbert from Randolph S. Churchill'. I had no idea until then that he had written half a dozen books. A month later he gave me another of them, *The Rise and Fall of Sir Anthony Eden*, inscribed 'Martin from Randolph'. I had been accepted as part of his team.

There were two other researchers in those early days. One was 'the Duke', whom I assumed as a result of Randolph's nomenclature to be a real duke, which he was not. His name was Michael Molian, and his sense of humour buoyed me up on difficult days. The other was Martin Mauthner, who had just completed the research in South Africa into Churchill's Boer War days.

The top floor of the house, where I had a large bedroom, also contained the main research room, with a magnificent view across the Vale of Dedham, housing Winston Churchill's press cutting books. There was also a secretaries' room on the top floor, presided over by Eileen Harryman, whose work in typing out the Churchill papers was continuous. The Churchill papers themselves were housed just outside the house, in heavy filing cabinets in a specially-built strongroom. Much of my work was done in Randolph's library, next to his own study. This latter was the centre of the enterprise, linked to all the rooms except the strongroom by a system of buzzers, so that Randolph could indicate, room after room, that he was in search of someone to join him. The intensity and length of the buzz gave some clue as to his mood.

It was at Stour, and under Randolph's gaze, that I learned much about history, and even more about Churchill. The method of work was rigorous. During my early visits I had to read through several files of original material, which I would 'sign out' of the strongroom and take to the upstairs workroom. Then I would have the letters in the files typed out, either by Eileen Harryman, or one of several secretaries who were on the payroll at various times, chief among them Barbara Twigg, who reached Stour in 1963 and went on to what Randolph called 'the bitter end' ('I hope, dear boy, you will be a "bitter ender"?' he once asked me, but I failed him in that regard). 'Miss Twigg', as we knew her at Stour, was with Randolph when he died. Later she became a senior producer with Yorkshire Television.

As soon as the material I had chosen was typed out (Randolph insisted on every document being typed out in triplicate), I would read the typed version to him, standing at an upright desk, just behind his armchair. The desk had belonged to Disraeli. As I read, he would fire questions at me, which I would jot down in the margin. It was then my task to find the answers.

Every aspect of the letters excited Randolph's imagination and prompted him to want to know more. The questions led me into a realm I had hardly visited during my undergraduate years at Oxford, the personalities, governments and wars of late Victorian England. After each hour or so of reading, I was expected to disappear, bury my head in the reference books, and emerge with all the answers in place. Sometimes I hardly knew the meaning of the questions, let alone how to tackle them.

Who was the 'Strong' referred to in a letter of January 1893? Why was Churchill writing from Lugano in August 1893? What Cabinet post did George Shaw-Lefevre hold in January 1894; had he held any earlier posts; what became of him?* What...? Who...? When...? I had to find, or at least to seek, the answers to a dozen questions each time I read a file to him, sometimes more.

Work could begin in mid-morning, after lunch, before dinner, or after dinner. Randolph never tired of asking the questions, and was always eager to hear the answers. 'Why have you taken so long, dear boy?' was a frequent complaint, even when it seemed to me I had been extremely quick. I did my best, but often floundered. Michael Wolff, whose task was to ensure that volume one of the biography, from Churchill's birth in 1874 to his escape from a Boer prisoner-of-war camp in 1900, was ready for the printer within two years, was often as exasperated as Randolph by my lack of knowledge.

I was given responsibility for the preparation of short biographical notes for every person who was mentioned in Churchill's letters: the person he was writing to, the people in the text of the letter, those referred to by name and those referred to by the office they held. This proved a hard task at first. I was used to reading secondary works in which the historian had already established the facts, or, if he had failed to establish them, had left them vague and blurred. Randolph wanted accuracy and detail: at least four or five lines for every person, however obscure.

I was unfamiliar with most of the reference books. Randolph's library, next to the drawing-room, was rich in nineteenth- and twentieth-century political history. Every day's work at Stour was an exploration for me. During my three days each week in Oxford doing my own researches on the roots of appeasement (which became a book) and teaching, I began to welcome the moment when I would be on my way back to Stour, and to the biographical queries. Slowly at first, it seemed to me, and to Randolph far too slowly, I began to master the world of reference books. How cross Randolph could be, in those early days, when I revealed ignorance, as I did on my first

---

* The answers to these queries were: Charles Powlett Strong, a Harrow contemporary of Churchill's who was killed in action in the Boer War; Churchill was travelling in Switzerland with his tutor Mr Little, of Merton College, Oxford (Lord Randolph Churchill's college, and mine); Shaw-Lefevre, a leading Liberal politician, was then President of the Local Government Board. In 1906 he was created Baron Eversley. He died in 1928 at the age of ninety-seven.

working visit, of *Who Was Who, Debrett's, Burke's Peerage, Kelly's Handbook, Webster's Royal Red Book*,* the Army and Navy Lists, and other basic works of reference. On my second visit he asked me to look something up in *Cruden's Concordance*, and when I looked 'yours truly bewildered' (as he used to describe it), he exploded with indignation. How was it possible that someone educated at Oxford was not familiar with the concordance to the Bible? (He was equally puzzled that I did not play a musical instrument. 'Are you musical?' he asked me on my first night at Stour, and he added: 'All Jews are.' He was amused by the fact that, when I joined him, all four of his researchers were Jews.)

Within a few months I had learned how to follow up the thinnest clue. Every fragment about a person could be put with another fragment, and built up into three or four lines of detail, if one knew where to look. I also learned how helpful libraries and institutions could be, and how many obscure or difficult queries could be answered by correspondence. One of the discoveries-through-correspondence that gave Randolph particular pleasure was the copy of his father's examination marks at the Royal Military Academy, Sandhurst, which was sent from the academy in 1964.

The young Churchill had dramatically improved his marks in the course of a single year, from December 1893 to December 1894. Military topography had been one of his best subjects. His marks in tactics, as well as in the study of fortifications had been very high. His horse-riding skills had been judged exceptional.† The young cadet's conduct had also steadily improved, from 'good but unpunctual' to 'unpunctual' (half way through the year) to 'good'. Most remarkable, as the librarian at Sandhurst pointed out in a covering letter, Churchill had come within 24 marks (out of 2,720) of receiving the Sword of Honour for his year: he only failed to attain that coveted prize because the winner had received a bonus of fifty marks for already being an Under Officer.

* *Webster's Royal Red Book* 'Comprising Court Guide, Peerage, House of Commons, Ambassadors &c, &c' was (and is) indispensable for its listing of all house- and flat-holders street by street, so that in 1914 for example, a letter signed 'Edwin' from 17 Queen Anne's Gate could be identified as coming from Edwin Lutyens, the architect (but a letter signed 'Edwin' from 24 Queen Anne's Gate was from the Liberal MP Edwin Montagu).
† Churchill continued to play polo until his fiftieth birthday.

The image of the backward cadet could no longer be sustained, even though, thirty years after this discovery, it is still being perpetuated.

Randolph was particularly pleased to find in the material preserved at Sandhurst a precise record of his father's height: 5 feet 6 $^7/_{10}$ inches. After Churchill's death, each new public statue seemed to add to his height, until, in Parliament Square, he is a giant!

I first made my journey from Oxford to East Bergholt as a research assistant on 25 October 1962, my twenty-sixth birthday, taking the train through London. Two weeks later I bought my first car, from Michael Wolff, and made the first of many three-hour cross-country drives. A week later Randolph came to Oxford, to persuade the dons at Merton to let me work for him half the week, which they agreed to do, being staggered by the kindly yet interested way in which he quizzed them about the College's finances, as if this was the one subject in which he was really interested.

My diary shows that during Randolph's visit to Oxford I went with him to lunch with the Regius Professor, Hugh Trevor-Roper, and then on to tea with A.J.P. Taylor. I also gave a small sherry party for three undergraduates whom he wished to meet: one of them, 'Aitken' in my diary, was Lord Beaverbrook's great-nephew Jonathan, now Minister of State for Defence Procurement. Three days after Randolph returned to Stour I followed, staying with him for four nights. I was back at Stour a week later, when he drove me to see the grandson of Admiral Lord 'Jackie' Fisher, who lived at the Admiral's former home, Kilverstone Hall, in Norfolk. But the grandson, while wanting to be helpful, had only a few papers, much to Randolph's, and my disappointment.

On the drive back a typical Randolphian episode occurred. As we entered Thetford, Randolph said to me, 'My kinsman the Duke of Grafton lives here.' The duke was a very distant relation indeed. The two men had only met once or twice in the past forty years. We found the house (a fine mansion, Euston Hall) and drove in. I rang the bell and the duke himself came to the door. 'I am your kinsman, Randolph Churchill,' announced my boss ('we ought at least to get a drink out of him,' he had told me in the car). The elderly duke looked somewhat alarmed, but after only the minutest of hesitations let us in, and produced the necessary beverages to lighten the remaining journey back to Stour.

In December I drove to Wilton near Salisbury, where Churchill had stayed on many a Whitsun in the 1930s (and where that festive occasion was known as 'Winstontide'). The visitors' book proved a marvellous source of Churchill dates and friendships; as did Lady Juliet Duff, a relative of Clementine's, who gave me lunch that day and recalled her many encounters with the Great Man. I was soon back at Stour to make my report, and to do some more footnotes.

Work for Randolph could be somewhat forbidding, especially as I never seemed to know what he expected of me. Merely mispronouncing a word could annoy him intensely. I was fortunate that my research work since I had graduated two years earlier had already taken me into the world of pre-war personalities and archives, so that I was able to combine my own interest in the policies leading up to the outbreak of war in 1939 with my work for Randolph. The more I went on with my old interests, the more I saw how closely Churchill had been bound up with every aspect of British history.

Randolph did not mind that I continued with my own researches: indeed, he encouraged them and was always keen to learn what I had discovered. On 21 December, in London, I went to see the journalist and leader-writer Ian Colvin, to discuss my work on appeasement. It emerged that Colvin had been among those who had brought Churchill information about Germany before the outbreak of war in 1939, and had accompanied to Churchill's home at Chartwell the Gauleiter of Danzig, Foerster, to whom Churchill had given a dire warning with regard to any German attack on Poland. A week later I went down to Trafalgar, just south of Salisbury, where I stayed for three nights, amid heavy snow falls, with an Oxford friend of mine whose father, Lord Chandos (formerly Oliver Lyttelton), had been a member of Churchill's wartime and post-war governments. The warmth of his recollections of Churchill made a strong impact on me. On New Year's day 1963 I was back at Stour for five nights.

Such was the pattern. It made for a hectic, but a fascinating life. Casting his mind forward to the volume which would cover the First World War, Randolph wanted me to assemble material on the

Dardanelles and Gallipoli. He had been disappointed that our visit together to Admiral Fisher's grandson had yielded almost nothing in the way of archival material, and no personal letters. The grandson had told us that all the archives were in Scotland. Randolph now asked me to fly north to look for Churchill's letters to Fisher. Their importance was this: in October 1914 Churchill had brought Fisher back to the Admiralty as First Sea Lord at the age of seventy-four. In May 1915 Fisher's sudden departure from the Admiralty building, into hiding, had precipitated the political crisis which led to Churchill's own departure from the Admiralty, at the height of the Gallipoli campaign, arguably the most bitter moment of his career, and at the time regarded by many well-informed observers as the end of his career.

It was 14 January 1964. I had never flown in Britain before, my only previous experience of air travel having been a terrible monsoon-battered night flight from Calcutta to Bombay via Nagpur five years earlier. At least I did not have to contend with the monsoon this time, though Randolph's expectations, and his irascibility when those expectations were not fulfilled, could, I knew, be monsoon enough.

On reaching Edinburgh airport I was met by my host, the Duke of Hamilton. He was a quiet, shy, pleasant person, who drove me in his own car, an elderly Rolls-Royce if memory serves, into Edinburgh, then apologized for having to make a short detour in order to collect some papers in his office. The 'office' turned out to be his room in Holyroodhouse: unknown to me until later, as 14th Duke of Hamilton (and 11th Duke of Brandon) he was the Premier Peer of Scotland and Hereditary Keeper of Holyroodhouse, the Queen's residence in Edinburgh. This had been the reason for the detour.

From Holyroodhouse the duke drove me into the countryside, to his own castle, Lennoxlove, the name of which had so pleased Randolph. It was indeed a romantic name for a romantic castle, complete with turrets and a high tower. The muniment room was in the tower. But before we went in, the duke stopped the car in the long driveway, and began to explain why Admiral Fisher's papers were at Lennoxlove. Fisher, it seems, had lived for many years with the Duchess of Hamilton, the duke's mother. She had been his love and his confidante. When Fisher died, all his letters had gone to her. She had guarded them as tenaciously as she had guarded his memory.

Fisher had clearly been a controversial old cuss, had made many enemies, and was the object of many accusations and rumours, among them, that his mother had been a Malaysian woman, hence his oriental appearance and his nickname, 'The Old Malay'. What the duke was leading up to, as we sat in his car, was this: some people believed that he, the duke, was not the son of the 13th Duke of Hamilton, but of Fisher. All he asked of me was that, if I should discover this to be the case, I would tell him first. He doubted that he was Fisher's son; but he would at least like to be the first to know. With that, we entered the castle.

I was taken straight to the muniment room. Dozens of files were on the table awaiting me. In them were hundreds of handwritten letters from Churchill to Fisher, history's gold. I began to open them, to read them, to work out how I should note down their contents. As I did so, the duke entered the room. Mr Churchill was on the telephone, and wanted to speak to me. I left the room, which had no telephone, and took the call in the duke's study. Randolph was in a foul temper.

> 'Why haven't you telephoned me?'
> 'I've only just begun work, I have the letters here . . .'
> 'What is in them?'
> 'I haven't had time . . .'
> 'I'm not interested in your excuses. What is in the letters?'
> 'I told you I . . .'
> 'For God's sake, can't you do what I ask you. What do I pay you for, to be sloppy?'

I shouted down the line that I could not hear him, that the connection was bad, that there was a terrible crackle on the telephone at the castle end. I heard a snort, and he put down the phone. I was so angry that I took a sheet of Lennoxlove notepaper and drafted a letter setting out my timetable since leaving Heathrow. My letter (which I never sent) ended: 'I do not regard my action as "sloppy". I am sorry you should have taken this view. Such accusations make research very disheartening.'

Three hours later, when I had something to report, I telephoned Randolph. 'I do hope I didn't shout at you earlier, dear boy?' he said in his most apologetic voice. 'I only wanted to know what lovely grub you had been finding'.

'Lovely grub' was Randolph's phrase for all our discoveries. History was for him a feast, full of delicious morsels. And so, despite his unpredictable rages, it became for me.

The Fisher papers at Lennoxlove provided many insights into Churchill's work at the Admiralty both before and during the First World War. There was his search, in which he enlisted Fisher's help in 1912, for a secure source of oil fuel for Britain's warships: the choice was the oil of Persia, and the result, that very Anglo-Persian Oil Agreement signed just before the outbreak of war in 1914 of which my Oxford tutor had said nothing.

It was Fisher's personal energy that most attracted Churchill to him, and led Churchill, against much naval opinion, to bring him back to the Admiralty in October 1914 as First Sea Lord. The dynamism was real, the enthusiasm extraordinary, but, as the letters showed, both were laced with a streak of wildness. At times that wildness lent itself to the successful preparation for war at sea, in new construction and greater inventiveness. When it came to strategy, Fisher wanted a massive naval and military assault against Turkey. When the naval attack against the Dardanelles was in its planning stage, it was Fisher who sent Britain's newest and most powerful battleship, the *Queen Elizabeth*, to join in the action. But, as the enterprise faltered, Fisher bolted – literally – leaving the Admiralty building for an unknown destination, and alerting the Conservative opposition leaders to the fact that he had gone, that a crisis had arisen which they could exploit. This they did at once, demanding a coalition government in which they would hold high office, and the removal of Churchill from the Admiralty. There were those in the Conservative Party, especially at its centre, who had never forgiven him for joining the Liberals in 1904, and for taking the political initiative against them as one of the most outspoken and popular anti-Conservative speakers of the election campaign in the following year.

The most moving letters at Lennoxlove were those which Churchill wrote to Fisher, demanding, urging, pleading with him to return to his post, to make a renewed effort to see the Dardanelles through to success and to renew the partnership that had achieved so much in six months of war. But Fisher resisted every appeal, the Liberal Prime Minister, H.H. Asquith, invited the Conservatives to join the Government, and Churchill was relegated to a sinecure: the Chancellorship of the Duchy of Lancaster.

From Lennoxlove I returned to Oxford. I was now in Randolph's good books, for a while at least. Buoyed up by his enthusiasm even more than by his goading, I went to the Bodleian Library to see Asquith's private archive and transcribed, in the obligatory pencil, the many handwritten appeals from Churchill to Asquith, begging to be allowed to stay at the Admiralty, pointing out that Fisher had been an early enthusiast of the Dardanelles campaign, and asking to be allowed at least to defend the policy in Parliament. But Asquith was obdurate. A new government must be formed, the Conservatives bought off by high positions in it, and Churchill removed from the work to which he had given his greatest effort. He was forty years old.

The anguish that was almost tangible in Churchill's long, handwritten letters made a great impact on me. In these letters he poured out his inner feelings with intensity, holding back nothing, and risking the derision of the Prime Minister. But in the same Asquith archive at the Bodleian were other letters, written almost a decade earlier, in which Churchill poured out other ideas, aimed at changing the life of ordinary people. Randolph was so excited when I brought my pencilled copies of these letters to Stour, and read them aloud to him, that I can picture the scene as I write these words: I standing at the upright desk in his drawing-room, Randolph in his deep armchair below me, a fire blazing in the grate, his eager voice calling out after each letter. 'More dear boy, read on, box on'; and when something in a letter particularly pleased him: 'Wonderful. Lovely grub.'

One of Churchill's letters to Asquith that I read one evening, a handwritten letter of 1908, was a plea for State intervention in the life of the less well-off; not for fragmentary improvement but for a comprehensive social policy to establish minimum standards both of labour and leisure, what Churchill called 'a sort of Germanized network of State intervention and regulation'. As I reached this last phrase, Randolph asked me what the German system was at that time.

'I'm afraid I don't know.'

'Then for goodness sake *do* find out. What do you think I pay you for?'

So, from pleasure to anger, from appreciation to demands, and for me the start of another quest, leading to yet more knowledge, to be duly imparted, and, hopefully, to elicit praise. It was not always easy, even after a hard search and many hours, to get that praise. Sometimes the details which I felt answered the question satisfactorily merely convinced Randolph that I had been slacking, not getting to the bottom of the issue, 'wasting your time and my money'. I could be cast down and crestfallen. But I persevered, though often when he was particularly critical, even abusive, of my lack of effort, I would vow that I would never come again to Stour, that I would resign once I was safely back at Oxford. He seemed to sense these moods, and would make sure, before I drove away, to slip in some word of appreciation, to express his eagerness to hear my next discovery.

During my visit to Scotland to see Fisher's papers, Randolph had also given me the instruction, noted in my diary: 'Telephone Duchess of Buccleuch, contact Duchess of Atholl'. The latter, known because of her outspoken support for the Spanish Republicans as the Red Duchess, had supported Churchill at the time of Munich, and been supported by him after Munich when her own constituents turned sour. She had several letters from Churchill, expressing his support and giving her encouragement. Her husband had fought at Churchill's side at Omdurman. The Duchess of Buccleuch, 'Mollie', had been a friend of Churchill's all her life, and of Randolph's too. Sitting in the drawing-room of her magnificent pink palace, Drumlanrig, she told me a story which, when I brought it back to Stour, raised many laughs, and with them my own stock rose. Churchill had stayed with the Duchess in Scotland one weekend early in 1939. As he left, she asked him if he could give her some advice. Neville Chamberlain was coming the next weekend to address the local Conservatives. Where should she set up the podium? 'It doesn't matter where you put it', Churchill replied, 'as long as he has the sun in his eyes and the wind in his teeth.' She did a fine and affectionate imitation of Churchill's defective 's': 'Shun in hish eyesh . . .'

In mid-February, once more in the course of my own work, I went to Denham Place for lunch with Lady Vansittart, whose husband 'Van', when head of the Foreign Office in the 1930s, had brought many secrets and much encouragement to Churchill. On the following day I drove to Ibstone House, in the Chilterns, for lunch with Rebecca West, who recalled the impact on her of Churchill's support for the anti-Nazis in Yugoslavia, through his pre-war newspaper articles. A week later I took my notes from these latest peregrinations to Stour.

On my next visit to Stour, in April, Lady Churchill came to lunch, and spoke about her impressions of 'Winston' when they had met at a dinner party in 1906. He had spent much of the time talking to the woman on his other side, and she was not impressed, especially when he offered to send her the biography of Lord Randolph Churchill that he had just written, and it never arrived. I accompanied Lady Churchill by train to London. She asked me about working for Randolph. I think she was afraid that I would report that work was not going well, but in fact, as it seemed to me progress was being made 'on all fronts', as Randolph liked to say, I told her so.

Towards the end of April, I called on Christabel Lady Aberconway at her house in South Audley Street. Again, my quest had nothing to do with my work for Randolph, but was part of my own continuing historical researches. As always, however, Churchill quickly entered the discussion (normally as soon as I said that I worked for Randolph). Lady Aberconway had known Churchill before 1914. During lunch she recounted a story about Churchill, aged twenty-one, making his first public speech. It took place in London, after the foyer of the Empire Theatre, used by 'ladies of the night' (as Lady Aberconway called them), was suddenly closed by the management. The ladies gathered angrily outside. Churchill arrived, stood on a soap-box, and cried out: 'Ladies of the Empire! I stand for Liberty!'

I sent this story to Randolph in the post: he liked to be kept informed of progress on a daily basis, and could be vexed if he heard nothing from me after such an encounter. Going through some old notes while writing this chapter, I found that he had this story typed out on a foolscap sheet, headed:

From M. Gilbert,
23 April 1963.

Having had such a document typed out, if he felt in the mood Randolph would then dictate an introductory sentence or two, some-times a paragraph. By this means his two volumes were built up. Sometimes Randolph would dictate his own recollections of his father. On these occasions I would stand at the Disraeli desk and write his words down as he dictated them. His idea was to insert these recollections in the volumes when the time came. The time never came for Randolph, and my notes remained unused. One of them, which I print here for the first time, was from Churchill's 'wilderness years', when he was out of office. These were Randolph's words, as I wrote them down:

> In 1935, while staying at the Château de l'Horizon in the South of France, I went one night with my father to the Casino in Cannes. By five in the morning I had won £200 and my father £500.*
>
> We left the casino, but could not find a taxi. 'Let's walk back along the beach, it is only four or five miles,' my father said, and off we went, reaching the Château at half past six. My mother, who had never approved of my father's gam-bling, was still asleep. Father went into her bedroom, woke her up, and showered her bed with 1,000 franc notes.

Another of Randolph's recollections was of the summer of 1929, when he, his father, his uncle Jack and Jack's son Johnny had travelled through Canada and the United States, going by train from Van-couver to San Francisco. Some months earlier his father had agreed to write an article for the *Strand* magazine and had fallen far behind with the delivery date. As Randolph told it:

> I remember how on a very hot train journey in California, or perhaps further north, he shut himself up in his own small compartment and wrote the article. He had for at least the last thirty years had the habit of dictating every-thing, but he had no secretary with him. In two or three

---

* The combined winnings of father and son were the equivalent in 1994 of £18,000.

hours he wrote, in his own hand, an article of two or three thousand words, which he read to us at dinner.

He did not do this so much because he needed the money; he had a sense of guilt which he felt he must expiate.

I remember complimenting him on the article when he read it to us. 'You know I hate to go to bed at night feeling I have done nothing useful in the day. It is the same feeling as if you had gone to bed without brushing your teeth.'

When Randolph recalled his father one felt very close indeed to the real Churchill. All the researchers shared this sense of proximity.

After I had been working for Randolph for six months, a new face appeared, that of Andrew Kerr, one of his very first researchers from the start of the enterprise in 1961, who rejoined the team. Andrew was jack-of-all-trades and master of all. He soothed the ruffles of aggravated secretaries (towards whom Randolph could be fierce), cooked when the cook was sacked, gardened when the gardeners were ill, drove to the shops for emergency supplies, and kept the work itself going when, for one reason or another, no researcher was there to answer Randolph's buzzer. For we worked on a shift system, sometimes with only a few hours' overlap, and when one or other of us was unable to come, there might be no one in the house at all for several days at a time. There were different types of distractions: after the Labour victory in 1964 Michael Wolff began to help Edward Heath in the struggle for the return of a Conservative government, and I, having by chance come across a cache of private diplomatic letters, started research on a biography of Sir Horace Rumbold, who had been ambassador in Berlin when Hitler came to power in 1933.

In June 1963 my travels on Randolph's behalf took me to Lee-on-Solent to spend the day with Admiral Sir Richard Bell-Davies. He had been one of the young Royal Naval Air Service pilots who taught Churchill to fly just before the First World War. In 1915 he had won the Victoria Cross, landing on the Gallipoli Peninsula to scoop up a British soldier who was being marched into captivity by the Turks. Later he became an Admiral. In recounting Churchill's efforts in 1913 to advance the techniques of military aviation, and the initial resistance to those efforts by the War Office – until war broke out and they were suddenly keen – he commented: 'They pissed on Churchill's plant for years. How could they then expect it to grow in a week?'

In the course of his Churchill work, Randolph would ask for notes and outlines for things that he was preparing outside the biography. One such effort, on which I worked quite hard, was a film script on the life of Hitler which was commissioned by Granada Television. The scheme, under which he would be the presenter, and which he looked forward to enormously, was abandoned after he quarrelled with the producer the first time they met, in a Granada studio in London. 'I refuse to work with a woman', he said, and walked out – to the Café Royal. I also helped him with the fortnightly articles he was writing for the *News of the World*. I became more and more a resident of Stour and less and less at Merton: in March 1964 I spent thirteen consecutive days with Randolph. Several of my friends wondered whether I could possibly survive unscathed, that is to say, without being sacked, but I did.

I enjoyed delving into current affairs for Randolph's newspaper articles, and listening to the visitors whom he invited to Stour to talk politics. It was as a very contented, open-eyed fly on the wall that on different occasions I heard Randolph's brother-in-law Christopher Soames (then Minister of Agriculture), Lord Home (later Prime Minister), and the Secretary of State for War, John Profumo, talk about events at Westminster.

Westminster was seldom far from Randolph's mind. On 8 November 1963 his friend and neighbour John Hare was raised to the peerage as Baron Blakenham. As a constituent, Randolph decided to promote a possible successor, Lord Beaverbrook's great-nephew Jonathan Aitken, then an undergraduate at Christ Church, Oxford, who also lived in the constituency. We 'ghosts' were put to work manning the telephone as Randolph put through mellifluous calls to the members of the selection committee, some of whom were audibly terrified when they were told (sometimes by me) 'I have Mr Randolph Churchill on the line.'

Randolph dictated a magisterial letter to the constituency chairman, extolling the young Aitken's qualifications as a parliamentarian. At the age of twenty, however, Aitken was not yet eligible to take his seat. Randolph was not deterred by this. He telephoned the Clerk of the House of Commons, who found precedents for those elected before they were twenty-one: they waited until their twenty-first birthday and then descended upon the Commons. 'These country bumpkins will be perfectly happy to wait until you take your seat,' Randolph told Jonathan. In the event, another candidate was chosen.

As a result of this episode, which for a while absorbed all Randolph's energies, I learned something about constitutional history. A decade later Jonathan was elected for Thanet; at the time of writing he is a minister in John Major's Government.

Like his father, Randolph was an exacting taskmaster but a generous employer. At a time when he was paying me a good salary, he wrote to me in Oxford from Stour: 'Looking at my salary book I see that you are being scandalously underpaid,' and proposed a generous increase, from £850 a year to £1,250. When a research assistant had angered him and was sacked at midnight, the next morning on the breakfast table was a blank cheque signed by Randolph for the young man to fill in. Kindness and anger were inextricably mixed up in his brain, the first warm and encouraging, the second sometimes frightening in its intensity.

A source of constant amelioration was Randolph's friend Natalie Bevan. The colourful, animated pottery figures that she made, some of which (including four large trumpeting elephant candle-holders) graced Randolph's table, reflected her own colourful character. When storms brewed, her presence could avert the worst dramas. Her arrival at Stour was something much to be looked forward to. She was always ready with words of comfort for us researchers when Randolph made life difficult.

Research at Stour was as far from any dry-as-dust archive or ivory tower as one could imagine. On the outside of the house, overlooking the terrace, Randolph had affixed a plaque with Constable's words, 'I am come to a determination to make no idle visits this summer nor to give up any time to commonplace people. I shall return to Bergholt.' Were we, Randolph's researches, 'ghosts' and 'paid hacks', among the 'commonplace people' when storms raged? We certainly felt as much. It was Natalie who, on so many occasions, raised both our spirits and his; or, in raising his, raised ours.

In the summer of 1964 the work load was lightened by the arrival of an enthusiastic young American, George Thayer, who later wrote a book on extremist right-wing groups in Britain, and worked for a Congressman on Capitol Hill. His career was cut short by his early death from cancer.*

The method of work at Stour involved dozens of memoranda sent from Randolph to his researchers, and between researchers. 'MW to MG' would be the heading on frequent instructions from Michael Wolff to me. In September 1964 all four researchers (Michael Wolff, Andrew Kerr, George Thayer and myself) and the four secretaries on the payroll at the time received a collective exhortation, one of Randolph's (and his father's) favourite verses:

> The heights of great men reached and kept,
> Were not attained by sudden flight,
> But they, while their companions slept,
> Were toiling upwards in the night.

Randolph's personality, with its exhortations and eccentricities, kept the team on its toes. On one occasion a telegram arrived in which the address was given not as East Bergholt but Beast Bergholt. He announced at once that he was now 'the Beast of Bergholt'.† How eagerly we researchers, when one of his storms burst, would run away from our 'Beast' and find an hour or two's sanctuary in the outside strongroom. Being just outside the house it was clear of the buzzer. He seldom visited it: one visit was arranged for a television crew, and we (the researchers) were terrified that he would find something amiss in the arrangement of the materials in the filing cabinets, but all went well.

Randolph liked to hear every story that one gleaned when away from Stour. I remember how amused he was when I reported back a chance conversation with a man I met who was then in the Ministry

---

* George Thayer's first encounter with cancer led to the amputation of one of his legs. Shortly after that, he wrote to me from Washington: 'Don't fret about me. I'm getting so agile on my sticks that I now wonder why I ever needed a second leg. Besides, I'm about to get a fancy leg (parts of which, incidentally, were invented by an associate of Von Braun's at Peenemunde), which will make me the terror of the neighbourhood.'

† In 1968, shortly after I began work on the Churchill biography at my house just outside Oxford, The Map House, a letter from a stationery shop arrived, addressed to The Mad House, much to the inmates' amusement.

of Aviation. My note of the conversation reads: 'The King, with a cold, was returning in car with WSC after accompanying Princess Elizabeth to the airport. King's heavy cold. WSC advised King to take strong drink. King said doctors only allowed it after dark. WSC: "My doctors won't let me drink before breakfast, but I do."'

Neither my research successes nor the humorous asides were proof against Randolph's inevitable anger. One day when I was at Oxford, a telegram reached the College Lodge informing me that I had been sacked. The reason for my sacking had nothing to do with my researches. Some grouse had reached Stour, by rail, as a gift from the Secretary of State for War, John Profumo. Having probably been shunted onto a siding for too long during their journey, they were no longer edible; this only became clear when they were at table. At the end of a letter to the minister, thanking him for some historical material he had sent (the fifty-year rule for public documents meant his permission was needed to see government archival material even for 1914), I mentioned the fact that the grouse were off. On receiving my letter he had telephoned Randolph to offer some more.

Profumo's call revealed that I had, unwittingly, broken a house rule, unknown to me at the time: 'I cannot have people who are working for me and who come to my house complaining about the food behind my back to people who had sent it. I cannot abide the idea that anyone staying and working in the house does not have his primary loyalty to myself. If you blab about the food in a mischievous way you might, for all I know, blab about graver matters.' If I wanted to work on research in Oxford and elsewhere at a reduced salary, I should contact Michael Wolff. 'But I do not wish you to come back here.'

Advice came that same day from Andrew Kerr: 'Suggest you write groveller.' I did so, and received a telegram from Randolph in reply: 'Thank you for your letter. The matter is closed.' 'Welcome back,' he said when I next returned to Stour. 'I am sorry about what happened. We won't speak about it again. Now tell me dear, what have you brought me to read?'

There was a sequel to this episode six months later when Profumo resigned. Randolph was shocked by the virulence of the newspapers, and by the way in which the Profumos were to all intents and purposes besieged in their own home. In strictest secrecy, so that it never reached the ears of any journalist or the lens of any press photographer, he offered Stour as a sanctuary. I still have the instructions we were all given, headed with the codename 'Operation Sanctuary', marked 'Secret', and explaining how we were to look after 'OGs' (Our Guests).

Randolph would leave the country to be with his father on board Aristotle Onassis's yacht *Christina*. 'Our friends will seek to come here to Stour unobserved.' If they were observed 'admission of the Press to the house or garden will be denied.' If interlopers broke into the garden 'they will be requested to leave.' If they refused, the police would be called, 'during which time our guests will retire upstairs. We will not stand any rot.'

The Profumos were to be treated as if they were in their own home. Randolph's staff were instructed not to 'blab' in the village. If the Profumos wished to go abroad 'they should fly from Southend to Dieppe and should charter a car on arrival on the continent and "disappear none knows whither".' In fact there was never any idea in the Profumos' mind that they would go abroad, despite newspaper speculation. Randolph, as usual, was trying to cover all possibilities.

I was impressed by Randolph's gesture, one of real affection and goodness. I knew that, as a young MP, Profumo had been one of the Conservative Members who voted against Neville Chamberlain on 8 May 1940, making possible Churchill's premiership two days later. At that time he was the youngest MP. He had entered the Commons only two months before the decisive vote and had not yet made his maiden speech. When I pointed this out to Randolph, he urged me to write it up and to send it not to one newspaper but to all of them. I did so, and about a dozen papers published it. It was my very first published foray into public life.

Two years later, when I was looking through wartime photographs of Churchill at Carthage in North Africa, I spotted Profumo in the foreground of one of them. He was taking a photograph of his own, of Churchill holding up his hat on a stick. I wrote to him to ask if I could see the picture. He replied: 'I would have been more than delighted to let you have the result from my side of the camera, but alas this, along with many other, to me, interesting photographs which I had had processed by an RAF photographic unit which was with us in North Africa, are at the bottom of the Mediterranean as a result of a bloody German submarine. I suppose I mustn't grumble as it might have been me as well!'

Randolph's generous nature, like his father's, could be stirred by a tale of injustice. One afternoon a pupil of mine at Oxford was pictured in a London evening newspaper, and pilloried, for a drug-related offence. I brought Randolph the newspaper that same afternoon. After I had told him the young man's story he telephoned the editor and demanded the removal of the offensive photograph. It was taken out in the later editions.

I learned at Stour that history was concerned with character and humanity, as well as with facts and achievements.

III

'Box On!'

In January 1965 Winston Churchill suffered a massive stroke in his London home, at the age of ninety. I was in the United States at the time, at the start of a six-month sabbatical from Randolph, and learned the news in Albuquerque, New Mexico. Turning on the radio in my hotel bedroom, I heard the announcer's brisk voice: 'Britain's war leader stricken: more after this message from our sponsor.' Pause. Then, to music, 'Winston tastes good, like a cigarette should.' I have never forgotten that moment, nor the advertiser's jingle.

Nine days later Churchill died. I was then in South Carolina, where I was to teach at the local state university. I telephoned Randolph with condolences. He was determined not to let the biography languish. What should I do, I asked (thinking he might want me to get back for the funeral)? 'Box on!' he said. The biography would continue, and our efforts would be redoubled. But he was already unwell, and at his father's State funeral a few days later he had to be helped by his mother during the long walk through the streets of London following the coffin.

Under the original agreement between the Churchills and the publishers, Randolph could publish nothing until a year and a half after his father's death. This meant that the work since 1961 had been influenced, and in some ways impeded, by a general sense of lack of urgency. Every author needs the spur of a deadline for handing in his manuscript: Randolph's deadline depended upon an unknown factor. Now that this factor was known, an alarm clock had begun to tick. Not only could his first volume now be published any time after January 1966, but the publishers began to press for assurances that this date would be met.

On the day after his father's funeral, Randolph flew with Andrew

Kerr to Marrakech, to take up the writing in the same hotel, La Mamounia, in which his father had written many chapters of his war memoirs. A clear and taut timetable now entered into Randolph's life. As the date for the completion of volume one drew closer, the life of the team became more and more frantic. Looming above volume one was the question of the remaining volumes. In all, four were planned. The publishers wanted to bring them out annually. Randolph, with volume one under control thanks almost entirely to Michael Wolff's unstinting efforts, wondered how the subsequent volumes would ever get done. On several occasions in my presence he wrote down a column of timetables and plans of work, with parallel lines listing payments and bonuses.

Volume two was to cover fourteen years, from the Boer War to the outbreak of the First World War. In November 1965 a new researcher was taken on, 'pudding boy', a young American whose love of a rich dessert endeared him to sweet-toothed Randolph. He was Frank Gannon, later to be a member of President Nixon's staff, and after the outbreak of the First World War were those of a pioneer. He is now a professor of History in Australia.

Hardly had Frank Gannon joined the team in order to help Randolph meet the publisher's deadline, than there was another blow to Randolph's efforts to master the mass of documents needed to tell his father's story. On 1 January 1966 the Prime Minister, Harold Wilson, replaced the fifty-year rule for official documents by a thirty-year rule. No longer would ministerial records for, say, 1940, be closed until 1990, and thus far beyond the reach of Randolph and his team. With the new rule we would have to wait only four years, for example, until 1969, to see the files for the outbreak of war.

Wilson's decision opened up a gold mine of documents for all modern historians. But Randolph quailed at the thought of having to go through a mass of official records in addition to his labours in the Churchill archive. I made a sally into these records, then housed in Chancery Lane, and brought back what I thought were several fine nuggets from Churchill's work at the Admiralty. 'This', said Randolph 'is for thesis writers.' I was put out by his dismissal of my efforts. Only later, when the responsibility for going through these files was mine, did I realize what Randolph had sensed instinctively, that the amount of extra work involved would be formidable, and that the wealth of extra material might well extend considerably both the size and the timetable of the biography.

As Randolph confronted the new mass of material to be selected and read and woven into his narrative, he took on four more researchers. Each was an Oxford graduate: Paul Addison, himself a future Churchill biographer; Robert Taylor, who prepared the background materials for Randolph on Churchill's social reforms, and was to become the industrial correspondent of the *Observer*; Alan Thompson, who went into the BBC, and died of cancer in his forties, just as his career was beginning to flourish; and Cameron Hazlehurst, who later published an indispensable guide to the papers of British Cabinet ministers, and whose researches into British politics during and after the outbreak of the First World War were those of a pioneer. He is now a Professor of History in Australia.

The enlarged team worked at whatever Randolph wanted done during any particular week. This might be biographical notes, proof-reading of main or document volumes, background papers on a min-isterial crisis, or the reading aloud of the latest discoveries. But even as the team was enlarged, so Randolph's literary-political diversions grew. In 1963 he had written a book on the fall of Harold Macmillan and the emergence of Lord Home: this gave him an appetite for further 'quickies', as he called them. In 1967 he wrote a book on the Arab-Israeli six-day war. For this effort Randolph's son Winston, then aged twenty-seven, and a newspaper correspondent, wrote the military sections, while the Boss, determined to write the book in no less time than than it had taken the Israelis to win it, took on several extra researchers, including John David, a young Indian Jew who was then an undergraduate at Oxford, and who subsequently became, and remains to this day, a hermit in the Negev desert.

For the last fifteen months of Randolph's life he was also helped by Tom Hartman, who had been working as an editor for a London publisher. Randolph had no faith in the editorial capacities of the Churchill publishers, Heinemann, and wanted someone to take charge of the editing and production side, and to do so at Stour. Tom quickly became one of his friends, and was drawn into wider responsibilities. I did not envy him when he was asked to do what I had done four years earlier: biographical notes. But when Randolph persuaded Heinemann, after great reluctance on their part, to publish in addition to the narrative volumes a parallel series of 'companion' volumes of documents, the number of biographical notes needed increased by leaps and bounds. Tom worked like a Trojan: for the past quarter of a century he has been a distinguished publisher of military books at Leo Cooper, including several editions of Churchill's early military books.

It was not only the research (and the researchers) that created a varied and exciting life at Stour, but also the visitors. I remember watching entranced as one of the most attractive Conservative thinkers of the time, Iain Macleod, while listening to some account by Randolph of contemporary political skulduggery, suddenly kicked the table leg and exclaimed 'I hate the Tory Party.' Hoping to show my worth as a researcher, I disappeared to the muniment room for some minutes and returned with a letter written by Churchill to a Conservative friend in 1904, which I proceeded to read aloud to my Master and the minister. In the letter was the sentence 'I hate the Tory Party, its men and its methods.' Randolph commented: 'We Churchills have never been Tories, though we have often found the Tory Party a useful vehicle.'

On two occasions the editor of the *Sunday Telegraph*, Donald McLachlan, came to dine. Randolph was excited that the paper would be serializing his volumes, and was, after some initial disagreements, willing to run stories from time to time about the progress and the discoveries. On the first visit, McLachlan's widow has recalled (in a letter to the *Sunday Telegraph* in 1982), after dinner 'Martin Gilbert was installed at what Randolph proudly stated was Disraeli's reading desk. Gilbert, although recognized as a brilliant historian, was far from self-confident, or experienced. From time to time he mispronounced a word or name, and we both thought Randolph cruel to humiliate him by correcting him in public. After each interruption the pug dogs would break into a chorus of barking, and when peace was restored, Randolph would say: "Box on, dear boy."'

On McLachlan's second visit he came alone. Randolph, still hoping to be asked to write several articles about the book, wanted to make a good impression. We ghosts were instructed to be on our best behaviour. A fine dinner was commanded from the cook-housekeeper then in residence. Its climax was to be a baron of beef, ordered from Randolph's favourite butcher.

McLachlan arrived. The talk turned, as so often at Stour, to
Neville Chamberlain and appeasement. Randolph spoke angrily
about the pre-war editor of *The Times*, Geoffrey Dawson, for cutting
out parts of the despatches of his Berlin correspondent, Norman
Ebbutt. The visitor, in a quiet voice, dissented. Ebbutt's despatches
were not cut because they told the truth about Nazi Germany, but
because they were sometimes too long. Randolph looked puzzled. It
was an act of faith at Stour to denounce Dawson for hiding the truth
about Hitler's Germany from the British people. We, Randolph's
minions, wondered what would happen. The visitor went on in his
quiet, but now also firm voice, to say that it was not Dawson who
had cut the despatches but our visitor himself. It was he who, as a
young sub-editor between 1933 and 1935, who had spent most of
1931 and 1932 in Germany, and had been for several months in
1934 in charge of the paper's Berlin office, had decided to trim the
Ebbutt despatches, which had been 'far too long'.

The cutting of the Berlin despatches was a central point in the
perfidy of the appeasers. Now the 'villain' had revealed himself, and
done so without realizing what he had done. I looked at Randolph,
but he had risen from the table and was already at the sideboard,
where the baron of beef was awaiting, his back to us. Suddenly he
turned towards the table, brandishing the carving knife, shaking and
trembling, and exploded with a bellow of fury: 'Shits like you should
have been shot by my father in 1940.' The stress on the words 'shits'
and 'shot' was fearsome to hear. Then he lunged towards the editor,
who had to dodge round the table, until Randolph hurled the carving
knife on to the floor and strode out of the room. We never saw him
again that night. In the morning McLachlan left the house.

What was the truth about the Berlin despatches? I have little doubt
that the sub-editor had cut them because they were too long, and
without any malicious political intent whatsoever. But Dawson himself took a definite view that Hitler was not to be antagonized, and
that *The Times* should even try to please him; and perhaps the period
during which our visitor was responsible for how long the items
should be was not the same period during which the cuts had been
made for reasons other than length. One of the discoveries of which
I was most proud, partly because it gave Randolph so much pleasure,
and partly because it was so self-explanatory, and for the

anti-appeasers so self-condemnatory, was a letter Dawson had written in 1937 to a friend which I found in the Scottish Record Office in Edinburgh: 'I should like to get going with the Germans. I simply cannot understand why they should apparently be so much annoyed with *The Times* at this moment. I spend my nights in taking out anything which I think will hurt their susceptibilities and in dropping in little things which are intended to soothe them.'

The focus on appeasement at Stour had a reason: Randolph regarded his own, as well as his father's, attitude at that time as very much their joint 'finest hour'. He was appalled that my Oxford tutor had virtually ignored his father's part in the pre-war appeasement debate. Together, he and I would rectify that omission. He could hardly wait to reach the 1930s. Often, in dictating passages for volumes one and two, he would break off with a long digression about the inter-war years. It was this period that excited him most, and where my own discoveries, like the Dawson letter, gave him most pleasure.

In the corridors of a Foreign Office depository near Waterloo Station, I came across a dozen green box files stuffed with letters written from the general public to Duff Cooper, at the time of his resignation in October 1938. Randolph was thrilled. These should all be published, he said, as a roll of honour of those who had opposed the Munich surrender. He asked me to read them aloud, and tears coursed down his cheeks as I did so. These writers were the heroes, the patriots, the men and women who had refused to kow-tow to Hitler, who had rejected the Government's grovelling stance. To Randolph's delight, one of the letters was from a young lecturer at Manchester University, A.J.P. Taylor, later the distinguished historian, and my own tutor at Oxford. What delighted Randolph was to contrast Taylor's total rejection of appeasement in 1938, with his apparently less harsh judgements on the men of Munich in his most recent book on the origins of the Second World War. 'I will tease him with this mercilessly when we meet,' Randolph said to me, and I had no doubt he would, though I had equally little doubt that Taylor would defend himself tenaciously. Still, Randolph would win, he would reassert his concern for that elusive entity, truth.

The talk about appeasement often deflected Randolph from his work on the pre-First World War period, but was fun for me. And more than fun: I learned a great deal from him about the moods and personalities of the time. Was a person 'sound'? Then he opposed any compromise with Hitler, and would receive, so Randolph promised and intended, a good write-up in the inter-war volume.

Alas, Randolph was not to get beyond 1914 in the writing, though he did set me to put together the materials for the First World War, and often discussed them with me, as I read them aloud to him from the Disraeli desk. Again, to be 'sound' was to have wanted the naval attack on the Dardanelles to succeed. His first political memory, at the age of four, was saying his prayers at Admiralty House: 'God bless Mummy and Papa. God bless the Dardanelles, and make me a good boy. Amen.' Later, at Eton, as he recalled in his memoirs, 'I said to another boy (it makes me blush to recall the episode) "Will you be my chum?" He said no. I said, "Why not?" He said, "Your father murdered my father." I said, "What do you mean?" He said, "At the Dardanelles."'

Randolph had begun to look forward to writing about the Dardanelles almost as much as about appeasement. At the beginning of 1967 he asked me to prepare a day-by-day chronology of his father's ten months at the Admiralty from August 1914 to May 1915, and to weave into it the documents from the Churchill papers. He also wanted me to track down those who had known his father on the Western Front in 1916. On 14 January 1967, four years to the day after that flight to Scotland when I had incurred his wrath, I wrote to him from Stour (he was then in Barbados):

> I had lunch on Thursday with Sir Desmond Morton and we talked for three hours mostly about the First World War and his early encounters with your father at Plug Street and Verchocq.* I will be dictating an account of this interview to Miss Twigg which I will show you on your return, together with my General Hakewill-Smith

---

* Plug Street was the Belgian village of Ploegsteert, where Churchill commanded the 6th Royal Scots Fusiliers from January to June 1916. Verchocq was the château near Faucquembergues which he used as his French headquarters when he was Minister of Munitions in 1917 and 1918.

interview. I am also trying to track down your father's Permanent Under-Secretary of State when he was at the War Office; although he is over 90 I am told he is still alert and I hope to have more to report on this after I leave Stour.

Randolph returned from Barbados keen to continue. His son Winston had begun work selecting the documents for the Chanak section: the period, in 1922, when Churchill as Secretary of State for the Colonies sought to prevent the Turks from overrunning the British controlled Zone of the Straits. My priority was the Dardanelles. As each month's material was assembled, I would read aloud to Randolph from my efforts. He would still make pungent comments, on his father's foresight, Asquith's pusillanimity, Fisher's eccentricities, but he was no longer well. A doctor told him that if he did not stop drinking wine and spirits he might die within a year. He obeyed at once, and watched in anguish as his guests continued to enjoy the contents of his cellar, while he abstained. An operation on his lung revealed no malignancy, but it was a time of worry and discomfort.

Rumours that Randolph was seriously ill spread through Clubland.* One day he was telephoned by the owner of the Telegraph newspapers, Lord Hartwell, who said without too much ceremony that as Randolph was now apparently too ill to complete the Churchill biography, that task would devolve upon Lord Birkenhead, Hartwell's brother-in-law. Randolph was indignant, but it soon emerged that as the effective copyright holder of the Churchill papers, as far as their publication in serial form was concerned, Lord Hartwell (whom Randolph had known since they were children) had the right to nominate his successor as biographer. The Telegraph newspapers, which Hartwell owned, had acquired these rights in 1961.

Randolph fell into a decline, punctuated by bouts of feverish activity. He was depressed by the realization that he was most unlikely to finish the one great work on which his heart had been set for so

---

* Randolph so hated the phrase 'seriously ill' that I blench to use it even now. In earlier years, when asked by journalists how his father was, he would say: 'Sir Winston is seriously well.'

long, and vexed that he could not determine his successor. He did ask me, late one night, if after his death I would help his son Winston finish the book, if events conspired to such an outcome, and I agreed with alacrity, but he had a deep suspicion that a family succession would not happen.

Twice that summer his spirits rose particularly high: first when he and his son Winston wrote their almost instant history of the Arab-Israeli war, *The Six-Day War*, and again when Robert Kennedy telephoned from Washington to ask if he would be willing to write the official biography of the late President Kennedy, who had been assassinated four years earlier. Thrilled by this commission, by which he would be the first person to use the Kennedy papers, and to do so exclusively, Randolph sat up late one night dictating to me a series of notes about the Kennedy biography, 'Project K' as he called it. One of the notes reads:

> Asked by Robert K and Mrs JFK to be the official biographer and use the papers (first use).
> Will MG help (a) visiting USA, possibly this autumn, probably March 1968, (b) writing the volume on K as politician, the power struggle, while RSC does K the statesman.

Randolph made plans for a two-volume work: Kennedy the statesman, which he would write, and Kennedy the politician, which I, 'MG', and no doubt other willing ghosts, would prepare. We would take a house in Washington and do the work there. The Churchill biography would be done in tandem. Randolph would pay a substantial salary with handsome bonuses as each volume of Churchill was finished. All this was discussed late into the night, but it came to nought.

Early in July 1967, while I was still piecing together more Dardanelles material, and was spending a few days in Oxford getting it ready for a reading at Stour, the telephone rang, well after midnight. I decided to let it ring, but its persistence alerted me to the caller. It was Randolph. 'We're writing about the war,' he said. 'I know,' I answered, as calmly as I could having been roused from my sleep. 'We're writing about the war,' he repeated, even more loudly. 'I know,' I replied. 'I'm bringing the next lot of readings down on

Monday' (it was then a Thursday). Then I put the phone down, and went back to bed.

The phone rang again. 'Not that war,' Randolph exploded, 'the new war.' My task, he said, was to write the first chapter: 'I want 5,000 words, the history of the Jews from Moses to Nasser.'

I tried to work out how much work and how many weeks would be needed for such a task. 'Can we discuss it when I come down on Thursday?' I asked. 'No', he bellowed. 'You will bring the 5,000 words with you, finished, on Thursday. We can polish it together over the weekend.'

I did as I was bidden. It was surely not my best effort, though it did appear in his book as chapter one. I also had to prepare a digest of all British Press opinion from mid-May until the outbreak of the war on 6 June. The history had to be typed out on azure paper, the press digest on green. The Dardanelles was never taken up again. The strain of working at Stour had begun to tell on me, and I wanted to move ahead with a few books of my own: indeed, that bizarre first chapter 'From Moses to Nasser' became the impetus for a historical atlas that I drew during the following year and then published: an *Atlas of Jewish History*, it is still in print, now in its sixth edition. I certainly have Randolph to thank for that, but I felt so tired by the twice-weekly drive across country to Stour (through Buckingham and Bletchley and St Neots) that I told him I could go on no longer. I was exhausted. 'Lie back and dictate like a Pasha,' he said, but I had had enough. Randolph was upset at my departure, and generous: he wished me well in my career and offered to help in any way he could.

There was one more act to be played in Randolph's story. On a visit to Washington to make plans for his work on the Kennedy biography, and as his health continued to deteriorate despite his having stopped drinking alcohol, he was introduced to a famous American clairvoyante, Jeane Dixon. After warning him that he might not live very much longer, she insisted that he had one final and magnificent task to perform: not his father's biography or even the Kennedy book, but the first step on the road to the reconciliation of Arabs and Jews.

Randolph, a keen Zionist, was excited. He at once flew to Morocco, where he saw King Hassan, and encouraged the King to be the conduit for peace. Although no immediate improvement took place in the Arab-Israeli conflict, King Hassan later emerged as a force for conciliation. Within a decade of Randolph's visit, two senior Israelis, Moshe Dayan and Yitzhak Rabin, both made that same journey, in secret. Twenty-five years after Randolph's last act, Rabin as Prime Minister and his Foreign Secretary, Shimon Peres, made the journey openly, with a guard of honour to welcome them at Rabat airport. As I watched that scene on television, I thought of Randolph's initiative, undertaken in such odd circumstances, yet with Randolph's typical tenacity and enthusiasm.

Early in 1968 I was drawn back into Randolph's orbit. I did not return to Stour, but we spoke from time to time on the telephone about various tasks that I could do for him. I began to interview some of those who had served with his father on the Western Front, and to prepare a historical brief about his father's period as Minister of Munitions. I sent him notes about what he might read as background for that period. On 29 April he telephoned me from Stour. 'I've been very depressed and low,' he said. 'There's always a lamp burning for you here.' I was about to go on holiday to Portugal, and told him I would come to Stour on my return. A week later, on a beach in the Algarve, I was handed a telegram. It was from Andrew Kerr. 'Randolph died this morning.'

I flew back on the following day. Randolph's brother-in-law Duncan Sandys was on the flight. In sending him a note of sympathy I added: 'It feels strange to be flying back to East Bergholt for the last time. He always called at awkward moments during the five years I devilled for him.' On the following day I returned to Stour for Randolph's funeral. Among the mourners were three who took me aside and spoke with warmth about the Boss: Harold Macmillan, Aristotle Onassis and Quintin Hogg (later Lord Hailsham). It was such a sad moment. Randolph was only fifty-seven. 'There were more genuine tears at his funeral at Bergholt than for many a more successful man,' Quintin Hogg wrote to me shortly afterwards.

Immediately after the funeral, I flew back to Portugal. 'Young' Winston had generously paid the fare for Randolph's devoted secretary, Barbara Twigg, so that she could have a week in the Portuguese sun. When I returned to London, Winston told me he would like to try to finish his father's work. I said that I would gladly help him set up a team, and guide it on its way, though I did not want to be a ghost any more. The British publishers of the biography, Heinemann, did not realize at first how keen Winston was to continue with his father's work. They thought that Michael Wolff, who had been with Randolph since 1961, would be the best person to finish the job, and he, having asked me to tea at a hotel in Victoria, invited me to undertake the document volumes.

Michael was to be disappointed in his hopes, a disappointment to which Edward Heath referred in his remarks at Michael's own memorial service a decade later, in 1976. His career at the very centre of Conservative Party policy-making had been brought to an abrupt end when Margaret Thatcher became Party leader: she had no place there for someone so devoted to her predecessor. Michael's early death at the age of forty-seven was a terrible shock to his own family and to his friends. He was the first of my contemporaries and colleagues for whom I wrote an obituary.

It was in the bright sunshine outside St Margaret's, Westminster, after Randolph's memorial service, that the chairman of Heinemann led me to one side and explained that they had decided that 'young' Winston should be the author, as 'Churchill, by Churchill and Churchill' now seemed to them a good way to stir up interest in the remaining volumes. As I had done when Randolph had asked me the same question, I agreed to give what support I could. But when Winston's name was put up to Lord Hartwell he replied that whereas the publishers had the right to nominate Randolph's successor, he, Lord Hartwell, had the right to veto their nomination, and that he had already appointed his brother-in-law Lord Birkenhead to the job.

Many weeks of impasse followed. Looking at my diary of those weeks (it runs to more than a hundred pages) I see that I wrote several letters to the publishers on Winston's behalf, pointing out that his father had asked me, shortly after that awful telephone call, if I would be willing to help Winston to keep the biography on the road, should Lord Hartwell's wishes somehow be frustrated. I also did a diary piece for *The Times* in which I wrote: 'Randolph's team survives; building on their many years' collective experience, there is little doubt that Winston could complete the richly woven tapestry of personal and political documentation along the excellent lines which his father had so carefully planned.' Such advocacy was in vain. Lord Hartwell was adamant and no decision was reached.

The delay began to threaten the momentum of publishing schedules. This led the American publishers, Houghton Mifflin, to enter the fray, in the person of one of their most senior people, Paul Brooks, who, after interviewing me, asked me to finish the job.

Still Lord Hartwell refused to budge. I was summoned to his presence on the top floor of the Daily Telegraph building in Fleet Street. He seemed shy and nervous, hesitating as he spoke, yet determined to end the impasse once and for all. I had earlier sent him some of my own books, including *The Appeasers* and *The Roots of Appeasement*, and a short volume of documents, *Britain and Germany between the Wars*. They were in a pile on the floor, together with the manuscript of a biography I was then writing, *Sir Horace Rumbold, Portrait of a Diplomat*.

After offering me a cup of tea, Lord Hartwell asked if I would be willing to be Lord Birkenhead's assistant in completing the biography. I declined. He then asked me if I would do the next volume, the one which would include the Dardanelles, and leave the rest of Churchill's life for Lord Birkenhead to write. Again I declined. He then asked me if I would co-author what remained with Lord Birkenhead. Mumbling something about my first book having been co-authored and that being enough for me (though in fact I had greatly enjoyed co-authorship) I again declined.

It was late afternoon. I had to catch a train back to Oxford. Lord Hartwell asked me if I could think of a solution. He then sat and waited. Tea was brought in. I realized that I would never get back to Oxford unless I said something. But I could think of nothing to say. The sun was flooding through the room. For a long time we were silent. The tea things were taken away. Then, in desperation I think at the thought of missing my train, I made the following suggestion: Lord Birkenhead, a noted one-volume biographer (of, among others, Lord Halifax and Lord Cherwell) would write a single-volume biography of Churchill based on the papers of which Lord Hartwell was the effective copyright holder. I would finish the multi-volume work on which Randolph had embarked. Lord Birkenhead's book would be short and stimulating. Mine would be long and academic.

Lord Hartwell was relieved. We parted, and a few weeks later, the scheme I had outlined was put into effect. The Churchill papers were brought across country from Stour in a pantechnicon, under police escort and put, for safety, into the basement of the Bodleian Library. They were calculated to weigh as much as fifteen tons. I advertised for a secretary, bought several tens of thousand sheets of foolscap paper (they ran out less than a third of the way through my work), and contemplated the future with some trepidation as well as excitement.

As I began work in the Bodleian, Lord Birkenhead came to do his work at my side. We got on well together, and he entertained me with his own recollections of Churchill, which went back to the early 1920s. But he was a sick man and after a number of visits he never came again. His one-volume biography was later taken up by his son, the 3rd Earl, but he too died before it could be completed.

My own course was now set. I gave up a commission I had been offered just before Randolph died, to write the official biography of Sir Stafford Cripps, and began work on that very period of Winston Churchill's career that Randolph had begun so much to look forward to writing, the Dardanelles.

IV

The Dardanelles

Throughout 1966 and the first half of 1967, at Stour and in Oxford, I had worked on the chronology of the Dardanelles for Randolph, plotting on large sheets of paper the day-by-day events, with notes of the telegrams sent to and from London, the decisions of the War Council, and the course of the fighting on the Western and Eastern Fronts and at sea. All the relevant documents in the Churchill papers were selected by me, typed out by Randolph's secretaries, in triplicate at his insistence, and put into manila folders with holes punched in the top left hand corners, after which they were held in place with green Treasury tags. This method, devised by Randolph, could not be varied.

On each visit to Stour, I would stand at the Disraeli desk and read Randolph the most recent file. He would punctuate (and sometimes puncture) my reading with comments, pointing out the gaps that he wanted filled, and asking for biographical notes about all those mentioned.

By the time of Randolph's death in June 1968 my Dardanelles folders were very full indeed, as far as his method of working was concerned. They were almost ready for him to use as the basis to dictate the series of reflective linking passages that he liked to insert between the documents. These passages constituted his narrative and reflective segments of the biography, and almost its only non-documentary sections: they were his characteristic growls of approval or disapproval of his father's actions; as well as commentaries, often caustic, on the actions, or lack of them, by the other Cabinet ministers.

When I took over from Randolph, I felt that such linking passages, however clear or outspoken, were not enough. They constituted, in the end, commentaries on the documents, rather than a narrative, or

47

an analysis. The documents were of course fascinating, and also voluminous. Most of them had appeared, though sometimes only in fragments, in many previous books. I decided that I would take my manila folders with me to the Dardanelles themselves; hoping to bring the subject alive in my mind.

In the introduction to the first volume, Randolph had chosen what he called the 'Theme of the Work'. This was a phrase that he had found in Lockhart's biography of Sir Walter Scott: 'He shall be his own biographer.' Actually – and Randolph had flared up when I pointed this out – Lockhart had gone on to say 'as far as possible', recognizing that other people's words must also be a part of any rounded work. Randolph, too, had often departed, in fact, from the more rigid method implicit in Lockhart's short phrase, for he too had wanted us 'young gentlemen' researchers to seek out, and he had then enjoyed reading, and including, some quite savage comments by Churchill's critics. Even so, I felt that it was more than just a matter of a juxtaposition of Churchill's words and those of his opponents.

What could be done for the Dardanelles campaign, and then for every subsequent controversy with which Churchill was involved (and there were far more than I had realized), was to explain exactly what he was trying to do, why he wanted to do it, how he set about it, and the way in which he confronted the various obstacles, whether of nature or of individuals, that were found along the way. I wanted to be able to establish the chain of events and circumstances within which he worked: the essential context that would show to what extent he was alone, part of a particular line of thought, ahead of his time, or (as was often the case) beset by critics who would not hesitate to resort to smears and innuendoes in order to try to discredit him.

The method I devised for my own work, which I thought might last a decade (but which still continues after more than two) was this: I would read every single page of the Churchill papers, and photocopy every document in them that seemed to me to be necessary, either to establish the narrative, or as a candidate for inclusion in the document volumes which were to accompany each narrative volume. The work of photocopying involved hundreds of hours of work, principally by my research assistant Susie (later my wife), by William Sturge (who photocopied all the Second World War documents), and by Larry Arnn and Sue Rampton, who undertook the bulk of the photocopying for the post-1945 period.

These documents came from Churchill's original working files, arranged over the years by his own staff into various themes, Literary, Political, Personal, Official, Speeches, and Financial. Some of these files, which could contain between half a dozen and fifty sheets of paper, were arranged annually, others, such as the Political Correspondence, had been filed in both annually and alphabetical order. Some files contained the newspaper and magazine articles Churchill had written during a single year. Others contained his financial accounts over several years. Family and political letters could be wrongly filed. Sometimes a secretary had not recognized a signature, or known into which category the letter should be put.

The system had been used over so many years, and the papers stored at different times in so many different vaults, both in banks and at Chartwell, that it varied, and could be muddled. Some files had letters in them that related to material in other, not necessarily adjacent, files. I remember finding in one file the first page of a letter to Churchill from General Sir Ian Hamilton (written from the Dardanelles). But the letter was incomplete. Many months were to pass until, in quite a different file, and under a very different date, I found the second and final page.

As soon as the photocopying of the Churchill papers was done for any year or episode of Churchill's life, Susie and I took the photocopies and arranged them in strictly chronological order. Each day's set of material was put together, and where possible arranged within the time-scale of the day: morning, noon, afternoon, evening, night. Each month's set of materials had a metal foldback clip of its own. On busy weeks in Churchill's (and the nation's) life, such as the first week of August 1914 or the first week of May 1940, each day had a clip of its own, often a bulky one. In this way, we could then mull over the materials and gain a sense of the sequence of events, the influence of one event (perhaps a single letter, or of a piece of information reaching him) on another: the daily and changing pressures and patterns.

This chronological method revealed many gaps. In a particular letter, Churchill or a colleague writing to him might refer to a Cabinet decision. We then had to find that decision, and incorporate it in the relevant clip, ready to be quoted or referred to in the narrative. This meant Susie and I spending hundreds of hours at the Public Record Office, sitting side by side, going through the files of Cabinets, War Cabinets and Cabinet Committees, and of each ministry of which Churchill had been a member: between 1914 to 1929 he held six different portfolios.*

This Public Record Office material, which had only been made available under the 1 January 1966 Thirty-Year Rule, and was vast, was slowly photocopied, brought back to my desk, and incorporated in the expanding clips. Then we set off to the archives of those who were involved in each phase of any episode, from the Prime Minister of the day (Churchill served under four Prime Ministers†) to other ministers, civil servants, parliamentarians and observers of the event which we were trying to describe.

The material that we gathered and brought back to Oxford covered every aspect of British and European history, including crucial moments in Britain's relations with Ireland, India, Russia and the Middle East. The negotiations and activities with which Churchill was involved included the arming of United States forces in 1917, the post-1918 Versailles settlement, the War Debts negotiations of 1924, the evolution of the Locarno Treaties in 1925, the attempt to sustain France in 1940, and the 'Big Three' conferences at Teheran, Yalta and Potsdam. There was new material to be woven in for key moments in domestic policy, the economy, and defence, as well as many personal vignettes. I only began to write a chapter when I felt that the gaps had been filled sufficiently for a true account of what had taken place, and Churchill's part in it.

I wrote each chapter by hand, in ink. It was then typed out by a secretary, read by several scrutineers, among them two of Churchill's former Private Secretaries, Sir John Colville and Sir David Hunt, and sent to those who might have some special knowledge of its subject matter. John Barnes at the London School of Economics was of particular help in reading through the disarmament section while

---

* First Lord of the Admiralty (1911–15), Chancellor of the Duchy of Lancaster (1915), Minister of Munitions (1917–18), Secretary of State for War and Air (1919–21), Secretary of State for the Colonies (1921–22), and Chancellor of the Exchequer (1924–29).

† Campbell-Bannerman, Asquith, Lloyd George and Baldwin.

it could still be improved. Edward Thomas was an essential and patient guide to all matters relating to wartime signals intelligence. Thus enhanced, the chapter would be retyped.

My next task was to send the chapters to those who had actually taken part in the events which it described, or to go to see such participants and discuss with them what they remembered. Susie and I would travel far and wide (including as far as India) to find those who could look at the chapter with the eye of a participant in the events it described. From such eye-witnesses could come myriad benefits: the addition of atmosphere and mood, the names and addresses of others who were also present but of whom I had no record, the spotting of factual error that could then be checked against contemporary documents, and, again and again, the shy or chance reference to an original document, diary or letters written at the time, that could add strictly historical material, and which had hitherto not seen the light of day. Thus, after Sir Edmund Spears, who had been on the Western Front with Churchill, had given me his recollections, he produced on my second or third visit two tiny pocket diaries that he had written at the time, from the front, describing Churchill's actions and points of view at a critical time in his life.

I can insert at this point a cautionary tale. I asked one of those who had known Churchill best, and longest, Clementine's cousin Sylvia Henley, whom I had met several times at Stour, if I could talk to her about her recollections of the Dardanelles. Certainly, she said, and we arranged that I would call on her at her London flat, Melton Court, South Kensington, in two weeks' time. I arrived from Oxford full of anticipation of gems to follow. Hardly had I sat down than Mrs Henley, who was then in her mid-eighties, said enthusiastically: 'I am so glad you let me have two weeks before we met. I have been refreshing my memory by reading Max Beaverbrook's book on 1915,' whereupon she proceeded to give me a detailed and accurate summary of all that Lord Beaverbrook had written. Her own memories were now well submerged beneath Beaverbrook's persuasive writing and distinctive narrative.

Normally the recollections that I was able to gather were vivid, helpful and entertaining. Adding them to the material in the Churchill papers, the government archives, and the private archives (and sometimes newspaper accounts), Susie and I could discuss together, and hopefully resolve, every mystery, every obscurity, and every evolution of policy. I would then fill my pen and write the chapter.

In addition to what became six narrative volumes, I continued work on the sets of document volumes, known as companions, which Randolph had begun. The aim was, and still is, to make available to students and scholars, and to the general reader who enjoys the raw material of history, a comprehensive selection of the letters, documents and other contemporary materials covering all periods of Churchill's life and career. In 1966 Randolph had published the first set of two companions, for the years 1874 to 1900. When he died two years later, a set of three companions, from 1901 to 1914, had been compiled and assembled by two of his assistants, Cameron Hazlehurst and Paul Addison, and by José Harris. My first task as Randolph's successor was to get these three books ready for the printer: it was a task that absorbed much of my time throughout November and December 1968 and January 1969.

Since then I have produced nine further books of documents, and have just sent a tenth volume to the printer: *Never Surrender*, which goes from May to December 1940. Work on these volumes, which are fully annotated, has involved as much work as for the main volumes, and has also called for stout extra hands. In myriad biographical tasks, I was helped at different times by Sidney Aster, Kate Fleming, Taffy Sassoon, Larry Arnn, Rachelle Gryn and Abe Eisenstat. Among those who helped with proof-reading, a substantial task, was Nigel Viney of Heinemann, my friend and contact there for many years.

To ensure that all this work went smoothly, to track people down, and to follow up archival queries, involved a formidable amount of correspondence, filing, sorting and retrieving. To do this over a twenty-five-year period, secretarial help was an indispensable and daily asset. In 1968 Sarah Graham set up the correspondence and archival system without which this present book could not have been written. During the following twenty-five years the secretarial tasks were carried out by, among others, Judy Holdsworth, Wendy Rioch, Penny Houghton, Sue Rampton and, for the Churchill War Papers document volumes now in progress, Kay Thomson. I am particularly aware of the importance of secretarial help, having seen just how dependent Churchill was on similar help for the smooth working of his own 'factory' (as he called it) about which I have written in chapter nine.

Within a year after of taking over from Randolph, I completed the first, rather tentative, draft of volume three. With it I flew to Istanbul, where for the first time in my life I was an official guest of a foreign government. The Turkish Ambassador in London, Zeki Kuneralp, himself a keen historian, had arranged the visit, having quizzed me carefully over a lunch as to whether I was somehow anti-Turk. I told him that twelve years earlier I had spent several months in Turkey, had taught English at a summer school on the top of Mount Uludag, the Mysian Olympus, above Bursa, and had nothing but fond memories (which was true) of travelling to the furthest eastern lands, to the then sealed Turkish border with the former Soviet Union.

On reaching Istanbul I was warned by the young Turkish diplomat who met me that a recent outburst of anti-American feeling made it important that I should make clear, to anyone I spoke to, that I was English and not American. This was especially true, he said, when I was at my hotel, the balconies of which overlooked the swirling waters of the Bosphorus far below. On the following day I was taken to the naval museum in which I saw charts of the Dardanelles minefields, in which it was clear just how close the Anglo-French naval force had come to penetrating them in the assault of 18 March 1915. There was also a note about the desperate shortage of ammunition of the Turkish mobile shore batteries: by a bizarre quirk of historical irony, the Imperial Russian intelligence service had reported this very fact to the Tsar. And in the Second World War, trying to show Churchill some goodwill during a stormy Moscow meeting, Stalin had repeated this to Churchill.

Somehow Stalin had understood that Churchill's Achilles' heel was the Dardanelles, and felt that a kindly reference to that campaign would be a means to win him over. In March 1915 Churchill, then only forty, but at the height of his powers and popularity, had pinned his hopes on the swift and relatively bloodless defeat of Turkey. As First Lord of the Admiralty he had been in charge of the Royal Navy for the previous four years of peace, bringing it to a peak of war preparedness. It was clear from the records of the War Council (Asquith's War Cabinet), which are available at the Public Record

Office, that Churchill had confidence in the ability of British and French warships to push past the Turkish minefields and forts at the Dardanelles, that narrow strip of water separating Europe from Asia, a few miles from ancient Troy. Through the records of the War Council, then available for study at the Public Record Office, I was able to follow not only Churchill's arguments from week to week, but also those of his (mostly much older) Cabinet colleagues. With Turkey knocked out of the war, Britain and France would, as they believed, be able to strike at the German and Austro-Hungarian monolith from the south, drawing onto the side of Britain, France and Russia three hitherto neutral states, Italy, Greece and Bulgaria. For the Greeks, the prospect of the fall of Turkey would make Constantinople a prize worth fighting for. The annexation of Eastern Thrace would be the spur for the Bulgarians to fight. Italy, once she committed herself, would be able to control, and even to annex, the Adriatic coast of Austria-Hungary.

Not only the War Council records, but the Foreign Office papers, and Lord Kitchener's War Office files – all at the Public Record Office – showed the precise evolution of the British naval attack at the Dardanelles. The British Ambassador in St Petersburg, in a telegram that reached London in the early hours of 2 January 1915, stressed, as a matter of urgency, that such British action would give the Russians a means of countering the Turkish advance into the Caucasian provinces of the Tsarist Empire. This point, as the records showed, had been taken up at once by Kitchener, who wrote to Churchill that morning: 'Do you think any naval action would be possible to prevent Turks sending more men into the Caucasus and thus denuding Constantinople?' Kitchener's letter was a catalyst in the concept that Russia might be helped on its Turkish Front by some British action at the Dardanelles, and that Constantinople might be the prize of victory.

The Admiralty archives provided the next piece of the jigsaw puzzle. They showed that Admiral Fisher, the First Sea Lord whom Churchill had just brought back to the Admiralty, had suggested a substantial naval and military assault against Turkey, including a naval attack at the Dardanelles and a military landing at Gallipoli peninsula. Fisher's papers at Lennoxlove – the ones that Randolph had sent me to see in 1964 – made clear that Churchill was at first hesitant about the new Turkish strategy. He wrote to Fisher, in reply to the Admiral's plan to land troops at Gallipoli: 'I would not grudge 100,000 men because of the great political effects in the Balkan peninsula: but Germany is the foe, and it is bad war to seek cheap victories and easier antagonists.'

That same week, as the Admiralty telegrams showed, Churchill asked the Admiral on the spot if something might be done by ships alone. In reply, the Admiral expressed his willingness to try some form of naval assault. Churchill became convinced that something decisive for the outcome of the war could be done. As the naval plans progressed and the planning obstacles were overcome, Churchill's keenness grew. Even the volatile Fisher had moments of dramatic enthusiasm, going so far as to urge that the most modern British battleship of all, the *Queen Elizabeth*, instead of 'uselessly' test-firing her as yet untested fifteen-inch guns into the ocean at Gibraltar, should test them against the Turkish forts at the Dardanelles. (This letter I had found in a small suitcase at the Royal Naval College at Greenwich, part of the 'archive' of one of Fisher's colleagues, Admiral Oliver.)

By the end of February, Churchill was borne further along the path of the swift defeat of Turkey by the incredible enthusiasm of every member of Asquith's War Council. The Council minutes show how each minister saw some specific gain for what seemed only a small risk. One minister, Lewis Harcourt, the Secretary of State for the Colonies, went so far as to circulate to his cabinet colleagues a paper entitled 'The Spoils'. I found this paper in Harcourt's son's house at Stanton Harcourt outside Oxford. It was in a small tin box of papers that had been neatly folded away and tied up with red ribbons fifty years earlier. The spoils for the defeat of the Ottoman Empire were to be the Empire itself, with Britain gaining the lion's share, including Palestine. Amid these enthusiasms, Churchill, to be on the safe side (to 'make assurance double sure', one of his favourite Shakespearean phrases), pressed for military as well as naval action. But Kitchener was emphatic that troops were not needed: the naval attack would do the trick.

Uneasy at this, and asking for his dissent to be recorded by the Cabinet Secretary, Churchill agreed to go ahead with ships alone. When, a few days later, Kitchener showed no interest in providing air support, in the shape of the army's fledgling Flying Corps, Churchill stepped in with the even smaller, but keen, Naval Air Service, which he had helped to establish as an independent air fighting force four years earlier. One of the young pilots, Richard Bell Davies, was to win the Victoria Cross for rescuing a captured soldier from the clutches of a Turkish Army patrol. Davies, when I found him in retirement on the south coast during my Randolph days, was as indignantly sure as many other survivors of the campaign that if only Churchill had been allowed to continue, victory might have come. Instead, the naval attack had been called off by the Admiral on the spot after several ships hit mines, and 650 men drowned, 600 of them on the French warship, the *Bouvet*. The naval attack on the Narrows was never renewed, even though minesweeping continued, and, in Churchill's view, a second naval attack could have been mounted with the still considerable naval forces gathered there. But the Admiral, after first agreeing to try again, decided not to take what he regarded as too big a risk. Churchill sent several telegrams urging renewed action, but did not have the authority to overrule the man on the spot.

The military attack that followed a month later became bogged down, despite great individual heroism, in incompetence and disaster. The Gallipoli Peninsula, to which I was even then on my way, became within nine months the graveyard of more than 60,000 soldiers. By then Churchill was out of office, himself serving as a soldier on the Western Front. But the stigma of Gallipoli never left him.

Churchill was never to shake off the charge of recklessness with regard to the planning and execution of the Dardanelles attack, even though the main charges almost always concerned the military attack, not the naval one. First at Stour, and then in my own study at Oxford, I read and re-read the War Council's deliberations. How clearly Churchill had understood the dangers and sought to avert them. But Kitchener's refusal to let the first naval attack be accompanied by a military landing, followed by his decision to throw troops ashore a month later, altered and hampered the original conception. It was errors of navigation in putting some of those troops ashore, and the lack of clear orders as to what they should do once they had landed, which many did without serious opposition, that proved the fatal flaw. Over that aspect, Churchill had no say, though he was soon to be widely assumed to be responsible, and to bear the blame.

All these factors, some already a part of history since 1923 through Churchill's own second volume of *The World Crisis*, some new, were in my manila folders as I flew from Istanbul to Ankara. I had been told that I could meet Ismet Inönü, who had been Ataturk's lieutenant at the Dardanelles and was later his successor as President. At the time of my visit in 1969 Inönü was under house arrest. I waited in my hotel for three days, while various Foreign Ministry emissaries told me how difficult it would be to see the former leader. On the fourth day a diplomat and a soldier came to escort me to Inönü's house. By then I had my own driver, Behçet Kosluler, who was to drive me across Anatolia to the Dardanelles on the following day. (When he finally deposited me back at Istanbul airport several weeks later, Behçet suddenly became very confidential, told me how much he admired the English, and asked if he could come with me, and be my driver in England. With great regret I had to decline.)

Behçet drove through Ankara to Inönü's house: the soldier sat next to him, his rifle pointed awkwardly in my direction. We came to a driveway, at the entrance to which was a small armoured vehicle. As we reached the front door, Inönü emerged, a diminutive figure, striding forward to meet his guest. The car stopped. Behçet hurled himself out of the driver's seat and prostrated himself before Inönü, calling out in tones of reverence, 'Pasha-m', 'my general'. Inönü lifted him back onto his feet, and we proceeded indoors.

There was a secretary present, who took notes of everything Inönü said, but not, so it seemed to me, of anything I said. I later learned that this was Bulent Ecevit, then the Secretary-General of Inönü's banned Republican People's Party, later himself a prisoner in the dreaded Mamak jail, and subsequently Prime Minister. Inönü told me that Ataturk had always insisted on speaking the language of the visitor, and that he, Inönü, would therefore speak to me in English. I was flattered, though he quickly lapsed into French. He had two points that he wanted to make about Churchill: that the naval attack at the Dardanelles had come to within an ace of success, and that he, Inönü, had thought at the time that the Turkish naval forces would have been decimated in the Sea of Marmara, exposing Constantinople itself to the vastly superior naval forces of the Entente (a British submarine had, a few days before the March attack, crept below the minefields and nets, penetrated the Sea of Marmara, and sunk two ships off the capital, causing consternation, and winning its captain the Victoria Cross).

Inönü made the point which Churchill had made at the time, in vain, that in the immediate aftermath of the setback of 18 March, had the Admiral tried again, he would have had a good chance of success. The Admiral was John de Robeck. Churchill, who loved nicknames, had quickly dubbed him Admiral 'de Row-back'.

I made one more call while still in Ankara, to Ataturk's house. His former secretary, Afet Inan, whom I was told by my diplomat escort had been his last and favourite mistress, showed me his library. I opened the drawer in which he had kept his maps. There was his working map of the Dardanelles, a 1911 British military map, printed in Cairo. So it was not the British alone who had to rely on other people's efforts: Lord Kitchener's nominee to lead the military forces in April 1915, General Sir Ian Hamilton, had taken out with him the 1908 Baedeker guide book to Constantinople and Asia Minor. This worthy Leipzig volume was hardly the most useful guide to a military campaign which had to start on a coastline disfigured (from an invading soldier's point of view) by cliffs and gullies constantly altered by tides and erosion.

I browsed about Ataturk's bookshelves. Shortly before his death he had hoped to welcome Churchill to Turkey, and his Private Secretaries, two of whom I met on this visit, had collected Churchill's books for him to read. There on the shelf was the Dardanelles volume of *The World Crisis*, which Churchill had published in 1923. At the point where de Robeck had refused Churchill's request to make a second attack on the minefields, Ataturk had written in the margin a Turkish phrase, 'History is ruthless to him who is without ruthlessness.' But Churchill did not have the authority to order the Admiral to make the second attack. He could urge and cajole, but he could not impose action. Fearlessly grasping the moment of decision when things could go either way: that was what Churchill was prepared to do. But his Admiralty advisers would not let him overrule the Admiral on the spot, that was clear from the Admiralty records. In the War Council, Churchill could not make progress against past prejudice and present doubts combined. I had seen in the archives of the ministers concerned that as things began to go wrong, they began to back away from their earlier support and to forget their initial strong enthusiasm.

All this was in my mind as Behçet drove me out of Ankara and across the Anatolian plain, through the Graeco-Turkish battlefields of 1922, and past some of the secret British airstrips of 1942, to the city of Çanakkale (the former Chanak). From there, based at a hotel on the Asian shore, we crossed each day by ferry to the Gallipoli Peninsula, to the edges of the 1915 naval minefields, to the general location of the mobile howitzers, and to the sites of the heavy gun emplacements, all of which had been knocked out during the March attack or been left with virtually no ammunition. Some of the guns were still there, pointing out across the water. It became clear how very far into the Dardanelles the ships had penetrated, and how close they were to the final obstacles where the narrows turn into the Sea of Marmara, and open water.

Together with Norman Pemberton, the Commonwealth War Graves custodian, we visited the beaches at which the military landings had taken place in April, and again in August, 1915. We climbed the heights, at Cape Helles and at Anzac, which those landings had failed to capture. At Cape Helles we stood in silence by the naval monument, looking out on an absolutely placid sea, beneath which still lies the detritus of the great warships that had been sunk. We stopped at almost every cemetery, read the names on so many of the gravestones, and marvelled at the work of maintaining trees and flowers and shrubs in such a hostile landscape. At Y Beach I found wild irises, and put a few in the relevant pages of the British official history. At Cape Helles I saw the grave of one of Churchill's army friends from the turn of the century, Lieutenant Thomas Frankland, a fellow prisoner of the Boers captured during the armoured train ambush, and one of the first to be killed in the W beach landings.

It was easy to understand, at that place, Churchill's terrible sense of frustration and of anger, that if only the naval attack had been tried a second time, if necessary a third time, then the terrible slaughter on the beaches and in the trenches of the peninsula could have been avoided. It was all the more understandable when, on opening my manila folders on the Peninsula itself, I reread Churchill's reasoning for attacking Turkey at the Dardanelles: that it would end the slaughter and the stalemate that had begun to be the curse of the Western Front. 'Are there not other alternatives', he had written to Asquith on 29 December 1914, 'than sending our armies to chew barbed wire in Flanders?'

I returned twice more to the Dardanelles. Each time, I contrasted the stunning beauty of the contemporary scene, the remoteness and grandeur of the Peninsula, and the serene beauty of the scattered graveyards, with the terrible slaughter and hardship that had taken place there on the cliffs and in the gullies. I also continued to reflect on the vision of shortening the war that had led Churchill to support a short, swift, successful naval attack. A superior naval force had been within hours, perhaps even minutes, of victory. But failure in the Narrows, the transfer of authority from Churchill at the Admiralty to Kitchener at the War Office, and the subsequent throwing ashore of vast armies, had brought about by far the blackest moment in Churchill's career, publicly and personally.

On my last visit to Gallipoli, with Susie at my side, there was an unexpected diversion from research. In one of the tiny villages near Suvla Bay we saw a local newspaper on a teahouse wall with a photo-graph of Elizabeth Taylor, much to the excitement of the villagers, who believed that the actress was on her way to the Peninsula. The article that went with the photograph, however, was about Queen Elizabeth.

The Queen, Prince Philip and Princess Anne were in fact on their way to Chanak. Susie and I packed our duffle bags and made the journey southward to Cape Helles. In preparation for the royal visit a tarmacked road had been specially laid from the village of Sedd-el-Bahr to the British naval monument overlooking the entrance to the Dardanelles. We waited for some time with a few Turkish soldiers and their officer until a bus was seen hurtling along the road. It pulled up at the monument and out jumped two dozen journalists. Susie and I were pushed to the side and a few moments later the royal car arrived, and many Turkish dignitaries.

The Queen laid a wreath. We heard Prince Philip say to an aide, 'I suppose they made this road specially for us.' There was a brief ceremony. Norman Pemberton took charge of the signing of the Cape Helles visitors' book. Then the royal car sped away, followed at highest speed by the journalists' bus.

We were left alone again, with a single Turkish naval officer, who was disconsolate that he, alone among his senior colleagues, had not been invited to dine on board the Royal Yacht *Britannia*. It had been a moment of modern sound and fury beyond the normally silent battlefield. Within a few minutes the scene had returned to its haunted beauty, and we were on our way back to Oxford to work on Churchill's story; to May 1915, when Asquith gave way to the Conservative pressure to create an all-party government.

The Conservative ministers had been in the political wilderness for ten years. They did not want to remain there any longer. A serious shortage of shells on the Western Front, and the threat of a controversial parliamentary debate on the Dardanelles, caused Asquith to lose his nerve, and to agree to a coalition. The Conservatives had very few conditions:the first and most emphatic was that Churchill, their foe from the day that he crossed over to the Liberal benches in 1904, must go. Asquith gave way.

When I returned to Oxford from the Dardanelles, I did not know why Asquith had succumbed to Conservative pressure. The Churchill letters that I had found in his personal archive revealed only Churchill's anguish, and that of Clementine, at his imminent fall from high office, and from the direction of war policy at a crisis moment.

Shortly after my return to Britain, with the image of the Dardanelles still vivid in my mind I received a visitor. She was a tall, attractive, amusing and voluble woman, who had written to me out of the blue, introducing herself as a friend of Randolph's and a cousin of Clementine's. Her name was Judy Montagu. I took her out to dinner at one of my favourite Oxford restaurants, the Sorbonne, its dining-room somewhat dark and romantic, as befitted its reputation. Judy, as she asked me to call her, had brought with her, somewhat surprisingly, a laundry basket. I assumed that it contained her overnight clothes (she had booked into the Randolph Hotel). Hardly had we sat down however, and before the waiter could take our order, she bent down and opened the laundry basket, bringing up to the table a folder full of letters.

The letters were handwritten, in an elegant hand that I recognized at once as Asquith's. They had been written to her mother, Venetia Stanley, Clementine's first cousin. The letters covered the whole period of the planning and execution of the Dardanelles. They were incredibly detailed, often telling far more about the course of the discussion in the War Council than the official record had done. There was a letter for virtually every day, sometimes two and even three letters in any one day. Not only had Asquith revealed to Venetia, at the time, the evolution of the Dardanelles, but he was particularly fascinated by Churchill, recounting to her Churchill's conversations, moods, plans, interventions, all in detail and with great colour. Then, in the week that the Conservatives demanded Churchill's head on a plate, there was a terrible change in the correspondence, hitherto caressing in its tone and seductive in its intention. Venetia, tired of Asquith's unrelenting attentions, had taken the one decisive step open to her to shake them off and to turn her back on them once and for all. She had informed him that she intended to marry. Her husband would be none other than the man they had both often laughed about and even mocked, Edwin Montagu, a dark, tall, ugly, 'unattractive' (an Edwardian codeword for Jewish) member of Asquith's Government. Not so long before, when Venetia had called on Montagu, Asquith had penned her the following note, which Judy showed me that evening:

> Venetia, though a Christian child
> Sprung from an Aryan stem
> Frequents – too easily beguiled –
> The silken tents of Shem.

Now Venetia would marry the mocked-at Montagu, did not want Asquith to write to her again, and wanted no more to do with him. He was devastated. Whatever dreams he had harboured of intimacy with her (he was sixty-two and she was twenty-seven) were shattered. Their drives together in his car along the Embankment were over. His tempting confidence of daily war policy-making would have to stop. He did not know which way to turn. Hitherto he had sought her advice about every political crisis. He had bombarded her each day with the most secret war news, and with his most detailed thoughts on war policy and politics. Now he could confide in her no longer. When Lloyd George, the Chancellor of the Exchequer and the second most powerful member of the Liberal team, went to 10 Downing Street to insist that the only way forward was to accept the Conservative demands, bring them in, and sacrifice Churchill, Asquith had no strength left but to acquiesce. No sooner had Lloyd George left than Asquith wrote to Venetia:

> Never since the war began had I such an accumulation (no longer shared!) of anxieties . . . one of the most hellish bits of these most hellish days was that you alone of all the world – to whom I have always gone in every moment of trial & trouble, & from whom I have always come back solaced and healed & inspired – were the one person who could do nothing, & from whom I could ask nothing. To my dying day, that will be the most bitter memory of my life . . .
>
> I am on the eve of the most astounding & world-shaking decisions – as I wd never have taken without your counsel & consent. It seems so strange & empty & unnatural: yet there is nowhere else that I can go, nor would I, if I could.

Shortly after Asquith wrote this letter, Churchill appeared in his room, full of confidence that he could deal effectively with any House of Commons debate on the Dardanelles, that he could set out the documents that would show that his actions had not been irresponsible, that he could rout the Conservative critics, and, even though he had been deserted at that very moment by Admiral Fisher, could not only defend what had already been done, but find a replacement for Fisher and see the naval attack through to success at the Dardanelles. Asquith heard him out, then said, as if he had heard nothing, 'No, this will not do. I have decided to form a national government with a coalition with the Unionists, and a very much larger reconstruction will be required.' Before Churchill could plead with Asquith to let him stay in charge of the navy, the Prime Minister turned to him with the words 'What are we to do for you?'

With these seven words, Churchill knew that his days at the Admiralty, perhaps even his days in public life, were over. He never knew that Venetia, whose company he always enjoyed, and was to go on enjoying for many years, had broken Asquith's heart and destroyed his will to fight. Judy, the daughter of Venetia and Edwin, having read these letters aloud to me in such a stentorian voice that the whole restaurant ended up listening, put them back in her case, and I escorted her to the Randolph Hotel. My only sadness, amid the excitement of such a historic goldmine, was that 'my' Randolph was not there to share in the discoveries. How he would have loved them, listened to the letters again and again, and no doubt woven them into his narrative, as I was about to do into mine.

Churchill left the Admiralty under a black cloud of Conservative hostility, abandoned by his Liberal leader's unexpected and sudden 'What are we to do for you?' which he was never to forgive. Clementine, outraged, sent Asquith a long, handwritten letter, one of those that I found preserved among his private papers at Oxford, begging him to allow Churchill to remain as First Lord. 'If you throw Winston overboard', she wrote, 'you will be committing an act of weakness and your coalition government will not be as formidable a war machine as the present Government. Winston may in your eyes and in those with whom he has to work have faults but he has the supreme quality which I venture to say very few of your present or future Cabinet possess, the power, the imagination, the deadliness to fight Germany.'

In one of his last letters to Venetia, Asquith had described this appeal as 'the letter of a maniac'. I remember reading the letter itself, and Asquith's comment, to Lady Churchill, at one of our lunches at her flat in London where I would give her an account of my progress. She was pleased that she had written so forcefully, and that her letter had survived. After I had read it, she spoke, as if it were only yesterday, of the stormy, angry, frustrating atmosphere of that terrible time. 'The Dardanelles haunted him for the rest of his life,' she said. 'He always believed in it. When he left the Admiralty he thought he was finished. He didn't believe he would ever be asked back into government. I thought he'd never get over the Dardanelles. I thought he'd die of grief.'

Appointed in June 1915 to the sinecure of Chancellor of the Duchy of Lancaster (though a later Chancellor of the Duchy wrote to me in bemused protest that I had used the word 'sinecure' for his Cabinet post), Churchill was unable to exert any further influence on the continuing battles at Gallipoli. The shadow of the Dardanelles haunted him, as did Asquith's behaviour in throwing him over, as he saw it, without giving him the chance to defend his policies in Parliament.

There was one last act to be played in the drama of the Dardanelles. In my search for understanding, it was one of the most moving and instructive episodes in the saga. Churchill had complete faith that when the documents were known to the public his actions would be seen to have been farsighted and potentially decisive for the war. Repeated appeals to Asquith to allow him to publish the documents were turned down. He therefore began to collect the documents himself, and to ask others to help him piece the story together. In the late summer of 1915 he thought for a while of leaving England and going to the Dardanelles himself, to report on the situation there for the Cabinet. Asquith and Kitchener gave permission for this journey, but when the Conservative ministers heard of it by chance, just as he was setting off, they vetoed it.

Before the Conservative veto, Churchill had written a letter 'to be sent to Mrs Churchill in the event of my death'. The letter survived among her papers. After making financial provision for Clementine and their three children, Churchill wrote: 'I am anxious that you should get hold of my papers, especially those which refer to my Admiralty administration. There is no hurry; but some day I should like the truth to be known. Randolph will carry on the lamp.'

Churchill had faith that the 'complete record', as he called it in this letter, would be to his credit; that there was indeed a 'truth' that existed, could be found, and could be known. He had done the best he could, with the records then made available to him, to tell the Dardanelles story in his second volume of *The World Crisis*, published in 1923, in which he printed in full many of the letters and documents that he himself had been able to assemble. I was sad, on reading his letter to Clementine, that there was now no way Randolph could carry on that particular lamp, of telling the story, as he had been so eager to do. It was also sad that the false story had been for far too long an integral part of popular misconception, making it almost impossible to lay it to rest even until today. But I was pleased that Churchill had written 'I should like the truth to be known,' thus echoing the belief of the Victorian bishop and historian, Mandell Creighton, a Fellow of my own Oxford college, Merton, on whose tomb are inscribed the words: 'He tried to write true history.'

V

The Muse of Painting

While I was working for Randolph at Stour, I spent as much time as I could in his library, trying to absorb myself in every facet of his father's life. One of his books was a catalogue entitled *Churchill, His Paintings* by David Coombs. Three or four of these paintings were hanging on the main staircase at Stour; I saw them every time I went up to bed, or when I was summoned, as sometimes happened, to read to Randolph in his bedroom in the morning. Three of them were identified as 'Hoe Farm'. From their date, 1915, they were clearly the earliest that Churchill had done.

Shortly after Randolph's death I pieced together the story of Hoe Farm. Forced to leave the Admiralty and to abandon all his plans for a victory at the Dardanelles, Churchill found a weekend retreat far from the political turmoil of London and his sense of failure. It was called Hoe Farm, and lay in the fold of a steep hill deep in the Surrey countryside. I went there after each of my visits to the Dardanelles. The house had originally been a fifteenth-century cottage, converted at the turn of the century by Edwin Lutyens into a comfortable and secluded residence. It was a far cry from the beaches and gullies of Gallipoli, yet the line between them was a straight one.

My first glimpse of Hoe Farm was of a cosy, idyllic red brick house with an evergreen arch gate. To reach the house the visitor has to leave all main and minor roads, driving finally along a short country lane that leads nowhere but to the gate. Invited by its owner, Arthur Simon, in the spring of 1970, I arrived when the flowers around the pond at the end of the driveway were all in bloom, when the lawns beyond were a lush green, and the tall trees rich in foliage.

Here was Churchill's rural hideaway after the disastrous weeks in which he had been told by Asquith that his dreams of successful war policy-making were over, that he was not to remain at the Admiralty, and that the incoming Conservative ministers were to hold the very positions of authority from which he was to be excluded. These were the ministers who, for the decade after he had left their party, he had criticized, rebuked, castigated and, at times, humiliated: the peers whom he had mocked for being the cast-off relics of a dead system, and the opponents of Irish Home Rule whom he had belittled for their lack of vision.

Hoe Farm, rented for the summer, was Churchill's bolt hole, made all the more seductive by the hot summer weekends that followed his departure from the Admiralty. In a letter to his brother Jack, then on Sir Ian Hamilton's staff at Gallipoli, he wrote before one weekend: 'It really is a delightful valley and the garden gleams with summer jewellery. We live very simply – but with all the essentials of life well understood and well provided for – hot baths, cold champagne, new peas, and old brandy.' Randolph, recalling Hoe Farm fifty years later, told me of a game his father used to play, Bear, in which Churchill would be chased by his and his brother's children around the garden. But neither the 'essentials of life' nor Bear could mask the reality of the fall from influence and command that he felt so sharply.

Like Randolph, Clementine also had memories of Hoe Farm, but they were different ones: of her husband stooped in deepest thought, pacing up and down the long grass path at the top of the garden, from the copse of young trees at one end to the wooden summerhouse at the other, beneath the oppressive line of the hill above. Nothing could distract him. She despaired of ever seeing him unworried. His depression frightened her. Not even the weekends out of London seemed to bring him comfort or relaxation.

As a schoolboy Churchill had enjoyed sketching and been proud of his skill at it. In one of the letters that I first saw in the cold, inhospitable muniment room at Blenheim, the first of the many pots of archival gold, was a letter to his mother dated January 1890: 'Papa said he thought singing was a waste of time, so I left the singing class and commenced drawing.' He was studying drawing for an extra hour each week, in the evening, and had been drawing 'little landscapes & bridges & those sorts of things'. He was ready now to begin shading in sepia.

Churchill was then fifteen. Not until he was forty did he have the good fortune, amid the unwonted and accursed leisure that followed his departure from the Admiralty, to take up drawing again. In one of the most moving of all his recollections, which he first published as a magazine article in the 1920s, he wrote:

> When I left the Admiralty at the end of May 1915 I still remained a member of the Cabinet and of the War Council. In this position I knew everything and could do nothing. The change from the intense executive activities of each day's work at the Admiralty to the narrowly measured duties of a counsellor left me gasping. Like a sea-beast fished up from the depths, or a diver too suddenly hoisted, my veins threatened to burst from the fall in pressure. I had great anxiety and no means of relieving it; I had vehement convictions and small power to give effect to them. I had to watch the unhappy casting-away of great opportunities, and the feeble execution of plans which I had launched and in which I heartily believed. I had long hours of utterly unwonted leisure in which to contemplate the frightful unfolding of the War.
>
> At a moment when every fibre of my being was inflamed to action, I was forced to remain a spectator of the tragedy, placed cruelly in a front seat. And then it was that the Muse of Painting* came to my rescue – out of charity and out of chivalry, because after all she had nothing to do with me – and said, 'Are these toys any good to you? They amuse some people.'

The muse of painting that summer Sunday was Churchill's sister-in-law Lady Gwendeline Churchill, who had set up her easel in the garden at Hoe Farm and was sketching the pond and garden. Churchill watched her and was fascinated. She at once suggested that he use her son Johnny's watercolour set to do something of his own.

---

* The muses were the nine Greek goddesses of inspiration. There was no muse of painting. The recognized muses were of epic and heroic poetry (Calliope), history (Clio), love poetry (Erato), music and lyric poetry (Euterpe), tragedy (Melpomene), songs or hymns to the gods (Polyhymnia), dance (Terpsichore), comedy (Thalia) and astronomy (Urania). I am grateful to my friend Erich Segal for these facts.

My search through his bills revealed that as soon as he was back in London he purchased an easel. Then, four days later, he bought a mahogany palette, oil, turpentine, paints and brushes.

On his next weekend visit to Hoe Farm, after another frustrating week in London, where his views had once more been ignored by the Cabinet of which he had so recently been such an influential member, Churchill set up his new easel. As he later recalled, in his magazine memoir:

> The next step was to *begin*. But what a step to take! The palette gleamed with beads of colour; fair and white rose the canvas; the empty brush hung poised, heavy with destiny, irresolute in the air. My hand seemed arrested by a silent veto. But after all the sky on this occasion was unquestionably blue, and a pale blue at that. There could be no doubt that blue paint mixed with white should be put on the top part of the canvas. One really does not need to have had an artist's training to see that. It is a starting-point open to all.
>
> So very gingerly I mixed a little blue paint on the palette with a very small brush, and then with infinite precaution made a mark about as big as a bean upon the affronted snow-white shield. It was a challenge, a deliberate challenge; but so subdued, so halting, indeed so cataleptic, that it deserved no response. At that moment the loud approaching sound of a motor-car was heard in the drive.
>
> From this chariot there stepped swiftly and lightly none other than the gifted wife of Sir John Lavery. 'Painting! But what are you hesitating about? Let me have a brush – the big one.' Splash into the turpentine, wallop into the blue and the white, frantic flourish on the palette – clean no longer – and then several large, fierce strokes and slashes of blue on the absolutely cowering canvas. Anyone could see that it could not hit back. No evil fate avenged the jaunty violence. The canvas grinned in helplessness before me. The spell was broken. The sickly inhibitions rolled away. I seized the largest brush and fell upon my victim with Berserk fury. I have never felt any awe of a canvas since.

Churchill's Private Secretary, Edward Marsh, who came down on the next painting weekend, described in his memoirs how the new enthusiasm was 'a distraction and a sedative that brought a measure of ease to his frustrated spirit'.

In *Churchill, His Paintings*, David Coombs reproduced four of the paintings that Churchill did at Hoe Farm: Lady Gwendeline in the garden, the inner hall (which was wrongly catalogued), a view of the house and garden, and the drive and pond. I went to see this latter, possibly the very first painting that Churchill completed. It was at Stype Grange, on a high plateau of the Berkshire Downs, then the home of the industrialist Sir Charles Clore, owner of the Ritz. The painting had pride of place in his study.

A few minutes' walk from 41 Cromwell Road, where Churchill was living after being forced to leave Admiralty House in 1915, with his own family, his brother's family and his mother, was Lavery's house and studio in Cromwell Gardens. Churchill spent more and more time there as the autumn of 1915 turned into winter, learning from the master. In 1941, on Lavery's death, a portrait was found there: it was Churchill's portrait of Lavery in his studio, an incredibly ambitious and attractive work for a beginner. It is reproduced in colour in *Winston Churchill, His Life as a Painter*, by Churchill's youngest daughter, Mary Soames, who quotes Lavery's comment in his memoirs:

> I know few amateur wielders of the brush with a keener sense of light and colour, or a surer grasp of the essentials. I am able to prove this from experience. We have often stood up to the same motif, and in spite of my trained eye and knowledge of possible difficulties, he with his characteristic fearlessness and freedom from convention, has time and again shown me how to do things. Had he chosen painting instead of statesmanship I believe he would have been a great master with the brush.

Churchill was to find solace in painting whenever things were rough for him. He even set up his easel in his reserve billets in Flanders in the early months of 1916, painting while German shells exploded in the nearby village: one of these paintings can be seen at Chartwell.

In March 1920, while he was Secretary of State for War, and also for Air, Churchill had gone on holiday with a military friend, General Rawlinson, to Mimizan, in the French Atlantic region of the Landes. 'Tonight we painted by the lake at a new place,' he wrote to Clementine. 'The general paints in watercolours and does it very well. With all my enormous paraphernalia, I have so far produced very indifferent results here. The trees are very difficult to do. How I wish Lavery were here to give me a few hints; it would bring me on like one o'clock.'

A year later, in March 1921, as Secretary of State for the Colonies, Churchill presided over a Middle East conference in Cairo. He again took with him on his travels his painting apparatus, and, during a Sunday respite after eight gruelling days of talks, set up his easel near the pyramids, and was painting once more. As Clementine travelled with him, there were no letters as there had been from Mimizan, to describe the scene. But the local press was there to report the event, and I was pleased to find in Churchill's own voluminous Press Cutting books a faded copy of the *Palestine Weekly* which described how, during a ride on a camel, accompanied by T.E. Lawrence (Lawrence of Arabia), Churchill 'was thrown by his mount and grazed his hand badly, but insisted on continuing, made several sketches at Sakkara, and accompanied by Colonel Lawrence, camelled back to Mena House'.

In December 1921 and January 1922 the *Strand* magazine published two articles by Churchill on 'Painting as a Pastime'. These were later reprinted in his book *Thoughts and Adventures* (1932) and as a book on their own, *Painting as a Pastime* (1948). An extract from these articles of seventy years ago was taken up by the art historian Ernst Gombrich in his book *Art and Illusion*. Gombrich noted that no professional critic had seen the nature of the problem of the relationship between the object painted and the work of art itself more clearly than Churchill, who had written in 1921:

> It would be interesting if some real authority investigated
> carefully the part which memory plays in painting. We
> look at the object with an intent regard, then at the palette,
> and thirdly at the canvas. The canvas receives a message
> despatched usually a few seconds before from the natural

object. But it has come through an office en route. It has been transmitted in code. It has been turned from light into paint. It reaches the canvas a cryptogram. Not until it has been placed in its correct relation to everything else that is on the canvas can it be deciphered, is its meaning apparent, is it translated once again from mere pigment into light. And the light this time is not of Nature but of Art.

Dismissed by the electorate of Dundee in 1922, Churchill took his first painting holiday in France, setting up his easel at Cassis, on the South Coast. In subsequent years he painted at Eze high above the Riviera, and at Cannes on the Mediterranean shore.

Throughout 1923 and most of 1924 Churchill suffered a two-year political wilderness, out of Parliament, in which he had sat since 1901. Although painting was a solace for political isolation, it became more than that: a companion in good times as well as bad, a holiday relaxation, something to be enjoyed in different lights and landscapes. He delighted in bright colours. His themes were full of nature's movement, reflecting scenes of ponds, the shore, woodlands, rivers and peaceful landscapes.

In 1932, when Churchill had been out of office for more than two years, and had little prospect of being invited to serve in the MacDonald-Baldwin National Government, he was asked to be the guest of honour at the annual Royal Academy dinner. His speech was cast in the form of a painting survey. Of the Prime Minister, Ramsay MacDonald, whose persistent search for disarmament he strongly opposed (MacDonald had left London for the five-power disarmament conference at Geneva nine days earlier) he said, reading from notes set out in what his secretaries called 'psalm form':

His works are well known;
    regret not more of them at home.

Exhibiting so much in foreign galleries,
    that we miss his productions here.

Believe he has several most important masterpieces
    on Continent,

which are still unpublished;
>> look forward hopefully their arrival and his return.

Churchill went on to say that for a long time he had thought there was 'too much vermillion' in MacDonald's pictures. He was glad that the Prime Minister had abandoned his earlier 'lurid sunsets of empire and capitalist civilizations' for paintings in which the red was replaced by blue, a colour that MacDonald now used, like Sargent, 'not only for atmosphere, but even as foundation'. As for Stanley Baldwin, the Conservative leader under whom Churchill had served as Chancellor of the Exchequer, one had to admit, Churchill said, that there was 'something very reposeful in his twilight studies in half tone'.

Speaking of his own painting-politics, Churchill said:

> But sure you will ask
>> why am I not exhibiting this year
>>> why no important pictures on the line?

> Frankly, differences with the Committee
>> and this year
>>> not submitting any of my works
>>>> for their approval

> Joined the teaching profession –
>> sort of Slade School

> We have a fine lot of young students
>> and glad to assist them
>>> in learning some rudiments
>>>> of parliamentary technique

> Still a few things on easel
>> which I hope some day
>>> to present to public.

From Baldwin came a charming note a few days later: 'I am glad to think that although my own preference is for still life and half-tone, I do enjoy the bright and sometimes fierce lights in which you revel, and no one will be more interested than I when you come to exhibit the work which is still on your easel.' My wife and I chanced upon Churchill's reply in the Baldwin papers at the Cambridge University Library. 'I was very glad that my chaff did not vex you. My shafts, though necessarily pointed, are never intentionally poisoned. If they cut, I pray they do not fester in the wound. I am also glad to feel that although we have differences, we have not had any misunderstandings.'

Those 'differences' were to keep Churchill out of office for another eight and a half years. But his painting flourished. Among the painters who helped him perfect his technique (which Francis Bacon once told me was not to be scorned) were Sickert (who introduced him to the panafieu technique of painting over a black and white photographic image projected on to a screen), Neville Lytton, and three French painters, Marchand, Segonzac and Maze.

In 1968, as I began work in Oxford on my own blank canvas, I was urged to make contact with Maze, the sole survivor of that French trio, by an unlikely painters' friend, the subsequently much-abused head of Bomber Command, Sir Arthur Harris, who lived near Oxford and was helping me understand the controversies over wartime bombing policy, in which Churchill had not always taken his side. Harris knew Maze well (both Maze and his son had worked on Harris's staff in the war) and urged me to visit him. I wrote, and soon found myself driving into another idyll, not unlike Hoe Farm, but further south, in the tiny village of Treyford, in a fold of the South Downs not far from Goodwood racecourse.

For me, perhaps the greatest single marvel of the search for Churchill has been the friendships that grew up as a result of it, and which flourished quite apart from their Churchill context. For the next ten years I was to return many times to Paul Maze's cottage, to delight in his company, to be entertained by him and his wife Jessie, to learn not only about Churchill's painting but about many aspects of Maze's life and adventures, and to return refreshed to my desk.

Maze was born in Le Havre in 1887. He was a prolific and lively impressionist-inspired painter of horses at Goodwood, of guardsmen on Horse Guards Parade, of yachts at Cowes, and, when I knew him, of his local Sussex landscape, its rolling fields and serene gardens. He had first met Churchill in 1915 on the Western Front. 'He was in a very dangerous sector,' Maze told me. 'I remember very well the canvas screen on the road that had been put up to hide the movement of troops. Bullets thumped. He looked at me, and pointed at my French helmet. He was wearing one too, most unusually for a British officer. "You and I both have good taste," he said.'

When they met again, in 1918, Maze was on the staff of General Gough ('Goughie') to whom he was devoted, and Churchill was Minister of Munitions, responsible for providing the guns, shells, tanks and aircraft for the war zone. He spent some hours at Gough's headquarters and was impressed by what he saw.

Churchill and Maze met for the third time in 1920 in the South of France, Churchill was working on his war memoirs, *The World Crisis*.

> 'It must be like digging up a cemetery,' Maze commented.
> 'Oh yes,' Churchill replied, 'but with a resurrection!'

Maze's cupboards, which he opened with such zeal, contained item after item for my search. The first letter from Churchill to Maze was written in 1927, after Churchill had published the volume of memoirs in which he told the story of Gough's command in 1918. In reply to Maze's letter of congratulations, Churchill wrote: 'I was so glad to hear that you are enjoying my new volume, and especially that you appreciate what I have written about Gough. It has been pleasant to receive several letters from friends of his to the same effect.' Churchill was then Chancellor of the Exchequer. 'With the Budget looming ahead', he wrote, 'I have no time for painting just now, but when that burden is lightened I shall hope to go back to it and to drink again at the fountain of your knowledge.'

In 1932, when Churchill was out of office and free to paint to his heart's desire and solace, Maze painted a picture of Churchill while the latter was himself painting at a château near Dreux, St Georges-Motel. Churchill's subject was the mill of the château, the Moulin de Montreuil, where Maze had a studio. Four French painters were visiting Maze that day: Vuillard, Segonzac, Simon Lévy and Boussingault. Maze delighted in telling me how, that lunch time, he and his friends set off to the park to find Churchill, who had been painting the woodland: 'He was battling with a canvas which, with his temperament and his prodigality with paint, he had already overcommitted.'

'Come to my rescue,' Churchill asked the painters, handing each of them a brush, and telling them what he wanted each to do to rescue his picture. 'Roaring with laughter', Maze recalled, 'we got going, watched by Vuillard who stood seriously aside with a smile.' When the painting had been amended to Churchill's satisfaction, he insisted that they all sign it. Many years later it was to cause a mini-sensation, and fetch a good price, at Sotheby's.

I once sent Maze three pages of notes that I had found, dating from the early 1920s, from Neville Lytton to Churchill, giving advice about painting. Maze wrote to me in reply:

> The whole of the three pages are taken from books on technique, and every great painter develops his own technique which comes from his personal approach. The pity about Winston's painting is that he had been under the influence of too many people when he began, Lavery one of the worst as he was slick & superficial. Knowing that Winston painted only between crises, it was a refuge for him, and all I ever attempted was to simplify his method and reduce his means and insatiable appetite for colour. He would have eaten a tube of white he loved the smell of it so. With his brushes and paint, he forgot everything, like a child does who has been given a box of paints.

In 1934 Churchill wrote an introduction to Maze's memoirs of the Western Front, *A Frenchman in Khaki*, a book in which, Churchill said, were 'the battle scenes of Armageddon recorded by one who not only loved the fighting troops and shared their perils, but perceived the beauties of light and shade, of form and colour, of which the horrors of war cannot rob the progress of the sun'.

Maze became a frequent visitor to Chartwell, the country home Churchill bought in 1922, his beloved refuge from the stress and storms of London. In one of our talks, Maze recalled Clementine saying to him during one visit, 'I've got Winston four secretaries for the weekend – because he's so busy.' This fact became self-evident when the host failed to appear for much of the day: he was dictating the chapters of a book. 'Finally he came down', Maze recalled, 'and said to us, "If only I had two more secretaries, I could have done another five thousand words."'

At Chartwell, and at St Georges-Motel, Churchill and Maze discussed the growing Nazi menace. Maze told me, more in sorrow than anger: 'Every idea was held against him by jealous people. Gallipoli was their monument.' On one occasion, when Churchill and Maze were at a dinner-dance in London, a young Conservative MP asked if he could join their table. 'He just turned to Winston and said, "It's no use your going on as you do about Germany. No one trusts you." He then got up and went back to the dance. Winston turned to me and said, "Let them talk."'

When Léon Blum came to London in May 1939, Maze found the French leader depressed by the lack of vision of those British politicians whom he met. Maze also took Blum to see the editor of *The Times*, Geoffrey Dawson. 'Who is that man, *that German?*' Blum asked Maze afterwards. 'So I said to Blum, "I'll give you a tonic", and we went to see Winston at Chartwell. After their meeting Blum said to me, "Now I know that there is a reserve somewhere in England." It was like a blood transfusion for him.'

Maze and Churchill were again painting in Normandy in August 1939. Maze showed me the small pocket diary that he had kept during the visit. In it was an entry for Sunday 27 August 1939:

> Winston came to paint the Moulin. I worked alongside him. He suddenly turned to me and said: 'This is the last picture we shall paint in peace for a very long time.' What amazed me was his concentration over his painting. No one but he could have understood more what the possibility of war meant, and how ill prepared we were. As he worked, he would now and then make statements as to the relative strength of the German Army or the French Army. 'They are strong, I tell you, they are strong,' he would say. Then his jaw would clench his large cigar, and I felt the determination of his will. 'Ah!' he would say, 'with it all, we shall have him.'

On the following night Maze was shocked when another British visitor at the château, Sir Evan Charteris, Chairman of the Tate Gallery, walking up to his bedroom, turned to Maze with the words:

'Don't listen to him. He is a warmonger.' From material in the British Government's archive, I later learned that Hitler, at that very moment, was warning a visiting Englishman that Churchill's return to the Cabinet would seriously set back the possibility of maintaining peace. Four days later, the German Army invaded Poland.

The events of that week were engraved on Maze's memory. On 29 August, a day Churchill had hoped to devote to painting, 'a boy from the Post Office handed to Winston a telegram from his brother John. He read it and handed it to me: "Advise return. There might be a job for you." This seemed to stir him, as if confirming the reality of his being out of office.'

Maze remembered how Churchill was depressed when he left the château later that day to return to England, still only a back-bench MP. As it was most unlikely that there would be a place for him in government, he was contemplating handing over Chartwell to the Red Cross, or to the army, and moving with Clementine into one of the cottages in the grounds. As Churchill left, Maze handed him a letter marked 'only to read when you are over the Channel', in which he wrote: 'Don't worry, Winston, you know that you will be Prime Minister and lead us to victory.' Jessie Maze, reading the letter before it was sealed, told her husband, 'This will cheer him up.'

Maze was still at the Moulin on 3 September, when he heard on the wireless of Britain's declaration of war on Germany and, for him the most welcome news, that Churchill had been brought back to the Admiralty. 'My dear Winston', he wrote that day, 'I feel happy to know that the responsibility of the navy is in your hands at this juncture. I am writing this only a few yards from the spot where your easel stood ten days ago – now we are at war and we can meet the future with true confidence.'

I found this letter among Churchill's private papers. Maze had kept no copy. I sent it to him in June 1969, almost thirty years after he had written it.

Paul and Jessie Maze escaped from France as the German armies swept southward. Reaching England on board the French warship *Courbet* (the sister ship of the *Bouvet* that had been sunk at the Dardanelles with the loss of 600 French lives), he joined the Home

Guard, becoming Adjutant to a battalion at Petersfield. After he had gone up to London to see Churchill, his battalion was sent fifty rifles, some machine guns and ammunition. Churchill also gave him a cigar. 'I told him, I'm going to make the men shoot for it.' Impressed by the efforts of the Home Guard, for whose welfare he worked with a painter's zeal, Maze suggested to Churchill that he should make a broadcast to them. 'As it appears to have been well received', Churchill wrote to him, 'you have the satisfaction of adding this to the services which you have rendered to them.'

In 1942 Maze sent Churchill a small painting that he had done specially for him. 'My dear Paul', Clementine wrote in reply, 'Winston is enchanted with the lovely watercolour of the proud American flag. I have hung it in his bedroom where he can see it when he looks up when he is working in bed.' In 1944 Maze was seconded to Bomber Command Intelligence, his painter's eye an asset to those studying aerial photographs of Germany. By coincidence, Churchill's daughter Sarah, herself an artist, was working at the same task, at RAF Medmenham.

With the coming of war in 1939 Churchill had put painting aside. Only once, while he was recuperating from pneumonia in Marrakech in 1943, did he paint a picture, of the snow-capped Atlas mountains. After the war, and the electoral defeat of 1945, painting was again a pastime and a solace for him. After 1955, in retirement, it was his last regular activity, most happily in the garden at Chartwell, in his study at Hyde Park Gate, or at the Villa La Pausa in the South of France, where the ancient olive trees in the villa grounds, and the Mediterranean coastline far below, were his favourite subjects.

In 1958 Maze invited Churchill to paint alongside him in Sussex. 'I wish so much Winston could come down to you for the day,' Clementine wrote. 'But alas his strength is sadly diminished and he grows weaker week by week. The strain of the war years is showing now.' In 1960, in the South of France, he set up his easel for the last time, in the garden of Lord Beaverbrook's villa, La Capponcina. Forty-five years had passed since that first timid experiment in Hoe Farm. Since then, Churchill the painter had been part and parcel of Churchill the man; his energies, when denied ministerial tasks or political power, could focus on colour and line, light and shade, and the making of a thing of beauty. 'Happy are the painters,' he had written in his article in *Strand* magazine, 'for they shall not be lonely. Light and colour, peace and hope, will keep them company to the end, or almost to the end of the day.'

VI

Soldiers and Soldiering

With Churchill's departure for the Western Front in November 1915 he became a soldier again after fifteen years in politics. What sort of a soldier had he been, and what sort of a soldier would he become? For 'Churchill the soldier' there are two remarkable sources: his hundreds of extremely frank letters to his mother, his grandmother and later to his wife, and the hundreds of newspaper and magazine articles, many of them despatches sent from the field of battle, scribbled down in pencil or ink in a tent, or in a telegraph office, often within sight and sound of the event.

From his first experiences as a soldier in the 1890s Churchill had not only seen, but had reported on the ugly side of war, and on the determination of subject peoples to resist oppression and occupation, at whatever cost. The first war he saw at close quarters, as an observer with the fighting troops, was a Spanish military attempt to put down the Cuban revolt. He was twenty-one. 'The more I see of Cuba', he wrote in a despatch to the *Daily Graphic*, one of his very first journalistic ventures, 'the more I feel sure that the end demand for independence is national and unanimous.' As to the fighting itself: 'Whatever may be the result, the suffering and misery of the entire community is certain.'

Churchill's first experience of being in action, on the North-West Frontier of India, was a searing one. On that occasion, it was in the archive at Blenheim Palace that the evidence of his attitude survived, in his long, handwritten, intensely personal letters. He was twenty-two. 'I cried when I met the Royal West Kents on the 30th September,' he wrote to his mother, 'and saw the men really unsteady under the fire and tired of the game, and that poor young Browne-Clayton, literally cut in pieces on a stretcher – through his men not having stood by him.' Writing to an army friend of some of the terrible things he had seen, he noted: 'The Mohmands need a lesson – and there is no doubt we are a very cruel people.' The Sikhs, who were in action alongside him, 'put a wounded man into the cinerator & burnt him alive. This was hushed up. I feel rather a vulture. The only excuse is, that I might myself be the carrion.' Churchill also told his mother, about the Mohmand tribesmen: 'They kill and mutilate everyone they catch and we do not hesitate to finish their wounded off. I have seen several things which have not been very pretty since I have been up here – but as you will believe I have not soiled my hands with any dirty work – though I recognize the necessity of some things.'

After describing the cruelties of battle, Churchill referred to its other aspect, one which he never attempted to disguise, telling his mother: 'Meanwhile the game amuses me – dangerous though it is – and I shall stay as long as I can.' But the cruelties were an ever-present factor: to his grandmother Frances, Duchess of Marlborough, he confided, also in a letter preserved in the archive at Blenheim:

I wonder if people in England have any idea of the warfare that is being carried on here. It is so different from all one has been led to expect – that I do not doubt there are many people who do not realize for instance that no quarter is ever asked or given. The tribesmen torture the wounded & mutilate the dead. The troops never spare a single man who falls into their hands – whether he be wounded or not.

The field hospitals and the sick convoys are the especial targets of the enemy and we destroy the tanks by which alone water for the summer can be obtained – and employ against them a bullet – the new Dum-Dum bullet – of which you may have heard – the shattering effects of which are simply appalling. Indeed I believe no such bullet has ever been used on human beings before, but only on game – stags, tigers etc.

The picture is a terrible one, and naturally it has a side to which one does not allude in print.

I wish I could come to the conclusion that all this bar-

1. Churchill and his wife see the Queen and Prince Philip into their car,
10 Downing Street, 4 April 1955 *(see page 3)*

2. Randolph Churchill on the telephone, cigarette in hand, Stour,
East Bergholt, February 1965

3. John Profumo, back to camera, takes a photograph of Churchill in North Africa, in the Roman amphitheatre at Carthage, 1 June 1943 *(see page 31)*

4. *Top:* Churchill, his grandson Winston, Randolph and Aristotle Onassis on board *Christina*, 1963 *(see page 31)*
5. *Above:* Paul Maze reminiscing, 1969 *(see pages 74-9)*

6. Madame Planche in her *estaminet*, fifty-four years on *(see page 87)*

7. The author with the owner of Burnt Out Farm, Joël Wgeux, and his son, Ploegsteert, 1970 *(see page 87)*

8. *Left:* Jock McDavid, one of the young officers in Churchill's battalion headquarters, Ploegsteert, January–March 1916 *(see page 92)*

9. *Below:* Edmund Hakewill Smith, the youngest officer at Ploegsteert *(see pages 39, 91 and 96)*

10. Francis Napier-Clavering, the Royal Engineer who was with Churchill on the Western Front *(see pages 93-4 and 98-9)*

11. Emery Reves greeting Churchill on his arrival in Paris during the Munich crisis, October 1938 *(see pages 109-10)*

12. *Left:* Professor Frederick Lindemann, later Lord Cherwell

13. *Below:* Desmond Morton

barity – all these losses – all this expenditure – had resulted in a permanent settlement being obtained. I do not think however that anything has been done – that will not have to be done again.

For Churchill, it was the war in the Sudan in 1898 that marked most dramatically the contrast between the cruelty of battle and its excitement. In 1898 his first instinct was an eagerness to see action. Again, the letters at Blenheim, bundled up before the turn of the century, and preserved unread for more than half a century, held his thoughts as if preserved in aspic across the years. Embarking on the journey towards the scene of battle, he wrote to his mother: 'I have a keen aboriginal desire to kill several of these odious dervishes. I anticipate enjoying the exercise very much.' Travelling up the Nile, drawing ever closer to Khartoum, he wrote again: 'I am very happy and contented and eagerly looking forward to the approaching actions.' And after the battle of Omdurman he wrote to his mother of the cavalry charge itself, 'I told my troop they were the finest men in the world and I am sure they would have followed me as far as I would have gone and that I may tell you and you only – was a very long way – for my soul becomes very high in such moments.'

Describing to his mother the way in which several of his friends had been killed and mutilated, he confessed that these things had made him 'anxious and worried during the night and I speculated on the shoddiness of war. You cannot gild it. The raw comes through.'

Such sentiments did not remain in the shelter of a private letter home. Churchill also wrote a remarkable, vivid and personal account of the Sudan campaign, which he called *The River War*. Its two volumes are seldom read today, yet in their pages are many sentiments unexpected from a young soldier who had felt the exhilaration of battle and victory. There was a great deal in this book, as in so many of Churchill's published works, that added substantially to the search for his character and opinions. Churchill told his readers:

> The statement that 'the wounded Dervishes received every delicacy and attention' is so utterly devoid of truth that it transcends the limits of mendacity and passes into the realms of the ridiculous.
>
> I was impatient to get back to the camp. There was

nothing to be gained by dallying on the field, unless a man were anxious to become quite callous, so that no imaginable misery which could come to human flesh would ever have moved him again.

I may have written in these pages something of vengeance and of the paying of a debt. It may be that vengeance is sweet, and that the gods forbade vengeance to men because they reserved for themselves so delicious and intoxicating a drink. But no one should drain the cup to the bottom. The dregs are often filthy-tasting.

Churchill never lost these sentiments. 'The treatment of the wounded', he wrote to his mother in a private letter, also at Blenheim, 'again disgraceful.' And of Kitchener, a man 'without much of the non-brutal elements in his composition'. After careful reflection Churchill decided to print the truth as he saw it, that the victory at Omdurman, as he told his mother, 'was disgraced by the inhuman slaughter of the wounded and that Kitchener is responsible for this'. In *The River War* he wrote: 'The stern and unpitying spirit of the commander was communicated to his troops, and the victories which marked the progress of the River War were accompanied by acts of barbarity not always justified even by the harsh customs of savage conflicts or the fierce and treacherous nature of the Dervish.'

The realization that opinions such as these would be unpopular did not deter Churchill from publishing them. 'I do not think the book will bring me many friends,' he wrote to his cousin Ivor Guest, in a letter preserved in the Guest family archive. 'But friends of the cheap and worthless everyday variety are not of very great importance. After all in writing the great thing is to be honest.'*

The Boer War confirmed Churchill's feelings about the essential cruelty of battle. In his next set of newspaper despatches, written to the *Morning Post*, he declared: 'Ah, horrible war, amazing medley of the glorious and the squalid, the pitiful and the sublime, if modern

---

* This letter from Churchill to Ivor Guest came to me as a result of a saleroom purchase, and the kindness of the purchaser, in this case David Satinoff, a collector of Churchilliana. The scrutiny of saleroom catalogues has proved a crucial element in my search for Churchill. I have given some examples of this in the chapter 'Inkwells of Gold'.

men of light and leading saw your face closer, simple folk would see it hardly ever.' His instinct, as victory came nearer, was for a conciliatory peace. 'I would treat the Boers with all generosity and tolerance,' he wrote to his paper after the relief of Ladysmith, 'even to providing for those crippled in the war and for the destitute women and children.'

In 1901, within three months of entering Parliament, Churchill was telling his fellow MPs, including the leaders of his own party and government, about the nature of war. His many hundreds of parliamentary speeches, recorded in the pages of *Hansard*, have been a fine barometer of his thoughts. On that early occasion, young, new and under the scrutiny of his political elders and betters, in whose hands his career then rested, he said: 'I have frequently been astonished since I have been in this House to hear with what composure and how glibly members, and even ministers, talk of a European war,' and he went on to warn that a European war could only end 'in the ruin of the vanquished and the scarcely less fatal commercial dislocation and exhaustion of the conquerors.' Mighty populations would be 'impelled on each other', each individual would be 'embittered and inflamed'. The resources of science and civilization would 'sweep away everything' that might mitigate the fury of the combatants. 'The wars of peoples will be more terrible than those of kings.'

The First World War was to bear out this terrible forecast, and Churchill was to be a witness of it, not only from Whitehall but also from the parapet.

There were frequent occasions before war came in 1914 when, at times of jingoistic enthusiasm, Churchill struck an unpopular note. I had read, in the vast archive of the Cecil family at Hatfield House, a letter that he wrote to one of his closest Conservative friends, Lord Hugh Cecil, in 1904, in which he stood out against the enthusiasm generated by Colonel Younghusband's action in Tibet, when he killed six hundred Tibetan peasants blocking his path on the road to Lhasa. The peasants were virtually without weapons when the British machine guns were turned on them. 'Surely it is v'y wicked to do such things.' Churchill wrote to Cecil. 'Absolute contempt for the rights of others must be wrong. Are there any people in the world so mean-spirited as not to resist under the circumstances to which these poor Tibetans have been subjected. It has been their land for centuries, and although they are only Asiatics "liberty" and "home" mean something to them. That such an event should be greeted with a howl of ferocious triumph by Press & Party must be an evil portent.'

Churchill wrote a similar letter of distress five years later, when, as President of the Board of Trade, he was the Kaiser's guest at German Army manoeuvres. This letter was to his newly married Clementine. It was one of thousands of letters that she made available for the biography. This particular letter contained a reflection that summed up the dual nature of Churchill's attitude to war, and his ultimate rejection of it. 'Much as war attracts me & fascinates my mind with its tremendous situations', he wrote, 'I feel more deeply every year – & can measure the feeling here in the midst of arms, what vile & wicked folly and barbarism it all is.'

This sentiment was sustained and intensified by the First World War. 'All the excitement dies away, and there is only dull resentment,' he wrote to his wife after his own first experience of trench warfare.

It was at the end of November 1915 that Churchill left fog-bound London for the Western Front, describing himself with some wit on his arrival at General Headquarters at St Omer as 'the escaped scapegoat'. In 1969 a former staff officer at St Omer, General Sir Ivo Vesey (then aged ninety-three) told me that Churchill said to him there, 'I am never going to have anything more to do with politics or politicians. When this war is over I shall confine myself entirely to writing and painting.' Churchill's cousin Sir Shane Leslie, whom I visited in Brighton in 1970, told me that Lady Randolph (his Aunt Jennie) was going round London saying, 'You want my Winston to have a bullet in him, that's what you all want.' Leslie commented, 'The truth is that many of them did.'

A former Lieutenant of Hussars on active service in India and the Sudan in Queen Victoria's reign, a Yeomanry Captain who had regularly attended camp and manoeuvres before the war, Churchill was given the rank of Lieutenant-Colonel. At St Omer his friend Sir John French was Commander-in-Chief of the British Expeditionary Force. Fifty-four years later I went to the house at 41 Cromwell Road, his brother Jack's house, from which he had left for Victoria Station, Folkestone, Boulogne and St Omer. My aim was to follow, geographically at least, in his footsteps, though the Clean Air Act of 1956 made it impossible for me to replicate the London fog.

During that research journey, and again in the following year, I visited the places where Churchill had stayed, first at St Omer, then in training with the Grenadier Guards, then in billets behind the lines with the battalion he was to command, the 6th Royal Scots Fusiliers, and finally at the farms that became his headquarters in the trenches. Each time I went, I took with me the recollections of the soldiers who had been with him there, and whom slowly I was tracking down. Among those I met in Flanders was Madame Planche, who as a young girl had dispensed Le Stout du Pays to Churchill's battalion at her mother's *estaminet* when the men were in reserve at Moolenacker, and was still (in 1970 and 1971) in the same *estaminet*, then as the proprietress.

I also met Joël Wgeuw, the owner of the farm which Churchill had made his frontline observation post, named on British military maps as Burnt Out Farm. 'Thrice burnt out', he quipped when I told him this, as he showed me the last traces of concrete wire. The farm had first been burnt down in battle in 1914, then in 1940, and again in 1945.

I was primarily guided in my search for those who had known Churchill in Flanders by the many long handwritten letters he had written to Clementine Churchill almost daily from the Western Front. She had kept all these letters, some still in their envelopes. In one of them, written a month after his arrival at St Omer, Churchill told her about an expedition he had made, while waiting for an active command, to the French front line. His guide was a young English cavalry officer, Captain Edward Louis Spears, whom he had met before the war and now quickly befriended. 'I believe Spears & I are the only Englishmen who have ever been on this battle-torn ground,' he told Clementine.

Spears had become a Brigadier-General in 1918 and a Member of Parliament in 1922. He also became one of Churchill's close personal friends. In 1940 he brought General de Gaulle back by air from France to Britain as German forces swept through Paris. Later he served as Churchill's personal representative in Syria and the

Lebanon. After I wrote to him in 1969, Spears invited me by telegram to lunch with him at his home at Warfield in Berkshire. As we sat in the spring sunshine a few weeks later in his rose-filled garden, far from any hint of violence or war, he recalled that very expedition:

> Mostly Winston looked. If there was a question to be put, he put it. There was a place I took him to at Notre Dame de Lorette. It was a ridge and a declivity. The French kept attacking it, but nobody had ever been known to come back alive. This interested Winston considerably. He wanted to know why, why, why.
>
> The Germans had realized the importance of the counterslope, of having trenches within fifteen yards of the top of the hill on the far side, and shooting like rabbits at anyone who popped over the top. It was a terrible place. I got wounded there myself. Winston had an inquiring mind of rare quality. He always turned up with some new invention – once it was a bullet-proof waistcoat. On another occasion a bullet-proof raincoat which would have sunk anyone wearing it in any sea.
>
> Winston was very curious, very inquisitive to see what the French were doing. It was a time when they were experimenting with all sorts of devices, like a moving shield which you pushed along in front of the infantry. But when Winston mentioned the idea of tanks the French said: 'Wouldn't it be simpler to flood Artois and get your fleet here?'

Churchill's initiatives in mechanical warfare were part of the story I was piecing together. More than a year before his meeting with Spears, he had encouraged a team at the Admiralty to examine all possibilities for protecting men behind a shield or using mobile armour, had found the money for their experiments, and had combated with his enthusiasm the negativism of the War Office. After the war, a Royal Commission recognized his predominant role: a part of which he was understandably proud. In Asquith's papers at the Bodleian Library was a letter which he had sent to the Prime Minister in January 1915, asking for work to begin on a trench-spanning car:

It is most important that the motor transport and armed motor-cars should be provided to a certain extent with cars carrying the means of bridging small cuts in the road, and an arrangement of planks capable of bridging a ten- or twelve-feet span quickly.

It would be quite easy in a short time to fit up a number of steam tractors with small armoured shelters, in which men and machine guns could be placed, which would be bullet-proof. Used at night, they would not be affected by artillery fire to any extent. The caterpillar system would enable trenches to be crossed quite easily, and the weight of the machine would destroy all wire entanglements.

Forty or fifty of these engines, prepared secretly and brought into positions at nightfall, could advance quite certainly into the enemy's trenches, smashing away all the obstructions, and sweeping the trenches with their machine-gun fire, and with grenades thrown out of the top.

They would then make so many *points d'appuis* for the British supporting infantry to rush forward and rally on them. They can move forward to attack the second line of trenches.

A month after listening to Spears as he sat in his armchair telling me about Churchill and the French Generals' scepticism about his tank idea, I returned to his house and read him this letter. He chuckled. I asked him why. He told me it brought back to his mind the boundless energy of his friend, and the often bewildered response of those around him to 'Winston's latest'. Although a lifelong admirer of Churchill, Spears once confided in me that 'even Winston had a fault'. My ears pricked up: every biographer searches for just such a clue, the flaw, the Achilles' heel of his hero. 'What fault?' I asked. 'He was too fond of Jews,' Spears replied. It was only after Spears's death that I came upon a personal telegram from Churchill to Spears, sent in 1942, warning him 'against drifting into the usual anti-Zionist and anti-Semitic channel which it is customary for British officers to follow'.

Spears not only gave me his recollections but, as he came to know me better, produced two tiny First World War pocket diaries. In them he had noted down Churchill's remarks to him during their journeys together. In one such note, from December 1915, he had recorded Churchill's view: 'Thinks we will have disasters in Serbia, Dardanelles & Baghdad – but we will win in end as ruin is better, so all England thinks, than a bad peace.' This was a foretaste of what Churchill was to say in 1940, believing then that despite the setbacks that would still surely come, the British public would not want to make peace with Hitler.

Two days after he had made this diary entry, Spears recorded another conversation with Churchill: 'We talked literature. Mostly French & politics – I made out a case for the House of Lords & he downed it – no agreement reached. He said some fine things about democracies, their answer to finer calls. Talk on religion – told him my views & he his – he believes he is a spirit which will live, without memory of the present, in the future.'

After I had visited him four or five times, always entranced by his rose-bedecked garden, Spears felt sufficiently at ease to show me his most precious possession, a letter Churchill had written to him towards the end of 1916, when Spears had been seriously wounded for the fourth time. 'You are indeed a Paladin', Churchill wrote, 'worthy to rank with the truest knights of the great days of romance. Thank God you are alive. Some good angel has guarded you amid such innumerable perils, & brought you safely thus far along this terrible & never-ending road.' Churchill's letter ended: 'But my dear why don't you write. I sh'd so value y'r letters and it w'd be such a pleasure to me to receive them.'

While he was still at General Headquarters, Churchill was offered command of a brigade (four battalions, in all about 5,000 men) by the Commander-in-Chief, Sir John French. But even while Churchill was waiting to learn the name of his brigade, French was dismissed by Asquith. When the outgoing commander, on the visit to London during which he learned of his dismissal, raised the question of Churchill's future command, Asquith replied: 'Perhaps he might have a battalion.' Not a brigade but a battalion; not 5,000 but less than 800 men were to be under his command. Churchill, already let down by Asquith in May and again in November 1915, was stunned by this off-hand demotion by the man who had been his friend and supporter for a decade. It was the last straw. 'I feel that my work with Asquith has come to an end,' he wrote to Clementine. 'I have found him a weak and disloyal chief. I hope I shall not ever have to serve under him again.'

The battalion Churchill was offered was the 6th Royal Scots Fusiliers: 800 men, mauled by battle, war-weary, with only one regular soldier left among their officers. They were then in training: he had two weeks to get them ready for the return to the trenches. When I began my work, there was one published account of this phase of Churchill's life, *With Winston Churchill At the Front*, published in 1924 by an anonymous officer. He was, in fact, as the British Museum catalogue revealed, Andrew Dewar Gibb, later Leader of the Scottish Nationalist Party. He was still alive in 1969, but too ill to see me. In his book was the initial complaint of the battalion, men mostly from Glasgow: 'Why could not Churchill have gone to the Argylls if he must have a Scottish regiment! We should all have been greatly interested to see him in the kilt.'

One by one, over the course of two years, I tracked down the surviving officers of Churchill's battalion. The sole surviving regular officer when Churchill arrived was only nineteen years old: 2nd Lieutenant Edmund Hakewill Smith. He had graduated from Sandhurst in June 1915, twenty years after Churchill's graduation. To talk to him, I drove to Windsor Castle and entered the precincts for the first time: Hakewill Smith was then Lieutenant-Governor and lived within the battlements in the Mary Tudor Tower. Recalling that moment when Churchill was announced as their new commander, he spoke to me of the 'horror' with which the news had been met. He also remembered the lunch that Churchill gave to the officers of his headquarters staff on the day of his arrival:

> It was quite the most uncomfortable lunch I had ever been at. Churchill didn't say a word: he went right round the table staring each officer out of countenance. We had disliked the idea of Churchill being in command; now, having seen him, we disliked the idea even more.
>
> At the end of the lunch, he made a short speech: 'Gentlemen, I am now your commanding officer. Those who support me I will look after. Those who go against me I will break. Good afternoon gentlemen.'

> Everyone was agreed that we were in for a pretty rotten time.

It did not take more than a few days for Churchill to begin to impress his battalion with his determination to help them.

I drove to Scotland to meet another of the young officers who had greeted him so warily on that first day. His name was Jock McDavid: a volunteer in 1914, he was eighteen when Churchill arrived, and had just been promoted full Lieutenant. In his home at Helensburgh, overlooking the Clyde, he recalled Churchill's time in training:

> After a very brief period he had accelerated the morale of officers and men to an almost unbelievable degree. It was sheer personality. We laughed at lots of things he did, but there were other things we did not laugh at for we knew they were sound.
>
> He had a unique approach which did wonders to us. He let everyone under his command see that he was responsible, from the very moment he arrived, that they understood not only *what* they were supposed to do, but *why* they had to do it.
>
> No detail of our daily life was too small for him to ignore. He overlooked nothing. Instead of a quick glance at what was being done he would stop and talk with everyone and probe to the bottom of every activity. I have never known an officer take such pains to inspire confidence or to gain confidence; indeed he inspired confidence in gaining it.

Churchill's only serious disagreement with his officers was over military discipline. He had been moved by the stories he heard of the sufferings of his battalion at the Battle of Loos six months earlier. His first question to the first troublemaker who came before him on a charge of indiscipline was: 'Were you in the battle?' When the man replied 'Yes' the charge against him was dismissed.

The officers were at first surprised by this generous act, then horrified when, as McDavid told me, 'everyone then said they had been at Loos.' Robert Fox, one of the battalion's Lewis-gunners, sent me the transcript of a radio broadcast he had made in 1964 in which he referred to this unusual aspect of the new commanding officer's approach to discipline: 'Churchill was scrupulously fair to any man before him on a charge. I remember once, when acting as escort, I heard him cross-examine the NCO giving evidence against the man, with all the skill of a counsel at the Bar. The evidence did not satisfy him, so he dismissed the charge and gave the NCO a homily on the virtues of exactitude.'

Dewar Gibb wrote in his book that Churchill was 'quite wrong' to side so openly with the rank and file: 'It is difficult to see how his ideas on this matter could receive sanction without serious detriment to the one essential of discipline, viz, prompt obedience to orders.' But Churchill was never the conventional soldier, any more than the conventional statesman. He knew from his own experience of war what torment men went through on the battlefield, and he had an instinctive sympathy for the rank and file, whether soldiers in the army or sailors at sea.

A further glimpse, through recollection, of this unknown aspect of Churchill's attitude to crime and punishment in the field came my way from the young engineer once attached to his battalion, Lieutenant Francis Napier-Clavering, whom I went to see at his home near Bishop's Stortford in Hertfordshire. He told me of the occasion when a notorious trouble-maker, Fusilier Fargus, had been in conflict with a sergeant. The result was black eyes and broken teeth for the sergeant. For such indiscipline dire penalties were usually exacted. When Fargus came before Churchill, the commanding officer who had once been Home Secretary asked him:

> 'Why did you do it?'
> 'I don't like the sergeant, Sir.'
> 'Why don't you like the sergeant?'
> 'I don't like him.'
> 'Haven't you got a reason?'
> 'I just don't like him.'

Napier-Clavering recalled how 'to everyone's surprise Fargus was not punished at all, but merely received an admonition and was then dismissed. The sergeant-major was white and speechless. Churchill didn't have a clue about punishment.' Whether Fargus was asked if

93

he had fought at Loos, Napier-Clavering could not recall. 'My dear', Churchill wrote to Clementine, who was worried that he might be too severe in his punishments, 'don't be at all anxious about my being hard on the men. Am I ever hard on anybody? No. I have reduced punishment both in quantity, & method.' My search for Churchill was showing how true this was.

Not only punishment, but comforts and leisure, were Churchill's concern during those two and a half intense weeks of training. On the morning after his arrival he had told the eight hundred rank and file, 'You men have had a hard time. Now you're going to have it easy for some time – I hope.' These were not mere words, as Robert Fox explained:

> Huge stocks of clothing arrived at the quartermaster's stores. We all needed new rig-outs. We got them. Steel helmets were by then being issued to the British Army. We were among the first to get them. We found, too, a vast improvement in our rations. Bully beef and biscuits were only memories.
>
> There were no parades after mid-day. The rest of the day was given over to rest and recreation. A field was rolled out more or less flat and goal-posts erected. Jerseys and footballs arrived from somewhere. Games were arranged against neighbouring units. The Fusiliers won them all. Churchill took a great pride in his team. He rarely missed a match.

The culmination of these efforts came on 16 January, when Churchill arranged a combined sports day and concert. 'The officers & men have taken a lively interest in both affairs,' he wrote to Clementine on the day; 'it is odd no one has got any up for them before.' A piano had been procured from somewhere, new songs were practised and various games were devised with somewhat macabre local touches such as 'the bomb throwers'. 'I will let you know how it goes off,' he told Clementine. 'I think they want nursing & encouraging, more than drill-sergeanting.'

The last surviving member of Churchill's headquarters, his batman John McGuire, recalled in an interview with the BBC in 1990, when he was in his mid-nineties: 'Winston Churchill was the world's most horrible singer, and he started to sing "Me Old Tarpaulin Jacket"* and it was terrible, and the boys they were clapping and they were as pleased as could be. He was a real man's man.' All his life, Churchill enjoyed singing the music hall songs of his youth, and his school songs: their actual words, which most people could only hum, he knew by heart.

On 24 January 1916 Churchill set off from the battalion's reserve billets on horseback, at the head of his men as they made their way towards the frontline trenches. It was the anniversary of his father's death. 'I thought much of father on Jan 24', he wrote to his mother a few days later, '& wondered what he w'd think of it all. I am sure I am doing right.' On 26 January he and his men reached the front line just beyond the Belgian village of Ploegsteert, known to the soldiers as Plug Street. With him was a young Liberal baronet, Sir Archibald Sinclair, like himself an enthusiast for flying, whom he had befriended before the war, and who came with him as Adjutant.

For the next three and a half months Churchill was to share every facet of the lives of his men, first for seven days in immediate reserve in the village, then for seven days in the front line. His headquarters in the front line was a much-battered farmhouse known as Laurence Farm. From Laurence Farm he would walk along the paths and trenches to the edge of no man's land. Jock McDavid, appointed Assistant Adjutant, often accompanied him: 'I have seen him stand on the fire step in broad daylight', McDavid told me, 'to encourage the Jocks, and to prove to the man on the fire step how little danger there was of being hit.'

Churchill decided to go out one night into no man's land, across the open fields to the battalion's forward posts, situated in the shell craters which pitted the landscape between the two armies. McDavid had never forgotten that moment:

---

* The first verse is: 'Wrap me up in me old tarpaulin jacket, And say a poor buffer lies low, Get six stalwart Lancers to carry me, With steps mournful, solemn and slow.' Another song Churchill often sang, both in the trenches and long after the war, was: 'Wash me in the water You washed your dirty daughter, And I'll be whiter than the whitewash on the wall.' In his old age Churchill wanted to make a gramophone record of all the songs of his youth and army days, having remembered them with a perfect recall for the words and verses (if not perfect pitch). To the best of my knowledge the record was never made.

The Colonel's first visitation of our posts in no man's land nearly brought the whole British Army into action. Clad in his long trench waterproof, shining knee-high trench boots and blue steel helmet, with his revolver and powerful flash-lamp attached to his web-belt, he preceded me on the journey through the wire. All went well until we were within a few yards of the first post. Then enemy machine-gun fire swept the sphere of operations.

We all made a dive for the shelter of the shell crater, which was now somewhat overcrowded, and consequently we had to keep in a crouching position. Suddenly a blinding glare of light appeared from the depths of the hole and with it the CO's muffled request to 'Put out that bloody light!' It was only a matter of seconds before he realized his crouching posture was responsible for pressure on the contact switch of his own flash-lamp, and corrective action quickly followed.

This excursion into no man's land was not an isolated example. Hakewill Smith told me of several similar incidents:

> He would often go into no man's land. It was a nerve-racking experience to go with him. He would call out in his loud, gruff voice – far too loud it seemed to us – 'You go that way, I will go this . . . Come here, I have found a gap in the German wire. Come over here at once!' He was like a baby elephant out in no man's land at night.
>
> He never fell when a shell went off; he never ducked when a bullet went past with its loud crack. He used to say, after watching me duck: 'It's no damn use ducking; the bullet has gone a long way past you by now.'

Churchill seemed unmoved by the racket of the bombardment, even when German shells fell nearby. Lieutenant Kemp, the signals officer, McDavid and Hakewill Smith were daily witnesses of this. 'He used to sit on one side of the farm,' McDavid recalled. 'Hakewill Smith and Kemp put on the hits of the day on a little portable gramophone. He would sit for a while just beating time, just ruminating.' He even set up his easel in the courtyard of the farm and began painting. The officers were amazed, as Hakewill Smith recalled:

> Winston started painting the second or third time he went up to the farm. Each time we were in the line he spent some time on his paintings. Gradually, too, the courtyard became more pitted with shellholes. As his painting came nearer to completing, he became morose, angry, and exceedingly difficult to talk to. After five or six days in this mood, he suddenly appeared cheerful and delighted, like a small boy at school.
>
> I asked him what had happened, and he said 'I have been worried because I couldn't get the shellhole right in the painting. However I did it, it looked like a mountain, but yesterday I discovered that if I put a little bit of white in it, it looked like a hole after all.

While I was still working for Randolph I had met Sir Desmond Morton, one of those who between the wars had brought Churchill detailed information about the Government's failure to rearm with vigour, and about Germany's military and industrial preparations for war. In the Second World War, Morton had been Churchill's liaison with the Secret Intelligence Service.

Morton invited me to lunch with him at the United Services Club. He told me that he had first met Churchill on the Western Front, when, as a major in the Royal Artillery, he was told to visit a particular battalion commander to arrange an artillery barrage. On asking a private soldier the way to this particular battalion headquarters, Morton was told, 'You will find that one in the middle of no man's land.' It was Churchill and his headquarters staff at Laurence Farm. Morton found Churchill busy painting. They discussed the proposed barrage, which Churchill intended to be a heavy one. Morton suggested, respectfully, that before the bombardment began Churchill should consult with his brigadier, but Churchill replied, 'I have no faith in brigadiers.'*

---

* Twenty-five years later when Morton, then himself a brigadier, was at Downing Street, urging upon Churchill the importance of some point which had been made by a number of field marshals, Churchill remarked: 'And what, my dear Desmond, are field marshals, except promoted brigadiers?'

The officer in charge of the fortifications at Laurence Farm, and of the trenches in front of it, was Napier-Clavering. When we met at his home in Hertfordshire he told me how surprised he was at Churchill's close attention to the details of the work: most commanding officers in his experience were content to leave the matter in the hands of the competent engineer. But from the first day at the farm Churchill was alert to the potential hazards and dangers. 'The trouble with these dugouts', he told Napier-Clavering on that first day, 'is they are not whizzbang proof.'

The young officer promised to do his best to fortify the dugouts. Churchill's next question to him was: 'How much earth do you need to stop a bullet?' 'You want at least three feet,' Napier-Clavering replied. 'Well', said Churchill, 'we'll go up to the front line tonight and have a look. Bring with you a stick three feet long.'

After dinner Churchill and Napier-Clavering left Laurence Farm, walked along the communication trench, and reached the front line. Once in the forward trench, they clambered on to the parapet and walked along it for the whole length of the battalion's line. Napier-Clavering had never seen an officer take such a passionate interest in the details of trench engineering, but there was more to come, as he recounted:

> Up went a Verey Light. Churchill was on his knees measuring the depth of the earth with the stick. The Hun machine guns opened up, belly high. Why the hell we weren't killed I just don't understand. I didn't want to die; I wanted to kill some of the Hun first.
>
> 'For God's sake keep still, Sir,' I hissed. But he didn't take the slightest notice. He was a man who had no physical fear of dying.

During the days that followed, Napier-Clavering continued his work of improving the parapets, under Churchill's constant surveillance, fortifying the dugouts and trying to arrange an effective drainage system for the trenches. In the evenings, when they were dining, Churchill often questioned him, not only about his own work but also about how the Royal Engineers ought to be run. Hakewill Smith told me of one occasion when Churchill asked: 'Why haven't we got a trench digger? We want a trench digger. Something that would crawl along and dig out a trench in five minutes.' Not to be outdone, Napier-Clavering decided to ask his own questions:

> I said to him one night, after the necessary number of ports, 'Could you tell us, Sir, what advantage it would be to us to win the war?' There was silence for three minutes. Then for the next twenty minutes he gave us a parliamentary speech. At the end of each paragraph he looked up, and looked at everybody in the room to see what the effect was. His language was so absolutely marvellous. I was only twenty-two at the time. My eyes were standing out like hatpins.

Churchill was similarly impressed by Napier-Clavering. 'This young fellow was lunching with us,' McDavid told me:

> Winston started giving a dissertation on a new type of vehicle he was keen on. A 'Caterpillar' Winston called it; it could get over the humps and over the wire. He used the various condiment sets to explain what he meant. He had this idea that a tracked vehicle could cut the German wire, or drag it through and make a gap. We all thought it an airy fairy idea. 'If it amuses him, let him go on talking about it,' we thought, 'but it is a damned silly idea.' It was away up in the clouds. But the young engineer officer took it up with him. He was the only one who encouraged him to talk about it. He realized that it was a possibility. They had quite a discussion together about it.

The effect of trench life on Churchill was profound. As the weeks passed the conditions under which his men were living impressed themselves harshly upon his mind. At Laurence Farm he could do nothing to express the anger which he felt at the indignities which the war was imposing upon exuberant boys, transforming them into tired men and driving them to despair or killing them in the steady, unstoppable slaughter. By personal intervention, by leniency and by kindness he tried to lessen in some small way the burden his men bore. They appreciated the efforts he made on their behalf. A young private, Reginald Hurt, wrote to me (after my appeal for recollections was published in the Scottish papers) with two recollections of

Churchill's command. The first incident took place while the battalion was in the trenches:

> I was on sentry duty that night, which meant standing on the fire steps of the frontline trench, and looking out towards the enemy lines. It was a bitterly cold, wet night and very quiet as regards action, and in a weak moment I stood my rifle up against the parapet; in a corner of the trench.
>
> I then marched up and down on the fire step trying to get some warmth into my arms and legs, when suddenly someone jumped down behind me from the top of the parapet. Fortunately for me and my sleeping colleagues, it was Sir Winston Churchill and his Adjutant, Sir Archibald Sinclair and not a German patrol.
>
> The next five or ten minutes were amongst the unhappiest of my life, all because my rifle *was not* in my possession. I received, and deservedly, the most severe reprimand I can recall. Finally he asked me my age, and on learning that I was one of the youngest soldiers in the battalion, and had been in the trenches at the age of eighteen, his anger evaporated and he became almost paternal.
>
> My punishment was much less severe than that meted out to a corporal on sentry duty in the next bay, found doing almost the same as myself, who was demoted to the ranks, because he was both a time-serving soldier and an NCO, and should have set a better example.

The second incident that Private Hurt wrote to me about took place in reserve:

> Whilst acting as a company runner, I was walking along what had been Plugstreet's main road, when I saw the OC coming along in the opposite direction. I gave him the usual smart salute, and had passed along about a dozen paces when he called me back and asked why I was limping.
>
> I explained that my feet were sore because of the bad condition of my boots, and that when I had applied for a new pair the quartermaster said they would last another three months.

The OC took a letter from his tunic pocket, detached the envelope and wrote on it, 'Quarter-master Sgt. B. Company, supply bearer with one pair of boots *immediately*,' and signed it.

Churchill's concern for his men, repeatedly described to me by the men themselves, was to be reflected in his subsequent speeches when he returned to the House of Commons in the summer of 1916. Any search for the opinions and feelings of a public man must include a careful scrutiny of his parliamentary speeches: they are often a neglected aspect, yet one which, certainly in Churchill's case, can throw a shaft of light on the portrait.

The men in the trenches, Churchill told his fellow MPs in the summer of 1916, were facing 'the hardest of tests that men have ever been called upon to bear'. Enormous sums of money were being asked for by Asquith to keep the war machine working. 'I say to myself every day, "What is going on while we sit here, while we go away to dinner, or home to bed?" Nearly 1,000 men – Englishmen, Britishers, men of our own race – are knocked into bundles of bloody rags every twenty-four hours, and carried away to hasty graves or to field ambulances, and the money of which the Prime Minister has spoken so clearly is flowing away in a broad stream.'

Two months later, Churchill raised another matter in the Commons that derived from his frontline experiences: the question of honours and awards. 'I am not concerned with the honours and rewards of the Staff and of the higher ranks', he said, 'because, I believe, they are tolerably well provided for at the present time. It is the privates, the non-commissioned officers and the regimental officers whose case requires the sympathetic attention of the House and of the Secretary of State. Honour should go where death and danger go, and these are the men who pay all the penalties in the terrible business which is now proceeding.'

For the rest of his life Churchill was to write, and to speak, in the most human terms, about that 'terrible business'. He had seen it at first hand on too many occasions to be able to thrust it from his mind, or to ignore it in the evolution of policy. In May 1944, when John J. McCloy, an emissary from Roosevelt, came to discuss the imminent Normandy landings, Churchill took him late one night to the bombed-out chamber of the House of Commons. Forty years later, when we met in New York, McCloy told me:

> Churchill used the word 'hecatombs'. He said: 'I can't endure the Hecatombs that I saw in World War One. I can't take the risk of that. If you think I'm dragging my feet, it is not because I am afraid of casualties, it is because I am afraid of what those casualties will be. No one can accuse me of a lack of zeal. I cannot endure the loss of another British generation.'
>
> He described himself as a sort of 'sport' in nature's sense as he said most of his generation lay dead at Passchendaele and the Somme.*

What McCloy could not know was that Churchill had, at the time of the Somme and Passchendaele, urged Lloyd George's Government not to embark upon offensives that would only be met by superior defences and massive counter-attacks. He had opposed the 1916 Somme offensive and the 1917 attempt to reach Passchendaele and sweep round to the sea. In March 1917 he had spoken in the Commons of 'those dismal processes of waste and slaughter which are called attrition'. But he was still not back in government and his voice was not listened to. In anguish he had written in 1916 to his cavalry friend Sir Archibald Sinclair (later Leader of the Liberal Party and Secretary of State for Air from 1940 to 1945): 'There will be no galloping through.'

The harsh struggle continued for two more years: there was indeed no swift victory. In 1940 Churchill realized, not through guesswork but through his experiences from 1914 to 1918, that the war would be a long and violent one.

After the defeat of Germany in 1918, as after the defeat of the Boers in 1902, Churchill spoke publicly against a harsh peace with Germany. When he did so in 1918, as in 1902, he faced the hostility

---

* Two months after McCloy's visit to London, both he (as Roosevelt's Under-Secretary for War) and Churchill were separately asked to bomb the railway lines leading to the concentration camp at Auschwitz. Churchill's response, in a letter to Eden, was: 'Get anything out of the Air Force you can, and invoke me if necessary.' McCloy's response to the same request was 'Kill it.' I have written about this episode in my book *Auschwitz and the Allies*.

of the articulate majority of his constituents. But he did not modify his views to suit the call of the hour. A year later he offered a French municipality, for its war memorial, the phrases that most reflected his own philosophy:

> In War: Resolution,
> In Defeat: Defiance,
> In Victory: Magnanimity,
> In Peace: Goodwill.

The municipality rejected these words, finding magnanimity and goodwill too much to bear.

In March 1920, in a personal letter to Clementine, Churchill commented on *The Realities of War* by Philip Gibbs, which she had found a disturbing book: 'If it is monotonous in its tale of horror, it is because war is full of inexhaustible horrors.' Churchill's own published account of the battles on the Western Front, in *The World Crisis*, were described by J.M. Keynes as 'a tractate against war – more effective than the work of a pacifist could be'. Few people read them today. I was encouraged to do so, and to read them aloud, by a young American scholar, Jim Meriwether, when I taught at his university in South Carolina for six months in 1965: a sabbatical from Randolph during which, thanks to Jim, my own knowledge of Churchill's writings and opinions was greatly augmented. Having heard of Churchill's death on the last day of a journey through the American West, I was back at South Carolina on the day of his funeral. Jim recalls, in a recent letter, 'It will be twenty-six years ago this month since you and I stayed up most of the night drinking single-malt Scotch, and taking turns reading to each other favourite passages from Churchill's writings. In retrospect, I don't think there was a better way to observe his passing from this world.'

Two passages from *The World Crisis* which Jim and I read aloud to each other that night engraved themselves on my memory. Both reflected Churchill's attitude to war. Reflecting on the celebrations in Trafalgar Square on Armistice Day, the beginnings of which he himself had witnessed from his room in the Ministry of Munitions' building, the former Hotel Metropole in Northumberland Avenue, Churchill wrote:

Who shall grudge or mock these overpowering entrancements? Every Allied nation shared them. Every victorious capital or city in the five continents reproduced in its own fashion the scenes and sounds of London.

These hours were brief, their memory fleeting; they passed as suddenly as they had begun. Too much blood had been spilt. Too much life-essence had been consumed. The gaps in every home were too wide and empty. The shock of an awakening and the sense of disillusion followed swiftly upon the poor rejoicings with which hundreds of millions saluted the achievement of their hearts' desire.

There still remained the satisfactions of safety assured, of peace restored, of honour preserved, of the comforts of fruitful industry, of the home-coming of the soldiers; but these were in the background; and with them all there mingled the ache for those who would never come home.

The second passage was from the final chapter of the fifth volume of *The World Crisis*, where Churchill wrote:

Mankind has never been in this position before. Without having improved appreciably in virtue or enjoying wiser guidance, it has got into its hands for the first time the tools by which it can unfailingly accomplish its own extermination.

That is the point in human destinies to which all the glories and toils of men have at last led them. They would do well to pause and ponder upon their new responsibilities.

Death stands at attention, obedient, expectant, ready to serve, ready to shear away the peoples *en masse*; ready, if called on, to pulverize, without hope of repair, what is left of civilization. He awaits only the word of command. He awaits it from a frail, bewildered being, long his victim, now – for one occasion only – his Master.

These passages, so resonant to the voice, were so much more than rhetorical flourishes. The sentiments and the warnings of war's terrors, its aftermath and its possible recurrence, are heartfelt. These sentiments are seen strongly in a newspaper article that Churchill wrote in July 1920, when the Red Army approached Warsaw. The Prime Minister, Lloyd George, had threatened to declare war on Soviet Russia if the Red Army continued its westward march. Much as he hated Bolshevism, Churchill, then Secretary of State for War, opposed any such ultimatum. In the *Evening News* he set out his belief about the British people: 'They are thoroughly tired of war. They have learned during five bitter years too much of its iron slavery, its squalor, its mocking disappointments, its ever-dwelling sense of loss.'

To the very end of his long political career, Churchill maintained this view. Though it fell to him to lead Britain through a second destructive war, he was always aware of the cruel nature of war itself, and understood its consequences. 'You are piling up an awful load of hatred,' he warned General Eisenhower in a secret message in 1944, when several towns in northern France, road and rail centres for the German Army, were being bombed as a preliminary to the Normandy landings.

Much of Churchill's political efforts were to find policies to prevent war, but on several crucial occasions he was unable to convince those with whom he worked that his approach was the right one. In 1914 he had failed to persuade Asquith's Liberal Government to allow him to open secret negotiations with his opposite number in Germany, Admiral Tirpitz, with a view to defusing the naval crisis and, hopefully, averting war. In 1932 he had failed to persuade Ramsay MacDonald's National Government to redress Germany's legitimate grievances before she was strong enough to redress them unilaterally and by force. In 1934 he failed to persuade Stanley Baldwin's Conservative-dominated Government to build up the air force sufficiently to deter Germany from action, and after 1937 he failed to persuade Neville Chamberlain to build up an alliance of threatened states in order to deter Germany from war.

The avoidance of war was Churchill's constant and determined aim in each of these initiatives. That he failed in each of them was a source of bitterness and even anger for him. Volume one of his war memoirs, *The Second World War*, reflects this bitterness. Shortly after the war, when he was asked to send Baldwin, then aged eighty, a birthday letter, he declined to do so, writing to an intermediary:

'I wish Stanley Baldwin no ill, but it would have been much better if he had never lived.' In my long search for Churchill, few letters have struck a clearer note than this one. Churchill was almost always magnanimous: his tribute to Neville Chamberlain in 1940 was among the highpoints of his parliamentary genius. But he saw Baldwin as responsible for the 'locust years'* when Britain, if differently led, could have easily rearmed, and kept well ahead of the German military and air expansion, which Hitler had begun in 1933 from a base of virtual disarmament. Churchill saw Baldwin's policies, especially with regard to Royal Air Force expansion, as having given Hitler the impression, first, that Britain would not stand up to aggression beyond its borders, and second, that if war came Britain would not be in a position to act effectively even to defend its own cities.

Churchill believed that if war could be avoided, then statesmen had the responsibility to take every step to avoid it. Once war became inevitable, however difficult it might be to wage it, it had to be waged with every ounce of energy and determination. 'Arms and the Covenant' had been his motto in the 1930s, and was the title of one of his pre-war volumes of speeches. His theme throughout the 1930s had been not the need to make war, but the need to preserve peace, and to do so through a League of Nations willing to confront an aggressor, and by this very willingness, able to deter aggression. In Baldwin's papers at the Cambridge University Library, Susie and I found a letter from Churchill, written in 1926, in which he explained his philosophy of deterrence: 'Short of being actually conquered, there is no evil worse than submitting to wrong and violence for fear of war. Once you take the position of not being able in any circumstances to defend your rights against the aggression of some particular set of people, there is no end to the demands that will be made or to the humiliations that must be accepted.'

My search made clear that despite the image of Churchill as a man eager to resort to force, his main theme in each decade had been to try to settle international disputes by negotiation. 'The aim is to get an appeasement of the fearful hatreds and antagonisms which exist in Europe and to enable the world to settle down. I have

---

* Churchill often used this phrase for the years 1933 to 1939: 'And I will restore to you the years that the locust hath eaten,' Joel 3:25.

no other object in view,' he told the Dominion Prime Ministers at their conference in London in 1921. The records of that conference became available to public scrutiny under the Public Record Act of 1965, while Randolph was still alive. In 1925, as the records opened in 1965 also showed, Churchill had dissuaded his Cabinet colleagues from negotiating a Franco-British pact aimed to secure the French border against Germany, and had been instrumental in widening the pact so that Germany was drawn into it as an equal partner, signing at Locarno a series of agreements whereby Britain, France, Belgium and Germany mutually recognized their common frontiers.

The *Hansard* for 1950 already set out what Churchill's view had been during the Korean war, when he told the House of Commons: 'Appeasement in itself may be good or bad according to the circumstances. Appeasement from weakness and fear is alike futile and fatal. Appeasement from strength is magnanimous and noble, and might be the surest and perhaps the only path to world peace.'

'How easily men could make things better than they are – if only they tried together!' Churchill had written in a private letter to his wife before the First World War. Two world wars were to mock his hopes, but not his faith that in the end man would see reason, even if it took, as in his later life he believed it would, the frightening power of the atomic and hydrogen bomb to affect the relationships between the Great Powers. He was still alive when Macmillan, Kennedy and Khrushchev took the first steps at nuclear *détente*. 'I have followed the tangled negotiations as best as I can,' he wrote in 1958 to Macmillan, who liked to keep him in touch with developments. For so much of his life, he had picked up the pieces of the failures and follies of others: now others were taking over from him the task of saving mankind from self-destruction.

VII

The Inhabited Wilderness

When I began to examine Churchill's ten years out of office, between 1929 and 1939, I shared the general view that these were the 'wilderness years'. This phrase has become so attached to that particular decade of Churchill's life that I used it myself for two books: a short single-volume study, *Winston Churchill, the Wilderness Years*, published in 1981; and one of the inter-war document volumes of the official biography, *Winston S. Churchill, Companion Volume Five, Part Two, 'The Wilderness Years'*, also published in 1981 (and now something of a bibliographic rarity).

Following the defeat of the Conservatives at the General Election in May 1929, Churchill, while retaining his seat at Epping, was, with all his fellow Cabinet ministers, out of office. Within a year he had fallen out with the Party leadership over its decision to support the Labour plan for Indian self-government. Churchill was in the United States when the Conservative leadership decided to support the plan; he was not consulted and was unable on his return to persuade Baldwin to reverse this stand. In 1931 a national government was formed, with Ramsay MacDonald as Prime Minister and Baldwin as the most senior Conservative in the Cabinet. In the Commons, a Conservative majority after the General Election of 1931 ensured that the National Government was predominantly Conservative. This was reinforced after the General Election of 1935, when the Conservatives received by far the largest number of seats, and an overwhelming majority. By then, Churchill's opposition to Indian self-government had been nullified by the passage of the India Bill, but since 1933 his main dispute with the Government was over what sort of defence policy was needed in the face of growing German rearmament. He did not receive office in 1935, though he had expected, and hoped, to be brought back. He remained a Member of Parliament, but a back-bencher.* The British declaration of war on Germany on 3 September 1940 found him still out of office.

The wilderness years lasted almost a decade. The more I delved, however, into what Churchill was doing during that decade, the less apposite did the concept of wilderness appear. Of course, he was out of office, and out of favour with the political establishment, but he was throughout that decade a Member of Parliament, and an active and forceful one. As the decade wore on, he became a kind of one-man unofficial opposition, complete with his centre of operations at Chartwell and a 'Cabinet' of former colleagues, friends, civil servants and political well-wishers. His fortnightly newspaper articles, and frequent magazine articles, on every aspect of European and world affairs, gained an extraordinarily wide circulation. Sometimes a single article would be printed in as many as twenty European newspapers in a single week. This achievement was the work of a Hungarian Jew, Imre Révész (later Emery Reves), who had gone to see Churchill early in 1937 to offer the services of his Paris-based newspaper circulation service.

I had first met Reves at Stour, when he gave Randolph an account of his work for Churchill and I took notes. Susie and I went to see him at his villa in the South of France, La Pausa above Roquebrune, where Churchill was a frequent visitor in the late 1950s. In 1981, as he was dying, he asked to speak to me again, and I flew to Switzerland, to the hotel where he was staying at Montreux. At each of our talks, Reves told me how he had recognized the quality and clarity of Churchill's arguments even before they met, how he regarded those arguments as of paramount importance in the debate about democracy that was then raging, and how he was determined to place them as widely as possible. This he had done with consummate success.

When I visited Reves at his villa in the South of France, among the photographs he showed me was one of him meeting Churchill on his arrival in Paris by air during one of those visits when Churchill,

* Although a back-bencher, Churchill was the senior Conservative Privy Councillor (having been elected to the Privy Council in 1908, while a Liberal). He sat on the non-ministerial section of the Conservative front bench, just across from the gangway, and therefore only one place away from Stanley Baldwin from 1935 to 1937 and from Neville Chamberlain from 1937 to 1939.

at odds with Chamberlain, tried to persuade the French Government that Britain would, despite appearances to the contrary, stand up in the end to the Germans.

Reves also stressed Churchill's ability, if telephoned at Chartwell with an urgent newspaper commission in, say, France, to produce something within hours and have it telephoned across to Paris.

It was in the House of Commons that Churchill was most effective. At a time when the chamber of the House of Commons was often, as today, almost empty for much of any debate, his outstanding speeches quickly filled the chamber. The knowledge that he was to speak quickly brought dozens of MPs from the tea rooms and bars. Once, after Churchill had spoken with particular forcefulness, a disgruntled Conservative minister commented, 'Here endeth the book of Jeremiah.' This prompted his neighbour to remark, as MPs, the masterful speech having ended, flocked out of the chamber: 'Followed, I see, by Exodus'.

Churchill's own humour could reduce MPs to tears. On one occasion, a few months after Chamberlain's return from Munich, during a debate on Palestine, the Secretary of State for the Colonies, Malcolm MacDonald (who told me this story himself) had reached the end of a difficult speech and was descanting lyrically about the land itself, all controversy behind him. He had come to a passage of which he was particularly pleased, 'Bethlehem, where the Prince of Peace was born', when Churchill's voice was heard from his seat below the gangway: ' "Bethlehem?" I thought Neville was born in Birmingham.'

Churchill was capable, each time he divided the House during the debates on India, of getting fifty and even sixty Conservatives to join him in the lobby against their own leaders and government. Nor was he isolated socially: people delighted in his company, newspapers paid him exceptionally well for his articles, his opinions were sought on innumerable occasions by the press, and increasingly by civil servants, senior officers from all three Services, and even government ministers. His knowledge about what was going on in foreign affairs and defence preparedness was formidable, often embarrassing the Government in debate.

When I began my work on the inter-war volumes, it was important to know where Churchill got his information from. Randolph's friend Lord Hailsham, a former Lord Chancellor and the son of a Secretary of State for War in the 1930s, spoke with scorn in a BBC television film about Churchill (of which I was the narrator, but sadly not the arbiter) of a 'very highly paid official who fed him accurate information and which of course was contrary to what was strictly proper'. This was said in 1990, fourteen years after the relevant volume of my work was published. Hailsham had no idea of the man's identity. The description 'very highly paid' was a characteristic example of the pre-war style of character assassination, no doubt handed on from one generation to the next. Civil servants were not all that highly paid, nor was this one. But who was he?

The Churchill papers held a clue, but it was nothing more than three brief entries in a visitors' book, and two thank-you letters. The visitors' book at Chartwell revealed that on 24 March 1935 Churchill had a lady visitor. Her name was Ava Wigram. Her husband Ralph, then aged forty-five, was the head of the Central Department of the Foreign Office, with special responsibility for Germany. Wigram had intended to go down with his wife but had been unable to get away from his desk. After her visit, Ava Wigram wrote a thank-you note, which contained the phrase, 'The things I told you at Chartwell were for yourself alone.'

What were these things? What lay behind this thank-you letter? Why had Wigram not been able to go to Chartwell himself? Two weeks later, on April 7, Wigram did visit Chartwell. What had these men discussed in the remoteness of rural Kent? Had Wigram acted alone? He returned there at the end of April, after which visit Mrs Wigram wrote again: 'I do not know how to express to you my gratitude for your kindness to me and Ralph. It has been a very real joy to us to go and see you at Chartwell & to talk things over with you.' That same day, in the House of Commons, Churchill made a devastating, detailed and unanswerable attack on the Government for having allowed Germany to overtake Britain in the air. It was essential, he ended, to retrieve 'the woeful miscalculations of which we are at present the dupes, and of which, unless we take warning in time, we may some day be the victims'.

Susie and I had no idea what Wigram had told Churchill, or why. But there was a path to follow, and she commuted from Oxford to Kew, searching the files in the Public Record Office for the answer.

When it came, it was astonishing. On 16 March Hitler had announced the re-introduction of compulsory military service. On 19 March, in the House of Commons, the Government had insisted that Britain still had a margin of superiority over the German Air Force. In the Foreign Office, Wigram knew that the Government's own information gave the lie to this: that it was known in Whitehall that the German Air Force had in fact already overtaken that of Britain in first-line strength, and also in reserve strength. In his anguish, he decided to take this information to Churchill, whom he had seen from time to time in the Foreign Office visiting his own boss, the Permanent Under-Secretary of State, Sir Robert Vansittart. From the documents that Susie found, it was clear that Vansittart shared Wigram's deep unease, both about German intentions, and about the Government's refusal to reveal them, and to mislead the House about them.

Ava Wigram's visit of 24 March had been the start of a determined attempt by Wigram to put Churchill fully in the picture. That very day, as Susie discovered in the Foreign Office files, new information had reached the Foreign Office of Hitler's rapid air expansion, and Wigram had been obliged to remain at his desk: hence his inability to go down to Chartwell, where his wife had represented him. His own visit on 7 April had enabled him to show Churchill the most recent secret documents about German air expansion, each of which Susie found in the Foreign Office files, and the contents of which had served as the bedrock of his speech of 2 May. This included a masterly paper by one of Wigram's assistants, Michael Creswell, a distinguished First World War pilot, in which, with tables and statistics culled from Air Ministry Intelligence, he showed that the German air factories were already 'practically organized on an emergency wartime footing' and that German productive capacity would enable the German Air Force to surpass Britain's home defence force by the end of the year. 'They will have the additional advantage', Creswell pointed out, 'of possessing entirely new material throughout.' On 18 March Wigram had noted on Creswell's memorandum: 'I do not believe that the British people will not defend themselves at whatever inconvenience or danger if they realize the necessity. The problem is surely to make them realize.'

Churchill was the instrument that Wigram chose to alert the

British public to the reality of German air power. On 6 April, the day before his postponed visit to Churchill, he had seen another secret communication, sent from the Air Ministry to the Foreign Office, admitting that Britain's existing first-line air strength was no more than 453 aircraft, in contrast with the Air Ministry figure of 850 German first-line and immediate reserve aircraft for that same date. Reading these figures, Vansittart had minuted: 'These figures should be known to every member of His Majesty's Government. I beg the Secretary of State to ensure that they are thus known.'

Wigram was determined that Churchill should know them too. The Air Ministry memorandum, which Susie had found in the Foreign Office papers, together with Vansittart's note, was one of the papers that he had taken down to Chartwell on the following day. Henceforth, Wigram and his wife were to be frequent visitors to Churchill's London flat at Morpeth Mansions and at Chartwell, and Churchill became a frequent visitor to their home in Lord North Street. As a result, his knowledge of the actual relative air strengths of Britain and Germany was always absolutely up to date, and based upon the Government's own most secret assessments.

Wigram's activities had not gone unnoticed. Even before we had unravelled the story of what precisely he had done for Churchill, and the sequence of events that led him to Churchill's study, I had gone to see his widow, then Ava, Viscountess Waverley, at her home in Lord North Street. These were her recollections, as I set them down in March 1969:

> In about 1935 Walter Runciman* said to me: 'Baldwin feels it would be better if Ralph did not see so much of Winston. It isn't good for him. He is the head of an important part of the Foreign Office. It is wrong that he should tell Churchill what is going on. If Ralph persists in seeing Winston he may be sent off abroad to a distant post where Winston could not get at him.'
> I said, 'Is it a threat?'
> 'No,' he said, 'a warning.'
> But Runciman and Baldwin knew that I couldn't leave

---

* A pre-war Liberal Cabinet colleague of Churchill's, Runciman was President of the Board of Trade from 1931 to 1937. He was created Viscount in 1937.

my invalid son. They wanted to use the threat of a foreign posting to get me to put pressure on Ralph to stop seeing Winston. So I said to Runciman, 'Ralph will go on seeing Winston as much as he likes, and he will tell him what he likes too.'

Lady Waverley also recalled how 'very hurt' Churchill had been when Baldwin appointed Sir Thomas Inskip as Minister for the Co-ordination of Defence:

> I wanted Winston to meet as many ministers as possible, to discuss his ideas with them privately, to feel less isolated. So I arranged a lunch for Runciman, Ralph and Winston. Somehow Sir John Simon* heard of it. That day he kept Ralph busy at all sorts of absurd telephone calls abroad.
>
> So Runciman and Winston lunched alone with me. Runciman was very stiff, very cold. Winston said almost nothing. He was very down.

Churchill admired Wigram for the risks he was prepared to take: risks which made Churchill extremely well informed about the inner debate and factual reality of Britain's air policy. Then, early in 1937, Churchill began to warn publicly of deficiencies in the running of the Air Force at home. There were rumours that a serving officer had brought him material, even that he was in contact with the Intelligence services, and that people came to see him who, had their visits been known at the time, would have been severely castigated, even court-martialled.

I remember an uncomfortable evening at Churchill College, Cambridge when the naval historian Captain Stephen Roskill, attacking me as if I were somehow Churchill's representative, told me in no uncertain terms how improper had been the actions of serving officers in bringing Churchill secret information. Roskill was the biographer of Lord Hankey, the Secretary to the Cabinet, and had seen a rebuke by Hankey to Churchill about this very matter. But

---

* Another pre-war Liberal Cabinet colleague of Churchill's, he was Foreign Secretary from 1931 to 1935, Home Secretary from 1935 to 1937 and Chancellor of the Exchequer from 1937 to 1940. Created Viscount in 1940, he served as Lord Chancellor throughout Churchill's wartime premiership.

the rebuke gave no clue as to who the officers might be. Indeed, Hankey was particularly angry that Churchill would not reveal their names to him. Nor did Roskill know.

I was bemused by Roskill's indignation as I worked through the Churchill papers finding out who these officers were, and what precisely they had done. The clue came in a pencilled note from his secretary Violet Pearman, in one of the files on defence policy. It was dated 20 May 1936, at the height of the defence and foreign policy debates, and a year after his parliamentary speech to which Wigram's information had been the key. A serving Air Force officer, Mrs Pearman wrote, would like 'a talk with you very soon', and she went on to explain, reflecting the officer's own nervousness, 'As a service officer you would appreciate his position. He did not wish to write, but thought a talk was better. Would you speak to him tomorrow, if possible? He would come to the Flat or the House.'

The 'Flat' was Morpeth Mansions in Victoria. The 'House' was Chartwell. 'He would confidently say you would be much interested in what he had to say. When can he come to see you?' Mrs Pearman then gave the officer's telephone number and extension at the Air Ministry.

I went at once to Churchill's desk diaries, the month-by-month cards on which his secretaries listed his engagements. In the square for Monday 25 May Mrs Pearman had written: '7, Squadron Leader Anderson at flat.' Here was the clue that unlocked a series of remarkable boxes. I went back at once to the Churchill papers, and found, in a special section, a file marked 'Anderson'. In it were innumerable Air Ministry documents. Once more, I combed the telephone directories. Once more I was fortunate, not only that Anderson was still alive, but that he lived on the south coast, at Chichester. Within twenty-four hours we had spoken. He was exceptionally nervous, not at all happy that I knew his name, and quite thrown by the thought that he was no longer the anonymous villain of Roskill & Co.

I persuaded Anderson to come up to London. I was so nervous myself that I booked a table at a restaurant in Jermyn Street that proved far too grand for him, as well as for me. He met me in the street, looking agitated and ill at ease, clutching a large brown paper parcel. We went into the restaurant, where, although it was lunch time on a sunny day, the room was dark and there was an air of gloom. I spent some time telling Anderson about my own work, and about what I already knew of Churchill's contacts at the time he had first gone to see him. I was able to point out that on the day of Mrs Pearman's message to Churchill, he had dined with Desmond Morton, the head of the Government's Industrial Intelligence Centre, who for more than three years had been providing Churchill on a weekly basis with material about German military, air and naval preparations. A week before that he had again lunched at Morpeth Mansions with Ava Wigram. Anderson was only slightly assuaged. What I did not tell him was that Wigram's widow had, a few years earlier, given me a harrowing description of how a Cabinet minister, meeting her at dinner, had given her a ferocious warning of the dangers to her husband's career if he went on seeing Churchill.

Although he had made the journey from Chichester to London to see me, Anderson seemed reluctant to talk. We ate hardly anything. As the final course was being taken away, he opened the brown paper parcel. In it were documents of the sort that I had seen in Churchill's papers, with notes on them as to when he had taken them to Churchill and discussed them with him. He told me about that first meeting in the flat at Morpeth Mansions. On that occasion he had brought with him Air Ministry charts and statistics which made clear that with regard to the Air Force, too few observer-navigators were being trained, educational standards were falling, and current plans were inadequate to provide the number of observers needed to confront Germany in 1937, 1938 or even 1939.

At this first meeting, Anderson gave Churchill a seventeen-page foolscap memorandum, the theme of which was that not enough was being done 'to fit the RAF for War'. He also produced fourteen pages of statistical information setting out the RAF programme in both personnel and aircraft. He recalled, as we sat in the dark restaurant, how frightened he had been, giving such material to someone who was such a vocal and persistent critic of the Government.

Churchill had understood Anderson's dilemma. He could not encourage him to divulge secret material, but he did not feel able to discourage him. He gave Anderson an assurance that the facts Anderson gave him would not be used in public, but only as the basis for general assertions, or in direct correspondence with ministers. Anderson was welcome to come to see him at any time, or to come down to Chartwell. Churchill may have realized that the initiative for Anderson's approach to him came from Mrs Pearman herself. She had already met and been attracted by this able, anguished soul, and had realized that he was tormenting himself over the neglects and failures of British air policy. This was the very area about which she knew her own master, for whom she had worked since 1929, to be so concerned, and yet unlike the German aspect on which Wigram was helping, he had little information. She must have encouraged Anderson to do what he had done, risking his career, but making it possible for a person of high standing to take on the cause of the state of preparedness of the Air Force.

At the age of forty, Anderson felt that he had failed to alert the Air Ministry to the need for greater efficiency and preparedness. His whole life had been one of service. As an infantryman he had been badly wounded on the Western Front in 1916 and forced to spend a year in hospital. Transferred to the Royal Flying Corps, he won the Distinguished Flying Cross in 1917. In 1934 he had become Director of Training at the Air Ministry. His ability to contribute to Churchill's fund of secret knowledge was considerable.

On 27 July the Air Ministry circulated to senior officers a comprehensive chart of past expansion schemes, together with the most recent scheme which the Cabinet had accepted, by which Britain was to have 1,736 first-line aeroplanes for Home Defence by March 1939. Anderson immediately gave his copies of the chart to Churchill, who henceforth was able to calculate in detail the precise British air figures, and to use them confidentially in his correspondence and discussions with Cabinet ministers.*

Each phase of Churchill's battle to stimulate greater production, training and rearmament, whether in parliamentary speeches, deputations to the Prime Minister, or approaches to individual ministers, was backed up by the material that Wigram, Anderson and Morton were giving him. Morton lived a few miles away across the fields

---

* After I pieced together Anderson's story, he asked me to come to his home in Chichester to tell his grandchildren. Until then he had been too shy, and also too frightened, to tell them about his true Churchill connection.

from Chartwell, and would call at the weekends, walking along the country lanes carrying a bundle of British Intelligence surveys of German arms production.

Morton was a man who believed in mystery. He had already told me of his service as an artillery officer in the First World War, when Churchill had met him, but even in the 1970s was reluctant to divulge very much about his contacts with Churchill. In 1916 he was shot through the heart at the Battle of Arras, but lived. He was, apparently, one of only two such lucky survivors.* Churchill had met him again on several occasions in 1917 and 1918 when he served as ADC to Sir Douglas Haig, and Churchill, as Minister of Munitions, was a frequent guest at Haig's headquarters. Morton had entered the world of Intelligence in 1919, when Churchill, then Secretary of State for War, had put him in charge of a War Office Intelligence-gathering section, covering Germany, Eastern Europe and Bolshevik Russia. The Foreign Office also used Morton's services in this connection. In 1929, when Churchill was Chancellor of the Exchequer, and concerned with the large purchases of raw materials by a disarmed Germany in foreign markets, Morton became Head of the Industrial Intelligence Centre, a sub-committee of the Committee of Imperial Defence, whose terms of reference were 'To discover and report the plans for manufacture of armaments and war stores in foreign countries'.

From the moment that Hitler came to power, Morton brought Churchill details of German industrial production, and, as it grew by leaps and bounds, of German aircraft production. These figures were always denied by Baldwin and his ministers. But Churchill knew that they came from the same Intelligence source that was providing the ministers themselves. When Morton gave me lunch at his London club in 1966, while I was still working for Randolph, he was far too discreet to enter into these details. But much later, when I was working through the Churchill papers, I found a clue. Among the notes that Churchill dictated after the war, when writing his war memoirs, was one in which he wrote about an episode directly linked

---

* Randolph later told me that on many of Morton's visits to Chartwell he would play tennis with Clementine, watched by Churchill's children, who had been told that because he had been shot through the heart he might drop dead at any moment. This possibility kept their minds focused on the game, or at least on the Major.

to the knowledge that Morton was giving him about the German Air Force:

> I happened to see Mr Baldwin in his own room at the House on some other matter and we had a friendly chat. I thought I would give him a hint in private and I told him 'speaking as an old colleague' that he was not getting the true information. He had better be careful. He had better look into the matter himself, personally. He had better look below the top officials at the Air Ministry who informed him. He had better see some subordinates for himself and cross-question them.
>
> 'You are being misled,' I said. 'The truth does not reach to ministerial levels.' I could hardly say more, without endangering my sources of information, which were in fact his own Secret Service.
>
> Mr Baldwin seemed suddenly impressed. I knew him very well. For five years we had worked closely together. He gave me a piercing look and I thought I had struck to the core. We parted on our usual friendly terms; but nothing seemed to come of it.

Morton had gone on providing Churchill with the secret information that reached him. My search for Churchill became, for a while, a search for Morton, who was no less enigmatic in the archives than he had been in person. My break came in the first week of March 1975, when Harold Wilson's Private Secretary, Marcia Williams, informed me that the Prime Minister had given permission for me to see the Morton papers. It emerged that these were still being kept under lock and key at Downing Street. On 14 March I presented myself at Number 10 and was taken downstairs to the rooms at the back, overlooking the garden. It was in these 'garden rooms' that Churchill's wartime secretaries had worked. Here, in a securely-locked metal filing cabinet were Morton's papers. The drawers were opened. I read and took copious notes, watched by a young civil servant in Wilson's office (later, as Secretary to the Cabinet, he was to be the senior civil servant in Britain). While I was transcribing the documents the Prime Minister himself arrived. I had just come across a handwritten letter from Churchill to Morton, dated October

1947, in which he wrote: 'I am anxious to make some mention in my memoirs of all the help you gave me – and I think I may say the country – in the critical pre-war years.' This was the clue I had been searching for. 'When I read all these letters and papers you wrote for me, and think of our prolonged conversations', Churchill told Morton, 'I feel how very great is my debt to you, and I know that no thought ever crossed your mind but the public interest.'*

In preparation for a deputation of senior Conservatives to Baldwin in July 1936, both Morton and Anderson helped Churchill to draft his statement. He was also helped, in analysing their material, and in presenting it with a sharp, accurate focus, by Professor Lindemann, who was almost always at Chartwell during the visits of the informants, and who invariably gave Churchill his own scientifically-presented projections based on the material Churchill had been given.

Lindemann and Churchill had met shortly after the First World War. Within a few years their friendship had become one of great trust and intimacy. After Lord Birkenhead's death in 1930, Lindemann became Churchill's closest friend and most frequent non-family guest at Chartwell. Clementine liked him, and the children were fascinated by him. His father was from Alsace but had emigrated to Britain in the 1870s. Lindemann had been born in Germany (at Baden-Baden) only because his mother, an American, was taking the cure there. Before the First World War he had studied physics in Berlin and physical chemistry in Paris. After the outbreak of war he was one of the organizers of the kite balloon barrage for the defence of London. In 1919 he became Professor of Physics at Oxford, a post he held until 1956, residing at Christ Church.

From 1935, Churchill was a member of a secret sub-committee of the Committee of Imperial Defence, responsible for examining the most recent developments and possibilities of Air Defence Research. At his suggestion, Lindemann was made a member in 1936. Lindemann was fertile in ideas, particularly for aerial mines to be dropped in the path of incoming bombers, for infra-red detec-

---

* The Morton papers were subsequently transferred to the Public Record Office at Kew, under the reference PREMIER PAPERS 7, and remained closed for many years. While preparing this chapter, I found the note I had made of that particular excursion.

tion of night-flying aircraft, and for the placing of a 'cloud of sub-stance' in the path of an aeroplane 'to produce detonation'. Lindemann and Churchill gave their support to Robert Watson-Watt, the inventor of radar, who was finding support hard to come by and had appealed to Churchill for the establishment of 'emergency machinery' to develop radar.

Given official access to the secret workings of research against air attack, Lindemann and Churchill were both vexed by what they saw as the 'slow, timid and insignificant' pace of research, as Churchill described it privately to Sir Thomas Inskip, newly appointed Minister for the Co-ordination of Defence. Churchill's frustration on the committee, paralleled by Lindemann's scientific keenness to act with greater speed and imagination, was another factor in his growing sense of isolation and anger. To be, in this one instance on the inside, and yet to be so effectively outside, the world of defence preparation and priorities, was vexatious. The archives of the Air Defence Research sub-committee were made available to the public while I was working on the inter-war years: they became an integral part of my understanding of Churchill's concern for anti-aircraft defence, and his closeness to Lindemann.

Considering the strength and length of their friendship, there were surprisingly few letters from Churchill to Lindemann in Churchill's papers, and equally few from Lindemann to Churchill in Linde-mann's papers at Nuffield College, Oxford. How to find out about their friendship was a problem. Lindemann had died in 1957. Unmarried, he had been served for many years by a devoted valet, Mr Harvey. One day I received, out of the blue, a letter from Harvey, in which he offered to help me. It turned out that he lived near Oxford station, five minutes drive from where I was working.

Harvey came to see me several times to talk about his Master, whom he adored. Nor was he the only person who spoke warmly of a man whom most of his Oxford university colleagues found stern and difficult. One of the most memorable mornings of my researches was spent with Churchill's daughter Sarah at her London flat, as she reminisced about 'Prof' and revealed through her own enthusiasm how close he had been to them all. Often the children would ask him to recount his wartime exploit, when he learned to fly in order to take up a plane himself to investigate the aerodynamic effects of spin, and thereby to try to prevent, by personal scientific experiment, the almost always fatal spins and side-slips to which aircraft were then prone. One episode Sarah told me of gives a picture of this Oxford academic and dour don in the relaxed atmosphere far from university high tables. Here are her words:

> The dear Prof was a vegetarian, a bachelor and a teetotaller, all of which things my father greatly deplored, but which slight imperfections he tolerated because of the value he placed on the Prof's splendid mind and friendship. He was part of our Chartwell life. It is hard to remember an occasion on which he was not present. His exterior was conventionally forbidding – the domed cranium, the close-cropped, iron-grey hair which had receded as if the brain had pushed it away, the iron-grey moustache, the sallow complexion, the little sniff which took the place of what normally would have been a laugh, yet he could still exude a warmth that made scientific thinking unfrightening.
>
> Prof had a gift of conveying a most complicated subject in simple form. One day at lunch when coffee and brandy were being served my father decided to have a slight 'go' at Prof who had just completed a treatise on the quantum theory. 'Prof' he said, 'tell us in words of one syllable and in no longer than five minutes what is the quantum theory.' My father then placed his large gold watch, known as the 'turnip', on the table. When you consider that Prof must have spent many years working on this subject, it was quite a tall order, however without any hesitation, like quicksilver, he explained the principle and held us all spell-bound. When he had finished we all spontaneously burst into applause.

Over the years I made a special effort to ask those who had known Churchill well to tell me about Lindemann. They all told the same story, that of closest friendship. Churchill's nephew Johnny, a painter and raconteur, told me when we talked at his home in London about his uncle: 'He swore by Lindemann. Anything that was a query, which Winston did not know, he would say "What do you think about that Prof? What is that about?" If Prof said it was all nonsense, Winston believed it to be nonsense.' Conversely, when Lindemann spoke to Churchill about scientific developments, Churchill questioned him about them in great detail and built upon the facts to construct themes and arguments.

In 1924 Lindemann had told Churchill about the future power of nuclear fission, Churchill was so struck by his exposition that he wrote a magazine article in Nash's *Pall Mall* about a bomb no bigger than an orange that would have the power to 'blast a township at a stroke'. In this same article, inspired by Lindemann's interest in rocketry, Churchill asked: 'Could not explosives even of the existing type be guided automatically in flying machines by wireless or other rays, without a human pilot, in ceaseless procession upon a hostile city, arsenal, camp, or dockyard?'

By the time of the defence deputation of July 1936, Churchill had augmented his own scientific knowledge, which was far from minimal, by contact with Lindemann over more than a decade. The material brought to him by Anderson and Morton lent itself to Lindemann's scrutiny. Were the figures being presented in the most scientific and accurate manner? What lay behind them? What could be deduced from them? All this was discussed by the two men weekend after weekend, and with a remarkable sense and unity of purpose.

At the deputation, Churchill spoke of the relative air strengths of Britain and Germany, stressing the enormous efforts being made in Germany to train pilots and to practise 'night-flying under war conditions'. This he knew from Morton. He then criticized Britain's air training facilities and educational standards. No doubt they would improve with time, he said, and he went on to ask: 'Shall we have time?' Far better to encourage long-term engagements and higher educational standards. 'Everything turns on the intelligence, daring, the spirit and firmness of character of the air pilots.'

Churchill went on to make the point on which Anderson had been so insistent, that observer-navigators must also be trained in much larger numbers, and with a much higher standard of education and intelligence. 'To use pilots as observers', he said, 'is almost to halve your pilot strength.' Churchill then asked whether all the squadrons in the Air Force list were up to full strength. 'I have heard of one', he said, 'that had only 30 airmen instead of 140.' This had, of course, come straight from Anderson.

Churchill continued: 'It is disconcerting to hear that many of our regular squadrons, not new ones in process of formation, but regular long-formed squadrons, are far below their strength, and have a large proportion, if not the whole, of their reserve aircraft either taken away for service in the flying training schools or unprovided with the necessary equipment or even, in some cases, without engines.' Again, Anderson was the source. Lindemann had scrutinized the figures.

During the autumn of 1936 Churchill's sources of information on defence were widened. That October, Brigadier Hobart, a leading tank expert, visited Morpeth Mansions. On the previous day a Royal Air Force pilot, Squadron Leader H.V. Rowley, who had just returned from a visit to Germany, wrote to Anderson of all he had seen while he was the guest of the German Air Ministry. 'The development of air power in Germany', he wrote, 'has left me in a somewhat dazed condition but with one fact firmly in my mind and that fact is that they are now stronger in the air than England and France combined.' Anderson at once sent Rowley's letter to Churchill, knowing that 'Papa' (as Anderson called Churchill in his letters to Mrs Pearman) was even then preparing for a defence debate. Among the other materials which Anderson sent Churchill was a 'Diagram Showing Peace Organization of the Royal Air Force', marked 'For Official Use Only': it showed the exact location of all operational, training and administrative units, and the chain of command.

As a result of the material that was being brought to him, it had become clear to Churchill that should war be a possibility either in 1937 or 1938, Britain would not have sufficient air defence or air power to resist a major attack, or to counter-attack. A second deputation was even then preparing to see Baldwin once more. In the five days leading up to it, Churchill's principal source of information was again Anderson. In a series of notes which he dictated to Mrs Pearman for 'Papa', Anderson set out the precise state of Air Force construction under the current expansion scheme. In the first of these notes he listed in one column the total number of bombers in existence, as stated by the Government, in a second column the actual mobilization strength as of June 1937, and in a third the planned mobilization situation in March 1939. The first column, Anderson added, 'is "shop window-dressing" for Parliament'.

Before Churchill made his presentation, Anderson dictated two more notes to Mrs Pearman, one on the state of British service aircraft, the other on German air and pilot strength. He also passed on to Churchill a document which he had received, under seal of secrecy, from the head of the Air Ministry German Intelligence Section, Wing-Commander Goddard. The information in the document was shocking. According to Goddard, his superior, the Chief of the Air Staff, Sir Edward Ellington, would only accept German first-line air strength as 550 bombers and 250 fighters, a total of 800. Yet in addition, Goddard pointed out, both the bomber and the fighter squadrons of the German force 'have 100 per cent reserve in aircraft'. Goddard's information showed both the strengths and weakness of the German situation. 'Their accepted pilot strength is 8,500,' Goddard had reported. 'It is agreed that few of these have been fully trained in the full arts of applied flying, i.e., bombing, gunnery, etc. But they are capable nevertheless of piloting an aeroplane and dropping bombs over a target, such as London. These reports are obtained direct from the Secret Service through agents.'

From the figures in Goddard's document, it was clear that the 372 British bombers, which would be fully operational in June 1937, would have to be the comparable figure to the German 800, quite apart from the question of how far the further 800 German reserve bombers could also be counted as first-line.

This revelation of British weakness in the air was known only to a handful of senior Air Force officers, and now, thanks to Anderson, it was known to Churchill. In 1976 I corresponded with Goddard about this episode. He wrote bitterly of Anderson, of whose general activities in giving Churchill information he had become aware at the time: 'He would have some names of his associates in what he regarded as patriotic work.' Goddard did not know that he himself had been an unwitting associate.

Anderson was sailing very close to the wind; he became frightened that somehow the figures he was giving Churchill could be traced back to him, and then to Goddard. 'Comdr. Anderson told me very seriously that he had never been frightened in his life before,' Mrs Pearman wrote to Churchill. 'He does not know whether they are suspicious of him, and may try to trace him. The figures are accurate, and so accurate and staggering, that he thinks this is the reason those who know are frightened of facts coming out.'

Throughout 1937 Anderson visited Churchill both at Morpeth Mansions and Chartwell, bringing with him more documents and memoranda relating to the state of Air Force training, machines and personnel. As we sat together in the restaurant, all the other patrons having left, and the waiters becoming impatient for us also to leave, Anderson became more and more animated. Memories of Churchill's kindness and attentiveness began to flood back. 'You would give Churchill a new idea, he would say nothing. Two hours later, while feeding the goldfish he would come out with the flaw in what you said. He had the power to use the unconscious mind. He said to me once, speaking of Britain, and, as it were *to* Britain: "You came into big things as an accident of naval power when you were an island. The world had confidence in you. You became the workshop of the world. You populated the island beyond its capacity. Through an accident of air power you will probably cease to exist."'

Anderson had become aware, within six months of first bringing material to Churchill, that great danger lay along that path for him personally. As I prepared to say goodbye to him, he told me: 'Churchill brought me into the family life at Chartwell. He did it to protect me. He could then say – he is a member of the family. One day when he was in bed he said to me: "I know what is troubling you. It is loyalty to the Service and loyalty to the State. You must realize that loyalty to the State must come before loyalty to the Service."'

As Goddard, at the German Intelligence Section of the Air Ministry, realized, Anderson drew his materials from many sources. One of these, he told me, as I walked with him to the station for his return journey to Chichester, was a senior officer in Bomber Command. He was reluctant to tell me his name. At the last moment, as we reached Victoria Station, he told me: it was Group Captain Lachlan MacLean. As soon as I was back in Oxford I went down to the basement of the Bodleian library, where I read again, with a new insight, an eight-page memorandum, in Churchill's defence files for 1937, written by Lachlan MacLean, then the senior Air staff officer at the headquarters of Bomber Group. The document made it clear that it had been sent to Churchill from Anderson.

MacLean's memorandum was critical of many aspects of Air Force development, including long-distance navigation, maintenance work and pilot training. 'Lacking modern aeroplanes and adequate equipment', he wrote, 'not only are we not ready for War, but our whole training for War must wait on the provision of such aircraft and equipment.' Were war to come in the next three, or even five years, he added, 'we shall be powerless to retaliate, at any rate in the air.'

MacLean, like Anderson, had begun the First World War as a soldier. He too had been wounded on the Western Front. He too had then transferred to the Royal Flying Corps, and was in action in the Middle East, driving the Turks from Palestine, and being mentioned in despatches. Returning to England at the end of the war, he was in charge of a Royal Air Force Training Depot Station. I hastened to make contact with him. Anderson told me that he thought that he was living in South Africa. In the course of my researches I was already in touch with the South African Air Force veterans' association, which soon located MacLean for me. We began a vigorous correspondence, in the course of which he told me that he had not known at the time that Anderson had sent his memorandum to Churchill, but that his argument had at once 'impressed the latter, and he expressed a wish to meet me'.

Of his first meeting with Churchill, MacLean wrote to me:

> Accompanying Anderson I was introduced to Winston in his flat in Westminster and he congratulated me on the papers and we discussed the air rearmament. Subsequently, from time to time, Anderson would ask me to write a short paper on some point that Winston wished to make in a letter to the Prime Minister or in a speech in the House and I would let him have these papers and would perhaps go to Churchill's flat for a discussion. This situation gradually developed into my sending to Winston's personal secretary, Mrs Pearman, papers on the more significant events in the air rearmament.

Towards the end of March 1937, Churchill raised with Sir Thomas Inskip, the Minister for the Co-ordination of Defence (a job that many people thought ought to have gone to Churchill) the problem of Britain's first-line air strength, a problem which he had discussed with Anderson at Chartwell a few days earlier. On 22 March Inskip informed the House of Commons that as from 1 April there would be 103 squadrons based in the United Kingdom. But to Churchill himself, he wrote privately on 23 March to explain that, unfortunately, ten of the squadrons would be under strength in aircraft 'pending the delivery of further machines', and that some of the recently formed Auxiliary Air Squadrons would likewise 'not be up to establishment'. Inskip added: 'I feel justified in giving you, as a Privy Councillor, this further confidential information, especially as you have already had so much secret information in this connection.'

Churchill replied to Inskip on 26 March, accepting that there must be 'a great deal of reorganization and weakness during a period of rapid expansion', and sending him 'in personal confidence' a memorandum on air squadron deficiencies by 'a staff officer of the Air Force'. Churchill went on to give Inskip his own view on how these deficiencies should be tackled:

> I wonder you do not get a list made of everything that a regular Air Squadron should have – pilots, machines, spare engines, spare parts, machine guns, bombing sights etc. together with the reserves of all kinds which should be kept at the station. And then, armed with this, go down accompanied by three or four competent persons to visit, quite by chance, some Air Squadron by surprise. If then during the course of a whole day your people went through the list while you cross-examined the officers, you would have some information on which you could rest with some security.

'The reason why I am not dwelling upon these matters in public,' Churchill explained, 'is because of the fear I have of exposing our weakness even more than is already known abroad.'

Less than two months later, Churchill received a further document through Anderson: it was a six-page letter from MacLean to Anderson about the state of the Air Force. That summer, in an attempt to influence senior members of the Conservative Party about the continuing weakness of Britain's air defences, Churchill sent MacLean's January memorandum on air deficiencies to Lord Salisbury. He had already sent it to both Inskip and Chamberlain. In a covering letter to Salisbury, Churchill wrote: 'Inskip made the observation that things had improved since then. No doubt this is true to a small extent. I therefore two months ago asked the officer to write another impression bringing his view up to date. I will send you this from Chartwell tomorrow . . .'

Through Mrs Pearman, Anderson kept Churchill informed of Air Force problems. On one occasion, enclosing details of accidents caused by the inexperience of pilots, maintenance failures and lack of practice, he wrote to Mrs Pearman: 'Will you give the attached papers to Papa? He asked for them to be sent on.' Two weeks later, Anderson wrote again, sending Churchill the most recently compiled secret details of British and German aircraft production.

From the Cabinet minutes at the Public Record Office, and from Lord Hankey's papers at Churchill College, Cambridge, it became clear that the Government had become so alarmed at the accuracy and impact of Churchill's information, and so determined not to admit the failings and weaknesses to which he pointed, that efforts were made, and made with considerable success, to discredit Churchill not only by belittling his judgement but also by maligning his character. Again and again, ministers made veiled references to his alarmism, his exaggeration, even his drinking habits, while agreeing to steer clear of the actual matters that Churchill was raising.

The Cabinet minutes also showed that the impact of Churchill's criticisms was such that, on several occasions, the Cabinet's discussion centred around how to reply to them with sufficient care and detail as to remedy the defect that he had pinpointed. Far from exaggeration, as the Whips' Office and the detractors were putting about, Churchill's points were being met in secret conclave by a serious and constructive response.

Both the archives of individual Cabinet ministers (many of them at the Public Record Office), and Churchill's own archive, showed that the matters he raised, often directly with Cabinet ministers rather than in public, were central to British defence policy. Towards the end of 1937 MacLean sent him a note of what was about to be shown to the German Secretary of State for Aviation, General Milch, during his official visit to Britain. As a result of the detailed programme prepared for him, Milch would gain a clear picture of a whole range of deficiencies in both equipment and training. Outraged, Churchill sent MacLean's report (after deleting his name) to Sir Maurice Hankey, begging him to use his authority as Cabinet Secretary to get something done. Hankey was equally outraged, but not by the story of the Milch mission. Writing to Churchill in reply, he declared: 'It shocks me not a little that high officers in disciplined Forces should be in direct communication with a leading statesman who, though notoriously patriotic beyond criticism, is nevertheless in popular estimation regarded as a critic of the departments under whom these officers serve.'

Hankey's rebuke hurt Churchill, who had deliberately sent this secret material to someone in a position to act on it. MacLean himself continued to send material. At the time of Munich, when the serious deficiencies in Britain's bomber preparations were an inhibiting factor in enabling the Government to take a firm stand against Germany, MacLean had provided Churchill with regular information about the setbacks in training and the delays in expansion of the bomber force. In the immediate aftermath of Munich, MacLean was asked to write an official report on these deficiencies for his superiors. He did so, and also sent a copy to Churchill.

On the Sunday after Munich, MacLean was invited down to Chartwell. In a letter to me from his home in South Africa, he recalled, of this visit to Churchill:

> He was sitting in the garden, and he looked up at me and said, 'The British Empire is finished.'
> I said, 'Do you mean by that that we ought to have gone to war?' and he said, 'Of course we ought to have gone to war.' I protested that we were utterly unprepared for war, emphatically so in respect of the Air Force, as was apparent from my post-Munich report. He ignored all that and went on to explain that the Munich agreement meant we had sacrificed 40 or 70 (?) divisions of first-class Czech troops, and the Skoda factories. My comment was 'but surely that is like saying that we should have committed ourselves to war, and have let the Czechs fight for us.'
> This sounds 'pert' and rather like a wisecrack. It wasn't intended as such, and I don't think it struck Winston that way because when I was leaving that evening, he opened

a newly arrived packing case containing the author's copies of *Great Contemporaries*. Taking one out he signed it 'To Lachlan Loudoun MacLean from Winston S. Churchill.'

He saw me off and we parted on the most amiable terms.

The contrast between the Government's continuing assertion that British defences were adequate, and that Germany did not necessarily constitute a threat, brought more and more individual officials to Churchill's door. At the end of 1937 Michael Creswell, Wigram's former assistant at the Foreign Office, who had recently been serving in the British Embassy in Berlin, and was now a member of the Austrian desk at the Foreign Office, wrote to Churchill asking to see him. He could come to his flat any evening 'after seven', he said.* When they met, Creswell gave him, as he later told me, details about the German Army's most recent mechanized equipment. 'I was speaking so much out of turn,' Creswell reflected.

Creswell was not the only one. In the Churchill papers was a letter to Churchill a few weeks later from the Earl of Munster, who was distantly related to Churchill by marriage, and who asked Churchill to see a cousin of his, Group Captain Frank Don, who had just returned from three and a half years as British air attaché in Berlin. 'He has of course to be careful what he repeats to you', Munster wrote, 'but I know if you would care to meet him he would like to come to see you.' Again I went to the engagement cards and found for Sunday 20 February the note: 'Lord Munster and cousin to tea.'

Group Captain Don had died before I began my work, but Lord Munster, with whom I corresponded, had a clear recollection of what had taken place. Don had brought with him to Churchill, under seal of secrecy, the most up-to-date details of German air strength and productive capacity. As he was giving Churchill these details, a telegram arrived. Churchill read it, and told Don and Munster its contents: Anthony Eden had resigned as Foreign Secretary, in protest at Chamberlain's policy of appeasing Italy and neglecting the United States. That night Churchill was unable to sleep, recalling after the war, in his memoirs: 'From midnight till dawn I lay in bed consumed by emotions of sorrow and fear.'

* It is little more than a five-minute walk from the Foreign Office to Morpeth Mansions.

There was one other mystery in the Churchill papers, with regard to his contacts in the wilderness years, that seemed at first insoluble. In the summer of 1936 the head of the Foreign Office News Department, Reginald Leeper, had written asking to see him on a matter of some delicacy. The letter was in the Churchill papers. It began: 'Sir Robert Vansittart has asked me to write to you about a matter which he considers of national importance & which is closely concerned with the work of the Foreign Office. He has told me to ask you whether you would give me an appointment, so that I might explain to you what this matter is, in which he hopes very much to enlist your interest.'

Susie and I were surprised at such an approach, from the heart of officialdom, and from a government department whose previous ministerial chief, Sir Samuel Hoare, had belittled Churchill's warnings about Germany. But we could find no response in Churchill's papers to Leeper's approach, nor any clue elsewhere. The Foreign Office files at the Public Record Office proved a blank. The files of the Foreign Secretary at that moment, Anthony Eden, were also blank. There was, however, one other depository of material that might just yield some clue: the Foreign Office archive, then housed at Ashridge, Buckinghamshire. We drove there from Oxford.

The number of files to be looked through was daunting. At one point in the morning I thought of giving up. I told Susie we already had enough material for ten books on the 1930s, and we had to squeeze it all into one. She would not allow me even to think along such lines and we continued our search. It might have gone on for days, even months. My Oxford tutor, A.J.P. Taylor, had told me after my last tutorial with him, in March 1960, 'If you go in for historical research, you will work for weeks on end and find nothing.' Hitherto this had proved a false prognosis. Now, I felt, it would come true. But no sooner had I allowed these thoughts through my mind than Susie woke me from my reverie. Here it is, she said, and there it was.

The file she had found made it clear that Leeper had been asked by Vansittart to find somebody with the will and authority to present to a wide public the virtues of democracy and the need to defend it, if necessary by force. In a letter to Leeper, Vansittart had written of the need 'to educate our own people. We have only a very little while ahead of us in which to re-educate the men in many streets.' Churchill was the first person they decided to approach. Two civil servants of a government committed to appeasement were about to enlist the help of appeasement's most vocal critic. Once more I wished that Randolph could have been with us as we read the file.

I went back to Churchill's desk diary. It was in the mid-point of the wilderness years, 1936, Friday 24 April, one entry only for that particular day: 'Mr Leeper coming to lunch'.

Churchill agreed to act as these two dissident officials wanted him to. In his next major public speech, to a large gathering in Paris, he set out in his most powerful language the need to believe in, and to defend, democracy. The speech contained the phrase: 'Between the doctrines of Comrade Trotsky and those of Dr Goebbels, there ought to be room for you and me, and a few others, to cultivate our own opinion.' No aggression, from wherever it came, could be ignored. All aggressive action must be judged, not from the standpoint of Right or Left, but of 'right or wrong'. Churchill then declared: 'We are in the midst of dangers so great and increasing, we are the guardians of causes so precious to the world, that we must, as the Bible says, "Lay aside every impediment" and prepare ourselves night and day to be worthy of the Faith that is in us.'

For many people reading Churchill's speech in the newspapers, and for several historians since, it was yet another example of a man in the wilderness challenging from the outside those who were making government policy, and doing so from a lonely, isolated base. Now, as a result of a particularly unusual search, it was clear that the speech was the culmination of his contacts and collaboration with those at the centre of government information-gathering; that he had the active support and encouragement of at least two of the very people who were the Government's own advisers, who knew that his patriotism was impeccable, and who recognized (and welcomed the fact) that his voice was still heeded.

Among those for whom Churchill's speech meant so much was Ralph Wigram, then a dying man, the victim of polio which had left him a cripple as a young man and made every day's activity a struggle. It was in 1969 that I had gone to see his widow, Ava. She had subsequently married John Anderson, Viscount Waverley, first

Home Secretary and then Chancellor of the Exchequer in Churchill's wartime administration. She was now a widow again. We talked of her husbands and their careers. She told me that when her second husband died in 1958 Churchill telephoned her from Chartwell. After commiserating with her on Lord Waverley's death he was silent for a while, then said to her with what sounded like tears in his voice, 'For Ralph Wigram grieve'.

I asked Lady Waverley if she had a photograph of Wigram. Yes, she said, it was by her bedside. I was welcome to see and to use it. We went upstairs to her bedroom. The small photograph was in a frame on her bedside table. It showed Wigram and Churchill walking together in the garden at Chartwell, their backs to the camera. It was she who had taken it, with her box brownie. I picked it up and noticed, tucked in behind the frame, a folded letter in Churchill's handwriting. 'Oh that,' she said, 'that is the letter Winston wrote to me when Ralph died. Would you like to see it?'

Here again was a letter of which Churchill had kept no copy. Ralph Wigram, who had provided him with such crucial material about German intentions and preparations, had been a true friend:

> I admired always so much his courage, integrity of purpose, high comprehending vision. He was one of those – how few – who guard the life of Britain. Now he is gone – and on the eve of this fateful year. Indeed it is a blow to England and to all the best that England means. It is only a week or so ago that he rang me up to speak about the late king. I can hear his voice in my memory.
>
> And you? What must be your loss? But you still will have a right to dwell on all that you did for him. You shielded that bright steady flame that burned in the broken lamp. But for you it would long ago have been extinguished, and its light would not have guided us thus far upon our journey.

When I began my search for Churchill in 1962, Wigram and Anderson, and MacLean and Morton, Creswell and Leeper, were unknown heroes in the Churchill story. Twenty years later I was able to tell in detail the part they had played. Each had been so troubled by what he saw as the Government's neglect of Britain's defences that he was determined to alert the one man who he knew would try to do something about it.

Thanks to these men, Churchill had been a well-informed critic of the neglect of Britain's defences. Thanks to them, when he entered the War Cabinet in September 1939, and when he became Prime Minister in May 1940, he was fully aware of the intricate, distressing details of military and air preparedness, and of the exact, and exacting requirements needed to accelerate production sufficiently to avert defeat. Thanks to his informants, his wilderness years had been fully inhabited.

VIII

'Mr Deakin to Dine and Sleep'

In the course of my search for those who had brought Churchill secret information in the 1930s, I combed his monthly engagement cards to see when they had been to his London flat at Morpeth Mansions, or to Chartwell. On each month's card, whoever else was there, I always found, twice, three times, sometimes even four times a month (sometimes, that is, every weekend) 'Mr Deakin to lunch' or 'Mr Deakin to dine and sleep'.

Who 'Mr Deakin' might be was no mystery to me. In 1960, when I went as a graduate to St Antony's College, Oxford, to study first Soviet and then British Imperial history, Bill Deakin was my Warden. As I write these words the college is preparing to celebrate his eightieth birthday. No one person did more to encourage my historical researches in those early days or to sustain them later on. In my first month at St Antony's he gave me a golden key: the advice and encouragement to seek out those who had played their part in the events of the century, to go to see them, to talk to them, and to discuss with them the evidence that I had begun to piece together.

My very first journey was to Bath (the city outside which Churchill, at Claverton Manor in 1895, had made his first political speech) to see, at Deakin's urging, Sir Orme Sargent, a Foreign Office man who had been a fierce behind-the-scenes opponent of appeasement. His nickname, 'Moley', reflected his underground and unseen activities. In 1945, as Deputy Permanent Under-Secretary of State for Foreign Affairs, he had helped Churchill considerably to try to stem the growing tide of Soviet encroachment.

It was Deakin who had encouraged me to take up the offer of working at Stour, if only for the short time that it was likely to last. When Randolph took me on, Deakin felt that somehow a modest dynastic succession had taken place; twenty-six years earlier, in 1936, as a young Oxford don, he had become Winston Churchill's literary assistant. For the following twenty-five years, except for a break during the war when he was parachuted behind German lines to make contact with Tito, he had been at the centre of the web of all Churchill's literary efforts. He was a link with Churchill spanning almost exactly three decades. The very last person with whom Churchill had sallied forth to dine, to his beloved Other Club, scarcely two months before his death, was Bill.

My search for Churchill's research assistants concerned a substantial segment of his work: his literary writings. How did he write his many books and articles? (He used to say with a chuckle, 'By the time I was twenty-five, I had written as many books as Moses.') How did he organize his research help? What sort of literary boss was he? Before the First World War, a research assistant had helped him put together the documents for his life of his father, *Lord Randolph Churchill*. After that war, a number of helpers, including a retired Admiral, helped him assemble the considerable amount of documentation he wished to include in his six-volume account of the war, *The World Crisis*, which he began in 1919 and completed while Chancellor of the Exchequer between 1924 and 1929.

When Churchill left the Treasury in 1929 after the Conservative defeat at the General Election in May, he once more called upon literary help for his four-volume *Marlborough, His Life and Times*. Bill Deakin was the third of his inter-war literary helpers on this substantial work of history. The first was Maurice Ashley, son of one of Churchill's Board of Trade officials before the First World War. Ashley was twenty-two in 1929, an aspiring historian who had just completed three undergraduate years at New College, Oxford. I turned to him for help as soon as I reached 1929 in my onward march through Churchill's life.

Following the defeat of the Conservatives in May 1929, Churchill embarked on a four-volume biography of his ancestor, John Churchill, 1st Duke of Marlborough. As a first step, he approached Randolph's Oxford tutor, Keith Feiling, for help in finding a research assistant. Ashley was recommended, and accepted. 'Broadly speaking', Churchill wrote to him, 'my method will probably be not to attempt to "defend" or "vindicate" my subject, but to tell the tale

with close adherence to chronology in such a way and in such proportions and with such emphasis as will produce upon the mind of
the reader the impersonation I wish to give. I have, first of all, to
visualize this extraordinary personality. This I can only do gradually
as my knowledge increases.'

In the summer of 1929 Churchill left England for a prolonged
holiday in Canada and the United States. While he was away, Ashley
worked in the archive at Blenheim Palace. Shortly after Churchill's
return, Ashley was sent to Vienna to study the early eighteenth-
century archives. Churchill, meanwhile, had decided to write a sixth
and final volume of his First World War saga. For this, he remained
at Chartwell, surrounded by books and documents relating to the
war on the Eastern Front.

Ashley's journey to Vienna, Churchill wrote to him, 'I hope will
be pleasant to you and profitable to me'. The two men discussed
historical method by correspondence. 'The first thing to do', Churchill explained, 'is to see the old tale in a new light, and in its true
proportions, and then, as you put it, to exploit by research particular
points.'

Churchill was pleased when Ashley was awarded a First Class
honours degree at Oxford. He was less pleased with his socialistic
views. But, as Ashley later told me, he had on one occasion, in
introducing Ashley to Field Marshal Smuts, told the South African:
'He's a *terrible* socialist, but he's an awfully nice *man*.' To Ashley's
father, Churchill wrote: 'It must give you great pleasure to watch
his development. My son is very idle, and profits little by the life of
the University.'

Churchill's archive contains many hundreds of letters exchanged
between him and Ashley on the search for Marlborough, as well as
great quantities of correspondence with the publishers, and with
historians who were glad to comment on the chapters as they
emerged. In 1931 Churchill returned to the United States, where
he was knocked down by a car and seriously hurt, but once back at
Chartwell, he began work again: in his three and a half months'
absence Ashley had continued collecting material. One archive he
visited was that of the Duke of Portland, who had been shocked to
hear from his archivist of Ashley's 'very advanced ideas'. Churchill
replied: 'I hope my young man did not make himself a nuisance with

his silly ideas. They are however no bar to his competence and industry as an historical investigator.'

In 1932 Churchill travelled to Marlborough's battlefields in the Rhineland and Bavaria in search of inspiration, much as I was later to travel to the farms on the Western Front where Churchill had been billeted as a battalion commander in 1916, and to the Dardanelles. Ashley remembered his master's keenness about maps to illustrate Marlborough's campaigns: 'He insisted that maps must be absolutely clear and simple and not cluttered up.' Volume three alone had sixty-seven maps.

To expedite the process from typescript to printed page, Churchill took on to his staff a member of the publishing firm Harraps, C.C. Wood, who became a full-time member of the literary team, responsible for proof-reading of *Marlborough* volume two and beyond. From then on, the proof-reading process was known at Chartwell as 'wooding'. After much trying, I failed to find Wood or his executors: then, one day shortly after the birth of my first son, Eileen Wood, his daughter, turned up on my doorstep carrying a large cardboard box filled with notes and materials relating to the technical production of Churchill's books, a process that, when Churchill tired of it (as any author may) Wood saw through to completion.

While Ashley continued to provide Churchill with the documentary background needed for Marlborough, Churchill enlisted a naval assistant, Commander Owen RN, and a military assistant, Lieutenant-Colonel Pakenham Walsh. He also turned to Keith Feiling, who was summoned to Chartwell for an eight-day working session.

There was no record of what Feiling and Churchill discussed, simply a mass of chapters being polished and perfected. Imagine my delight when Feiling himself, then aged ninety, responded to my request for a recollection of those hard-working days, when Clementine was also a witness to the literary powerhouse, and an American millionaire friend, Bernard Baruch, was trying to save Churchill's investments in a collapsing market:

> The background was sometimes sombre, for he was in vehement opposition over India and felt it: very rarely there would be some petulance over trains, cars, or guests, which it seemed to me *she* bore angelically: once an

embarrassing outcry of hers 'If only you had stuck to the Liberal Party!' Not liked.

There seemed a good many telephone calls to Baruch in New York and some sense of financial botherations.

I began as to an undergraduate pupil and after a little grumbling his amazing quickness of intellect – as I thought – would seize the point at issue. After the first day or two he would call in a stenographer and get written down a summary of what he wanted to retain. And very entertaining – and often illuminating – those recordings sometimes were. I remember one very vividly – and my memory is accurate as to the two *names*, though I can only reconstruct the sentences: 'Robert Harley, Leader in the Commons, adept in its moods, intriguing, shifty . . .' Continuing – 'square brackets, Baldwin'.

There was another aspect to Churchill's life at Chartwell, a central feature, of which Feiling was a witness during his eight-day visit, and on later historical excursions. 'The only habitué I saw much of then', he told me, 'was Desmond Morton, and very much liked: W's solicitude for him was remarkable – I remember his crying out in horror at seeing M winding up his car handle (he had been shot through the heart, had he not?)' Feiling wrote to me: 'It was on one of the early morning or dawn hours on his quarter-deck that, waving his glass towards Morton, myself & one other I can't remember, he quoted Q Anne's famous sentence, "We four must never part till death mows us down with his impartial hand."'

In 1933 the first Marlborough volume was published. Ashley continued archival work on the second volume. He had become a member of Churchill's inner circle. In 1981 he was watching a Southern Television dramatization of my fifth volume, in which Robert Hardy played Churchill. He wrote to me at once about the scene in which Churchill was shown being taken ill at Chartwell in 1932 with a recurrence of paratyphoid: 'Churchill was pictured as building a wall at Chartwell, and Lindemann seeing how ill he was, before his being carted off to the nursing home. In fact, Churchill was sitting and talking to me at the time. Lindemann was not there, and I don't think Churchill was building a wall. What I do remember was seeing him carried out on a stretcher and his saying to me, "Don't worry, Ashley, I am not going to die."'

Ashley left Churchill's employ in 1934, first to work on the *Manchester Guardian* and then to embark on his own successful career as a historian. Among his books was *Churchill as Historian*, published in 1968, in which, in his autobiographical introduction, he described Churchill as 'always the soul of consideration, courtesy and charm. He expected one to work hard but not a quarter as hard as he worked himself'. Ashley added: 'He was a man of splendid humour with a capacity for living every hour of the day.'

In the Second World War, working for Military Intelligence, Ashley became a specialist in the order of battle of the Japanese Army. In his eighties he was angered by a newspaper article in which it was alleged that 'Churchill showed no consideration for servants, employees or assistants at all.' The article was a review of a book by William Manchester. Ashley wrote to the newspaper:

> I must be one of the few persons still alive who knew Churchill intimately during the years about which Manchester is writing. I was then his literary assistant, fresh from Oxford. He treated me with the utmost consideration, almost as an equal, was exceedingly generous and good humoured, wrote to my father kindly about me, and raised my salary when I told him I was in difficulties. His secretaries adored him. Although he kept his chief secretary, Mrs Pearman, working late at night, he always telephoned himself for a car to take her home. When she died he gave financial help to her only daughter.*

Talking to me about Churchill, Ashley mused (ten years before his dispute with Manchester): 'We were all in love with him; he was such a lovely man.'

After Ashley's departure the mass of documents still awaiting Churchill's scrutiny for subsequent volumes of Marlborough was so great that, as Randolph was to do after him, he decided that he needed a residential literary assistant who could live at Chartwell. Churchill's choice was a twenty-two-year-old Oxford graduate, John

---

* In fact, Mrs Pearman had two daughters.

Wheldon. 'He has been living with me for the last two months', Churchill wrote to the Duke of Marlborough in March 1934, 'and has made himself not only useful but agreeable.'

I was fortunate in finding John Wheldon quickly; he was in the London telephone directory and I wrote to him at once. 'At the time', he wrote to me in answer to my first letter, 'my one very mild grouse was being worked too hard to keep a diary – often made a sort of conceited vow to myself that I would not offer personal services in war conditions.' Both Churchills, he added, 'were phenomenally kind in keeping to the present when I felt that discretion might demand return to Marlborough. His stock exchange dealings, e.g., American market, and personal finances, and Diana, were the only closed subjects which I remember being conscious of.'*

There was one other subject that impinged on Wheldon's awareness, the frequent arrival, and cosseting with Churchill in the upstairs study, of the somewhat mysterious figure of Desmond Morton. On one occasion Morton brought to Chartwell some Intelligence files prepared by the Joint Intelligence Committee, which Morton received as part of his own official work studying German war preparations, but which he ought never to have taken down to Kent. Wheldon wrote to me of Morton's visits: 'His high patriotic motives were clarified fully when I was pledged to secrecy,' and he added: 'Though Sir Winston really had no guile – so far as I saw, in his domestic relationship anyhow (and this was a very great charm), presumably Sir Desmond had a normal ration at least.'

Forty years later, as we talked together in his London flat, Wheldon recalled how he and Churchill used to work. After dinner Churchill would dictate to Mrs Pearman or Miss Hamblin (of whom more in the next chapter) until two or three o'clock in the morning. He would begin work again at about seven in the morning, sometimes even earlier, seldom sleeping more than four and a half hours. 'In those days rural post was very early indeed,' Wheldon recalled. 'The house domestics used to bring the early post up to him. It included

---

* In 1935 Churchill's eldest daughter Diana obtained a divorce from her husband John Bailey, whom she had married three years earlier. Later in 1935 she married Duncan Sandys, a young Conservative MP (later Lord Duncan-Sandys).

proofs etc – he liked these – he required this as a kind of check on anything being done inside his office without his knowledge. He would sit up in bed reading it.'

Of the literary work in the evening Wheldon recalled: 'The great man dictated, no one was allowed to contribute a creative word.' The typescripts were then scrutinized by himself, Commander Owen, Colonel Pakenham Walsh, and, at a later stage, by the military historian General Edmonds. 'He always took criticism very, very meekly,' Wheldon added. 'One could say exactly what one liked in the way of criticism. This was partly because he knew he was not fully educated in the ordinary academic sense, partly it was temperament. He wanted the full critical value from subordinates.'

Wheldon remained in residence at Chartwell for more than a year. In a resumé of his career which he sent me – when I asked him for some notes from which I could compile my standard five- or six-line biographical note for each person when they first came into the narrative – he commented: 'All meals with the family, including quite frequent dining alone with the great man (when the ration of champagne between us was reduced to a "pint").' In a letter to me a few weeks later, reflecting on his time at Chartwell, Wheldon wrote:

> I had worked v. hard indeed, e.g., enabled during exceptional summers in '34 and '35 to put in extremely long hours by a basket *chaise-longue* in the terrace garden (which caused comments at first) – this somehow made practicable say a ten-hour day on papers (even more I think really, but this will seem exaggerated) and then two and a half or three hours listening to dictation, attentive to step in after dinner, with the massive frame of the great man often (example, several times a week) liable to become irked, sometimes even enraged almost, so that once or twice I did feel he could project himself on me in the low easy chair. Deakin told me he made a little story of my falling asleep (once, or more) as I was left to wake, or woken, without a word said.
>
> After such irritability – doubtless with real short-comings of mine – Mr C went far out of his way to be

143

extraordinarily kind; and always took the line – in my experience unique with superiors and employers – that there was positively nothing that one could think of to say that would give offence.

Wheldon's work coincided with the use of Chartwell by a group of Conservative MPs opposed to the India Bill, who would gather there to discuss their tactics in each successive debate. Wheldon told me: 'I was even allowed to be agnostic about the India Bill, on grounds (a) I had been brought up a Liberal and (b) could not take a view, not having been to India. Notwithstanding, for the quite frequent conclaves of Mr C's right-wing group, he always kept me present. As composition varied, if one of the MPs asked about my presence in relation to some confidential point, Mr C would just say I was completely reliable.'

In the summer of 1935 there was a crisis: one to which Wheldon was the witness, and of which his record is the only one that seems to have survived. The crisis was brought to Churchill's attention by his constituency chairman. As Wheldon wrote to me:

> Sir James Hawkey invited himself to lunch at Chartwell, and issued (diffidently) effectively an emphatic warning that Mr C's stand against Baldwinism (obviously air armament and India Bill) had already alienated even previously staunchest constituency workers etc. so that an official Conservative candidate was likely to be adopted to run against him unless he devoted time and considerable effort to the constituency. *Inter alia*, this caused the 'special line of Green Line coaches' to Chartwell for several hundred constituency workers, two fortune tellers in separate tents and catering by no less than Gunters (who were a *coup de canon*) – both the latter insisted on by Mrs Churchill.

As a result of Hawkey's warning, Churchill reduced the time he spent on Marlborough until after the 1935 General Election, and paid more attention to his constituents.

Wheldon returned to Oxford, working for another eight months half the week for Churchill, mostly at Morpeth Mansions, and half the week at Oxford (my exact time system with Randolph, and very exhausting it could be, but always rewarding). In 1936 he returned to full-time teaching at Oxford. In 1939 he went as an officer to France, where he was wounded during the Dunkirk evacuation. A member of General Alexander's staff at the beachhead, he suggested, when the question of the grave shortage of small craft became urgent, that Alexander send Churchill's nephew Johnny to see his uncle at Downing Street to explain the needs. It was only when he was on the destroyer crossing the Channel that Johnny discovered to his alarm, as he later recalled to me, that Lord Gort, the Commander-in-Chief and Alexander's superior, had sent his own ADC, Lord Munster, on the same mission. The two men had gone into Churchill's study at Number 10, Johnny still in dirty and damp battledress, Munster wearing immaculate dress uniform complete with Sam Browne. Munster was in fact also a relative of the Prime Minister, albeit more distantly and by marriage. All went smoothly, and orders were given for the deficiencies in small craft to be met, if humanly possible, in the few days that remained before the Germans overran the beaches.

For much of the rest of the war Wheldon was involved in the interrogation of British and French agents brought out of occupied Europe. During the Normandy landings he served as an Intelligence officer on Montgomery's staff. His memories of his time at Chartwell were an important portrayal of Churchill at work in the literary sphere. His successor as literary assistant was Bill Deakin, who began work at Chartwell in April 1936 and was quickly drawn into the Churchill family circle.

A friend since the days when I was a graduate student at St Antony's College and he was the college Warden, Bill now responded to the call for help with alacrity and zest. He was already living in the South of France, and on his relatively short visits to London, perhaps two or three times a year, he would find time to come for several hours, and sometimes for the whole day, to Susie's small *pied-à-terre* at Earls Court, where he would answer dozens of questions, recall dozens of episodes, and give encouragement for the task of putting everything in place. Sometimes I feared that our questionings would exhaust him, but he was always willing to delve into his memory for whatever we asked him about. Few people had been so close to Churchill over so long a period: it was our good fortune that Bill wanted so much to help, to set the record straight, and to see the 'real' Churchill appear in my pages.

Bill gave us a vivid picture of the work into which he had plunged during his first visits to Chartwell, first helping Churchill to finish *Marlborough* and then, when that task was done, working on another four-volume work, Churchill's *A History of the English-speaking Peoples*. In this task he worked with Churchill up to the outbreak of the war, and beyond.

Deakin, like Wheldon, had been recommended by Keith Feiling, who described him to Churchill (in a letter which, when I found it, gave Bill great pleasure) as 'a person of great spirit and courage'. 'I like Mr Deakin very much,' Churchill wrote to Feiling. A friendship had begun that was to last for three decades. In 1976, forty years after he began work for Churchill, Bill recalled during one of our long talks in London the pattern of literary creativity at Chartwell:

> The activities seemed to stimulate him. I never saw him tired. He was absolutely totally organized, almost like a clock. He knew how to husband his energy, he knew how to expend it. His routine was absolutely dictatorial. He set himself a ruthless timetable every day and would get very agitated and cross if it was broken.
>
> He would start the day at eight o'clock in bed, reading things: reading proofs. Then he started with his mail, which he would clear fairly rapidly before going back to whatever interested him. He would get back to his reading or his proofs and say to me: 'Look this up', 'Find out about this.' If there was something he wanted to hear about I sat at the desk in his library and read to him. At luncheon he did not come downstairs until the guests were there – he would never greet them at the door.
>
> His lunchtime conversation was quite magnificent. It was absolutely free-for-all. He did not restrain himself. After lunch if people were there he would shut off completely from politics, from writing. If he had guests he would take them around the garden. If there were no

guests he would potter off to his room. He never had exactly a siesta. Sometimes he would lie down for a few minutes. Between five and seven he would clear the mail he had dictated in the morning and sign letters but still there would be no work. He might play cards with his wife or Randolph. At seven he would bath and change for dinner.

Dinner at 8.30 was the event of the day. In very good form he could hold forth on any subject – memories of Harrow, or the Western Front – depending on the guests. After the ladies had left he might sit up with his male guests until midnight. He seldom talked about the work he was doing, though he might bring out something that had interested him.

At midnight, when the guests left, *then* he would start work. Work on Marlborough would go on to three or four in the morning. One felt so exhilarated. Part of the secret was his phenomenal power to concentrate – the fantastic power of concentrating on what he was doing – which he communicated. You were absolutely a part of it – swept into it.

Nothing was allowed to interfere with the night work. While he worked he would call up a secretary and start to dictate. I might have given him some memorandum before dinner, four or five hours before. Now he would walk up and down the room dictating. My facts were there, but he had seen it as a politician. My memorandum was a frame. It set him off, it set off his imagination.

Several of Churchill's notes to Deakin survive in the Churchill papers. One, written to Deakin at Oxford, is typical: 'I think the chapter requires to be enriched at various points and clamped together. Pray study the points marked and bring this back with you on Monday.' There was also, in the family papers, a letter from Churchill to Clementine (then on holiday in Austria) in which he wrote: 'Deakin arrives this evening so the pace will not slacken.'

Deakin was a witness to many of the comings and goings of those who brought Churchill information on defence. 'He never took anybody's information *totally*,' he recalled. 'He was *checking*.' Much of that checking went through Professor Lindemann, a man of a certain mystery, about whom Deakin told me: 'He was extremely witty, a most enchanting form of wit. He had a great contempt for people, it was arrogance of a courteous kind, but an absolute curiosity about things. He was a good companion to be with. He used to love Winston's staff.'

Deakin travelled with Churchill on several long journeys in France, where literary work and painting were combined. Lindemann was also a frequent guest on these excursions. On one occasion, when they were together at Aix-en-Provence, and Churchill wanted to do some painting, he called Deakin and said with a twinkle: 'Take the Prof away.'

In August 1936 Churchill was in Paris, working on the final proofs of his third Marlborough volume. Deakin was summoned to Paris by telegram to go through the proofs with him. They were joined at lunch by Georges Mandel, soon to be Minister for the Colonies (and eventually to be murdered by Vichy police). Deakin was ready to leave, to let the two politicians have their talk, but Churchill encouraged him to stay. It was, Deakin told me, a 'most depressing lunch', with Mandel listing, accurately enough, the catalogue of disasters that was likely to face France. 'There is a total breakdown of the balance of power in Europe,' Mandel told them, and Deakin commented: 'He spat it out.'

In the summer of 1938, as the Czech crisis loomed, Churchill completed the fourth and final Marlborough volume. Then, without a break, he embarked on his four-volume history of the English-speaking peoples. The contract date for finishing all four volumes was December 1939. Deakin worked with enthusiasm at his new task. It was, he told me, a massive and at times daunting undertaking. (He reminded me, as he spoke about his work, of my own days at Stour, with Randolph's enormous project looming in front of my eyes and on my desk.)

By the end of 1938 only twelve months remained before Churchill's new book had to be handed to the publishers. One of the bulkiest sections of the Churchill papers, a part of the Literary section, contained the many hundreds of files that were the daily correspondence and draft chapters of that endeavour. As I worked steadily through them, determined not to miss a single file or indeed a single sheet of paper, I came across the traces of one of Deakin's friends, a young Oxford don named Alan Bullock (later the biographer of Hitler, and of a parallel study of Hitler and Stalin), who agreed to prepare sections on the origins of the Empire in Australia and New Zealand. Maurice Ashley undertook to write a 10,000-word outline for the Stuart period, and another 10,000 words (twice the length of this chapter) on Cromwell. The Oxford historian G.M. Young, the biographer of Gibbon (and, after the war, of Baldwin), provided notes for the medieval period, and also for the reign of Queen Victoria. General Edmonds provided material on the American Civil War: Churchill was determined to have a full American dimension.

The Churchill papers gave me a day-by-day picture of historical teamwork. As the new book progressed, John Wheldon was called upon to prepare material on the Tudors. After waiting a while Churchill wrote to him: 'I am getting rather hungry for your notes on Henry VIII, which you so kindly promised to give me. Do not let the better be the enemy of the good. Remember "Sentimental Tommy" who lost his examination because he could not think of the right word in the opening sentence.'

Work continued throughout 1939. 'It is very hard to transport oneself into the past', Churchill wrote to Ashley that spring, 'when the future opens its jaws upon us.' The new book had a serious purpose. 'In the main', he wrote to Ashley, 'the theme is emerging of the growth of freedom of law, of the rights of the individual, of the subordination of the State to the fundamental and moral conceptions of an ever-comprehending community. Of these ideas the English-speaking peoples were the authors, then the trustees, and must now become the armed champions. Thus I condemn tyranny in whatever guise and from whatever quarter it presents itself. All this of course, has a current application.'

On the night of 31 August 1939, as each previous day that week, Churchill worked on his book. That night, as was his custom when writing at full flood, he dictated until the early hours of the morning. As he fell asleep, German bombers struck at Warsaw. He was woken up a few hours later by a telephone call from the Polish Ambassador, Count Raczynski: Poland had been attacked by Germany.

Churchill's life was transformed that night. Within three days

Britain was at war with Germany and Churchill was back in the Cabinet after a ten-year absence. But still the book contract had to be finished, and Deakin found himself summoned several times to Admiralty House to help piece the final chapters together. In November 1939 he received a note from Churchill: 'I am expecting to receive from you by the end of the week "Trafalgar", "Waterloo" (which includes a reference to the return from Elba) and the "Crimean War".' With those three sections done, only the book's preface remained. The contract would be fulfilled.

The final literary sessions for the history of the English-speaking peoples were held while Churchill was at the Admiralty. Thirty years later, in a lecture in Switzerland, Deakin recalled an evening's session in April 1940, which Churchill's engagement card shows began at eleven in the evening:

> Naval signals awaited attention, Admirals tapped impatiently on the door of the First Lord's room, while on one occasion talk inside ranged round the spreading shadows of the Norman invasion and the figure of Edward the Confessor who, as Churchill wrote, 'comes down to us faint, misty, frail'.
>
> I can still see the map on the wall, with the dispositions of the British Fleet off Norway, and hear the voice of the First Lord as he grasped with his usual insight the strategic position in 1066. But this was no lack of attention to current business. It was the measure of the man with the supreme historical eye. The distant episodes were as close and real as the mighty events on hand.*

'Please always count on me as a friend' was Churchill's final message to Deakin in 1940.

During the war Deakin parachuted behind German lines in Yugoslavia. He was at Marshal Tito's side during some of the fiercest battles between the partisans and the Germans. In 1946 he returned to Churchill's side to help organize a massive new venture, the six-

---

* Deakin first gave this account during a lecture at the University of Basel on 10 January 1969, at the invitation of the Swiss Winston Churchill Foundation. It was published by the Foundation in 1970 as a special supplement to the *Schweizer Monatshefte*, Zurich.

volume memoirs of the Second World War. A substantial new team
was enlisted to search for material in the archives and memoirs of
the time, and to prepare it in draft chapter form.

Churchill's capacity for organizing research help, and for pressing
ahead with dictation, writing and rewriting, was undiminished by
the long years of war. As Deakin told me, when I showed him from
among the Churchill papers some of the bulky files of material that
had been collected for this new venture, his master expected full and
detailed briefs to be put in front of him, virtual draft chapters, but
he then imposed on them his own style and tone, adding, either by
hand or dictation, many sections of vivid narrative and personal
reminiscence.

Among those who helped Churchill with his war memoirs after
1945 was a naval historian, Captain Gordon Allen. I had made contact with him in 1968 when we corresponded on naval matters con-
cerning Britain's declaration of war on Turkey in 1914, and
Churchill's swift and effective decision to seize the two super-modern
Turkish battleships then being completed on Tyneside, and almost
ready to steam to Constantinople. Alas, by the time I reached my
preparations for the years on which Allen's help was most needed,
he had died. He had, however, responded in a full letter to my
request in 1969 for some notes on his working days at Chartwell
and Hyde Park Gate.

'Churchill sometimes made his own drafts by dictation when no
one else was around', Allen wrote, 'but all these were freely open to
amendment by any of us. It was remarkable how he could amend,
say, my drafts by a few deletions of needless verbiage and by introducing his own characteristic wording or phrases make the whole text
into his own.' The determination to get the work done was always
evident: 'I have sometimes continued a conversation through the
bathroom door while he made his ablutions.' Allen's note continued:

> Churchill was very demanding and expected unlimited ser-
> vice from us, and also from his four excellent girl secre-
> taries. Two of these girls were always on duty until he
> chose to go to bed. He drove them hard but they wor-
> shipped him. As for us, no one could have been more
> gracious and appreciative of our work than he was, it was
> a real pleasure to serve him.

We were privileged people and could say what we liked to him. He was always ready to listen but was frequently argumentative. However, I soon learned that it was wiser not to press an argument if he was in that sort of mood but to let the subject drop for the moment. By returning to it later mutual agreement was nearly always reached.

The last of Churchill's literary assistants was Alan Hodge, whom Brendan Bracken recommended to him, and who from 1953 helped with the final revision of *A History of the English-speaking Peoples*, which had been left unpublished in 1939. Hodge died before I began my work, but there were many traces of him in the Churchill papers. In sending Hodge a paper on the Common Law on which he had taken 'a great deal of pains' before the war, Churchill wondered whether it should have a section on its own or be broken up at different places in the narrative, writing to Hodge: 'The theme of the growth of our Common Law, which is the inheritance of the English-speaking peoples as a whole, must however run through the story. It will take some art to tell this story to others than lawyers who know much of it already.'

Hodge and his wife Jane were frequent guests at Chartwell, and went with Churchill when he was working on the book in the South of France. After one long session at Chartwell in 1956, Jane Hodge wrote to Churchill, in her thank-you letter, that when her daughters asked her where she had been, 'I shall tell them that I have been visiting the world's kindest great man.'

Churchill had written his first book in the reign of Queen Victoria, his last in the reign of Queen Elizabeth II. Literary and research help had always been at hand, but so had his own powers of sheer hard work, his passion for the subject under scrutiny, and his unsurpassed talent with words.

IX

'God's Teeth, Girl!'

In my talks with Churchill's literary assistants I gained a picture of continual secretarial activity at Chartwell. Sometimes two and sometimes three secretaries would be at work there on any one day. Their shifts would usually begin soon after breakfast and would continue, with liberal breaks for Churchill's lunch, afternoon nap and dinner, until after midnight: sometimes until well after midnight. A rota system ensured that Churchill could maintain an unbroken pace of dictation for books, speeches and articles. The mass of his considerable correspondence was also dealt with mostly by dictation. Another secretarial task was the organization of a formidable filing and retrieval system. This was when he was out of office.

Secretaries are seldom mentioned in political biography either by work or name, yet they see their employers at close quarters, in all circumstances and moods, and at critical moments. Might not they too be of help in the search for the character of their employer?

The earliest example of secretarial help that I could find in Churchill's story came from a letter that he wrote to his mother, part of the vast cache of letters at Blenheim. It was the person to whom he had dictated the letter, John Milbanke, a fellow-schoolboy at Harrow. 'Milbanke is writing this for me', Churchill informed his mother, 'as I am having a bath.' Milbanke was then sixteen, Churchill fourteen.

Dictation in the bath was to re-emerge as a method fifty years later, when Churchill was Prime Minister. Milbanke became an artist, exhibiting at the Royal Academy. He won the Victoria Cross during the Boer War for saving the life of a trooper in his regiment. Fifteen years later he was killed in action at Gallipoli.

A succession of young men and women were to follow Milbanke, pencil in hand or fingers poised over the keyboard, to record

Churchill's thoughts, letters, speeches or instructions. His irascibility and intolerance have been stressed by some historians. Some years after I had shown his essential kindness, a distinguished historian still described him in a lecture at Oxford as 'a horrible man', with the emphasis on 'horrible'. How far this would be borne out in my own research, I had no idea in 1968. Having seen Randolph sometimes reduce secretaries to tears, and sometimes win their total devotion, I felt even then that the secretarial path was one that I ought to follow.

Pointers as to the importance to Churchill of secretarial help emerged in his private letters. In 1902, when he was a Conservative MP of less than two years standing, he wrote to his mother: 'My secretary has gone away to India (like a lot of other silly people!), so that I am very much stranded in regard to correspondence. Will you find out from Miss Anning whether she could come to me two days a week, let us say, and she could make what arrangement would be suitable to her.' Churchill added: 'It is essential that I should have someone that could answer the simple letters that I receive.' Miss Anning had worked for the Prime Minister, A.J. Balfour. She was to become Churchill's principal amanuensis for several years, taking dictation and writing out the letters in longhand: Churchill then signed what she had written out.

Many an auction house has sold as 'Churchill manuscripts' long handwritten letters in Miss Anning's neat script, in which Churchill's only contribution was the words 'Yours sincerely, Winston S. Churchill'. His dependence on her is seen in a letter that he wrote to his mother in the autumn of 1905: 'Miss Anning has buried herself in Scotland and this is the first time I have come in contact with shorthand, so do please forgive me.'

Miss Anning remained with Churchill when he became a Liberal and entered the Government. The letters that she filed have survived. A few of Churchill's letters were destroyed in August 1908, when he spent the weekend at Burley-on-the-Hill and a fire broke out during the night, burning down much of the house. He was staying there with his Private Secretary Eddie Marsh who, he wrote to his fiancée Clementine Hozier, 'lost everything (including many of my papers) through not packing up when I told him to'.

Marsh served as Private Secretary and amanuensis for many years.

Many important political letters were written out by him in his precise longhand and then signed by Churchill. At the Admiralty, Churchill took on the services of a male shorthand writer, H.A. Beckenham. When Churchill left the Admiralty he asked the Treasury if Beckenham could go with him to the Duchy of Lancaster: this was agreed. Beckenham returned to Churchill's side in 1918, and for the next four years took dictation of Churchill's war volumes, *The World Crisis*. I was unable to find out anything about him; I could not even discover what his initials stood for. When Churchill went out of office in 1922, following his defeat at Dundee, Beckenham disappeared from the files.

After many years of always remembering to look him up in reference books, however obscure, but never finding him, I wrote a letter to the newspapers, asking anyone who had known him to get in touch with me. Within a few days I had a single reply. It was from a civil servant who used to travel home by underground train from Baker Street every evening. He recalled that among his fellow commuters, with whom he would sometimes have a drink before leaving London, was Harry Beckenham. He remembered that Beckenham had worked in 1924 and 1925 as Secretary to the British Empire Exhibition at Wembley. The papers of the Exhibition had survived in the Public Record Office. In them I found Beckenham's letter of application for the job as Secretary. It gave me an outline of his career: he had been born in 1890 and entered the Admiralty when he was twenty. From 1912 to 1915 he had been Assistant Private Secretary to Churchill. Later in the war he had worked first for the Secretary of the Admiralty and then for Admiral Jellicoe. He had again worked for Churchill, as I knew, from 1918 to 1922. In 1924 he had gone to Wembley. He had died in 1937, at the early age of forty-seven.

With this information I was able to write a short biographical note, ensuring that at least Beckenham would be more than just a name. But I could take the search no further: perhaps, somewhere, there is a diary, or some notes and jottings, from a man who saw Churchill at close quarters at two dramatic stages in his life, and helped him with a major work of historical reconstruction.

I had another disappointment when I came across Beckenham's successor, Miss Fisher, who had worked with Churchill in 1923 and

1924. I knew what she looked like, because during his unsuccessful attempt to be elected to Parliament for the Abbey Division of Westminster (when he was said to have been rung up 'more often than anybody in the history of the telephone') she was photographed at his side taking dictation. When Churchill became Chancellor of the Exchequer at the end of 1924, she went with him to the Treasury, where she had held the rank of Junior Administrative Assistant from 1924 to 1929. In 1926 there is a letter from Churchill to Clementine in which he writes: 'Miss Fisher is going to stay, after having a rest cure on medical certification!'

From the Treasury files at Kew I found that Miss Fisher's first name was Lettice, but could uncover no further details. She too may have kept a diary or notes, but they have not yet emerged into the light of day. She worked for Churchill for seven years. She was succeeded in 1929 by Mrs Pearman, who remained with him for nine years, and in search of whom I made many forays. Two years after Mrs Pearman began working for Churchill, he took on a number two to help with the ever-increasing volume of secretarial work. Number two was Grace Hamblin, who, from my very first days until today, has been a stalwart help in guiding my steps on a hundred different biographical matters. After five years working for Churchill, Miss Hamblin had to leave Chartwell to look after her elderly mother. In his letter of recommendation to any future employer, Churchill wrote: 'She is not in any sense an ordinary stenographer, but can manage to keep track of correspondence.' That, in the mass of incoming and outgoing letters that Churchill's busy life generated, was a true talent. In the event, Miss Hamblin quickly returned to Chartwell, as Clementine's secretary, staying on until after Churchill's death, and becoming Chartwell's first administrator.

When I embarked upon the 1930s, Miss Hamblin was able to tell me about Violet Pearman, who had died in 1941, at the age of forty:

> In appearance she was tall and striking. She seemed to me to work like a Trojan – fast and furious, without stopping. I have never come across anyone who typed so fast! She was always surrounded by paper – a pile of 'work to do'

on one side and a pile of 'work done' on the other. She *ran* up and down stairs.

Sir Winston referred to her as 'Mrs P'. She was devoted to him, and very loyal. She seemed to be in charge of every single thing – not anything special, just *everything*!

Mrs Pearman was herself impressed by Churchill's powers of work. After his paratyphoid attacks in 1932 she wrote to one of Churchill's literary agents (who was pressing for a contract to be fulfilled): 'Mr Churchill is steadily improving, though progress is rather slow, but as usual nothing can keep him from work, and he busies himself a good many hours each day and gets through a lot.'

Churchill worked with Mrs Pearman at Chartwell, and at Morpeth Mansions in London, often taking dictation during the frequent car journeys between the two. She was at the centre of the constant flowing in of information and individuals during Churchill's efforts to alert the Government and the public to the German danger. Brendan Bracken, who often saw her at her employer's side, wrote to her in the summer of 1938: 'Your devoted service to Mr Churchill is beyond valuation. No one has helped him more than you during these last five years when he has been fighting an uphill battle for things very precious to England.'

Churchill took Mrs Pearman with him on his annual journeys to France where, while he painted and swam, she typed out the letters and articles that he had dictated to her. His personal, political, literary and financial correspondence was all within her compass. Her discretion was absolute. He sheltered her, too, from the buffets of ill-fortune with which her life was dogged: her husband, whom she had married during the war, had lost both legs in the fighting on the Western Front and been severely shell-shocked. The marriage was ending when Churchill took her on; she was living then in nearby Edenbridge with one daughter aged nine and another only two months old.

As a result of Miss Hamblin's help (for she had kept in contact with almost all those whose paths had crossed hers at Chartwell), I was able to meet both of Mrs Pearman's daughters. They came to see me, one of them carrying a small attaché case in which they had gathered together such letters and photographs as she had left them on her death forty years earlier. One of the letters was from Churchill. No historian searching for the character of his subject could ask for anything more remarkable; yet but for Miss Hamblin's effort on my behalf it would almost certainly not have surfaced.

Mrs Pearman, her marriage in ruins and her health shattered as a result of her husband's refusal to give her a divorce, even though they had been apart for more than ten years, suffered from abnormally high blood pressure. In June 1938 Churchill wrote to Clementine that a 'Dr Brand' had rung him up with the news that she would not be able to do any serious work for some months. 'All this causes me much perplexity,' Churchill confided.

I felt that I should try to find this Dr Brand and, through the *Medical Directory*, contacted all the living Brands. T.A. Brand was alive and well, living in the West Country. He wrote to me that Mrs Pearman had in fact suffered a cerebral stroke; that he had visited her at her home near Chartwell; and that Churchill had asked him over to the house. 'He said that he was very concerned about her and was very complimentary about her loyal service. He listened to my account of her case and of the poor prognosis. After having asked me various relevant questions, he then asked me what I thought of the very recent paper on high blood pressure by a Paris physician. I had to say that I had not seen this reported in the British journals. He then gave me a very lucid account of this and I was tremendously impressed by his command of quite rarified medical terminology which he used very accurately.'

Mrs Pearman was forced to take a year off. Churchill told her that he would pay her year's salary while she was away. In the letter that her daughters showed me, he wrote:

> Dearest Mrs P,
>
> I am so grieved at your illness – due I fear largely to your devotion to my interests and fortunes. I am sure that all you need is a good long rest without worries of any kind. Now do help in this. Lie absolutely fallow and you will recover. There is no need to fret about anything – though I don't pretend I do not miss you badly.
>
> Do not let your case be a burden. Why don't you tell your solicitor to come to me. I will have it all properly

looked after. Remember you can count on me for the £50
I promised.

All I want you to do is to get well, and this you can do
by a good holiday. I will look after you.

Yours affectionately,

Winston S. Churchill

From her cottage near Chartwell, Mrs Pearman had followed Churchill's efforts with admiration. After he had spoken publicly in the
summer of 1939 of the neglect of London's anti-aircraft defences,
she wrote to him: 'Every shock the Government has of this kind
brings to light the appalling lethargy over defence preparations of
which they are guilty. I wish you every success in your fight, and
only wish I were there to help you.'

Mrs Pearman died in 1941. One of her last letters was to con-
gratulate her former boss on a speech after he had returned to
the Admiralty. It was a speech, she wrote, with 'several shocks in it
for Hitler and his gang'. She was still living in Edenbridge. 'I
am very proud to hear your name spoken frequently in this small
market town by all sorts and conditions of men, and to hear the
pride and confidence which your presence in so vital a post brings
to all.'

After Mrs Pearman's death, Churchill made arrangements for her
monthly salary, at that time £12, to be paid to her daughter Rosemary, then aged eleven, and for a further seven years beginning in
1943 he paid £100 a year towards Rosemary's education.

Mrs Pearman's deputy, Miss Hamblin, had watched quietly from
her vantage point as the literary work proceeded year after year on
the Marlborough biography. She was twenty-four when she began
work at Chartwell. She stayed with Churchill for six years, before
becoming Clementine's secretary when Churchill went to the Admiralty, to help lessen the demands made on a minister's, and later on
a Prime Minister's, wife. She remained with Clementine from the
outbreak of the war in 1940 until after Churchill's death in 1965.

As I proceeded with my quest for Churchill the employer, Miss
Hamblin was a constant and valued source of information. When I
asked her about Mrs Pearman, she wrote me an account of their
work together on the Marlborough volumes:

My Senior and myself worked alternately with him long into the night. He would come from the dining-room at about 10 o'clock – refreshed and often jovial. It was very obvious that this was his best time for working and that he enjoyed these hours. He would become entirely immersed, and would dictate until 2 or 3 in the morning: sometimes very slowly, and always weighing every word, and murmuring sentences to himself until he was satisfied with them – then bringing them forth, often with tremendous force, and glaring at the poor secretary when driving home a point.

Often one of his 'young men' – a literary assistant – or sometimes a friend – Professor Lindemann or Mr Bracken – would be present during these sessions, and I am sure he liked to have human company at these times – if there were two of us so much the better.

There is no doubt he was a very hard taskmaster. He drove us. And he rarely gave praise. But he had subtle ways of showing his approval, and we wouldn't have had it otherwise. He worked so hard himself and was so absolutely dedicated to the task in hand that he expected the same from others. He accepted it as his right. And in time we who worked for him realized that in full return for the stress and strain, we had the rare privilege of getting to know the beauty of his dynamic, but gentle character.

At Chartwell, the hub of secretarial activity took place in the ground-floor room which Churchill called his 'factory'. 'He loved his office,' Miss Hamblin told me. 'He loved coming in and plonking down in the chair. He would welcome a guest at the front door, perhaps arriving for lunch, and say to them, "Do come in and see my factory." I remember well one such occasion when I happened to be alone: "This is my factory, and this is my secretary," – pregnant pause – "Hmm, and to think I once commanded the Fleet."' Miss Hamblin added, 'I don't think he meant me, he probably meant the room.'

In 1937, as the political situation in Europe worsened, and Churchill's political and literary work grew, he decided that he needed a resident secretary, in addition to Violet Pearman and Grace Hamblin, both of whom came each day from their homes nearby. His choice was Kathleen Hill, who was to stay with him for nearly ten years, including the whole of his wartime premiership. Mrs Hill was discreet and loyal. She saw Churchill every day, had a deep admiration for him, and was almost invisible. On one occasion he wrote in his memoirs of how, when some particularly bad news had reached him in the war, 'I was alone.' He was not: on that occasion, as on so many, Mrs Hill was also in the room, sitting at her desk with her typewriter ready should he decide to dictate something. 'I sat in the corner of the room silently and unobtrusively,' she told me. 'When he was upset I used to try to be invisible.'

Silent, unobtrusive but ever-present, Mrs Hill was a main factor in the smooth operation of his private office. She also knew what letters not to bother him with, and what letters had to be given to him for urgent attention. The public never knew of her. When Churchill left his London home on 3 September 1939 to return to high office after a ten-year absence, he was photographed on his doorstep. Mrs Hill was just behind him, clearly visible. But when the photograph was published in the newspapers the next morning, she was not there: she had been airbrushed out.

When I began my Churchill work Mrs Hill was one of more than five hundred people who answered my appeal in the newspapers (on 28 October 1968) for recollections and materials about Churchill. She was then curator of Chequers. I knew that she would be very busy, and yet I knew how important her recollections would be for me. 'I am sorry not to have answered your letter,' she wrote to me from Chequers after I had replied to her initiative, 'but my time has been fully occupied of late, owing to various Conferences being held here. I had vaguely wondered if I might perhaps meet you at the launching of HM submarine *Churchill*. As I shall be busy during the Commonwealth PMs' visits here during the first half of January, & then hope to join Grace Hamblin at Hove for a ten days' holiday, may I get in touch with you – say early in February?'

I was to see a great deal of Mrs Hill, to visit her at her home at Great Missenden, near Chequers, after she retired in 1970, and to correspond on many points of detail. She did not mind a telephone call for some small, or even large, enquiry. A visit to her flat was always rewarding. During one of our talks together she told me of the pattern of work during her first year, when she and Bill Deakin were in charge of their respective spheres of the history of the English-speaking peoples, and Churchill working against the clock, amid the pressure of Hitler's growing menace, to finish the book before war came:

> Sometimes he would dismiss me at two or even three in the morning. The idea was that I would get a rest in the afternoon. It hardly ever happened. I had never been in a house like that before. It was alive, restless. When he was away it was as still as a mouse. When he was there it was vibrating. So much happened that I, with my small brain, I was bewildered by it all. He could be very ruthless. He used to get impatient of delays. He was a disappointed man waiting for the call to serve his country.
>
> When he was bricklaying we used to take our notebooks and mount the ladder – even there he would dictate but not at length. If it was a long letter he would come down.
>
> Often we would dash up to the House of Commons, he dictating as we drove, and then we would type it out in the Commons. Sometimes we would pass the sheets in as he was speaking.
>
> I had originally hoped to find a post in a school combining school work with music supervision, and I remember thinking when he was in good dictational form – well, I have lost the music but I have got the music of words.

When another Churchill biographer borrowed the words 'bewildered', 'very ruthless' and 'impatient' from my talk with Mrs Hill, and did so out of context to describe Churchill thus, Mrs Hill telephoned me in some distress, saying that he had quoted her 'in all sorts of directions, but I never saw him. I never gave him an interview.'

In August 1938, after her worsening health forced Mrs Pearman to give up her work at Chartwell, her place had been taken by the twenty-four year old Mary Penman. Her recollections were also an important source for the year leading up to the war. 'I took my full share of the work', she wrote to me in 1978, 'and as I was young enough not to mind late nights, I did a large share of the night work when *A History of the English-speaking Peoples* was being dictated. I made many journeys with Mr Churchill in the brown Daimler, taking dictation as we travelled.'

Miss Penman had kept her shorthand notebooks and let me see them. In January 1939 she had travelled with Churchill to Paris and then on to the South of France. As well as the notebooks, she showed me her diary. I published extracts from it in *The Coming of War* document volume. It contained many delightful vignettes. At the end of the three-week visit Miss Penman travelled with Churchill from the villa where he was staying to the railway station at Monte Carlo. One piece of work had not been done, Churchill's fortnightly article for the *Daily Telegraph*:

> As we passed the Casino he ordered the car to stop although we had little time to spare before catching the train. He jumped out and ran to the Casino entrance, his clothes flapping about him in the strong wind, looking a little shabby and untidy.
>
> He disappeared inside briefly and then came out still running, he waved his right hand triumphantly to me and grinned as he leapt into the car beside me. 'I have just won enough to pay for our fares home – What do you think of that?'
>
> The *Daily Telegraph* article was still undictated and it was Tuesday evening. After dinner on the Blue Train Mr Churchill who was very tired went to bed in his berth and having called me into the compartment which was anything but spacious announced his intention to dictate the article.
>
> The only thing I could find to sit on was his hat box in which he packed his dirty linen, it was barely 12 inches high and the light was very poor indeed. Somewhere near to midnight the article was finished.

Early in August 1939 Miss Penman left Churchill's office to get married. Her successor was Mary Shearburn, who accompanied Churchill on his visit to France later that month. It was her future husband, Churchill's detective Walter Thompson, who later published her recollection of how, as she and Churchill were driving through the corn-filled French countryside with Churchill dictating to her, he fell silent, then commented sorrowfully and slowly, 'Before the harvest is gathered in – we shall be at war.'

That was on 22 August 1939. Nine days later Hitler invaded Poland. Mrs Hill was with Churchill at Morpeth Mansions that day, as he expected to be asked to join Chamberlain's Cabinet. 'He was pacing up and down like a lion in a cage,' she told me. 'He was expecting a call, but the call never came.' A day later Churchill was again First Lord of the Admiralty. The days and years of waiting were over.

On the evening of 3 September 1939 Churchill returned to the Admiralty, where he had previously lived and worked from 1911 to 1915. Mrs Hill went with him. 'He rushed up to the First Lord's room', she told me, 'and went up to a cupboard in the panelling. I held my breath. He flung the door open with a dramatic gesture – there, behind the panelling, was a large map showing the disposition of all German ships on the day he had left the Admiralty in 1915.'

It was Mrs Hill who had to sort through the flood of letters that reached Churchill from the public after his appointment to the Admiralty, and to decide which ones to put before him. One of these letters was from a young Conservative, apologizing for having tried to oust Churchill from his constituency earlier that year. '*Please* read this,' she wrote to Churchill, underlining the word 'please'. He did so, and then dictated to her his reply: 'I certainly think that Englishmen ought to start fair with one another from the outset in so grievous a struggle and so far as I am concerned the past is dead.'

In order to accelerate the work, Mrs Hill, instead of taking shorthand notes and then typing them out, typed directly on to Admiralty notepaper as Churchill was dictating. After May 1940 she did the same directly on to Downing Street paper. Somehow she had mastered the grunts and mumbles that were the inevitable accompaniment of his thought processes. The typewriter was a specially designed silent one, so that he would not be disturbed by any clack-clack-clack as she took down his words. One recollection that Mrs Hill gave me was an insight into Churchill's return to high office: 'When Winston was at the Admiralty', she told me, 'the place was buzzing with atmosphere, with electricity. When he was away on tour it was dead, dead, dead.'

Mrs Hill worked for Churchill at the Admiralty, at Downing Street and at Chequers. Bed was no barrier to work: in June 1940 one of the Private Secretaries,* summoned by Churchill, noted in his diary: 'He was lying in bed in a red dressing gown, smoking a cigar, and dictating to Mrs Hill who sat with a typewriter at the foot of the bed.' Recording another bedside scene five months later, at the height of the Blitz, the same Private Secretary wrote: 'He lay there in his four-poster bed with its flowery chintz hangings, his bed table by his side. Mrs Hill sat patiently opposite while he chewed his cigar, drank frequent sips of iced soda-water, fidgeted his toes beneath the bedclothes and muttered stertorously under his breath what he contemplated saying.'

Travelling with Churchill by car and train, Mrs Hill typed during the journeys whenever he had something to dictate. When he crossed to France in January 1940 the destroyer captain recalled his words as he went down to his cabin to work: 'I know it is not usual for ladies to be on the bridge of a destroyer in wartime, but I would be glad if you would give my secretary a cup of tea.' That secretary was Mrs Hill.

When Churchill crossed the Atlantic by battleship to see President Roosevelt in the summer of 1941 it was thought that a woman might be offended by the language of the sailors, and a male shorthand typist, Patrick Kinna, was found. Even on the roughest sea or air journeys, Kinna ensured that there was no unnecessary pause in the flow of ideas into memoranda, speeches, enquiries and instructions. Many years later, as we sat together over a cup of tea at the Charing Cross Hotel in 1982, he told me of how, when an army sergeant, he was called in for the first time to Churchill's cabin. Without looking up at the new arrival Churchill said in a low voice: 'This is a melancholy story.' Thinking that this remark was intended for him, Kinna laid down his pencil and replied, 'Oh dear! How unfortunate.' But Churchill had been dictating the first words of a minute on reported aircraft-carrier deficiencies. 'Well, *take it down . . .*' he shot back.

Kinna was present at several moments of tension: 'If you had the temerity to ask him to repeat a word he nearly killed you *with* words. It upset his train of thought. He never paused.' With Churchill's

---

* Jock Colville, then the Junior Private Secretary.

speech impediment, saying 'sh' instead of 's', it was not always easy to hear what he said. There was yet another problem for those who took dictation: the fascination of his remarks. 'Sometimes I just wanted to listen and not take it down,' Kinna told me. 'I found myself listening instead of taking it down.'

All those who worked for Churchill at closest quarters saw his sternest moods, born, in wartime, of fearsome problems and responsibilities. They also saw the character that lay behind those moods. In the summer of 1941 a new secretary, Elizabeth Layton, began work at Number Ten. I made the longest air journey of my life, from London to the Indian Ocean, to see her in her home in Port Elizabeth. With the diffidence that is one of her charms, she produced a bundle of letters she had sent to her parents during the war, when they were in Canada and she in London. 'I can't help feeling rather fond of him,' she wrote in one of her first letters. 'He is a loveable person, in spite of his impatience.' A month later, after an outburst of anger when she had twice misheard a word, 'he forgave me and was very amiable for the rest of the day.' This was the regular pattern. 'He was in a bad temper all week', she wrote during one of the most dangerous periods in the Western Desert, 'and every time I went to him he used a new and worse swear word. However, he usually rounded it off by beaming good-night at me, so one can't bear any malice or even let it worry one.' In one of her letters to her parents, Miss Layton described an episode with the Foreign Secretary, Anthony Eden:

> I was on early duty, and he was in bed, and he dictated in shorthand a two- or three-page telegram. Presently Anthony came in. I fidgeted around, longing to go, because it makes you feel very awkward when they start talking about their colleagues or opposite numbers in other lands, and so forth. But twice lately I've been told, 'Come back – what are you sneaking out for? I'll tell you when to go.' So presently he said, 'Now read that, and then she'll read you my answer.'
>
> I surreptitiously scanned the outlines and put in the commas and the full stops hastily, and wrote 'a' or 'the' above the dots because I never remember to differentiate.

Then he said, 'Now Miss Layton, read to the Foreign
Secretary. And don't gabble – read slowly – and don't
whisper – read out loud.' So I started off, trying to go
slow, and as loud as I thought suitable.

In a few seconds: 'No, No; *much* louder – he wants to
be able to hear it; and much slower. Come on now, Miss
Layton, come on.' So I took a deep breath and fairly
bawled it at him, about one word a minute.

I looked at the Boss, and there was a very definite
twinkle, so I sort of grinned back. He really does make
you laugh at times.

Fifty years later, Elizabeth Layton was to respond to a historian's
characterization of Churchill as 'deeply ambitious, egocentric, often
abominably selfish, difficult and ruthless' by sending a letter to the
journal in which the comment had been published:

Many years have passed since those days, but memory has
not faded. Ambitious? Yes, I suppose so; he could not
otherwise have reached the pinnacle from which he
inspired his country and the world. Egocentric and abominably selfish? No, these he was not, though he was quite
frequently inconsiderate, impatient (but he could be
patient too), and demanding. But if he demanded their all
from those who served him, he never spared himself in
his mighty task.

Difficult? Yes, but nowhere near impossible; he was lov-
able, and one forgave him for being difficult. He had such
an incredible storehouse of knowledge, such a quick intelligence, and yet something simple in his make-up too, so
that he could not always see when he was being funny –
he was unconsciously so.

Ruthless? *Chambers* defines this as 'pitiless, unsparing,'
and here again I must disagree – pitiless never, unsparing
possibly.

To try to cope with the pressures of war, in 1942 a new secretary,
Jo Sturdee, joined the inner team, as did, in 1943, Marian Holmes,
who let me see the diary she had kept during those years. It was an

exciting moment to read the day-by-day jottings of someone who had been at Churchill's side during many dramatic moments, and also during the routine work and moments of relaxation. Here is her first encounter:

> At last my initiation and baptism of fire. 11.30 p.m. Mr Rowan* introduced me very firmly and said twice 'This is Miss Holmes.' The PM was so absorbed in the documents he was reading that he did not hear and did not even look up. He went straight into dictating and I took it down on the silent typewriter.
>
> 'Here you are' – he still didn't look at me. I took the papers, he reached for more work from his despatch box and I made for the door. Loud voice 'Dammit, don't go. I've only just started.' He then looked up. 'I am so sorry. I thought it was Miss Layton. What is your name?' 'Miss Holmes.' 'Miss Hope?' 'Miss Holmes.' 'Oh'.
>
> He then carried on dictating directives and comments on various documents from his box, every so often glancing at me over his spectacles. 'That is all for the moment. You know you must never be frightened of me when I snap. I'm not snapping at you but thinking of the work.' This was said with a cherubic smile.

Unlike Elizabeth Layton and Marian Holmes, Jo Sturdee had written no letters home and kept no diary. She was not only discreet but self-effacing, a fine characteristic in any person, though not what the prying historian necessarily seeks. 'Alas my brain is utterly addled now, perhaps it always was,' she wrote to me when I made contact with her in 1974. 'So I warn you a meeting with me is never stimulating or amusing. And don't forget I was very junior & very stupid (I still am). It is thanks to many folk like Kathleen Hill, Grace Hamblin and John Martin† that I stayed the course. We were a happy, loyal circus though.'

Miss Sturdee made her contribution to the joyful circus and was a witness of it. In 1946, after Churchill's return from his 'Iron Curtain'

---

* Leslie Rowan, a member of Churchill's Private Office from 1941 to 1945.
† Churchill's Principal Private Secretary from 1941 to 1945.

speech at Fulton, Missouri, she wrote to one of his Private Secretaries, John Peck: 'He keeps us all dancing about and amused. I don't know that his holiday in America was much of a rest for him, but he seems to have come back refreshed and just as vigorous as ever.'

Churchill's concern for his secretaries showed itself in unusual ways. 'He would never let us carry things', Mrs Hill later told me, 'or run up and down stairs quickly. He was afraid we would get a heart attack.' When cross, he could be very cross: 'God's teeth, girl!' he once exploded when Elizabeth Layton twice typed the wrong word. One winter evening at Chequers, however, Marian Holmes noted in her dairy: 'PM was concerned when he discovered Elizabeth and me working in the Hawtrey Room without a coal fire. "Oh, you poor things. You must light a fire and get your coats. It's just as well I came in." He then lit the fire himself and piled it high with logs.'

Not only did Churchill's secretaries give many glimpses of his character and method of work, they were also present and have left a record of wartime episodes where their perspective added to the Churchill story. Elizabeth Layton and Marian Holmes had gone with him to Athens at Christmas 1944, when, by his personal example, he brought the warring Greek factions together round the conference table. At the start of that visit Miss Holmes was witness to an otherwise unrecorded episode. On board a British warship in Phaleron Bay, as a Greek Communist battery fired shells into the sea around them, the captain asked Churchill if he should return fire. 'The PM replied', noted Miss Holmes in her diary, '"I have come here on a mission of peace, Captain. I bear the olive branch between my teeth. But far be it for me to intervene with military necessity. *Return fire!*"'

Following Churchill's election defeat in 1945, Churchill asked Mrs Hill to work out a secretarial schedule for his life as Leader of the Opposition. Her note to her boss and his wife survives in the Churchill papers. 'I cannot conceive a plan', she wrote, 'whereby we could manage with less than three secretaries plus the assistance of Miss Hamblin at Chartwell on alternate weekends.' The plan devised by Mrs Hill was this: she and Miss Sturdee would work from 9.30 in the morning until 5.30 in the afternoon. Elizabeth Layton would begin work just after lunch and continue until 9 at night. On Friday nights Mrs Hill would return from 9.30 until midnight. 'While Miss Layton or I was in attendance upon Mr Churchill, Miss Sturdee could remain in the office to open and sort the post, answer telephones and obtain calls, receive callers, type letters and speeches, and help with filing etc.' At Chartwell, the off-duty secretary of the pair would 'answer telephones, prepare meals, wash dishes, make beds etc.' Only an employer who was much loved could have asked for, and been granted, such times and terms. 'He was so human, so funny – that always saved the day,' Grace Hamblin told me.

Mrs Hill's plan had to be given up when she was appointed Curator at Chequers, and Elizabeth Layton left for South Africa to be married. As I began my work on the post-war years I made contact with those under whom the office was reorganized: Elizabeth Gilliatt, Lettice Marston, and Jo Sturdee. They were, Jo later wrote to me, 'the first WSC secretaries, following with some trepidation our distinguished, older predecessors, in his new post-war private office.' Each one gave me many vignettes of work for the Leader of the Opposition, as Churchill had become, and of the often hectic, always interesting and sometimes hilarious work on the six *Second World War* volumes. Miss Shillingford also dealt with the voluminous constituency correspondence, and helped organize his birthday parties.

For the post-war years, Jane Portal, Chips Gemmell, Catherine Snelling and Doreen Pugh each gave me vivid glimpses of their boss. Each had worked with him for five years or more, itself a testimony to his qualities. One lady, not one of those who became devoted to him, who worked with Churchill for just under three months in 1931 while he was in the United States, did not like him. She made her objections plain when, nearly sixty years later, she was interviewed at length by the BBC. It was curious, and for me distressing, that the other secretaries, who were with him for so much longer, and saw him at his daily work, were given far less time to say their piece.* The overriding impression that his secretaries gave me was of a man who worked hard himself, drove them equally hard, but did so with humour and kindness, alert to their personal needs and quick to apologize for any outburst of anger.

---

* Her name was Phyllis Moir. In 1941 she published *I Was Winston Churchill's Private Secretary*. The only other book by one of Churchill's secretaries was by Elizabeth Nel (formerly Elizabeth Layton), *Mr Churchill's Secretary*, published in 1958.

The predominant mood which Churchill generated was described by Chips Gemmell, who worked for him in the late 1950s. 'I recall lots of laughter and comical situations,' she wrote to me. 'Jane Portal and I, aged 18 and 19, used to do weekend duty together at Chartwell (goodness knows why or how the old man put up with us) and we were usually paralysed with laughter from beginning to end. On one occasion we so disturbed a peaceful painting session that there was a fearful yell from the studio and the detective was summoned and told that the young ladies were getting over-excited and should be taken for a walk.'

Throughout his five years in opposition after 1945, Churchill worked on his war memoirs. By the summer of 1951 they were almost completed. A General Election was in the offing and he was determined to finish the work before then. In search of sun, he took his secretaries with him to Annecy and then to Venice. With him on the journey were several dozen trunks full of papers: the literary task. 'It was just slogging away on the last volume', Jane Portal later told me, 'because he had a premonition that he would be Prime Minister after the next election, a very strong premonition that he would get back: he talked about it all the time.'

The 'Churchill secretarial annals', as Jo Sturdee called them, included many unsung heroes: those who enabled him to maintain his extraordinary pace of political and literary work and productivity. Each secretary was witness to some important moment, some difficult decision, some thought process for which written evidence might not exist.* Reflecting on the pressure for Churchill not to remain at Downing Street for too long after his return in 1951, when he was

* Among Churchill's other secretaries at different times were Joan Taylor (at Chartwell in the late 1920s); Miss Tallens (who helped for a year in 1935 when literary and political pressures were particularly heavy); Olive Harrington (who was brought in when Mrs Pearman was taken ill in 1938, and who worked at Chartwell throughout the Munich crisis); Millicent Broomhead (who had a heart condition that made the frequent journeys to and from London impossible); Corporal Green, RAF (who, as deputy to Patrick Kinna, accompanied Churchill on several wartime overseas journeys thought unsuitable for women); and Anne Hipwell (after the war she went on to become an undergraduate at Southampton University); Maud Stanley; and Monica Graham (who undertook, in Churchill's London office and from her own home, the sorting and answering of tens of thousands of letters from the public). Throughout my work I was conscious of how Churchill's extraordinary productivity depended in such large measure upon these unsung labourers in the Churchill vineyard.

seventy-seven, Elizabeth Gilliatt told me: 'He could be up some days and down the others. He was variable. I never thought him too old for what he was doing.' She added, in summary of her boss's character after nine-and-a-half years with him: 'He didn't waste a single talent.' Even while he was having his portrait painted he would dictate to her, 'because he could not relax'.

Churchill's second premiership was a time of failing physical powers, accentuated by a massive stroke in 1953. But his powers of recovery, and his mental resilience, were seen most clearly by his secretaries. In 1955, for his final speech on defence, in which he told the House of Commons that Britain was to build its own hydrogen bomb, he spent several days preparing it. 'He dictated it all himself,' Jane Portal told me. The speech was an appeal for a summit of the confronting states, at which the question of nuclear deterrence 'could be put plainly and bluntly from one friendly visitor to the conference to another'. Churchill concluded: 'The day may dawn when fair play, love for one's fellow men, respect for justice and freedom, will enable tormented generations to march forth serene and triumphant from the hideous epoch in which we have to dwell. Meanwhile, never flinch, never weary, never despair.'

Churchill was then eighty years old. Five weeks later he left Downing Street for the last time as Prime Minister. With him as he drove away, the newspapers later reported (for they were on strike that week) was 'an unknown woman'. This was Elizabeth Gilliatt, one of his secretaries since 1945. The unknown women of his life had been an integral part of it for more than half a century. Nor was their task ended with his retirement. 'There was a secretary on duty every day but Christmas Day,' Doreen Pugh wrote to me of Churchill's final decade, throughout which she was at his side, and she added: 'Sir Winston never quite understood why he had to let us off on that day!'

Under Miss Pugh's direction were Gill Maturin and Delia Morton. Miss Morton was in charge of the letters from the general public, hundreds every week, including those from eccentrics and lunatics. 'It was fun,' she told me when we met at her house in London many years later. 'He loved the thank-you letters. We worked in this big room at Hyde Park Gate. "Poppa" used to appear, stand on the top of the stairs and greet us all. He would come over to me as I worked;

he was very fond of his "potty bins" as he called the P for Potty file.'

In 1958 Chips Gemmell joined the secretarial team. When we met in New York in 1990 she told me of her concern lest the current portrayals of Churchill turned him, as they were beginning to do, into someone dour and glum: not at all the man she had worked for.

I learned a great deal about Churchill from his secretaries. Every biographer of a public figure who depends on secretarial help, can only benefit by tracking down those often silent witnesses who sat at the receiving end of their subject's voice, and were witnesses to the aspirations, shortcomings and strivings of public life.

X

Private Secretaries

There were few efforts more rewarding in my researches than my search for Churchill's Private Secretaries. Just as they had been a part of Churchill's inner circle of confidence and friendship, so in my own life they became a much-prized source of encouragement and enthusiasm. All those who worked as Churchill's Private Secretary between 1905 and 1955 had quickly recognized his extraordinary talents: his intense patriotism, drive, and impatience not only at the slowness of others, but more frequently at his own failures, and at the often disappointing turn of events.

Churchill's first Private Secretary was Eddie Marsh, who came to him at the Colonial Office when Churchill was appointed a Junior Minister there in 1905. Churchill's friend Pamela Plowden told Marsh: 'The first time you meet Winston you see all his faults, and the rest of your life you spend in discovering his virtues.' Churchill delighted in Marsh's company, and took him with him to each of his successive ministries until 1922.

Marsh's private papers had been bought by the Marquess of Bath just as I began work for Randolph. One of the first research journeys I undertook on his behalf was to Longleat House, in Wiltshire, to see them. Marsh had also published diary extracts from his time with Churchill in his memoirs: I later found out that some of these were not in fact from a diary but, equally valuable to the historian, from a series of letters to the young Ivor Novello, later songwriter, actor-manager and composer. On 30 October 1918 Marsh wrote to Novello: 'It was yesterday that Turkey gave in and it will be Austria tomorrow – "a drizzle of Empires", Winston calls it, "falling through the air".'

The recollections of those who worked with Churchill as Private Secretaries were indispensable elements in the search for his moods, his conversation, his opinions and his character. The earliest such recollection reached me in 1968, after my newspaper appeal for information. It came from Sir Ralph Hawtrey, who had served under Churchill from 1924 to 1929 at the Treasury. His recollection, however, came from the period before the First World War when he was Private Secretary to the then Chancellor of the Exchequer, David Lloyd George. Hawtrey, who was eighty-nine years old when he wrote to me, recalled:

> When I was Private Secretary to Lloyd George in 1910–11, he and Churchill drove down one weekend to his house in Brighton, and I in the car had the opportunity of listening. Churchill began to talk about the next war. He described how, at the climax, he himself, in command of the army, would win the decisive victory in the Middle East, and would return to England in triumph. Lloyd George quietly interposed, 'And where do I come in?'

In 1919 Churchill became Secretary of State for War. While Marsh remained at his side as his Personal Private Secretary, the head of his War Office secretariat for the next two years was Sir Herbert Creedy. Having entered the War Office as a clerk in 1901, Creedy had become the Minister's Private Secretary in 1913. From 1924 until the outbreak of war in 1939 he was to be Permanent Under-Secretary of State for War. His whole working life was spent in Whitehall, most of it in the War Office building.

Creedy had just celebrated his ninetieth birthday when I took up my Churchill task. He lived in a small house in Oxford, immediately opposite my graduate college, St Antony's. I called on him there a number of times. His most vivid recollection concerned the outbreak of war in 1914, when he was Private Secretary to the newly appointed Secretary of State, Lord Kitchener, a formidable figure brought into the Government by Asquith, partly at Churchill's urging, to reinforce the Liberal war-making capacity. With Kitchener at the War Office it was assumed that the country was in safe hands, even by Conservatives with misgivings about the Liberals' ability to conduct a war which the Cabinet had been so hesitant to join.

In the first week of war Creedy accompanied Kitchener to his first Cabinet meeting. Soon after it began, Asquith asked him to give an account of the military situation. The Field Marshal looked up and – Creedy saw the surprise of all those present, including Churchill – proceeded to take out a pair of glasses, put them on, and then read out a prepared statement. The War Lord with glasses! Such a sight was a shock to preconceptions.

Churchill got on well with Creedy during those first months of war, and, knowing that he was absolutely trustworthy, used him as a conduit to Kitchener. In 1921, when he was already at the Colonial Office, Churchill enlisted Creedy's help with the evolution of a Middle East policy, and of a special Middle East department, that would enable law and order to be maintained in Palestine, Transjordan and Iraq. The hope was to satisfy rival Jewish and Arab aspirations without putting too great a burden on the British taxpayer.

'Mr Churchill's original idea', Creedy wrote in a memorandum at the time, 'was to have a sort of War Office of his own with military and military-finance departments. With characteristic thoroughness he wished to be completely master in his own household.' When Churchill was criticized by his successor as Secretary of State for War for wanting too much authority in the Middle East, Creedy, though now serving a new Minister, defended his old one with vigour: 'It was certainly Mr Churchill's intention, as expressed to me, only to work in consultation with the War Office.'

Creedy gave me an insight into Churchill's ability to win the loyalty of those who served him. The imagination, zeal and determination of the minister was a tonic to his civil servants: Creedy particularly impressed on me how much it meant to them to have a minister who would fight their department's corner in Cabinet, and do so with energy and skill.

At the Admiralty between 1911 and 1915 Churchill had the help, as well as Eddie Marsh's, of an official Admiralty Secretary, James Masterton Smith. In a letter to Venetia Stanley, Asquith noted two days before Christmas 1914: 'I am writing in the Cabinet Room at the beginning of twilight, and thro' the opposite window across the Parade I see the Admiralty flag flying & the lights "beginning to twinkle" from the rooms where Winston and his two familiars (Eddie and Masterton) are beating out their plans.'

There is a glimpse of how Masterton Smith regarded his master in a letter he wrote to Clementine a year later, when Churchill, having left the Government altogether, left England for the Western Front. 'Not even the high gods (whether their home be Fleet Street or Mount Olympus)', he wrote, 'can make things that have been as if they had never been, and to those of us who know and understand, Winston is the greatest First Lord this old Admiralty has ever had – or is likely to have. With those of us who shared his life here, he has left an inspiring memory of high courage and tireless industry, and he carries with him to Flanders all that we have to give him – our good wishes.'

In 1924 Churchill became Chancellor of the Exchequer. For the next five years, and five Budgets, his Principal Private Secretary was P.J. Grigg, unusually for that time a grammar school boy, who had been a Treasury official since 1913. They worked together in harmony and, as had happened with Marsh, Grigg found that duty soon combined with friendship and affection. It was Grigg who, when Churchill proposed a detailed plan for abolishing rates on all industrial enterprises as a means of stimulating growth, warned him: 'Altogether the Dardanelles situation seems to be re-creating itself. Everybody loves the idea, everyone but you is frightened at its boldness & magnitude. Everybody therefore stands looking on idly – perfectly ready to be pleased if it succeeds & equally ready to say "I told you so" if it doesn't & kick you downstairs.'

When Churchill left the Treasury in 1929 he wrote to Grigg: 'Your friendship is ever of great consequence to me, and my regard for you is deep.' Churchill never forgot Grigg's abilities or their friendship; in 1942 he appointed him Secretary of State for War. They remained in contact throughout Churchill's ten wilderness years. In 1930 Churchill sent Grigg a copy of his volume of youthful recollections, *My Early Life*. In his letter of thanks Grigg wrote of how, while reading it, 'I shall recapture some of the magic of those long evenings at Chartwell when you were in reminiscent mood & I exceptionally was content to listen in fascinated and happy silence.' Four years later Churchill sent Grigg the first Marlborough volume. 'Of all my masters you have been much the most generous to me personally,' Grigg replied, and added: 'How are you? Pretty sick at heart, I dare say, both at what is and what is not happening.' At the height of the Munich crisis in September 1938 Grigg wrote to Churchill from India (he was then Finance Member of the Viceroy's

Council): 'I do wish that you were in the Government but I daresay that unless & until war actually comes the minnows won't tolerate the presence of a Triton.'*

As Grigg suspected, it was not until war actually came that Churchill was brought back to the Cabinet. As First Lord of the Admiralty he again had a Private Office to serve him. In February 1969, four months after I succeeded Randolph, I went to see the former Parliamentary and Financial Secretary at the Admiralty, Sir Geoffrey Shakespeare, at his home in Chislehurst. 'At the Admiralty Winston got his finger in every pie,' he recalled. 'He worked from eight in the morning to three the next morning, with one hour's sleep after lunch. In this way he made two days out of every one day. When a man does that he becomes a tremendous force.' Shakespeare added: 'Winston was a terrific man of action. Nobody was allowed to sit on his bottom. You had to get cracking.' I asked Shakespeare if he could sum up the impressions that Churchill had made on him (they had first met in 1922). 'You couldn't be near Winston without being amazed at his vitality and resourcefulness,' he replied. 'The nearer you got to him, the more brilliant he was.'

Among the members of Churchill's Private Office at the Admiralty was Bernard Sendall. He came to see me in London in 1979, as I began detailed work on the opening months of the Second World War. 'One got caught up into the family,' he told me. 'You were treated as part of the family on the basis of complete trust, whether it was personal or official. One realized that if one did drop a clanger which incurred his wrath, it wouldn't last long, and he wouldn't bear a grudge against you, as long as you were doing your duty as best you could.'

Another member of Churchill's Private Office at the Admiralty, John Higham, came to my home in 1982, by which time I had managed to piece together a detailed narrative of Churchill's nine months as First Lord. He gave me this account of Churchill's Admiralty days:

> Everybody realized what a wider responsibility he had.
> The Admirals felt he had to be handled very carefully, but

---

* In Greek mythology, a sea deity, with the upper part of a man and a dolphin's tail. Tritons served as heralds for their father, Poseidon.

14. Churchill, Bill Deakin *(see chapter 8)* and Sarah Churchill on their way to Marrakech in 1948, to work on the war memoirs

15. *Left:* Maurice Ashley, Churchill's first inter-war literary assistant
(see pages 138-41)

16. *Below:* Charles Torr Anderson, a Royal Air Force officer who brought information to Churchill
(see chapter 7)

17. *Above:* Ralph Wigram, head of a Foreign Office department, who brought information to Churchill *(see chapter 7)* with Churchill at Chartwell, 7 April 1935

18. *Right:* Captain Gordon Allen RN, Churchill's post-war naval assistant on the war memoirs *(see pages 151-2)* with Churchill and Rufus at Chartwell

19. *Opposite above:* Lettice Fisher, one of Churchill's inter-war secretaries *(see pages 155-6)* at work with Churchill during the Westminster by-election, 1924

20. *Opposite below:* Violet Pearman, who worked for Churchill in the wilderness years *(see chapter 9)*, seen here during a moment of relaxation at the Château de l'Horizon near Cannes, 1937

21. *Above:* Kathleen Hill, Churchill's secretary from 1937 to 1945 *(see chapter 9)* leaving Morpeth Mansions with Churchill on the morning of 3 September 1939

22. *Above:* Eric Seal, Churchill's Principal Private Secretary from 1939 to 1941 *(see pages 180-2)* leaving the Admiralty building with Churchill on 5 September 1939

23. *Opposite:* Churchill's wartime Private Office on the garden steps at 10 Downing Street: *left to right*, John Colville, Leslie Rowan, Churchill, John Peck, John Martin, Miss Watson, C.R. 'Tommy' Thompson, Anthony Bevir and Charles Barker

T. L. Rowan. J. H. Peck. E. M. Watson. Mar~
Winston Churchill
J. M. Martin. Anthony
C. Thompson

24. Churchill in uniform, Paris, May 1947, after receiving the Médaille Militaire *(see page 203)*

25. Churchill, aged eighty-six, and Jane Montague Browne, a young diarist *(see pages 233-4)* on board Onassis's yacht, *Christina*, 1961

they weren't frightened of him. He was a tremendous tonic, everybody saw that – a tremendous nuisance, but there wasn't any resentment.

'The Old Man's off again.' But his baits were very real. They did lead him off on false tracks.

I don't think anyone ever felt he was an impossible man to deal with.

Certainly everyone was very conscious that he was regarded by his colleagues as trying to take the war over. They were pretty sensitive about that. There was a feeling that we were having to keep tabs on things that were not really our concern, that the war was being run from the Admiralty War Room, where the First Lord's charts were set out, and the movements of ships were plotted. Winston would go along at any time to see how things were going on. It was a kind of relaxation.

He was a great man for seeing the people who had done the job. This did a tremendous amount of good. He was a tremendous traditionalist. When he first came, he wanted the old map he remembered when he was there before. It was a useless map – but he loved it.*

You would go to the flat in Admiralty House. He would be there dictating in the raw to Mrs Hill. She had the Old Man pretty well buttoned up.

Of Churchill's frequently-argued plan to drop mines in the River Rhine to disrupt German barge traffic, Higham told me that, in his view, 'It was a very sensible thing. The French torpedoed it. They hoped the war wouldn't come – at all. It was an example of Winston's impetuosity for anything offensive. He pushed and pushed and pushed, which was all to the good – the admirable wish for the offensive, provided he had people to keep him on the rails. He didn't

---

* Was the map really 'useless', which is just possible, or is that the sort of thing that, years after the event, people say without very much thought? Many latter-day comments about Churchill by his contemporaries, as about other political figures when they come to be remembered, have an 'I-knew-much-better-than-he-did' aspect. They need to be treated as an amber light, with caution.

at the Admiralty; he dominated the Board. He did have as Prime Minister, with Brooke and the Chiefs of Staff. That is one of the reasons why we won the war.'

Churchill's Principal Private Secretary at the Admiralty was Eric Seal, who remained with him for the first year and a half of his premiership. His name was to be a source of affectionate amusement: when Churchill wanted him he would say to the nearest secretary: 'Fetch Seal from his ice-floe.' I was fortunate when I began work on the Second World War years to make contact with Seal's son, who was then British Naval Attaché in Egypt (he was present on the reviewing stand in Cairo during the military parade at which President Sadat was assassinated). He showed me his father's wartime letters home, as well as the recollections Seal had written in the 1950s. These included the following account of the end of Churchill's first day as First Lord:

> Churchill went off to sleep in his flat at Westminster; it was not for several days that he was able to establish himself in Admiralty House, so that he could pay a 2 a.m. visit to the Admiralty War Room on the way to bed. We arranged for telegrams and papers to be sent round to the flat by locked Cabinet Box. In some mysterious way Churchill's personality had begun to overlay us. We felt that he had already laid a firm hand on the navy. That was part of the magic of the man.

Seal's son also showed me a note his father had written after the war about working with Churchill. This note reflected the wider aspect of Churchill's character and motives:

> The key word in any understanding of Winston Churchill is the simple word 'liberty'. Throughout his life, through many changes and vicissitudes, Winston Churchill stood for liberty. He intensely disliked, and reacted violently against, all attempts to regiment and dictate opinion. In this attitude, he was consistent throughout his political life. He believed profoundly in the freedom of the spirit, and the liberty of man to work out his own salvation, and to be himself in his own way. His defence of the British

Government in India is not at variance with this idea; he defended British rule in India because he thought that it brought individual freedom in its train. He demanded for himself freedom to follow his own star and he stood out for a like liberty for all men.

All organized attempts to dictate to men what or how they should think, whether by the Nazis in Germany, or by the Communists in Russia, incurred his passionate hatred and fell under his anathema. In the last resort, this was the mainspring of his actions.

I quoted this passage some ten years ago in my book *Churchill's Political Philosophy*. It epitomized Churchill's intentions and actions through each decade. Although he had often to give orders, he was never a dictator: this was seen most clearly by his Private Secretaries, who often faced his anger, if a suddenly-required document could not be found or a much-needed fact could not be produced, but with whom he was always open and fair. They also saw the strain that responsibility could bring. 'Winston's been preoccupied, & a bit out of sorts recently,' Eric Seal wrote to his wife in December 1940. 'He has had a cold, which fortunately is now better. Also, the decision to take the offensive in Egypt weighed heavy upon him, although that, glory be, has been abundantly justified.'

Much was to weigh 'heavy upon him' between 1940 and 1945, that his Private Secretaries saw at close hand. Susie and I were not surprised to find, in the Baldwin papers at the University Library, Cambridge, a handwritten letter from Churchill to Baldwin, scarcely a month after he had become Prime Minister, which contained the phrase 'I cannot say that I am enjoying being Prime Minister very much.'

Under Eric Seal in the Private Office were John Martin, John Peck and John Colville. I got to know each of them well during twenty years. Each had seen Churchill at close quarters. Each had a clear picture of his vitality and judgement. It was Seal who expressed their general view when he wrote to his wife in May 1941, at a time of Cabinet changes: 'I am never really sure whether these moves of his are really bad, or whether they are strokes of genius! Judged by ordinary canons, they are often bad, but in his hands they often turn out to produce astonishing results. He has a wonderful touch for handling public opinion, & of course an unrivalled experience of public affairs. A civil servant inevitably has a more parochial view of administrative efficiency.'

John Martin, who in 1941 succeeded Seal as Principal Private Secretary, had begun work for Churchill in May 1940. He had spent his previous twelve civil-servant years at the Colonial Office. In 1936, as Secretary to the Peel Commission, he heard Churchill give secret evidence upholding the right of the Jews to become a majority in Palestine. It was while I was writing a biography of a member of the Peel Commission, Sir Horace Rumbold, British Ambassador in Berlin when Hitler came to power, that I first met John Martin. He lived quite near Oxford, at Watlington, and invited me over to lunch. He gave the impression of being very shy, and was certainly diffident: modest about his own contribution, and unwilling to embellish or invent anything about his master.

From time to time I give a lecture called 'The Perils and Pleasures of Research'. One of the principal pleasures was getting to know those with whom I first came in contact as a searcher of materials. How quickly the search could lead to friendship. I always enjoyed driving over from Oxford to spend time with John and Rosalind Martin, to absorb not only the Churchillian aspects but to relax in their friendly, cultured and wise company.

During one of our talks together after lunch, Martin told me how, early in his Downing Street days after a particularly strenuous evening during which everything seemed to have gone wrong, Churchill put his hand on his arm, regretted that there had been no time 'in all the rush of these days' to get to know him better, and added: 'You know, I may seem to be fierce, but I am fierce only with one man – Hitler.'

The Churchill desk diaries were mostly filled in by the Private Secretary on duty: I could therefore ask them about a meeting or journey which appeared in their handwriting. They had also noted down at the time, in short messages for Churchill or his staff, the times of travel and engagements at Downing Street or Chequers. As my experience grew, I knew that given a jolt to their memory with such an item, however brief, some recollection could emerge. My job was to find the facts of Churchill's movements, the details of what he said in Cabinet, his minutes and instructions on any particular day or theme. But the Private Secretary's recollection could add a further dimension of atmosphere, and also of detail, which was often lacking in the contemporary written record.

An example of this was John Martin's letter to me, after I had sent him a note of a visit Churchill made, with Martin as his duty Private Secretary, to the East Coast defences. All I knew was the date (26 June 1940) and the places (Southwold to Harwich). Martin added the colour and the mood, recalling 'the tremendous enthusiasm and delight with which Winston was welcomed wherever he was recognized. A large crowd collected outside the hotel where we stopped for lunch and gave him a rousing cheer. His early broadcasts as Prime Minister seemed already to have got his personality and leadership across to the entire population.'*

It was typical of John Martin that he added at the bottom of his letter, 'sorry to be so unhelpful.' In fact, each recollection was a vignette that added to the wider picture, making it possible at times to have some sense of what it must have been like at Churchill's side; to understand his emotions as well as his actions. Martin had also been a witness to the aftermath, in London, of the Royal Navy's attack on the French warships in harbour at Oran in July 1940. More than a thousand French sailors, who but a few weeks earlier had been allies in the war against Germany, were killed in the British bombardment, while their ships lay at anchor. 'I was in the House for the Oran statement, when all (except, I think, the ILP† members) rose and cheered for several minutes. There had been nothing like it, people said, since Munich. Churchill himself was quite overcome and his eyes filled with tears.'

There were also moments of relaxation that Martin reported in his letters home. One was on Christmas Day 1940, after a morning of work and dictation, 'from lunch time on less work was done and we had a festive family Christmas with the three daughters, two

---

* Since becoming Prime Minister on 10 May 1940, Churchill had broadcast twice: on 19 May and 17 June. His subsequent broadcasts in 1940 were on 14 July, 11 September, 30 September, 21 October and 23 December.

† The Independent Labour Party, which then had four members of Parliament.

sons-in-law, and one daughter-in-law* and no official visitors. For lunch we had the largest turkey I had ever seen, a present from Lord Rothermere's farm, sent in accordance with one of his last wishes when he died. Afterwards we listened to the King's speech and Vic Oliver played the piano and Sarah sang. It was the same after dinner. For once the shorthand writer was dismissed and we had a sort of sing-song until after midnight.'

A more sombre description, one of so many that John Martin was able to provide as an eye-witness, concerned the night in December 1941 that Churchill, at Chequers, heard on his small wireless set that Pearl Harbour had been attacked by Japan. A call was put through to Roosevelt, and the American Ambassador, John G. Winant, who was a guest at Chequers that weekend, spoke direct to the President to confirm the news. 'I was one of the small party dining with the PM', Martin wrote to me, 'the others being Winant, Harriman and Tommy Thompson.† Harriman and I chuckled afterwards about Winant's excited cries of "That's fine Mr President: that's fine." No doubt the President did not tell him on the telephone the full scale of the naval disaster; but in any case Winant's dominant reaction was one of elation at the certainty that the USA was now definitely in the war. Soon after the first excitement, I was able to obtain on the telephone from the Admiralty news of the Japanese attack on Malaya.'

No week went by over many years without my asking one of the Private Secretaries to comment on something that I had found in the archives, and wanted to know more about. They never let me down. Working with Churchill was clearly a tonic as well as a challenge. In giving John Martin a signed copy of one of his speech volumes, in July 1944, Churchill inscribed it: 'Keep jogging along.' To John Peck he said, after the sinking of the *Prince of Wales* and *Repulse* off Malaya in December 1941, 'We must KBO (Keep Bugger-

---

* The three daughters were Diana (Mrs Sandys), Sarah (Mrs Oliver) and Mary. The two sons-in-law were Duncan Sandys and Vic Oliver. The daughter-in-law was Pamela Churchill (Randolph was then in Cairo).

† Tommy Thompson was Churchill's former Flag Lieutenant at the Admiralty; he remained with him as aide-de-camp for the rest of the war. Averell Harriman was Roosevelt's personal emissary to Churchill, with special responsibility for American supplies to Britain.

ing On).' A variant of this exhortation, also recorded by Peck, was 'KPO' (Keep Plodding On).

The strains and ugliness of war affected everyone. John Martin told me that from time to time Churchill's daughter Sarah would come down to Chequers from her work at the Royal Air Force photographic reconnaissance centre at Medmenham. She would bring with her the most recent aerial photographs showing the damage that had just been done to the German cities. 'This used to be horrific,' Martin recalled. 'Sheet after sheet after sheet.' Richard Casey, Australia's representative in the War Cabinet, noted in his diary in the summer of 1943, after watching a film at Chequers showing the night bombing of a German city, that Churchill 'suddenly sat bolt upright and said to me, "Are we beasts? Are we taking this too far?" '*

It was not only for their recollections that help came from the Private Secretaries. Each of them had also kept a few notes and documents from his sojourn at Number Ten. At a time when Churchill had been ill, a Palestine Hebrew-language daily paper reported that an eighty-nine-year-old Jewess, Leah Vitkind, although medically unfit to do so, had 'made a vow to fast, if she should live to hear that Mr Churchill had recovered from his illness'. When Martin showed Churchill the newspaper cutting, he wrote on it: 'Thank her & tell her to begin taking nourishment again.' Martin had kept this note among his few prized momentoes of the war years.

From John Peck I gained another Private Secretary's perspective. He was with Churchill from the first day of his wartime premiership to the last, having become an Assistant Private Secretary during Churchill's closing weeks at the Admiralty. As I began my work on the war years, Peck, who lived in Dublin (where he had earlier been British Ambassador) would come to see me in London and spend many hours listening to my draft chapters, commenting, and suggesting wider lines of enquiry. It was he who, as I embarked upon Churchill's war years, advised me to hold the following in constant view: 'The scars left by the Dardanelles fiasco, and his determination

---

* In the summer of 1970, when I met Lord Casey at the Australian High Commission in London, he gave me a copy of the book in which this diary entry (for 27 June 1943) was published, *Personal Experience 1939–1946*, London 1962.

not to let ineptitude or bloody-mindedness at lower levels ruin aud-
acious projects for a second time.' It was for this reason, Peck
stressed, that Churchill's creation of a Ministry of Defence, with
himself as minister, was important. 'It gave him direct access to
the Chiefs of Staff. It was the Dardanelles complex: the brilliant
idea mucked up by bungling down the line. That was the origin
of the weekly reports that he wanted for everything. He wasn't
going to let the lower echelons of the public service muck up
his ideas.'

Peck was always fun to talk to: he has a penchant for witty stories
and wry reflections. He had also been very close indeed to the centre
of power. In one of our talks, as I began work on my seventh volume,
he recalled an aspect of Churchill's war leadership once the United
States had come into the war in December 1941 that he felt would
serve, as it did indeed serve, as a guide to my study of the many
thousands of documents. 'The first year of the American war was
very deflating and disillusioning for him,' Peck said. 'All the disasters
in the Far East and all the disasters in the Western Desert – the
tanks breaking down – all the sniping in Parliament – 1942 was a
terrible year for him. The possibility of Stafford Cripps leading a
revolt, Nye Bevan continually sniping, Stalin always ungrateful and
asking for more, the dispute among the Top Brass as to whether the
Pacific or Europe would have the priority, the sheer volume of the
meetings and the minutes only indirectly concerned with how to
beat Hitler – it was a bad year for him.'

John Peck finally laid to rest, for me at least, the belief that Churchill had spent the war in the underground rooms beneath the Old
Board of Trade Building at Storey's Gate. He had indeed spent a few
nights there, but did not like living underground like a troglodyte. 'If
living means working, eating and sleeping', Peck wrote to me in
1982 after reading one of my draft chapters, 'it was only a few weeks
before the Churchills moved to the relatively secure flat that had
been constructed on the ground floor of the government building
at Storey's Gate, *above* the "slab" which protected the underground
complex. It was this flat which with the Private Offices constituted
the "Annexe" that was his real residential base. No. 10 itself was
totally insecure from bombs, flying bombs and rockets; but Churchill
insisted on using No. 10 itself whenever it was reasonably safe to do

so, and sudden changes of venue for meals & meetings produced hair-raising escapes from chaos.'

The Private Secretaries would be awaiting a Cabinet minister or foreign statesman for a meeting at the Annexe, only to learn that the Prime Minister had gone to Number 10. Chaos was only avoided by a brisk move up King Charles Steps and through the Foreign Office courtyard to Downing Street, with the visitor alerted to the change of plan, if possible, before he actually arrived at the Annexe, and the Private Secretaries hoping that no one would notice anything untoward, and that they would not seem flustered.

In one of our many talks, Peck gave me an account of Churchill's wartime speech-making. I set it out here as he told it:

> There would be a big speech coming up. For days he would go broody. He wouldn't touch the work in his box. You had to jam things down his throat.
>
> After dinner he would say to his Private Secretary, 'I shall need two women tonight.' This was usually Mrs Hill and Miss Layton. Mrs Hill would come first. He would then sit down and dictate for one or two hours. He'd break off at about half time and start with the second woman, while the first one went away and typed out what he had already dictated.
>
> His own amendments tended to be minimal. He obviously had it all in his mind.
>
> Different sections would be sent off to the ministers concerned, with a deadline put to the minister's Private Secretary: 'Phone in your comments by . . .'
>
> There was often a damned short deadline, as Winston had left it so late. A Private Secretary would ring up to say that his minister wanted such-and-such changed. We'd either say, 'All right, we'll write it in' or 'Quite frankly, the Old Man isn't going to wear that. How strongly does your minister feel? Well, if he feels that strongly, he's going to have to fight for it himself.'
>
> You wouldn't make a change unless there was a good reason. We would add or change the passages that seemed to need it, from the various ministerial points of view.

Then he would pronounce himself satisfied. Then we
would send it back to Mrs Hill, to be typed in 'speech
form'.

John Peck had been with Churchill during the election campaign in
1945, when the Prime Minister, for the first time as a party leader
fighting a political campaign, travelled through England by special
train. His task was to keep Churchill abreast of the flow of material
on diplomatic and national issues. It was revealing for me to learn
how this aspect had continued at the most intense electioneering
time. 'He'd go off every day on his triumphal tour, then come back
exhausted to work on the telegrams. Everyone was convinced that
the Tories would win. "I suppose I must win another election for
them," he said.'

The Junior Private Secretary, who worked alongside Seal, Martin
and Peck, was John Colville, known as Jock. Alone of the others, he
had been Neville Chamberlain's Private Secretary before Churchill
came to power, having been seconded to Downing Street from the
Foreign Office in October 1939. He was to become a part of my
life sooner than the others: as a Churchill Trustee he vetted me
before my appointment, and within a few years was trying to help
me when the financial demands of the biography were no longer
met by the publisher's volume-by-volume advance, which had been
fixed by negotiations in 1967, on the eve of the oil price quadrupling
and inflation's evil triumph. I received no royalty for the volumes,
so the publisher's advance was the sole source of funding. Inflation,
the curse of all salaried people in the early 1970s, was not taken into
account by my paymasters.

Colville went into battle several times on my behalf. But it was in
vain. 'I've done all I can,' he told a mutual friend. 'There is nothing
more I can do.' When I learned this, I was touched.

I must admit to having been somewhat afraid of Colville, and it
was a very long time before I felt able to call him Jock. At first he
would receive me in his City office, a bankers' haven no doubt,
but formal and forbidding to a young historian. He was always so
impeccably dressed that I would automatically look down to see if
some crease of mine was out of place, or crumb visible. He spoke
with such authority about Churchill, and was so scornful (rightly of

course) of the mistakes and inventions of many writers, that I was petrified to be found wanting. He so frequently expressed to me his low opinion of historians ('you people almost never get it right') that I was sometimes inhibited even from asking questions, lest they revealed the abyss of my ignorance.

Looking back, I have no doubt that Jock Colville meant well, and wanted to help me. As each volume was ready to be printed, his neat, mostly pencil comments in the margin became more and more informative, as well as entertaining. I do not think there was a single aristocratic family, however minor, that he did not know enough about to correct any conceivable error I might make, of title, inherit- ance or relationship. Being a grandson of a Marquess of Crewe was no doubt a help. I almost dare not say which Marquess (in fact, the first, an Asquith creation), in case Colville's pencil rises up from the grave to correct me. We became friends, and although I remained inhibited by the generation gap to the end, I felt a deep sadness when, in 1987, within only a few moments perhaps of sending me a postcard from Winchester Station, he had a heart attack and died. I had known him for nearly two decades.

From the outset of my work in October 1968, Colville's writings and reflections, in pencilled notes, long handwritten letters, and in conversation, were invaluable. In January 1969 he sent me the copy of a speech he had just made in which the following passage appeared, which I soon came to realize was a true assessment of Churchill:

> He held strong views on most things: past, present and future. But he was fair to those who held the opposite views, however strongly he believed them to be wrong. He was not a believer in infallibility of any kind – even Churchillian infallibility.
>
> Of course he was certainly not infallible; but his convic- tions were more often justified than those of any statesman in my lifetime, and his countrymen, even his political opponents, had no doubt at all that he was the greatest man alive.*

* J.R. Colville, speech at the *Yorkshire Post* Book of the Year Literary Luncheon, 9 January 1969.

As I prepared the first draft of my first volume, volume three, I kept Colville informed of progress on a regular basis, following up his leads and suggestions, looking again in the archives for clues that he felt certain were there, and contacting the people he thought could help me. Sometimes my reports to him were rather short and breathless. I have found one from 1969 in which I wrote: 'I leave for Gallipoli on May 2nd. The Turks have promised archives and survivors galore.'

When I began my work on the war years, Colville told me that I was welcome to make what use I wished of his own wartime diary. This diary was already something of a legend. Everyone knew that he had kept it during his Downing Street years. No one knew what was in it. For me the first glimpse of it came when he wrote out by hand the September to December 1939 entries in which Churchill appeared. Then he found this copying wearisome, and asked if I could send a 'myrmidon' to whom he could dictate. Remembering with a glow of embarrassment my ignorance in Randolph's days, I had to look 'myrmidon' up. The dictionary told me: 'a faithful follower or servant'. It was typical of Colville, and others too, that they assumed I would, or could, delegate my search to others. At that time, as I explained to him, I did not have the resources to do this. I was also determined to see and hear the evidence for myself.

A new plan evolved: I would take the train from Oxford to London, walk from Paddington to his flat nearby, and sit in an armchair while he read each day's entry, rather rapidly. If there was something that I felt might be useful for me, I would ask him to read it again at a slower pace, and would then write it down. I had a number of sharpened pencils for this. After several such sessions, Colville himself suggested that I take the diary away and copy down what I needed.

Whether the readings in his flat stimulated Colville's subsequent inspiration I do not know, but before I had got very far into copying the entries for 1940, which were substantial, he decided to publish the diary. The resultant book, *The Fringes of Power: Downing Street Diaries 1939–1955*, became one of the two or three best-selling Churchill-related books. Although there were many weekends when Colville was not on duty at Chequers, and days when he was not at Downing Street, which are therefore blanks in his diary, the multitude of occasions when he was an eye-witness, or, more properly (or improperly!) an ear-witness, are covered in magnificent detail, with much verbatim reporting. 'I am filled with amazement', John Peck wrote to me when the diary was published, 'at the risks Jock was running in the matter of security, for which he should have been sacked on the spot if he had been caught.' 'I disapproved of his diary-keeping activity at the time', John Martin wrote that same month, 'but have to admit that I have much enjoyed reading the product and salute it as a valuable contribution to history.'

I much amused Colville on my return from a conference in Moscow in 1985 by telling him that among the historical facts I had gleaned there was that the penalty for keeping a diary, for a member of Stalin's staff, was death. No such penalty existed in London, though the keeping of diaries was not really allowed. On 3 February 1941, Colville received a minute which read: 'Mr Colville, Mrs Hill informs me that you are in the habit of keeping a diary, containing a close and intimate account of events in my Private Office and at Chequers. The keeping of private records of this sort is fraught with many dangers. Pray bring your diary for my inspection at 10 a.m. tomorrow. WSC.'

John Martin told me that Colville 'went green' when he read this minute. 'I think you'll find the diary stopped for a few days.' Shortly before obeying the summons Colville was told that the minute was not in fact from Churchill; it was a spoof, dictated and initialled by John Peck. Its origin was this, as Peck explained to me in a letter in July 1993 when he was reading the draft of this chapter (thus the mysteries continue to be unravelled). 'As a good civil servant Seal was seriously concerned about Colville's keeping a diary but found himself in a dilemma. Actually to forbid Colville to keep a diary was going to be a pretty drastic measure, and Seal felt too insecure to be certain of being fully supported by the PM. So he conceived the idea of commissioning me to do a fake minute. Seal insisted on my being present by chance when he gave Colville the minute, and I can confirm his moment of panic, but it was naturally treated as good clean fun and the diary continued.'

Colville's diary is an integral part of all accounts of Churchill's war years, including my own. But there was one crucial area of Churchill's daily wartime life that had no place at all in it: this was the contents of the locked yellow boxes that reached him daily, and for which, John Martin told me, 'not even the Private Secretaries had a key'.

The contents of the yellow boxes, as unlocked by Churchill himself, were mainly top secret summaries of the daily German radio messages, encrypted by the Germans on their ultra-secret Enigma machines. These were the daily German operational orders for land, sea and air action, often more than a hundred messages a day, sent by the highest coded secrecy, picked up by British radio receivers and analyses were then sent (by a code that the Germans never broke) decrypted and analysed at Bletchley by a formidable team; summaries and analysis were then sent (by a code that the Germans never broke) to the British Commanders-in-Chief in the field.

Churchill received a daily selection of the summaries and interpretations of the Enigma messages, later known as Ultra. These gave him, and the Chiefs of Staff to whom they were also sent, a remarkable window into the actual German orders and intentions, which had a twin impact: it gave worrying prior knowledge of attacks and initiatives against which there was often no real means of defence, and it enabled steps to be taken to prevent otherwise dangerous courses of German action.

The one man on Churchill's staff who knew the contents of the yellow boxes was Desmond Morton, who had an office at 10 Downing Street, and was in daily contact with the Secret Intelligence Service by whom the Ultra messages (as they became known) were distributed. When I met Morton at his London club in 1968, however, the story of Enigma was still secret, and he was far too discreet to divulge it. After the German invasion of the Soviet Union, Churchill insisted that Stalin was kept informed of these messages as they related to German military intentions on the Eastern Front. Only with the publication of the multi-volume official history of British Intelligence in the Second World War in 1979 did this aspect of Churchill's daily work become known. One of the authors, Edward Thomas, was my perspicacious guide on this essential aspect of Churchill's wartime decision-making.

In the late 1960s, as I began my work, every reference to intercepted top secret German radio messages had been removed from Churchill's papers by the Cabinet Office. In the early 1970s men like Eden and Montgomery could make no reference, either in their published memoirs, or in conversation with historians like myself, to this ultra-secret form of signals intelligence. They could not deal with it when discussing the decisions they and Churchill had made, even though it lay at the centre of those decisions again and again, at practically every turning-point of the war.

I was fortunate that by the time I came to write my two wartime volumes, the archives were open and the story could be told. One document that had been withdrawn from the Churchill papers shortly after they were transferred to Stour, and was opened to scrutiny just as I started work on volume six, was from Churchill's Principal Private Secretary to the other members of the Private Office, dated 28 September 1940: 'Will everybody please take note that from now on boxes will come regularly every day from "C"* marked "Only to be opened by the Prime Minister in person". This marking is not mere camouflage and is to be taken seriously. The boxes are to be put on the Prime Minister's desk and left for him to re-lock. They will be returned to "C".'

Wartime secrecy was maintained with such effectiveness that when, in 1941, Churchill went to Bletchley to meet those working there, John Martin, who accompanied him on the drive, did not enter the building. According to Morton, who went in with the Prime Minister, and who told this story to John Peck at the time, 'W was shown the cubicles where the mathematical geniuses were at work. In one a tall gaunt figure, ?Polish or Austrian? saw his door open and the PM peer round; rose to his full height, turned grey and then green, and was sick.'

I had one piece of pure luck in my search in the Enigma sphere. In April 1941 Churchill had sent Stalin a warning about German military designs on the Soviet Union: he published this fact in his memoirs. When I was in Moscow in 1989, I remembered one of my own footnotes, published in volume six in 1983. This pointed out that when Churchill asked Anthony Eden if Stalin had ever acknowledged the message of April 1941, Eden replied that Stalin had not. Eden added: 'This same attitude was adopted towards the later messages which, with your permission, I gave to Maisky, beginning several weeks before the attack.'

---

* Sir Stuart Menzies, Head of the Secret Intelligence Service.

What were these messages given to the Soviet Ambassador by Eden? I had not managed to find them. Did they derive from the top secret Enigma? The official history of British Intelligence in the Second World War was silent on this matter. Then the answer came unexpectedly from my Soviet host, General Dmitri Volkogonov, the biographer of Stalin. Yes, he said, the messages existed. They were clearly based on top secret German orders, and they had been passed on to Moscow. One message was of particular significance: on 11 June 1941, ten days before the German invasion of the Soviet Union, Stalin had been told the precise dispositions of the German units massed upon the Soviet border. This information derived from a British Intelligence study of the most recent Enigma signals. Churchill had passed the information to Eden for transmission to the Soviet leader. One of the very few Foreign Office officials who knew of the Enigma secret, Sir Alexander Cadogan, had given the information to Maisky, who had sent it on to Moscow. Another search had been concluded, this one by sheer chance.

Churchill continued to keep the needs of the Russian front in his mind: on one occasion he noted on a set of signals in his yellow box, relating to the war in the East: 'Has any of this been sent to Joe?'

The Private Secretaries, though they did not read the contents of the yellow boxes, had nevertheless to make sure that Churchill received them regularly. Even when he was overseas provision had to be made to get the top-secret material to him. I was fortunate to find in the Public Record Office, in a file full of dull administrative routine queries: one from a new Private Secretary, Leslie Rowan, asking what he should do with this material while Churchill was on his way to Roosevelt in August 1941. This gave me a valuable clue as to how the material was referred to, so that I could then be more alert to its presence.* It also introduced me to Rowan himself. 'He

---

* The Enigma-based materials were known as Boniface (a typical codename for an individual agent, and thus a disguise for this incessant stream of intercepted radio signals). They were sent to Churchill on this occasion, on his instructions, 'in a weighted case, so that they will sink in the sea if anything happens to the aeroplane'. Another set of material that Rowan had to get to Churchill was given the code 'BJ' (for 'brown jackets', the folders in which they were circulated): these were the intercepted and decrypted messages sent to and from foreign diplomats in London. These messages also provided Churchill and his advisers with an important (if clandestine) glimpse of German war policy. In November 1993 they were released for public scrutiny.

was by far the most talented and best suited for the task of all those who served as Private Secretaries during the Churchill régime' was John Peck's comment to me.

Rowan kept no diary and wrote no memoirs. Although, when I started my Churchill work, he helped me trace the story of the two Turkish battleships Churchill had seized in 1914 while they were being completed on Tyneside, he died before I had begun my detailed work. In 1968, in an essay in the volume *Action This Day: Working With Churchill*, he made a point which echoed the notes Seal had set down: Churchill's conviction 'that our democratic form of government was that under which freedom – the basis of all real human dignity and progress – had the best chance to flourish'. Rowan added: 'In many of his actions he was in fact dictatorial, though it is notable that he never once overruled the Chiefs of Staff. But when he gave orders in relation to the conduct of affairs, civil or military, he expected to be obeyed, or to be told, quickly and clearly, why he should not be.' It was not really dictatorial to ask to know the reason why one would not be obeyed!

There was one other Private Secretary with whom I made contact: his brief tenure, and somewhat illegible signature, had been a deterrent at first even to knowing his name. I cursed illegibility, and looked in vain in the indexes of the existing books about Churchill. He was in fact Paul Beards, brought in by Rowan in the early summer of 1945 from the War Office. When I began my work on 1945 he was living in retirement in Devon, and we corresponded. Among the episodes that he recalled was one shortly after he had joined the Private Office:

> On one occasion, when the others were at lunch and the PM had left his room in the Annexe, a signal came from the Australian Prime Minister to WSC. I was quite perplexed what to do about it but thought I should let the PM know at once it had come. I asked Sawyers (the butler) where the PM was and he said 'In the bath' (this was about 1 p.m.), and that the PM would like to see the signal at once.
>
> So I took it in to find the PM arrayed like a Roman Senator in a massive towel and he proceeded to read the signal.

Another of Beards's recollections was of the farewell-taking after the election defeat: 'I went into the Cabinet Room at No. 10 and WSC spoke for a few minutes to me. He said "Mr Attlee is a very nice man and you will be well with him. The Private Office is a most important mechanism in the machinery of the State and it is a little known and most useful experience to serve in it." He then got up and put his hand on my shoulder and said goodbye.'

The wartime Private Office was a small, self-contained and hard-working group of youngish civil servants. Three others were part of the inner circle of the Prime Minister's daily life: Professor Lindemann, at first head of the Statistical Office and later (as Lord Cherwell) a Cabinet minister, Brendan Bracken, at first Parliamentary Secretary and likewise later a Cabinet minister, and the Chief Whip, James Stuart. There was also another member of the Private Office, Anthony Bevir, who was in charge of ecclesiastical patronage. 'Everyone loved him,' was Peck's comment to me.

In 1951 Churchill became Prime Minister for the second time. Two further Private Secretaries, David Pitblado and David Hunt, both provided me with their recollections. 'The main point that I want to make is that it was fun to work for Churchill,' Hunt had written in his memoirs, where he commented, with regard to the question that Colville (who also returned to Number 10 in 1951) had addressed: 'He certainly drank the weakest whisky-and-soda that I have ever known.'*

Churchill was almost seventy-seven when he became Prime Minister for the second time. But even at that age, Pitblado told me when we met at his home in London, 'he took great pains on his speeches. They were always dictated, so that although he read them, they were always the spoken word. They took a long time to prepare, two or three weeks of labour. He would ask Jock and David and me to get bits and pieces from the government departments. Then there were

---

* Sir David Hunt, *On the Spot, An Ambassador Remembers*, London 1975: chapter four is called 'Private Secretary to Churchill'. For almost all my volumes, starting with volume four, David Hunt was a vigilant reader both of the typescripts and the proofs, finding innumerable errors of fact and transcription, always willing to add his own historical comments and recollections, and helping to make the search for Churchill both disciplined and enjoyable.

the little bits we would put in. Towards the end they were all thrown out. "This is very good,' he would say, "but . . .".'

During Churchill's second premiership, a former RAF pilot joined his Private Office: Anthony Montague Browne. He was to remain with Churchill until 1965. As Churchill became less and less able to attend to his correspondence, Montague Browne ensured that it was dealt with wisely and expeditiously. He was constantly at Churchill's side, a witness of many flashes of humour, wisdom and kindness in the declining years. In 1960, when Columbia Pictures gave Churchill £100,000 for the film rights of *My Early Life*, Montague Browne had been the main and tenacious negotiator on his behalf.* 'I handed the cheque to him,' he told me. 'It thrilled him. He sent for his cheque book and proposed giving me a quarter – £25,000. Knowing his true financial situation I declined. But it shows how he retained these generous instincts.'

Montague Browne helped me considerably with my final volume. He never minded (or certainly never gave the impression of minding) being telephoned at virtually any hour to be asked to help on some query. I was greatly impressed by the selfless efforts he had made on Churchill's behalf for so many years, in the latter years holding the fort during Churchill's extreme old age and failing health.

Among the frequent visitors to Chartwell during Churchill's last years was Jock Colville. He had served with Pitblado as Joint Principal Private Secretary from 1951 until Churchill's resignation in 1955. He remained a friend and frequent dinner guest until Churchill's death ten years later. From this latter period, one of the most moving episodes that Colville recalled was when I was writing about the aftermath of the Dardanelles. I had found a reference in Churchill's papers to a portrait painted after his return from the Western Front in the summer of 1916, when there was no place for him in government. The painter was William Orpen. In a letter that he sent me in May 1970, Colville recalled an episode that had taken place less than six years earlier:

> A few months before Sir Winston died I stayed with him
> at Chartwell for the night and dined alone with him. His

---

* The film was eventually made, by Carl Foreman, directed by Richard Attenborough, with the title *Young Winston*.

memory had already faded and conversation was exceedingly difficult. During the first two or three courses at dinner I tried every subject in which I knew him to be interested, without success. I even went so far as to say that Napoleon was, after all, the Hitler of the 19th century – an expression of opinion which would, in earlier days, have been greeted with an expression of wrath!

Finally, over the savoury, I looked at the Orpen, which was hanging in the dining-room behind Sir Winston's chair, and made the not very original remark that it was far and away the best portrait of Sir Winston that had ever been painted. Suddenly Sir Winston's brain cleared. His voice became exactly as it had been years before. He replied:

'I am glad you think so. I gave him eleven sittings, which is more than I ever had time to give to any other painter. It was in February 1916, at a very unhappy time of my life when I had nothing whatever to do. Rothermere gave me the portrait, which was very generous of him, and almost my only occupation was to sit to the artist.'

His mind then clouded over again and we had no coherent conversation for the rest of the evening.

A final gem from the Colville jewel box: he had been told by Queen Elizabeth the Queen Mother of a luncheon visit Churchill made to Buckingham Palace shortly after India and Pakistan had separated, India becoming a Republic and Pakistan, briefly, a member of the Commonwealth. 'He stood in the doorway of the drawing-room in which the King and Queen were awaiting him, bowed and said, "I believe that this is the first time I have had the honour to be invited to luncheon by their Majesties the King and Queen of Pakistan."'

Montague Browne was with Churchill to his last days. During that time, as their former Master's memory and strength faded, the Private Secretaries of the war years were always welcome. Leslie Rowan and his wife Judy, John Martin and his wife Rosalind, and John Peck and his wife Mariska, knew that whenever they were in London (Martin and Peck being often posted overseas) a telephone call to Churchill's London house, 24 Hyde Park Gate, would lead to a warm request for a visit.

In 1960 Churchill made his last visit to Washington. Thirty-three years later John Peck, who was then stationed in New York, recalled how he was invited down to the farewell dinner for President Eisenhower. 'When he finally went to bed Winston asked me to see him to bed and I went through the old familiar routine until lights out.'

In my search for Churchill, I was helped several times when his former Private Secretaries reacted to some account which they considered to be false. At the time of my own four-part BBC television series, in referring to the interview with Sir Ian Jacob of Churchill's wartime Defence Staff, *The Times* drew attention to Churchill's 'huge intake of alcohol'. In sending me this cutting, John Peck wrote: 'To me *The Times* notice gave a completely mistaken picture, based on a misunderstanding of Ian Jacob's statement that "he always had a bottle of champagne for lunch". I have already been challenged on this and I have said (i) Ian Jacob hardly ever had lunch with Winston so he could only have been quoting hearsay, (ii) even if Churchill had had champagne for lunch every day he would never have got through an entire bottle, and even if he had a glass or two by himself, I fear that Sawyers the butler would have ensured that none was wasted.'

Churchill's Private Secretaries were often disturbed by the misrepresentations that grew with the passage of time, and continue to grow. They had seen him at closest quarters, on a daily basis, over long periods of time. They had won his trust and he had gained theirs. For me, their help and their friendship were a precious link with the past.

XI

'A Loving, Generous Father'

Every author in search of a historical character tries to get as close as he can to those who knew the subject best. Closeness for a lifetime or closeness for a day can each divulge their touch of understanding. Memories and documents also tell their tale: proximity is the key. This is as true for medieval times or for the Victorian era as for the twentieth century, with the added bonus for the twentieth-century historian that it is possible to meet and correspond with those who were in the inner circle, or who touched it.

Churchill had a gift for friendship, as well as the ill-luck to make some lifelong enemies. I remember many years ago meeting an elderly duchess who impressed on me Churchill's utter wickedness in betraying the aristocracy when, in 1909, he took a leading part in challenging the powers of the House of Lords. Much later a distinguished baroness began her remarks, immediately after we had been introduced: 'Winston was wrong about everything.' Neither had known him well (not that their attitudes need necessarily have been different had they done so), but both gave me a sense of needing to find those who had been close to him, otherwise I feared I might flounder amongst such sharp opinions.

Once every month or so while I was writing volume three, I would take the train from Oxford to London, walk through Hyde Park, and present myself at Lady Churchill's flat in Prince's Gate. I was always nervous of what her reaction might be to whatever chapter I had brought with me to read aloud after lunch. During lunch she would talk about 'Winston' and I would take notes on my lap. She would often ask me about how the researches were going, about whom I had seen, and what I was finding in the archive. As I read aloud from my most recent draft chapter, she would make comments: they gave me a particular insight into her husband's distress at the failure of the Dardanelles in 1915. It was this episode that was to hang like a shadow over the years ahead. It was a plan with a purpose, to shorten the war, and it was one, she made clear to me, in which her husband had complete confidence. But it had dogged him relentlessly.

Lady Churchill spoke of her husband's great anger when two successive Prime Ministers, Asquith and Lloyd George, refused to allow anything like the full publication of the documents he had put together to show just how the enterprise had come into being.

From the first days of their marriage in 1908, not only Clementine's letters to her husband, but her handwritten notes to him, were a guide to his character. She had given her archive to her daughter Mary, not only as custodian, but as her future biographer. On one occasion Mary came to the lunchtime reading. Although I was never a part of the family circle, and perhaps as a biographer would have been inhibited in my comments had I been drawn too closely in, I recognized the importance of being allowed to see everything, to use it, and not to have to submit my drafts for scrutiny or censorship. Not every biographer is so fortunate. I was also fortunate that Mary Soames not only let me see these myriad letters and notes, but answered dozens, it may even have been hundreds, of queries arising from them.

In her notes to her husband, Clementine would set down in writing something that troubled her about his actions and behaviour, and give it to him to read. She felt, for example, before 1914, that it was rash of him to continue flying, in pursuit of his pilot's licence. In 1918, three weeks before the war came to an end, she advised him to turn his energies from his war-waging tasks as Minister of Munitions to peace-making plans. This has long been one of my favourite examples of her mastery of plain speaking, with charm, outspokenness and, above all, wisdom:

> Do come home and look after what is to be done with the munition workers when the fighting really does stop. Even if the fighting is not over yet, your share of it must be & I would like you to be praised as a reconstructive genius, as well as for a Mustard Gas fiend, a Tank juggernaut & a flying Terror. Besides the credit for all these Bogey parts will be given to subordinates.

Can't the men munition workers build lovely garden cities & pull down slums in places like Bethnal Green, Newcastle, Glasgow, Leeds, etc. & can't the women munition workers make all the lovely furniture for them, babies' cradles, cupboards etc.

Do come home and arrange all this.

The Prime Minister, David Lloyd George, had other ideas, appointing Churchill Secretary of State for War within weeks of the end of the conflict, and giving him three main responsibilities: the demobilization of several million men, the withdrawal of British troops from Russia, and the administration of British military forces overseas, on the Rhine, the Jordan and the Euphrates. But Clementine's advice did not fall on an unreceptive ear. In Lloyd George's archive is a letter that Churchill wrote to him, two months after Clementine's letter, stressing that in the creation of a Minister of Pensions the Prime Minister would need 'a sympathetic figure, "one who knows what they went through"', someone who could deal with a mass of detail 'in a humane & warm-hearted spirit'. Churchill ended his letter: 'I hope you will endeavour to gather together all forces of strength & influence in the country & lead them along the paths of science & organization to the rescue of the weak & the poor. That is the main conception I have of the Victory government.'

Clementine's letters continued to give her husband the benefit of her own Liberal upbringing and instincts. Shortly after he became Prime Minister in 1940, she warned him (in a letter that she decided not to give him, tore up, then pasted together and handed to him) that she had been told by 'someone in your entourage (a devoted friend)' that his colleagues and subordinates were becoming distressed by 'your rough, sarcastic & overbearing manner'. If an idea was suggested at a conference 'you are supposed to be so contemptuous that presently no ideas, good or bad, will be forthcoming'. This was not the Winston she knew. 'I was astonished & upset because in all these years I have been accustomed to all those who have worked with you & under you, loving you. I said this & I was told "No doubt it's the strain."' Her letter continued:

My Darling Winston – I must confess that I have noticed a deterioration in your manner; & you are not so kind as you used to be. It is for you to give the Orders & if they are bungled – except for the King, the Archbishop of Canterbury & the Speaker you can sack anyone & everyone. Therefore with this terrific power you must combine urbanity, kindness & if possible Olympic calm.

You used to quote: – '*On ne regne sur les ames que par le calme*' – I cannot bear that those who serve the country & yourself should not love you as well as admire and respect you. Besides you won't get the best results by irascibility & rudeness. They will breed either dislike or a slave mentality – (Rebellion in War Time being out of the question!)

Please forgive your loving, devoted & watchful

Clemmie

Despite the relentless strain of the Dunkirk evacuation, the fall of France, and the intensification of the air war, Churchill recovered his equanimity; the diaries and recollections of his staff attest to that. But Clementine remained vigilant, never hesitating to express her feelings when she felt it was in her husband's interest for her to do so. In 1947, two years after the war, she learned that he had instructed his valet to take his wartime Air Commodore's uniform for the ceremony in Paris at which he was to receive the *Médaille Militaire* (a signal honour for an Englishman). Her advice was succinct:

> I would like to persuade you to wear civilian clothes during your Paris visit. To me, air force uniform except when worn by the Air Crews is rather bogus. And it is not as an Air-Commodore that you conquered in the War but in your capacity & power as a Statesman.
>
> All the political vicissitudes during the years of Exile qualified you for unlimited & supreme power when you took command of the Nation. You do not need to wear your medals to show your prowess. I feel the blue uniform is for you fancy-dress, & I am proud of my plain Civilian Pig.

There is a curious sequel to this letter, part of the endless fascination of the search. In Churchill's private papers is a note to his valet in which he states: 'I shall wear civilian clothes and take no uniform at all.' Finding this, I wrote with some satisfaction in volume eight of the biography that he had deferred to his wife's advice. In the spring of 1982, however, the magazine *Finest Hour*, journal of the International Churchill Society, published an article by William E. Beatty, a professor at the Rochester Institute of Technology, Rochester, New York State, which undermined my confident statement. In 1947 Beatty had been studying at the University of Paris: his room overlooked the Hôtel des Invalides where Churchill was to receive his medal. As soon as the ceremony was over Beatty ran down the Esplanade des Invalides, where he took a number of snapshots of the cavalcade as it drove away from the ceremony. One of these photographs showed Churchill in uniform. My deduction had been wrong: he had not taken his wife's advice after all. He had, however, given up his original plan of wearing his Air Commodore's uniform, to which she had particularly objected. Beatty's photograph shows him in the uniform of the 4th Queen's Own Hussars, his old regiment, certainly a more suitable uniform for a military ceremony and award, but still not a 'plain Civilian pig.'

Churchill almost always deferred to his wife's advice. He wrote to her once, however, that it was 'too negative'. But he understood her concern that, at particularly difficult times, especially in war, the rougher edges of his character could be bruising. More often than not, when her advice came, he was full of praise for the guidance of his 'sagacious cat'.

Early in my search for Churchill I became aware of how close he had been to his wife and children: a closeness shown both by the time spent together, and intimate correspondence; an uninhibited and open relationship within the family circle. Churchill delighted in his five children. His letters about them radiate affection. But their lives were not without sadness and even tragedy. His fourth child, Marigold, born four days after the Armistice in 1918, died of meningitis before she was three years old. His eldest child, Diana, committed suicide when she was fifty-four. At the time of Diana's birth in 1909, Churchill had written to Clementine: 'I wonder what she will grow into, & whether she will be lucky or unlucky to have been dragged out of chaos. She ought to have some rare qualities both of mind & body. But these do not always mean happiness or peace. Still I think a bright star shines for her.' These were prescient words: many bright stars were to shine for Diana, but happiness and peace were to elude her.

Randolph's devotion to his father was complete: his happiest memories when we talked of the past were of the times when he and his father had travelled or campaigned together, above all in the anti-appeasement days. He also saw at closest quarters his father's kindness, not only in repeatedly paying his enormous bills, with the minimum of grumbling, but in seeking his well-being. Randolph told me how his father had taken him to see both the schools that he might go to, Eton and Harrow, so that Randolph could give his opinion on them; at the end of the journey he told his son that they had had more talk together in that one day than he, Winston, had had with his father in the whole of his life. A tenderness towards his son was ever-present. On one occasion, at Randolph's urging, the two of them had gone to the cinema in Tunbridge Wells. On the drive back Randolph felt ashamed that he had dragged his busy father away from his important work (he was then Chancellor of the Exchequer) to see what he thought had proved a trashy, slushy film. But Winston put his hand on Randolph's shoulder and said with gentleness: 'We must lend ourselves to the illusion.'

From time to time, from the first days of his own appointment as biographer in 1961, Randolph would dictate notes about his father, intending to use them when he reached the relevant stage of the biography. His death when the book had only reached 1914 made it difficult for me to use these: he would, after all, have polished or elaborated on them. One, which is dated 3 February 1961, contains a recollection of 1920, when Churchill was living in London at Sussex Gardens: 'Often before the children went to bed he would invite them into his bedroom and read aloud to them for an hour or more, sometimes making the children late for their bedtime and himself late for his dinner. When Diana and I were eleven and nine he would read to us *Treasure Island* and *The Lunatic at Large*, *Wee Willie Winkie* and other stories by Kipling, which used to make us all cry, especially *The Drums of the Fore and Aft*.'

In the course of my search for Churchill's relationship with his son, I had a particular stroke of luck. Finding in the Chartwell visitors' book for 1928 the signature of James Lees-Milne, I wrote to him (fifty years later) and he sent me his recollections of that visit.

They included a family portrait of a sort I had not seen elsewhere. Churchill was then fifty-four:

> Sir Winston, I recall, came in late to dinner after we had all started. He sat hunched up over his soup, which he ate aggressively, without speaking a word. Some provocative remark of Randolph's might induce him to bark angrily. I think Randolph, who even then adored and revered his father, enjoyed taunting him, as one might a bull from a safe distance. Randolph would repeat his monstrous opinion, and this would elicit long growls of contradiction.
>
> The rest of us young looked nervously down our shirt-fronts. Lady Churchill would gently check Randolph and assuage Sir Winston.
>
> Towards the end of the meal tension relaxed. By then I suppose Mr Churchill (which of course he was then) had dismissed from his mind the book which he was in process of writing. He became very sweet to the girls present, indulgent with the boys, and clearly very proud of Randolph's bursting self-confidence and intelligence.

Father and son could quarrel violently, particularly when Randolph would accuse his father of having unsuitable friends, that is those whom Randolph disliked. But after each quarrel there was a reconciliation. 'We have a deep animal love for each other,' Churchill once reflected. In 1968, Field Marshal Alexander told me of a moment of affection between father and son that he had inadvertently witnessed at a wartime airport, when, after a quarrel, the two of them had embraced in a moment of deep tenderness.

People often comment on how difficult it must have been to have such a famous father. This is surely true. But sometimes these comments are laced with unpleasant, even with cruel, references to Randolph's or Sarah's drinking. I knew them both, and knew (it was not a secret) how much each had suffered quite different blows to the 'blow' of having a famous father: Randolph through a war injury and the failure of his first marriage, Sarah in the tragic death by suicide of her second husband Antony Beauchamp, and the death through a sudden heart attack of her third husband, Lord Audley, after only fifteen months of marriage. Churchill invariably sought to comfort all his much-loved children whenever they were in distress. Reading of Sarah's arrest on Merseyside for drunkenness, he wrote to Clementine with understanding: 'I think they treated her very roughly at Liverpool and roused her fiery spirit.'

Sarah Churchill often recalled, when she visited me in Oxford, or when I called on her in London, the marvellous warmth of her father's affections. When she travelled across the Atlantic in 1936 with her first husband, Vic Oliver, of whom Churchill did not approve, he nevertheless took considerable trouble to ensure that Oliver, an Austrian Jew, would not be in danger if he made the crossing on a German ship. It was Sarah who, in a letter written from her air force reconnaissance unit during the 1945 election campaign, urged him to follow up his election broadcast on the dangers of a Labour government (they would bring in 'some form of Gestapo') with a promise to improve the nation's housing, and to offer a better life to all those who had suffered so much privation in the war. 'Don't think I'm a rebel!' she wrote, 'but I thought that as this morning there is not very much to do, I would try and put down what I see and hear, of what the people I live and work with feel.'

Churchill took his daughter's advice. In his second election broadcast a week later he promised that 'social insurance, national injuries insurance, and the national health service will be shaped by Parliament and will be made to play a dynamic part in the life and security of every family and home.' As to housing, about which Sarah had been especially concerned, Churchill declared: 'Every method, public or private, for houses, permanent or temporary, will be employed, and all obstructions, from whatever quarter they come, be they price-rings, monopoly, or any other form of obstacle, will be dealt with by the whole power of Parliament and the nation.'

The Gestapo speech is always quoted, the social reform pledge hardly ever.* This saddened Sarah, who, like all Churchill's children, saw at close quarters what she described to me as the essentially humane and constructive nature of his genius. She also saw that he, like all people, needed encouragement. After finding him cast down by a letter from a friend warning that his war memoirs were too full

---

* Churchill's 'Gestapo' broadcast was made on 4 June 1945, the Four-Year Plan broadcast on the 13th.

of documents, she told him not to pay any attention. 'You are the best historian, the best journalist, the best poet – shut yourself up and only listen to a very few, and even then, write this book from the heart of yourself, from the knowledge you have, and let it stand or fall by that. It will stand. Everyone will listen to your story. I hate to see you pale & no longer happily preoccupied.'

In a letter to Randolph shortly before her brother's death, Sarah recalled the poetry that their father had liked: 'Heroic poetry, poems with stories and legends. But there were other facets to his enjoyment, such as his appreciation of beauty – a compassion for humanity, as is embraced by the wrily humorous and philosophical ditties of Chesterton, Lear and music-hall songs.'

I learned a great deal from Sarah about her father's compassion, warmth and sense of fun. She had travelled with him to Yalta, from where her letters home were an important window on a sombre scene. 'Last night', she wrote to her mother on 6 February 1945, 'just before he went to sleep, Papa said "I do not suppose that at any moment in history has the agony of the world been so great or widespread. Tonight the sun goes down on more suffering that ever before in the world." '*

I saw Sarah at Stour with her brother, both of them recalling episodes of their youth at Chartwell and on family holidays in France. I travelled with her in the train to her brother's funeral, and saw how strong were the bonds of love in a family outsiders saw only as quarrelsome and divided. Above all, I had a sense of Winston Churchill's revivifying presence. His youngest daughter Mary, in her conversations with me, as well as (more importantly) in her letters to him, confirmed this impression. For that reason I ended the biography with her words, of which I hoped Randolph would have approved (he was always concerned with how he would end his final volume and final page): six months before her father's death, when he was in his ninetieth year, Mary wrote to him, on learning he was cast down by the burden of age, 'In addition to all the feelings a daughter has for a loving, generous father, I owe you what every Englishman, woman & child does – Liberty itself.'

---

* Sarah Churchill published her Yalta letters in 1981 in her book *Keep on Dancing*: in the copy she gave me she wrote 'for the long task, accept my little offer'.

As with Randolph, so with Mary, some of the most vivid recollections concerned the time of Hitler's pre-war aggression, from the Anschluss with Austria in March 1938 to Munich seven months later, a low point in Churchill's fortunes. In one of our talks together she recalled 'the feeling of tremendous frustration, that people *wouldn't* believe. It dominated the thought and the talk at Chartwell. It was so agonizing. From the Anschluss onward the kettle never came off the boil.'

Yet through it all, as Lady Soames remembered across the years, 'Papa had this enormous quality of never despairing.' As a result of the publication of his doctor's diary in 1965, the picture of Churchill as frequently and debilitatingly depressed had, by the time I began my work, taken hold in the general literature. It did not quite square up to what I was finding: a man often angered and saddened by the bad turn of events, but having unusual resilience to come back fighting within a short time; not someone incapacitated through mental ill-health or through excessive drinking.

As Susie and I worked our way through the detailed daily records of the war years, we came to the conclusion, borne in on us by what we were finding, that Churchill's exceptional resilience was a far more dominant feature of his character than his occasional down-heartedness. It was his courage in 1940 that inspired the nation. All those who worked with him at that time recalled, above all, his ability to lift the mood of a meeting by his sense of the possible, his humour, and his refusal to be cast down.

From a careful study of the archives, and from long talks with Churchill's colleagues, drink and depression seemed much exaggerated, yet much repeated (and embellished) in recent popular accounts. John Peck had already written to me about Churchill's alleged heavy drinking: 'Personally, throughout the time I knew him I *never* saw him the worse for drink. The glass of weak whisky, like the cigars, was more a symbol than anything else, and one glass lasted him for hours.'

I mentioned the depressions to Jock Colville in one of our earliest talks together. He wrote to me in April 1969:

I suppose that this hypothetical state of depression into which Lord Moran alleges Sir Winston used to fall will become accepted dogma. I therefore, some time ago, took the trouble to ask Lady Churchill about the theory. She was quite positive that although her husband was occasionally depressed – as indeed most normal people are – he was not abnormally subject to long fits of depression.

The expression 'to have a black dog on one's back' was one that my nanny used to use very frequently. I suspect that Mrs Everest must have used it too. It was a very common expression among nannies. I think that Sir Winston must have said on various occasions to Lord Moran: 'I have got a black dog on my back today.' Lord Moran, not moving very frequently in nanny circles, evidently thought that this was some new and remarkable expression which Sir Winston applied to himself.

If I am right – and Lady Churchill thinks I am – this does show what dangerous errors historians can make, by being ignorant of the jargon of an age preceding their own.

As my search continued, even though it seemed clear from this letter that Churchill did not suffer from clinical depression, I kept my eyes open for clues about his dark moments. In July 1911, three years after his marriage, he wrote to his wife, whom he was about to join at the seaside, that he had spoken to the wife of a cousin who had 'interested me a great deal by her talk about her doctor in Germany, who completely cured her depression. I think this man might be useful to me – if my black dog returns. He seems quite away from me now – it is such a relief. All the colours come back into the picture. Brightest of all your dear face – my darling.'

As he became older, the depressions came at times of particularly harsh burdens or disappointments: the worst being in 1931. Churchill had lost most of his savings in the American stock market crash. He was no longer a member of the inner counsels of his party. And he had been knocked down and badly hurt by a car while trying to cross the road in New York. It was the physical blow that was the most upsetting for him, and the catalyst to worry. Randolph had among his papers a letter from his mother written from the Bahamas, where his father was recuperating from the accident, in which she told him: 'Papa is progressing, but very slowly. I am sure he will be again as well as before, but he is terribly depressed at the slowness of his recovery and when he is in low spirits murmurs "I *wish* it hadn't happened." He has horrible pains in his neck and shoulders. The doctors call it neuritis but they don't seem to know what to do about it.' She also told her son how on the previous night his father had been 'very sad and said that he had now in the last two years had three very heavy blows. First the loss of all that money in the crash, then the loss of his political position in the Conservative Party and now this terrible physical injury. He said he did not think he would ever recover completely from the three events.'

Churchill did recover, to lead, from 1934, the parliamentary and public campaign against appeasement, to write more books, and to be considered by many as the man most suitable to be Prime Minister in a time of crisis that would need every ounce of vigilance and alertness. It was not until the General Election defeat of 1945 that depression struck again with its full force. His daughter Mary has recalled in her biography of her mother how, on his last weekend at Chequers, with power already behind him, and no daily work arriving in the black and yellow boxes, she saw 'with near desperation a cloud of black doom descend'.

Two years later there was despair of another sort, such as had struck him during the night following Eden's resignation in 1938; the despair and deep sadness based upon a penetrating insight into the likely course of events. This despair had been strongest in the inter-war years immediately after Munich, when he wrote to the French Prime Minister, Paul Reynaud: 'The question now presenting itself is: Can we make head against the Nazi domination, or ought we *severally* to make the best terms possible with it – while trying to rearm? Or is a common effort still possible? For thirty years I have consistently worked with France. I make no defence of my own country; but I do not know on what to rest today.'

The post-war world stirred equal if not worse fears in Churchill's mind. In December 1948 he wrote to Clementine from Marrakech, where he was writing his war memoirs: 'I continue to be depressed about the future. I really do not see how our poor island is going to earn its living when there are so many difficulties around us, and so much ill-will and divisions at home. However, I hope to blot this out of my mind for a few weeks.'

This was prescience, not depression. It was the response of a clever and sensitive person who saw and understood too much. But writing the memoirs, painting, exploring the Moroccan countryside, and playing cards in the evening, he was able to set his cares aside, and to enjoy the companionship of his family and friends, among whom 'Prof' remained a constant and stalwart presence.

Two further elements of deep sadness, difficult to shake off, came during Churchill's second premiership: that brought on by his stroke, when he was seventy-eight, which left him physically weak and unable to work as he had done hitherto; and that brought on by the continuation of the Cold War. It was Colville who noted in his diary shortly after Stalin's death in 1953, at a time when Eden was arguing in favour of retaining the strength of NATO: 'W is depressed by Eden's attitude (which reflects that of the Foreign Office), because he thinks it consigns us to years more of hatred and hostility.' Even more distressing for him, Colville noted, was a report from Washington that President Eisenhower was violently hostile to Russia and did not want to follow the path of conciliation that Churchill so desired to pursue.

For Churchill, depression was not so much a failure to keep the mind free from inner worries, as a reaction to the world's failures, and deep frustration whenever he was not in a position to influence them. This frustration welled up in the months following his resignation in 1955. Randolph was a witness of it one evening at Chartwell. He decided to write to his father a letter for him to see when he woke up. I found it in Churchill's personal files:

> Power must pass and vanish. Glory, which is achieved through a just exercise of power – which itself is accumulated by genius, toil, courage and self-sacrifice – alone remains. Your glory is enshrined for ever on the imperishable plinth of your achievement; and can never be destroyed or tarnished. It will flow with the centuries. So please try to be as happy as you have a right and (if it is not presumptuous for a son to say it) a duty to be. And,

by being happy, make those who love you happy too. All
on one sheet of paper! With devoted love, Randolph.

Amid all the storms of political life, and the problems of Britain and
the world, the 'loving, generous father' was not only part of my
voyage of discovery, but an essential element in the make-up of a
titan.

XII

'Genius and Plod'

Even those who saw Churchill in his youth recognized something of the 'genius, toil, courage and self-sacrifice' that Randolph listed in his letter to his father in 1955, in trying to cheer him up. Even while a schoolboy, his unusual qualities already marked him out as someone out of the ordinary. The first recollection I found went back to those schooldays and came from a fellow schoolboy.

When I began my work for Randolph in 1962 this recollection was already part of the large pile of material awaiting inclusion in the biography. But, as sometimes happened in those days and still happens today, things of importance were set aside by very reason of their importance, and somehow slipped out of sight. When Randolph came to write his first volume this particular recollection was not in the correct file. I found it only after the Churchill papers had been transferred to Oxford from Randolph's home at East Bergholt (where they were kept in the specially-designed strongroom just outside the house). The writer was Sir Murland Evans, and the year that he recalled was 1891. It was a summer's evening 'in one of those dreadful basement rooms in the Headmaster's House, a Sunday evening, to be exact, after chapel evensong'.

> We frankly discussed our futures. After placing me in the Diplomatic Service, perhaps because of my French descent from Admiral de Grasse who was defeated by Lord Rodney in the battle of the Saints, 1782; or alternatively in finance, following my father's career, we came to his own future.
>
> 'Will you go into the army?' I asked.
>
> 'I don't know, it is probable, but I shall have great adventures beginning soon after I leave here.'
>
> 'Are you going into politics? following your famous father?'

'I don't know, but it is more than likely because, you see, I am not afraid to speak in public.'

'You do not seem at all clear about your intentions or desires.'

'That may be, but I have a wonderful idea of where I shall be eventually. I have dreams about it.'

'Where is that?' I enquired.

'Well, I can see vast changes coming over a now peaceful world; great upheavals, terrible struggles; wars such as one cannot imagine; and I tell you London will be in danger – London will be attacked and I shall be very prominent in the defence of London.'

'How can you talk like that?' I said; 'we are for ever safe from invasion, since the days of Napoleon.'

'I see further ahead than you do. I see into the future. This country will be subjected somehow, to a tremendous invasion, by what means I do not know, but [warming up to his subject] I tell you I shall be in command of the defences of London and I shall save London and England from disaster.'

'Will you be a general then, in command of the troops?'

'I don't know; dreams of the future are blurred but the main objective is clear. I repeat – London will be in danger and in the high position I shall occupy, it will fall to me to save the Capital and save the Empire.'

Another of Churchill's fellow schoolboys, Tuttie de Forest (the illegitimate son of the Jewish philanthropist and railway builder Baron de Hirsch) gave me, when in his nineties, a similar account of Churchill's sense of a future at the centre of events. As I read through the Churchill family letters it became clear to what a remarkable extent the schoolboy, whose parents' guests were often from the very centre of British political life, moved with ease among the great figures and controversies of the time, eagerly discussing politics and international affairs with the Balfours and the Asquiths, the Harcourts and the Hicks Beaches. One of his earliest political debates, while he was a teenager and very much a Conservative, was with his Liberal uncle, Lord Tweedmouth, then Chief Liberal Whip.

Shortly after Churchill left Harrow in 1892, he had gone to see the laryngologist Sir Felix Semon, who advised against cutting the ligament that was constricting his tongue and producing the speech impediment from which he suffered all his life. Some years later, Semon recalled in his memoirs how immediately after Churchill had left his consulting room he told his wife: 'I have just seen the most extraordinary young man I have ever met. He is only sixteen years old, and is the eldest son of Lord Randolph Churchill. Without being handsome, his face is very intellectual. After informing me that he had just left Harrow, he added: "I intend to go to Sandhurst, and afterwards to join a regiment of Hussars in India. Of course it is not my intention to become a mere professional soldier. I only wish to gain some experience. Some day I shall be a statesman, as my father was before me."'

Churchill became a soldier: those who saw him in war were impressed by something more than his courage or enthusiasm. In search of more clues to his early development and character, I was struck by a letter he received shortly after his escape from captivity in 1899, from a gunnery expert, Captain Percy Scott, the Military Commandant of the Durban-Pietermaritzburg area. 'I am very proud to have met you', Scott wrote, 'because without any luck you have made a wonderful career. Though I did not shake hands with you in Pietermaritzburg I feel certain that I shall someday shake hands with you as Prime Minister of England. You possess the two necessary qualifications, genius and plod. Combined I believe nothing can keep them back.' Churchill was twenty-five when Scott wrote this letter. Scott, twenty years his senior, died in 1924.

At one point my search for Churchill's character took me to an early newspaper article written about him by one of those who knew him well. In 1898, just after his twenty-fourth birthday, a journalist friend, G.W. Steevens, who had travelled back with him from the war in the Sudan, published a profile in the *Daily Mail*. In it he wrote: 'At present he calls himself a Tory Democrat. Tory, the opinions, might change; democrat, the methods, never. For he has the twentieth century in his marrow.' What would become of him, Steevens asked, of a man who had not yet even stood for Parliament. 'At the rate he goes there will hardly be room for him in Parliament at thirty or in England at forty. It is a pace that cannot last, yet already he holds a vast lead of his contemporaries.'

Steevens went on to write of Churchill's 'queer, shrewd power of introspection, which tells him his gifts and character are such as will make him boom'. This sentence caused me a jolt, for when I read it, I had just been reading a letter Churchill wrote to Clementine from the trenches of the Western Front, nearly twenty years later, in which, after describing how he was nearly in the path of a German shell, commented that if the shell had struck him it would have been 'a final gift – unvalued – to an ungrateful country – an impoverishment of the war-making power of Britain which no one w'd ever know or measure or mourn.'

Seven years after the article by Steevens, and four years after Churchill entered Parliament, the first Churchill biography was published. I naturally read it with close attention: even Randolph had not been born when this first of his, and my, predecessors strode into print.* Its author, Alexander McCallum Scott was the same age as his subject, and had been excited by Churchill's espousal, as a young Conservative, of the basic tenets of liberalism. 'His sympathies are with labour as against the power of organized wealth,' McCallum Scott wrote. 'He is determined that capital shall be made the servant and not the master of the State. He believes that the true happiness of nations is to be secured by industrial development and social reform at home, rather than by territorial expansion abroad.' Of Churchill's future, McCallum Scott had this to say (in 1905):

---

* In the course of my initial work for Randolph I read Churchill biographies by McCallum Scott (1905, revised edition 1916), Bechofer Roberts (1927), H.V. Germains (1931), Hugh Martin (1932), Sir George Arthur (1940), Robert Sencourt (1940), René Kraus (1940), Lewis Broad (1941), Philip Guedalla (1941), Malcolm Thompson (1945), Guy Eden (1945), Virginia Cowles (1953), and Peter de Mendelssohn (1961). This latter, volume one of which went from 1874 to 1911 (no subsequent volumes appeared), was published in the same year that Randolph began his task. It was comprehensive and used at Stour as a basic work of reference. Several hundred other books deal in detail with aspects or phases of Churchill's life, or contain complete chapters devoted to him. There is a comprehensive list (398 pages) of books by and about Churchill, as well as newspaper and magazine articles by him, and his introductions to other people's books, in Frederick Woods, *A Bibliography of the Works of Sir Winston Churchill, KG, OM, CH*, revised edition, London 1969. This too, when it was first published in 1963, served at Stour as an essential handbook.

No one who has studied impartially the varied career and achievements of this young man can doubt that he was born to greatness. Wherever fortune has led him he has pressed forward to the very van. In every work to which he has put his hand he has excelled. He will ever be a leader, whether of a forlorn hope or of a great party.

Already in the House of Commons he leads by natural right which no man can dispute. He does the inevitable act which no one had thought of before; he thinks the original thought which is so simple and obvious when once it has been uttered; he coins the happy phrase which expresses what all men have longed to say, and which thereafter comes so aptly to every man's tongue. He is not simply a unit on one side or the other, and the transference of his vote counts for more than two on a division. He not only thinks, and feels, and speaks; he does, and the crowd who can only follow in beaten tracks do likewise.

'He *does* . . .' It was Churchill's positive actions that made the most immediate impact on his contemporaries. Yet two years before McCallum Scott's biography there is a glimpse of a rather arrogant Churchill through the eyes of the social reformer Beatrice Webb. In July 1903 (Churchill was then twenty-eight) she wrote in her diary of a dinner encounter:

First impression: restless, almost intolerably so, without capacity for sustained and unexcited labour, egotistical, bumptious, shallow-minded and reactionary, but with a certain personal magnetism, great pluck and some originality, not of intellect but of character. More of the American speculator than the English aristocrat.

Talked exclusively about himself and his electioneering plans, wanted me to tell him of someone who would get statistics for him. 'I never do any brainwork that anyone else can do for me,' – an axiom which shows organizing but not thinking capacity. Replete with dodges for winning Oldham against the Labour and Liberal candidates. But I dare say he has a better side, which the ordinary cheap

cynicism of his position and career covers up to a casual
dinner acquaintance.

Bound to be unpopular, too unpleasant a flavour with his
restless self-regarding personality and lack of moral or intellectual refinement. His political tack is Economy, the sort
of essence of a 'Moderate'; he is, at heart, a Little Englander.

Beatrice Webb's conclusion that evening was: 'No notion of scientific research, philosophy, literature or art, still less of religion. But
his pluck, courage, resourcefulness and great tradition may carry him
far, unless he knocks himself to pieces like his father.'

Within a year of this dinner, Churchill had crossed from the Conservative to the Liberal benches in the House of Commons. He had
been forced to give up Oldham but had been elected, as a Liberal,
for Manchester North-West. Within five years of that dinner with
Beatrice Webb he was President of the Board of Trade, at the centre
of the Liberal social reform revolution. The 'pluck, courage and
resourcefulness' she had noted in 1903 were serving him well.

Although now largely forgotten, several important acts of legislation and administration came from Churchill's initiatives. Indeed,
while I was working at Stour through the Churchill papers for the
years 1908 to 1911, it was Churchill the radical legislator that most
surprised, and excited me. By a bizarre coincidence, even as I was
studying these particular files, I was also trying to buy half an acre
of land just outside Oxford, on which to build a house. The problems
of the purchase were made more complicated by a piece of legislation, the Land Commission Act, that was at that very moment being
introduced by Harold Wilson's Labour Government. Under the new
act, the increased value of land bought as farmland and developed
as building land was to be taxed, and taxed heavily. This was one of
the exact proposals Churchill had put forward nearly sixty years
earlier. He had even suggested the identical, and for many people
swingeing, rate of tax: forty per cent.

It was in a speech at Edinburgh in July 1909 that Churchill had
set out his reasons and intentions. From my early days at Stour,
Randolph had impressed upon me the importance of the speeches
that his father made outside Parliament. There was, and still is (in
1993), no complete collection of these. I was fortunate that on the

top floor at Stour were not only the *Hansards* but enormous leather-bound press-cutting books. I spent many hours studying these. At Edinburgh, Churchill had called land ownership 'the mother of all other forms of monopoly'; the profits made from the sale of land 'positively detrimental to the general public'.

It was Lloyd George who gained the radical high ground in 1909 through his People's Budget. But the measures Churchill put on the statute book before the First World War made a marked improvement to the life of Britain. My search through the statute books and archives of the Board of Trade showed how he had set in train substantial statutory improvements in conditions of work on the shop floor. He created a national system of labour exchanges through which the unemployed could seek work and employers find a workforce. He arranged for government shipbuilding orders to be placed in areas of high unemployment. He considerably improved prison conditions, and drastically reduced the numbers of those in prison, introducing the principle of 'time to pay' for debtors, and reducing the number of young people sent to prison. He created the first compulsory arbitration system, whereby those engaged in an industrial dispute could have the benefit of an impartial arbitrator. He introduced reforms in the coal mines, including the provision of pit-head baths, hitherto non-existent. He laid the groundwork, and prepared many of the details, for what became known as Lloyd George's national insurance scheme. He made off-duty life for sailors, and also for airmen, more comfortable. The object of government, he insisted – before the First World War – should be not only to reduce hours of work, but to ensure 'sufficient hours of leisure'. After the First World War he introduced State-assisted pensions for widows and orphans, and reduced the income tax paid by those on the lowest incomes. His aim, he told his advisers at the Treasury in 1925, was 'to make finance less proud, and industry more contented'. His views on education, as relevant in 1897 as now, were that no barriers of class or creed should interfere with opportunity.*

---

* 'The object of governments should be the equal education of the whole people, not the advantage of any one sect,' Winston Churchill, handwritten pencil notes on a published parliamentary debate, 1897. 'Old-fashioned prejudices and snobberies can have no place in education or society,' John Major, radio interview, 22 January 1992.

The list of Churchill's reform measures is impressive. The Tory Democrat who became an active Liberal and then a Conservative again (at the age of fifty-six) could look with pride at the legislation he had put on the statute book. There was, however, something beyond legislation that drew me deeper in my search from its earliest days. Essentially, it was a deep well of kindness, an ability to encourage the young, and to enter sympathetically into other people's problems. Desmond Flower, the young publisher who supervised the printing of *The Second World War* and *A History of the English-speaking Peoples*, wrote to me in 1976: 'With all the stories of how impossible he could be in every way at times, not only in the heat of war, how come that I always looked forward to our next meeting and always found him so gentle with me? Particularly when we lunched alone together, which was hilarious.'

Churchill's generous nature was recalled by many of those who knew him well. Two months after I took over from Randolph, I went to see Field Marshal Earl Alexander of Tunis at his house at Winkfield, on the edge of Windsor Great Park. As a former private soldier, this was a somewhat nerve-wracking prospect for me. But Alexander quickly put me at my ease. Among the stories he told me was one about a Cabinet meeting in 1952, when Alexander was Minister of Defence. During the meeting Churchill began to run down the army and Alexander, whereupon Alexander burst out: 'That's all nonsense. You don't know anything about the army.'

Alexander told me: 'I was very outspoken. Winston just grunted. When I had finished my outburst I thought, "That's done it. I've overstepped the mark." That same night we were to dine together at a mutual friend's house. I was rather anxious. Winston came up to me and I began to apologize. Then a smile came over his face. "Dear boy", he said, "you said what you felt had to be said." And we sat down to dinner. He bore no malice.'

There was another indicator to Churchill's kindness in a letter he received in 1937 from the widow of a political opponent, Philip Snowden, a Labour Chancellor of the Exchequer and a formidable, and at times acerbic opponent. After Snowden's death, Lady Snowden, herself an active socialist (and a leading member of the temperance movement) wrote to Churchill: 'Your generosity to a political opponent marks you for ever in my eyes the "great gentleman" I have always thought you. Had I been in trouble which I could not control myself, there is none to whom I should have felt I could come with more confidence that I should be gently treated.'

There are rather few of whom this can be said, even outside the political fray. It marks a quality which, by its very nature, would remain little known beyond those who were its beneficiaries. In all the avenues of my search, finding this characteristic seemed to me the most rewarding.

XIII

Diaries and Diarists

When I started work for Randolph in 1962, I was in the early stages of writing a short book of my own, an anthology of British attitudes to Germany between 1933 and 1939. Randolph looked on my plan with an encouraging eye and was eager to hear what nuggets came my way. (Once, when he told me a story about his father, he hastily added, 'That is for *my* book, not *your* book.') I hoped to include in my volume (which I subsequently set aside; perhaps one day I will take it up again) hitherto unpublished contemporary letters from people who had visited Germany in the Nazi era, or had commented in their letters and diaries on the rise and dominance of Nazism before the outbreak of war. One of the people I approached in 1963 was Sir Harold Nicolson, who had been a Member of Parliament before the war, and a writer and journalist of distinction.

I went to see Nicolson at his flat in Albany, just off Piccadilly. He showed me a bulging folder full of handwritten and typewritten pages. It was an untidy bundle, but from the moment I began to look at it I saw that it was a historical goldmine. In the ensuing thirty years the number of published diaries burgeoned. Among them, the three-volume Nicolson diaries were a pioneer. When he first handed me his somewhat scruffy sheets of paper the idea of publishing diaries of that period had not taken hold. He told me he doubted that his late-night thoughts merited publication. If I wanted, I could take them away with me. He had no copies, so he would like them back in due course.

The Nicolson diary was so remarkable a document that I suggested to him that it ought to be published. The references to Churchill cast a vivid light on his parliamentary activities at the height of the appeasement era and during the first year of the Second World War. I wrote out each of those references in pencil in a large notebook;

when I was next at Stour I got mounting credit in the Boss's eyes as I read them out at the Disraeli desk.

Nicolson had been in the Commons for Churchill's first parliamentary speech after his return to the Admiralty and the War Cabinet in September 1939. The speech was made with the Prime Minister, Neville Chamberlain, looking on. Nicolson commented in his diary:

> The effect of Winston's speech was infinitely greater than could be derived from any reading of the text. His delivery was amazing, and he sounded every note from deep preoccupation to flippancy, from resolution to sheer boyishness. One could feel the spirit of the House rising with every word.
>
> It was obvious afterwards that the PM's inadequacy and lack of inspiration had been demonstrated even to his warmest supporters. In those twenty minutes Churchill brought himself nearer the post of Prime Minister than he has ever been before.
>
> In the lobbies afterwards even Chamberlainites were saying 'We have now found our leader.' Old parliamentary hands confessed that never in their experience had they seen a single speech so change the temper of the House.

Before the war, Nicolson had been a determined anti-appeaser. By contrast, R.A. Butler had been an enthusiast for conciliation with Germany even after Munich. He and Randolph had been quarrelling about it for thirty years. It was in an attempt to patch up that quarrel that 'Rab' invited me to spend a weekend with him at Trinity College, Cambridge, where he was Master. I took the train that used to run between Oxford and Cambridge, long since closed down and its bridges dismantled. Once more, Randolph was exceptionally curious to know what would emerge, even insisting that I telephone him from the Master's Lodgings when everyone else had gone to bed. In fact, 'Rab' kept me up almost as long after dinner as Randolph used to. He wanted me to see the diary he had kept, and which he produced for me after dinner to read aloud to him as he sat in his deep armchair, behind which a signed photograph of Neville Chamberlain was the only decoration.

I began to read out loud from the diary. Butler listened attentively for a while, and then began to doze. Finally he fell asleep. I went on reading aloud, but could not wake him, and from time to time I would break off to jot down one of the entries. In due course he woke up, and it was time for both of us to go to bed. Many years later I published a few snippets from the diary in volume six of the biography. To my surprise, I received a pained letter from one of Butler's biographers, insisting that Butler had never kept a diary. He had of course, and must either have caused it to be destroyed, or hidden it away where it still lies, or mislaid it. Until it is found, my few snippets remain the only evidence for its existence, and for his night thoughts.

For Randolph, the most fascinating, and as he saw it disgraceful, entry is that for 13 March 1940, written five months after the defeat of Poland, then under Gestapo rule. Butler was at that time Under-Secretary of State for Foreign Affairs. His boss, Lord Halifax, had discussed with him that day the outlook for a negotiated peace. Butler wrote in his diary: 'I said I would not exclude a truce if Mussolini, the Pope and Roosevelt would come in.' Butler also recorded Halifax's reply: 'You are very bold, what a challenging statement, but I agree with you.'

There was a sequel to my visit to Trinity College. Some months later I was invited to lunch by Lady Christabel Aberconway, one of those elderly Liberal ladies about whom Randolph would always sing: 'She was one of those flash-eyed "gels", one of the *old* brigade.' In the course of her recollections of Churchill in 1914, she told me that Butler had recounted the following story: in 1943 he went to see Churchill at Chequers. The Prime Minister was in bed with Nelson the cat snuggly curled up on his feet. 'This cat', Churchill told his about-to-be appointed Minister of Education, 'does more for the war effort than you do. He acts as a hot-water bottle and saves fuel and power.'*

I described briefly in an earlier chapter another diary success that I had in those early Randolph days, when, in the course of my

---

* Christabel Aberconway published this story (without mentioning Butler by name) as a footnote in her book *A Dictionary of Cat Lovers*. She gave me a copy of the book when we met in London on 18 February 1963.

own work on appeasement, I contacted Lord Harvey of Tasburgh, a distinguished diplomat. We had lunched together at his club in St James's, and I asked him various questions about British foreign policy in 1938 and 1939, which he answered in general terms. Later he invited me to his flat overlooking Hyde Park. I expected yet more general answers, but hardly had I sat down than he said, rather shyly, that he had been thinking over my earlier questions and refreshing his memory from a diary he had kept at the time. He then produced the diary and read out various extracts which he told me I was at liberty to note down. I did so, and took some fine nuggets with me to Randolph that evening.

Randolph, harboured an intense dislike of Anthony Eden for what he considered the pusillanimity of the Suez débâcle in 1956. He was much incensed by Lord Harvey's record of a talk with Eden in June 1941, in which Harvey recorded: 'He told me how difficult the PM was: in spite of splendid qualities as a popular leader, he had a devastating effect on planning.' The 'great need' of the hour was for a Minister of Defence 'independent of the PM'.

Harvey's diary contained many valuable descriptions. An entry during January 1942, as Japanese forces advanced into Malaya and Burma, reported Churchill's desire to fly to India to consult with Indian leaders about the formation of an assembly 'to work out a constitution after the war'. It was more than four decades since Churchill had been in India (Sir Alexander Cadogan, another diarist who referred to this plan when Churchill presented it to the War Cabinet, called it 'brilliantly imaginative and bold').* Harvey noted something else, that Churchill's doctors doubted he was well enough for such a long journey by air: 'His heart is not too good and he needs rest.' Eden told Harvey that Churchill had 'confessed that he did feel his heart a bit – he had tried to dance a little the other night but found he quickly lost his breath!' Harvey commented, on Churchill's determination to make the journey: 'What a decision to take, and how gallant of the old boy himself! But his age and more especially his way of life must begin to tell on him. He had beer,

* Sir Alexander Cadogan's diary, edited by David Dilks and an important source for the war years, was published shortly after I began my work.

three ports and three brandies for lunch today, and has done it for years.'

In the event, Churchill did not go, not because of his health, but because he felt that he ought to be in charge in London when, as was becoming inevitable, Singapore fell to the Japanese. That would be a testing time at Westminster. But Churchill was still to make many long and arduous journeys: to Moscow, to Teheran, to the Crimea, to the United States, and to North Africa.

I suggested to Harvey, as I had to Nicolson, that his diary ought to be published. At that time, however, the idea of publication did not appeal to a civil servant for whom the mere fact of keeping a diary was somehow frowned upon. After Harvey's death in 1968 his son wrote to me to say that the diary would be published; he had edited it in two volumes.

The children of diarists have been among my most helpful providers of material. Shortly after Randolph's death I asked Julian Amery if I could see his father's diary. Leo Amery had been at school with Churchill at Harrow. From 1924 to 1929 they had both served in Baldwin's Cabinet. In 1940 Churchill made Amery Secretary of State for India. Julian, who had fought and lost the Preston seat alongside Randolph in 1945, and was himself subsequently a Cabinet minister, let me delve into the enormous mass of his father's diaries in the basement of his London house. They too have since been published. They provided many insights into Churchill's thought. He and Amery had travelled together across the Atlantic in 1929, shortly after the fall of the Baldwin Government. During the voyage Amery noted in his diary Churchill's comment that his only consolation for the failure of the Dardanelles campaign 'was that God wished things to be prolonged in order to sicken mankind of war, and that therefore He had interfered with a project that would have brought the war to a speedier conclusion'. Churchill's other evidence that God existed, he told Amery, 'was the existence of Lenin and Trotsky, for whom a hell was needed'.

Amery also recorded a remark by Churchill that highlights his verbal wit. To Amery's suggestion that Churchill might find himself breaking away from the Conservative Party when the Party moved back to tariffs and protectionism, Churchill replied: 'I shall stick to you with all the loyalty of a leech.'

On that particular journey Randolph had also kept a diary. I was with him at Stour one evening when he asked me to read it aloud to him: he was then writing his own memoirs.* In this diary he recorded two of my favourite examples of Churchill's spontaneous remarks. When, one night, after a day driving through the Canadian woodlands, they saw from their hotel window in Quebec the Rother-mere paper mills all lit up, Churchill remarked: 'Fancy cutting down those beautiful trees we saw this afternoon to make pulp for those newspapers, and calling it civilization.' Two weeks later, in Calgary, after Randolph had criticized the lack of culture of the Calgary oil magnates, his father mused: 'Cultured people are merely the glittering scum which floats upon the deep river of production!'

Sometimes a diary could make a decisive difference to Churchill's story. This was particularly true of his two years as Secretary of State for War from 1919 to 1921. His principal military adviser at that time, and Chief of the Imperial General Staff, was Field Marshal Sir Henry Wilson, whom he had known since the turn of the century, and whose widow had published a highly-edited version of his diary in the 1920s. I was determined to see the full and unexpurgated original. Its custodian, Wilson's nephew, not only agreed that I could read his uncle's diaries, but, when I drove from Oxford to Hampshire to see them, told me I was welcome to take all twelve books away with me for as long as I needed them.

The Henry Wilson diaries were a crucial contemporary source for Churchill's actions and thoughts over a two-year period: when I finished my work on them the nephew agreed that they should be deposited in the Imperial War Museum and made available to all. One entry pleased me both for its content and its circumstances. In his own recollection of Armistice Day, 11 November 1918, written ten years later, Churchill wrote that he and Lord Birkenhead dined alone with Lloyd George that night. But Wilson had dined with them, noting in his diary: 'LG wants to shoot the Kaiser: Winston does not.'

As well as the diary, Wilson's papers included many of his letters, in one of which, to a fellow general, he wrote of Churchill: 'He has

---

* They were published in 1964 as Randolph S. Churchill, *Twenty-One Years*. The 1929 diary, the only one Randolph kept, is published extensively on pages 71 to 87.

many good qualities, some of which lie hidden, and he has many bad ones, all of which are in the shop window.'

When I began my work for Randolph in 1962 one of the most frequently consulted sources for the Dardanelles was General Sir Ian Hamilton's *Gallipoli Diary*. It was one of the most heavily thumbed books in Randolph's library. Wanting to see the original, I made contact with Mrs Mary Shield, the General's secretary in 1916, and his companion for the rest of his life. She invited Susie and me to her home in Hampshire and went out of her way to be helpful. There was, she said, no original diary. The General (to whom she was devoted) had not kept a diary at Gallipoli. The book I had seen and used, and of which I wished to see the original, had been written after the event.

In June 1916, seven months after Hamilton had been recalled to London, and more than a year after he had gone to Gallipoli, while preparing evidence for the Dardanelles Commission of Enquiry, he began to dictate what was headed 'The Private Diary of General Sir Ian Hamilton'. Mrs Shield showed me the typescript: the General had dictated it to her. He was aided in his reconstruction of past events by a brief factual account kept by his personal clerk at Gallipoli, Sergeant-Major H.G. Stuart, and by the official telegrams and letters that he had brought back from the Peninsula.

Mrs Shield told me that Hamilton had dictated quickly (which made her work all the harder), as he wanted his 'diary' to be ready for Churchill to use when he came to prepare his own evidence for the Commission. Thanks to Mrs Shield's secretarial efforts the work was ready in time for Churchill to cite it in his own evidence. Hamilton later elaborated on the details, and in places altered the contents of the recollections, which were published in 1920 with the misleading title *Gallipoli Diary*. Thanks to Mrs Shield, I was able to avoid the pitfall of using the diary as a genuine contemporary jotting, and to quote only from the 'original' June 1916 typescript, while alerting my readers to the nature of that document. To this day, however, the diary is quoted as if it were a genuine contemporary document, written in the heat of battle, or at least within sight of the battle (for Hamilton had spent much of his time watching the action for which he was responsible from on board ship).

Another published diary that I tried to find in its original form was that of Lord Riddell, the press proprietor and owner of the *News of the World* and *Country Life*. His three volumes, in particular the volume for the years up to 1914, contain many splendid episodes in which Churchill appears. I failed despite a long search to find the original, or even to ascertain if it still existed. The published version is illuminating for anyone seeking to draw a portrait of Churchill. Here is an entry from August 1911. Riddell was driving through South London with Churchill. 'He spoke enthusiastically of the day when the working classes would live in fine blocks of dwellings with central cooking and heating, swimming baths etc., subsidized by the State or municipality.'

In November 1911 Riddell and Churchill were playing golf together. 'He is a charming companion, full of witty, amusing, unexpected sayings – never dull, never tedious. I find him a most considerate and loyal friend. He is also kind-hearted. The other day we came across a worm on the golf course. Winston tenderly picked it up and placed it in the bracken, saying, "Poor fellow! If I leave you here, you will be trampled upon by some ruthless boot!"'

In search of unpublished diaries, I would turn to Churchill's visitors' book at Chartwell for whatever period I had reached, and write to those who appeared in it, on the off-chance that they had kept a diary. On one occasion I was particularly rewarded. The visitors' book showed that among the guests on 21 September 1928 was James Scrymgeour-Wedderburn, then twenty-six years old, and at the time of my work on the 1920s, Minister of State for Foreign Affairs and Deputy Conservative Leader in the House of Lords (as 11th Earl of Dundee). In response to my letter, asking for reminiscences, he said he could go one better: he had kept a diary of his visit. It was a gem, and included a glimpse of one of Churchill's closest friends, Professor Lindemann, about whom every reference is welcome, his presence being so often shadowy:

> Winston is building with his own hands a house for his butler, and also a new garden wall. He works at bricklaying four hours a day, and lays 90 bricks an hour, which is a very high output. He also spends a considerable time on the last volume of his war memoirs which he is writing. His ministerial work comes down from the Treasury every day, and he has to give some more hours to that.

It is a marvel how much time he gives to his guests, talking sometimes for an hour after lunch and much longer after dinner. He is an exceedingly kind and generous host, providing unlimited champagne, cigars and brandy.

Even poor old Prof, who is really a teetotaller, is compelled to drink ten cubic centimetres of brandy at a time, because he was once rash enough to tell Winston that the average human being could imbibe ten c.c. of brandy without causing any detectable change in his metabolism.

On the following day Scrymgeour-Wedderburn wrote another entry in his diary:

Last night I had the great privilege of two hours' conversation with Winston alone.

He began by asking how old I was. When I said twenty-six, he replied 'Ah! The age at which Napoleon was given command of the French Army of Italy,' and he then discoursed for some time on the changes in military tactics and strategy since 1795, and stressed the importance of the revolution brought about by the invention of tanks and armoured cars, which were incomparably superior to the cavalry for all purposes.

When he becomes engrossed in his subject he strides up and down the room with his head thrust forward and his thumbs in the armholes of his waistcoat, as if he were trying to keep pace with his own eloquence. If he shows signs of slowing down, all you have to do is to make some moderately intelligent observation, and off he goes again.

Many published diaries also contained insights for my search, but the editing of diaries is not easy, and not all published diaries are a full reflection of the original. I know from my own editing of the Churchill papers, which has now reached the Second World War, just how difficult and numerous an editor's problems can be: deciphering handwriting, finding (if they can be found) missing or misplaced pages, tracking down the information needed to explain obscure references, identifying people only mentioned by their initials or (often even harder) the initials of their job, and making sense of allusions to long-forgotten episodes.

Diaries do not always tell the whole story, or necessarily follow up a story. Nor can they always dispel myths: indeed, a diarist might be the first person to set down a myth, becoming the originator of error rather than error's enemy. One Churchill episode, widely repeated in diaries, letters and recollections – it may or may not be true – has long eluded me. When Churchill returned to the Admiralty in 1939 it was said that a three-word naval signal was sent to all ships, 'Winston is back.' Despite repeated trawling in the archives I have never managed to find this signal. If apocryphal, it must rank with Churchill's alleged reply to an Admiral who had protested that the provision of better conditions for ordinary seamen was 'against the traditions' of the Royal Navy: 'Traditions! What traditions? Rum, sodomy – and the lash!'

I once gave a graphic rendering of this reply (though it does not appear in any of my volumes) during an evening reception in Chicago, only to be unexpectedly and forcefully rebuked by my host, a retired ambassador, who insisted that the story was apocryphal. I felt ashamed to have been caught telling it, being always so scornful myself of unauthenticated stories.

The dilemma of establishing authenticity is ever-present with Churchill, around whom everyone naturally wishes to attach their favourite story. Certainly many of the widely-circulated stories of the 1920s, which were originally attached to long-forgotten characters like William Joynson-Hicks (Jix) and the 1st Earl of Birkenhead ('FE') are now given Churchill as their source to make them more interesting. Did Churchill ever say to Nancy Astor, 'If I were your husband, I would drink it?' after she had said, 'If I was your wife I would put poison in your coffee.' I have no idea, though several old-timers suggested to me that the original of Winston in this tale was in fact FE (a much heavier drinker than Churchill, and a notorious acerbic wit).

One often-repeated story is that in 1940, after a dispute with General de Gaulle, Churchill remarked, 'The greatest cross I have to bear is the Cross of Lorraine.' I published this in the first edition of my one-volume *Churchill: A Life*. Within a week of publication several readers had written to me to point out that the phrase was not Churchill's at all, but that of his liaison officer with de Gaulle, General Spears. They were right; hanging my head in shame, I amended my version for subsequent editions.

In the multi-volume biography, with every story which came to me through the prism of time and memory, I indicated in the text itself the nature of its source (as opposed to relegating the source to the back of the book). I felt that it was essential for the reader to be able to judge, on the page itself, the type of evidence being offered. Any fact or quotation, if introduced as coming from a diary, will alert the reader to the possibility that the word 'diary' covers certain all-too-frequent limitations: writing-up after the event, as in the case of General Hamilton; or the poetic licence of the diarist even when the words are written down at the time.

Perhaps the most disturbing discovery I have made on sources for Churchill's life came after I had finished the eighth and final volume of the biography, in which a major source, for me as for all historians of his last twenty years, was the voluminous diary kept by Churchill's doctor, Lord Moran. Throughout the period of my researches the diary was closed to historians. Then, after the completion of an authorized life of the doctor, it was brought to a leading medical library in London. I asked for the diary entry for a single date (I wanted to reproduce the published version in facsimile in the second of my Churchill Second World War document volumes). To my dismay, not merely for myself but for historical truth, I was told by the custodian of the papers that there was no entry for that day at all, even though an entry under that exact date appears in the published book. Even the entries that did exist, I was told, were 'not a diary in the accepted sense of the word'. The mind boggles at how much misinformation may have crept into the history books, mine included, by such routes. As in the marketplace for fruit and vegetables, so for diaries, *caveat emptor*, let the purchaser beware.

The very last diary that I traced was far from spurious. By chance, I had met its author during my days as a Randolphian 'ghost'. I had been giving a lecture, in my graduate hat, to the pupils of Tudor Hall, not far from Oxford. After the lecture a thirteen-year-old schoolgirl introduced herself. Her father, she said, had been Churchill's Private Secretary. My own work was then so firmly focused on the pre-First World War period, about which I had indeed been lecturing to the girls, that I smiled affably and forgot all about it.

Twenty years later, when I was putting the finishing touches to the final volume of the biography, and looking for contemporary evidence about Churchill's cruises on *Christina*, his Private Secretary at the time, Anthony Montague Browne, told me that his daughter Jane had been on one of them. Jane was the girl I had been introduced to at Tudor Hall. Her mother had made it a condition of her taking time off school that she keep a diary of the trip. This the seven-year-old girl had done. It included a charming passage which portrayed a very old man still able to enjoy life: at Port of Spain, Trinidad, she wrote: 'Sir Winston was cheered by the people on the quay.'

When the adults went ashore for a strenuous bout of sightseeing, or were down below dressing for dinner, or packing, Jane would stay on deck with Churchill. Among her treasures was a photograph of the two of them off the Canary Islands. In Jane's diary was a curious link with the previous 'diarist' of this chapter: on that same cruise she noted: 'Yesterday night I played snap with Lord Moran.'

Jane Montague Browne's diary entries, with their glimpses of Churchill's life at the age of eighty-six, were among the final pieces in my mosaic.

XIV

Harold Macmillan

When I began work with Randolph, the Prime Minister was Harold Macmillan. My first contact with him came at a distance. Encouraged to do so by Randolph, in July 1963 I had sent him a copy of my first book, *The Appeasers*, written with Richard Gott, my first Oxford pupil. Four days later Macmillan was photographed sitting in a train about to leave London for Derbyshire. The photograph was headed 'Case of the busy Premier.' The caption read: 'Mr Harold Macmillan rummages through the contents of a well-worn attaché case as he settles down on a train for Matlock at St Pancras Station, London.' The Prime Minister was leaving to spend the weekend at Chatsworth with his nephew, the Duke of Devonshire. In front of him in the photograph was a book that he had just taken out of the case. It was *The Appeasers*. On top of it was his spectacle-case.

As I recalled it when preparing this chapter, that was the last contact I had with Macmillan for at least a year. No doubt I would have written just that, but for the golden rule of historical evidence, which I learned the hard way in my search for Churchill: never fully trust any recollection. Beware of memory, even one's own! Looking through some old correspondence files I found that it was only two weeks after the 'Case of the busy Premier' that I wrote to him to ask, in connection with a book about refugees from Hitler that I was thinking of writing (but never wrote), about the help he was said to have given to Jewish refugees in Britain shortly before the Second World War. His Private Secretary, John Wyndham, replied that the Prime Minister had indeed given shelter to a number of refugees in 1938: 'He lent them a house on his estate.' The estate was Birch Grove in Sussex. Later I learned that in South Wales James Callaghan had also helped Jewish refugees, while in Grantham Margaret Thatcher's parents had taken in a Jewish refugee girl from Germany.

It was a different story when Churchill, as Chancellor of Bristol University, had written to his Vice-Chancellor to ask if Bristol would take a German Jewish dental student whose parents had appealed to him. The answer was a determined negative. Bristol University, it seems, did not want to open its doors any further even for its Chancellor. For several years I was concerned about the fate of the student. Did he get refuge somewhere? Did he survive the war? By chance, I mentioned the story, and the student's name, in a lecture in the United States, somewhere in the Midwest. After the lecture someone in the audience told me that the man lived in that very city. We met and corresponded. He could not believe that if Winston Churchill had written on his behalf, the Vice-Chancellor would not have complied. In my long search for Churchill, I found many occasions when, despite his intervention, his will was not executed.

I made a note of Macmillan's help for refugees in my file, where I found it while writing this chapter. When the political crisis of 1964 erupted and 'Macmillan Must Go' became the shrill cry of many in the Conservative Party, Randolph, himself a former Conservative MP, mounted a fierce pro-Macmillan campaign. As always happened during our Churchill work at Stour, which was itself hardly sluggish, the arrival of an outside cause created electric currents. 'We're off,' Randolph said one early afternoon, and proceeded to drive across country with me to Rab Butler's constituency at Saffron Walden. There, at a meeting addressed by his brother-in-law Christopher Soames, then Minister of Agriculture, Randolph stood quietly at the back until the local Party Chairman asked for questions. He then called out in his booming voice: 'What I want to know is – Is Mr Butler loyal to the Prime Minister?'

There was consternation on the platform. The Chairman tried to have the question ruled out of order, but Rab, recognizing his adversary, agreed to answer it, and, somewhat nervously, attested to his loyalty.

Randolph's efforts to keep Macmillan at Number Ten were intensified by his contempt for Butler, whom he accused of being one of the worst of the pre-war appeasers, a man who would have done anything, however dishonourable, to keep Britain out of the war. By contrast, Macmillan was Randolph's ideal of the patriotic anti-appeaser, the man who had fought throughout the First World War, and who had supported his father's call for rearmament in the 1930s. Hence the zeal to champion Macmillan's cause, even when it had almost no other champions.

I was a bystander as Randolph tried to mobilize support for the Prime Minister. I helped him, if only with points of grammar, with his newspaper articles demanding that all good Tories stand up and be counted on Macmillan's side. I waved him off from the lawn at Stour as he flew by helicopter to Macmillan's house at Birch Grove, then on to Lord Beaverbrook at Cherkely, then on to his father at Chartwell, in an attempt to show the flag. When Macmillan resigned, I watched as Randolph urged the Party leaders, mostly in long, late-night telephone calls, to support Quintin Hogg for Prime Minister. Anything to keep Rab out. Special lapel buttons were printed, with a blue 'Q' for Quintin on them, to be distributed at the Conservative Party Conference. Unfortunately for Randolph's campaign, though no doubt less decisively for Hogg's premiership, no pins were fitted to them, so they could not be affixed to the lapel. Hundreds remained in their boxes. I have one in front of me as a write.

In the event, the prize went to Lord Home. Randolph, a day or two before, had got the scent of it. He asked me to take notes as he telephoned to The Hirsel, Lord Home's house in Scotland, to see if he could learn what was going on at the source. The butler who answered the telephone gave Randolph one of the biggest chuckles I ever heard. Assuming that all callers must be peers, he replied to Randolph's request to speak to his master: 'My Lord, I am sorry, his Lordship is walking in the garden with Her Majesty.'

'Beat that' was Randolph's comment, as he mused whether 'Her Majesty' was the Queen or (more likely) the Queen Mother.

Five years after Macmillan resigned from the Premiership I met him for the first time, at Randolph's funeral. He asked me about the work and what would become of the biography, and offered to help with his own recollections if ever his help was needed. In 1970 he invited me to Birch Grove, where he spoke with enthusiasm of how he, a believer between the wars in the 'Middle Way' of Conservatism, and in the evolution of a fair and opportunity-based society, had been attracted to Churchill's social reform plans in the 1920s, including State-assisted pensions for widows and orphans. He also spoke with a certain scorn of Churchill's 'absurd Gallic sympathies'.

There was an elderly guest present at the lunch whose name I had failed to catch when we were introduced. During the conversation, Macmillan suddenly commented, with vigour, on how wicked the old Conservative Party had been. Did you know, he asked me, that in those days Prime Ministers even gave peerages to their in-laws? My indignation at this fact was nothing compared to the alarm it seemed to cause the older guest. I later found out that this was Viscount Stuart of Findhorn, ennobled by Macmillan in 1959, who was married to Macmillan's sister-in-law.

The question of peerages was one to which all twentieth-century British historians were introduced by Lloyd George, to whom one prospective peer is said to have sent the large cheque, the prerequisite of his peerage, signed not in his current name but in the surname he would only receive after he had been created a peer. Macmillan may have ennobled his sister-in-law's husband; Churchill ennobled his doctor, Sir Charles Wilson (created Lord Moran), and was rewarded within weeks of his death by the publication of his doctor's diary.

In 1972 I received a letter from Macmillan out of the blue. He had been reading the first of my Churchill volumes, covering the years 1914 to 1916, what he called in his letter 'the most critical and poignant years in the first half of Churchill's life'. As for so many of Macmillan's generation the First World War, in which he had fought for two years and been wounded, had been the testing time. Two months later he came to see Susie and me at the Map House. He was old and frail, but tenacious, insisting on mounting the stairs, which had rather a sharp turn in them, unaided. He spoke entrancingly about the inter-war years, of the struggle to keep up morale when so many MPs rejected the sense of urgency of danger. In 1936 he had been one of those back-bench Conservatives who argued that Churchill should be made Minister of Defence. In February 1938 he was one of twenty-two Conservative MPs who joined with Churchill to express their support for Eden's resignation by abstaining on a Labour Vote of No Confidence. In October 1938 he and Churchill were among thirty MPs who abstained after the Munich debate, in protest against what they saw as the betrayal of Czechoslovakia. Macmillan had also joined Churchill in opposing the adjournment of the House in the aftermath of Munich, telling his fellow MPs, in

Churchillian tones: 'We are being treated more and more as a kind of Reichstag to meet only to hear the orations and register the decrees of the government of the day.'

In November 1938, when Churchill appealed for fifty Conservatives to follow him into the Lobby in support of the immediate establishment of a Ministry of Supply, only two had done so, Brendan Bracken and Harold Macmillan. It was a humiliation for Churchill, and he felt it as such. Macmillan was proud that he had stood up to be counted, amid the frowns of disapproval from his party and its leaders.

In March 1939 Macmillan had joined Churchill, and thirty other Conservative MPs, in a call for a national government, to meet the growing danger of German aggression. A week later, when Italy invaded Albania, he had been with Churchill at Chartwell, where he witnessed the incredible energy of a man who had been out of political office for almost ten years, but who conducted the day as if he were in charge of a Service Ministry, calling for maps, telephoning the Prime Minister, sending an urgent message to the First Lord of the Admiralty, laying out a strategy to deter Mussolini from further aggression. 'He alone seemed to be in command,' Macmillan later recalled, 'when everyone else was dazed and hesitating.'

As Macmillan left the Map House, he asked, in his self-deprecatory way, if I would care to come to see him when I reached the Second World War years, if I thought he could be of help. As I did not see myself reaching this period for about eight or ten years, I said, without thinking, 'I will try to reach that volume as quickly as I can.' He smiled and replied, 'Don't hurry, dear boy, don't hurry.' I didn't. And he was still there to help me a decade later.

In 1974, on the eve of the General Election, Lord Stockton visited the Map House again. I had just reached Churchill's Exchequer Years, and his first Budget, in 1925. As a young MP, only just elected, Macmillan had spoken in the Budget debate and, *The Times* reported, had caught Churchill's own 'spirit of audacity' by giving the social reform measures his 'undubious and provocative acceptance'. I had written to Macmillan about this a few days before his visit. 'I recall not very much,' he replied. 'You would no doubt have documents that would jog my fading memory.' We sat in my study, I read him the documents I had found, including many of his own handwritten letters of which he had kept no copies at the time, and he reminisced.

It was eleven years since he had been Prime Minister. During his visit he correctly forecast a Labour victory and Harold Wilson's return to Downing Street. Once again I was having a tutorial on Churchill's time as Chancellor, this time from a former Prime Minister. During a brief encounter in 1925 he had mentioned to Churchill the possibility of stimulating industry by taking away the burden of the rates. It was a chance remark, but Churchill did not forget it. Two years later, when he embarked upon a major scheme to get rid of the rates on industry, he gave Macmillan a room at the Treasury. Macmillan's comments on derating as it evolved were of enormous help to Churchill in making the scheme acceptable to the Conservatives. 'I remember years ago', Macmillan later wrote to me, 'Churchill saying "I will be judged by the written word." With him conversation was an amusement, a mental stimulus and a way of probing and testing other people's thoughts. Although he did not appear to listen, he never missed anything. The origins of derating which he attributes to a chance remark of mine two years before is an example.'

It was from Chatsworth, where Macmillan had gone with *The Appeasers* in 1963, that he had sent Churchill in 1928 a long handwritten critique of the derating scheme. I read this to him as we worked together. His tired hooded eyes seemed, as he listened, to be transported back across the years. He chuckled aloud when I read the sentence in which he warned Churchill that opposition would come from those Conservatives who 'are anxious to see a policy of drift erected into a system'; men, Churchill added 'who suffer from "tranquillity" as men suffer from sleeping sickness'.

There was to be nothing tranquil about Churchill's reform plans. For him, in 1928, Macmillan's help was like a breath of fresh air. 'It is always pleasant to find someone whose mind grasps the essentials and proportions of a large plan,' he wrote to Macmillan from Chartwell, at a time when heavy storms had cut the roads to London. 'In fact', Churchill told him, 'the wireless was our only connection with the outer world; and that can be switched off at will – altogether a most unusual and by no means a disagreeable sensation.' For his part, Macmillan had been so attracted to Churchill's thinking that he told him: 'It will put fresh hope and enthusiasm into the hearts of all those who have supported the Conservative Party because they honestly believe it to be a party capable of constructive thought and progressive effort.'

During our talk, I told Macmillan about the problems I was having with my publishers, who had refused to take into account the rapidly accelerating inflation, with the result that I was being forced to find other literary work in order to subsidize the biography. In particular, I was having to subsidize work on the Churchill document volumes by doing other books, a time-consuming and distracting effort. Macmillan, a publisher himself (his father had published Churchill's two-volume *Lord Randolph Churchill* in 1906), was indignant on my behalf, as Jock Colville had earlier been.

A week later Macmillan telephoned from his home in Sussex. He had been in London that day, he told me, and had taken the opportunity of going to see my publishers to argue my case. They had sent him away without any satisfaction. 'Do you know', he said, 'they treated me like an underling.' Arguing that the scale of the biography was too long for commercial success, the publishers were also insisting that the whole of the Second World War should be covered in a single volume. Macmillan had opposed this, and successfully so, writing to me a few days later, 'At any rate two volumes has been agreed which is essential.'

As instructed by Macmillan in my Oxford days, I did not hurry. When I reached the Second World War he was still alive, and eager to help. He had seen Churchill at close quarters on several momentous occasions. On 8 May 1940, in the smoking-room of the House of Commons, shortly before Churchill was due to speak in defence of the Norwegian campaign and Chamberlain's Government, Macmillan wished him luck but hoped that his speech would not be too convincing. 'Why not?' asked Churchill. 'Because we must have a new Prime Minister,' Macmillan replied, 'and it must be you.' Churchill answered gruffly that he had signed on for the voyage and would stick to the ship. 'But I don't think he was angry with me,' Macmillan later commented. Two days later Macmillan was one of thirty-three Conservative back-benchers who defied the Party whips to vote against Chamberlain, thus accelerating Churchill's transition to power.

On May 10 Churchill became Prime Minister. Five days later Macmillan received his first government appointment, as Parliamentary Secretary to the Minister of Supply. As the war at sea intensified in 1941, Macmillan attended the Battle of the Atlantic Committee, seeking, like Churchill, to involve the United States more and more closely in the defence of the vital ocean supply lines. Of the seventeen members, at least three had American mothers: Churchill, Sir Archibald Sinclair (the Secretary of State for Air), and Macmillan himself, as did Lord Cherwell, Churchill's closest adviser.

In December 1942, following the Allied landings in North Africa and the ending of Vichy French rule there, Churchill appointed Macmillan Minister Resident. To Roosevelt, who sought to limit Macmillan's North African powers, Churchill wrote: 'He is animated by the friendliest feelings towards the United States, and his mother hails from Kentucky.' After the fall of Mussolini in 1943 Macmillan was appointed Minister Resident in Italy. His most dramatic moment came at Christmas 1944, when Churchill flew to Athens to try to persuade the Greek Communists, then fighting in the streets of Athens, to join an all-party government. Macmillan was at the airport when he arrived, and spent the first hours with him in the slowly freezing cabin, as a howling gale raged outside, discussing how to bring all sides to the conference table. The weather is often excluded from historical writing. But this picture of Churchill, wrapped in blankets and with his heavy overcoat on, struggling to make sense of the intricacies and imponderables of a civil war, was one for which the weather was a poignant addition.

One episode at the war's end troubled Macmillan in his later years. This was the repatriation of tens of thousands of Russians, then being held in areas liberated by the British, and sent back to the Soviet Union. Force had to be used to get most of them to go. For many, repatriation meant death or long terms of forced labour. One of those accused of direct complicity in the repatriation was a civil servant, Sir Patrick Dean, a close friend of Macmillan's. In September 1976 Macmillan asked me to see Dean and discuss what could be done to remove him from the controversy. 'I have urged him very strongly to make no reply to the newspaper attacks nor to the debate in the House of Lords,' Macmillan wrote to me. 'It seems to me quite improper that civil servants should either be accused, or expected to answer, accusations which are properly the function of ministers. The only two ministers concerned are now dead – Churchill and Eden. I have told Patrick Dean that the proper place for the answer to be made would be in the life of Churchill. You will have to deal with Yalta and especially the Yalta negotiations.'

Here was a strange situation. I, as Churchill's biographer, was to help Macmillan's friend by pointing the finger of responsibility at Churchill. The answers lay, as they do with as much as eighty-five or ninety per cent of all historical queries in Churchill's story, at the Public Record Office at Kew. Spurred by Macmillan's request, I went through the minutes of the War Cabinet. There I found that in the summer of 1944 Anthony Eden had argued in support of sending back to the Soviet Union the 1,500 former Soviet citizens, all of whom had fought alongside the Germans, and then been held as prisoners-of-war in Britain. During the discussion that followed, it was Churchill who said that the ambivalent position of these prisoners, as former allies of Germany, should be shown in the most 'extenuating' light and, if possible, their return delayed. Four days later Churchill wrote to Eden: 'Even if we are somewhat compromised, all the apparatus of delay must be used. I think these men were tried beyond their strength.'

Another set of files at Kew, the minutes of the wartime conferences, showed, however, that in Moscow in October 1944 Churchill had deferred to Stalin's insistence that all captured Russians be sent back. When, a week later, the British Embassy in Moscow raised various procedural matters, Churchill minuted: 'Are we not making unnecessary difficulties. It seems to me we work up fights about matters already conceded in principle. I thought we had arranged to send all the Russians back to Russia.' Three months later, while he was on the journey to Yalta, the War Cabinet discussed in his absence a new Soviet proposal that any reciprocal agreement to cover the repatriation of prisoners-of-war 'should be extended to all liberated Soviet and British subjects'. This increased the numbers involved from thousands to tens of thousands. Ministers accepted this Soviet proposal. As a result, any Soviet citizen who was liberated in western Europe, not merely those who had fought in the German ranks or aided in some way the German policy of persecution, could be 'repatriated' to Russia.

Churchill had taken no part in this considerable widening of the repatriation agreement. Those who did so included Clement Attlee, who took the chair at the meeting, and Ernest Bevin, who later, as

Labour's Foreign Secretary, ensured that the agreement was carried out in its wider form.

At Yalta, as the minutes at Kew made clear, it was the fate of former British prisoners-of-war who were even then being liberated by the Russians in the East that was uppermost in Churchill's mind during the repatriation discussions. The minutes record that he 'begged' Stalin 'for good treatment for them: every mother in England was anxious about the fate of her prisoner sons.' Worried about the situation of the British prisoners, he told Stalin that 'we wanted to send liaison officers to the Red Army to look after our men.' Stalin agreed without demur. He had got what he wanted with no dispute. Patrick Dean's task was to prepare the agreement for the signature of the leaders: this he did.

One author, Nikolai Tolstoy, has estimated that twenty per cent of all those repatriated to Russia, including those under the Yalta repatriation agreement, were sentenced either to death or to twenty-five years' penal servitude in labour camps; that a further twenty per cent were given labour camp sentences of between five and ten years; that perhaps fifteen per cent were sent as conscript labourers to various areas devastated by the war; and that up to twenty per cent were allowed to return to their homes.

Learning two months after Yalta that many of the British prisoners-of-war still in Russia were being subjected to harsh treatment, Churchill telegraphed to Stalin: 'There is no subject on which the British nation is more sensitive than on the fate of our prisoners in German hands and their speedy deliverance from captivity and restoration to their own country. I should be very much obliged if you would give the matter your personal attention, as I am sure you would wish to do your best for our men, as I can promise you we are doing for your men as they come into our control along the Rhine.'

The records at Kew made it clear that it was the ill-treatment of British prisoners-of-war, not the fate of repatriated Russians, that came top of the British agenda. I sent all this material to Macmillan, who realized that the accusations against Patrick Dean, unfair though they were, would not be lessened by the historical search. All that would happen, and it saddened him that this was so, was that Churchill would be criticized by many for having put the relatively unpleasant, temporary fate of Englishmen before the much more dire likely fate of Russians. Yet, he asked me over the telephone when he had studied what I sent him, 'How could Winston, how could any of us, not put the fate of our men first?'

Through Macmillan, I gained another insight into Churchill's story, and that of all leaders. Each day during my Churchill work I was conscious of how, despite the plethora of documents, there was still so much we do not know, and may never know. How many occasions there must have been when, for example, Churchill spoke after dinner, formally or informally, and of which no record survives. Where the record does survive, it scintillates and illuminates. Where there is no record, there is no light. Indeed, whole areas of his interests may remain quite unrecorded.

This was borne in upon me most recently when I was reading a biography of Macmillan. There was nothing in it – why should there have been? – about his attitude to the period of Mrs Gandhi's emergency rule in India. But at the height of that emergency period, Susie and I were guests at the farewell dinner given by the Indian High Commissioner in London, Mrs Gandhi's cousin, at which Macmillan was the guest of honour. At dinner's end the High Commissioner asked him to say a few words. He rose, spoke hesitatingly about the situation in India, said it was not for him as an outsider, as one of the nation that had ruled India from afar, to criticize the internal affairs of a fellow member of the Commonwealth, but still, when one looked at some of the things that were happening, one felt that something was not right. As he spoke, his voice gained in firmness and authority. The Indian diplomats listened with growing attention. Their guest of honour was defending democracy and arguing with considerable force that democracy had to be defended, that vigilance was essential, nowhere more so than in the world's largest democracy, India, where, for the moment, the democratic instincts had been subverted.

I listened mesmerized, wishing that a tape recorder had been running, or that I had brought a small notepad and a pencil with which to jot down some of the ringing phrases, the bold, wise assertions. I thought to myself: how often must Churchill have spoken on similar occasions, with no mechanical or human Boswell present, only a small group of listeners caught up in the force of his convictions, and realizing that they had listened to something rare, profound and extraordinary.

That evening recalled to my mind a file in the Churchill papers, Churchill's correspondence with the historian Lewis Namier, to whom he had sent some of the chapters of *Marlborough, His Life and Times*. Namier had criticized Churchill for making use in his narrative of imaginary conversations. Churchill agreed to delete these, but went on to tell Namier (the amateur guiding the professional): 'One of the most misleading factors in history is the practice of historians to build a story exclusively out of the records which have come down to them. These records are in many cases a very small part of what took place, and to fill in the picture one has to visualize the daily life – the constant discussions between ministers, the friendly dinners, the many days when nothing happened worthy of record, but during which events were nevertheless proceeding.' I see no reason to quarrel with this. Thanks to Harold Macmillan, my 'friendly dinner' in Kensington Palace Gardens was a case in point.

In December 1976, following the death of Sir John Wheeler-Bennett, I was asked to write Anthony Eden's biography. 'The news is most interesting – even exciting,' Macmillan wrote, in offering his services as publisher and inviting me back to Birch Grove 'to discuss certain aspects of the quest'. As we talked, it became clear to me just how much Macmillan had hoped to succeed Churchill as Prime Minister in 1955. He had been encouraged in this hope by Eden's recurrent illness, and his own promotion to Minister of Defence in the last months of Churchill's premiership.

At one point in our talk at Birch Grove that afternoon Macmillan expressed his fondness for Randolph, and recalled with affection Randolph's efforts in 1964 to drum up support for him. I then told him of how, after Macmillan's resignation, Randolph had half expected to receive a peerage in Macmillan's resignation Honours List, and had talked to me about what he would say in his maiden speech in the House of Lords, and what causes he would espouse. For some weeks he had felt that his ambition to return to Parliament was about to be fulfilled: he had been in the House of Commons for five years, elected unopposed in 1940 and defeated in the landslide of 1945. Macmillan expressed amazement that Randolph should have expected such an honour. But then he began to muse, and finally said, almost to himself, 'You know, that might not have been such a bad thing, what a pity I never thought of it.'

The friendships that were built up during my search for Churchill were built up gradually and imperceptibly. Macmillan, and Anthony Eden, whom I also met several times, belonged to a generation and a world far removed from my own. It was the First World War that had burned itself into their lives and killed so many of their friends. Through our unhurried talk, and their old-world courtesies, they found someone who clearly enjoyed listening to them as much as they enjoyed reminiscing. I recall how glad Eden was when, one lunch time at his home at Alvediston, in Wiltshire, I listened intently and took notes as he described how, early in 1941, he and not Churchill had urged Britain to throw its support behind Greece, then threatened by imminent German attack. That I would listen at all meant a great deal to him. That I took the story seriously was a special bonus. In my later archival work, after Eden's death, I found that his recollection was accurate.

In the course of historical research unexpected friendships grow up between unlikely people. Several of my fellow biographers have had this same experience. I knew it was so for me when, at Westminster Abbey, I was unexpectedly overcome with sadness on two separate occasions: the first at Eden's memorial service, the second at Macmillan's. It was a historical fact, explicable through their political rivalry, that they themselves had got on together so badly. The historian, unable to influence past events, has no need to take sides.

XV

Harold Wilson

During my first two years at Stour, Harold Wilson, then Leader of the Opposition, was much spoken of at Stour, not always with the distaste with which he was regarded by many Conservatives. In 1964, on the eve of the election that brought Wilson to power, Randolph sent him a pink tie as a gift, with a good-luck message ('The leader's tie is palest pink, it's not as red as people think.') I was on my way to Stour during the election campaign when, at Liverpool Street Station, I saw him in the train setting off for what was to be his triumphal Norwich speech. He offered to give me his signature but declined to sign my Conservative Party election manifesto. He settled for the *Evening Standard*, the ritual and essential gift I was bearing for Randolph.

I had first met Wilson in the summer of 1960, when I was working as a research assistant to the former *Manchester Guardian* correspondent in India, Taya Zinkin, then writing a book about British reflections on Indian independence. He invited us to the tea room in the House of Commons and I took notes as he talked about Anglo-Indian relations since 1947, when he had been President of the Board of Trade. He crossed my historian's path again three years later, while I was working for Randolph, and came across a reference to Wilson's father, James Wilson, a lifelong Liberal who had been Churchill's deputy election agent at North-West Manchester during the by-election of 1908, a by-election which Churchill lost. It was to Wilson senior that Churchill had made his then radical, and later much-quoted, remark: 'Had I the powers of a dictator, I would cause the word "Insure" to be inscribed on the lintel of every house in the land.'

Churchill died in 1965 during Wilson's first premiership. The passion of his parliamentary tribute annoyed many in the Labour

Party for whom Churchill was always an enemy. Intrigued though I was to know the reason for such a warm encomium, I little imagined that one day I would learn it from the man himself.

In June 1970 Wilson was defeated at the General Election. A few months later he asked me to read through the draft memoirs that he was writing about his premiership. Large batches of typescript, with handwritten amendments already in the margin of many pages, began to reach me at Oxford. In mid-December Wilson wrote 'to warn you in advance that should a large parcel arrive, you should not assume that it was a large box of cigars or other Christmas gift, with the subsequent disappointment when you find some 800 or 900 pages of script'. That winter I spent many days and evenings with him at his home in Lord North Street and in his room in the House of Commons.

Watching a Leader of the Opposition at work, and seeing how he was determined not only to hold on to the leadership of his party, which blamed him for the election defeat, but also to regain the premiership, gave me many glimpses of political life. Like Churchill, Wilson was a glutton for hard work, a voracious reader, and a witty commentator on the events and personalities of the time. Late-night working held no terror for either of them. Both men were also dependent for the smooth working of their private office on massive, unsung secretarial help. In Wilson's case there were times, while he was in opposition, that Marcia Williams had to dictate answers to more than two thousand letters a week, often working up to and beyond midnight in order to keep pace with the correspondence. For Wilson, as for Churchill during his wilderness decade, there was no State funding for this secretarial work: it was part of the financial burden of political life which, for Churchill in 1938, led him to the brink of financial ruin.

Wilson was basing his memoirs on the documents kept by his Private Office and was interested to know the sort of documents that Churchill had kept. But documents, he warned me, were not the whole story. Some turning-points were never recorded, and he then gave me an example of something which 'even I' would not find in the records. 'I was responsible for the Berlin airlift,' he said. 'It was done by me on a piece of blotting paper.' The year was 1951. The question was: could Britain fly in enough food and supplies to Berlin to enable it to resist the Soviet road and rail blockade? This is what Wilson told me:

> Ernie Bevin wanted to do it, but the Foreign Office were against it. They produced figures which showed that it could not be done. We had the figures in front of us at Cabinet. I said to Attlee: 'They're wrong, these figures; the Foreign Office have left a naught off.' 'You work them out then,' he said. I did the calculations then and there, on a piece of blotting paper at the Cabinet table. I worked out how many aeroplanes, landing every ten minutes, could fly in the required tonnage of supplies. 'Look', I said, 'the Foreign Office figures are wrong. It can be done.' 'Right', said Attlee, 'we'll go ahead with it.' And that was that.

I have often wondered if that story was true. On one occasion Wilson told me that the memoir title he liked best was Duff Cooper's *Old Men Forget*. But Wilson was far from an old man when he told me the Berlin airlift story: he was only fifty-five (two years younger than I am as I write these words). In my Churchill work, I have often had to balance the veracity of a story against its colour and charm. Memories are not necessarily lies. In 1906 Churchill had called an alleged lie a mere 'terminological inexactitude'. A much later Cabinet Secretary used the phrase 'economical with the truth'. As long as the reader's sense of scepticism is alerted by any sentence beginning 'He later recalled . . .' then no harm is done. Recollection, for all its tendency to error, has a charm that no amount of factual correctness can replace. Memory for facts can sometimes (though not always) be fallible, memory for colour and mood, less so. When Lady Churchill used to speak to me about an individual, she seldom told me a fact that I did not know, or sought to recall facts at so great a distance in time, but always gave such a vivid impression of the person she was recalling that it was as if they had just left the room.

Wilson enjoyed breaking off the work on his memoirs to tell me about Churchill. Their paths had crossed and clashed in September 1950, quite soon after Wilson's entry to Parliament. Churchill, then himself Leader of the Opposition, had attacked the Labour Government for having sold machine tools to the Soviet Union, under the

1947 Anglo-Russian Short-Term Trade Agreement. This agreement had been negotiated by Wilson as President of the Board of Trade (this had also been Churchill's first Cabinet post, in 1908). For Churchill, the Wilson Agreement, as it was known, represented all that was worst in post-war appeasement. It was 'intolerable', he told the House of Commons, 'that British troops today should be sent into action at one end of the world' – Korea – 'while we are supplying, or about to supply, if not actual weapons of war, the means to make weapons of war to those who are trying to kill them or get them killed.'

Wilson was proud of his battles with Churchill in the Commons: the rising Labour star in his thirties against the Conservative giant in his seventies. He was less willing to admit that the Soviet Trade Agreement might have been a mistake; indeed he must have told me a dozen times of his 'eighteen visits' to the Soviet Union before he became Prime Minister, of how the Russians trusted him, and of how he had befriended Kosygin long before he rose to power in the Kremlin. He also spoke with pride of how, when Prime Minister many years later, he had taken a tough line with his Russian hosts over such Jewish dissidents as the Panovs, the ballet dancers whose exit visas his advocacy helped to procure.

Seven months after Churchill's attack on the Soviet Trade Agreement, Wilson resigned from the Labour Government because of its increased defence spending. Aneurin Bevan resigned at the same time in protest against the introduction of Health Service charges. One of Wilson's favourite stories was of what happened next. Immediately after the two men had resigned Churchill went up to them in the Lobby and expressed his sympathy. Wilson recalled Churchill's remarks: 'We were facing a situation which was very much familiar to him, though, as he pointed out, we would never be obsecrated as he had been. We had gone out with honour. But he added, with a twinkle in his eye, that he and his party would make the most of the situation that resulted.'

That was not the end of the story. Later that evening Churchill's friend Brendan Bracken sought Wilson out. 'He had been charged, he said, "by the greatest living statesman, for that is what Mr Churchill is", to give me a message to convey to my wife. The message was that whereas I, as an experienced politician, had taken a step of which he felt free to take such party advantage as was appropriate, his concern was with my wife, an innocent party in these affairs, who would undoubtedly suffer in consequence; he recalled the number of occasions his wife had suffered as a result of his political decisions. Would I therefore convey to her his personal sympathy and under-standing?'

Wilson thanked Bracken for the message and went home. It was one o'clock in the morning. On learning of Churchill's concern, Mary Wilson burst into tears. When Wilson left home the next morning she asked him to see 'the old boy' and give him her thanks for his kind consideration. 'In the early evening I saw Winston in the smoking-room and went up to him, and told him I had a message from my wife. He interrupted me to point out that he had on one occasion been presented to her, otherwise he would not have pre-sumed etc.' Wilson then passed on Mary's thanks, whereupon Chur-chill immediately burst into tears, 'as he expatiated on the way that wives had to suffer for their husbands' political actions, going on to recall a number of instances over a long life'.

Wilson reached home that night at 2 a.m. Mary was still awake. 'I was asked if I had seen the old boy and thanked him. I had, and recounted the interview. She burst into tears again, and I was moved to say that whereas two days earlier I had been a Minister of the Crown, red box and all, now I was reduced to the position of a messenger between my wife and Winston Churchill, each of whom burst into tears on receipt of a message from the other.'

It was this episode, which Wilson so enjoyed recounting, that had led him to say in his parliamentary tribute to Churchill in 1965: 'Each one of us recalls some little incident – many of us, as in my own case, a kind action, graced with the courtesy of a past generation and going far beyond the normal calls of parliamentary comradeship.'

During Churchill's second premiership, unknown to Wilson at the time, Churchill pressed the Cabinet to try to establish better relations with the Soviet Union. After Stalin's death in 1953 he tried, though in vain, to persuade the United States to join him in the search for a meeting at the 'summit' (Churchill's word) with Stalin's successors. In 1954 Wilson visited Moscow on private trade business. Because Anthony Eden was ill, Churchill was also in charge of the Foreign Office. 'He called me across the smoking-room for a drink,'

Wilson recalled; 'He was eighty. "What we want", he said, "you tell them – is *easement*. We may not settle all our problems: we want EAZHMENT." Then the old statesman told me what to look for: consumer goods. If they were allocating more materials for the production of consumer goods, he went on, it was a sign that they were looking to a peaceful solution; it might mean, it did not necessarily mean, that they were having to take more notice of ordinary people.'

As I helped Wilson check dates and figures and the texts of speeches and agreements, I thought of how Churchill had also relied for such mundane essentials on a team of young men, headed by Bill Deakin, who had become his sole literary assistant in 1936, and was still working for Churchill twenty years later, at the head of a considerable team. My own servitude was to be of less than six months' duration, but it was none the less taxing while it lasted. Like Churchill, Wilson was determined that his memoirs should be accurate, full and informative, and that they should set out clearly what he had tried to do and what he had achieved. One day I told Wilson that I had to leave early, to give a lecture on the perils of historical research. 'Would you like to take a visiting card?' he asked; '"Also Representing Harold Wilson".'

Wilson worked hard and expected those helping him to work equally hard. But he loved to use the discussion on some paragraph as a peg for some personal or political digression. At one of our sessions we discussed Churchill's work at the Board of Trade. Wilson had been impressed that, almost a decade before he was born, a future Conservative leader had laid the foundations of national insurance. I read Wilson a letter Churchill had written to Lloyd George, then Chancellor of the Exchequer, proposing the creation of a Committee of National Organization, in order to 'reproduce for the defence of the country against poverty and unemployment, the sort of machinery that we have in existence in the Committee of Imperial Defence to protect us against foreign aggression.' Wilson was impressed.

In those early months of 1971, at the beginning of Wilson's long haul back to power, and with many in the Labour Party hostile to him, he was unexpectedly buoyant. Had not Churchill had a whole decade in the political wilderness? But I also saw another side to political history during those months, the uncertainties of life on the Opposition benches. That March, Anthony Barber introduced the

Conservative Budget. It was a success, causing considerable gloom in the Wilson entourage, where there was talk of a quick General Election and a Tory landslide. Wilson was downhearted that his own speech during the Budget debate had not been good. 'He had a cold, and he spoke for too long,' one of his staff told me that night, adding in desperation: 'Perhaps Labour is condemned to be the Opposition party for a decade.' But Wilson was not cast down for long. By the following afternoon he was working on a speech that he was to give in Perth, working 'harder than anyone I know', one of the inner circle reported.

There were those in Wilson's entourage who disliked his fascination with Churchill. During one of our working sessions, Marcia Williams pointed out to him that, in the first draft of his memoirs, he had devoted four pages to his description of Churchill's death and only four lines to the death of Herbert Morrison, once Labour's most popular figure. In his description of how President Johnson had invited him to attend the annual ceremony of switching on Washington's Christmas lights, Wilson had written that this was the first time a British Prime Minister had been so invited 'since Mr Churchill, twenty-one years earlier'. A member of staff wanted the Churchill phrase deleted. Wilson refused. In another chapter, despite my inevitable protest, he agreed to delete the phrase 'Churchillian expressions of defiance'. Also deleted, at the insistence of one of his staff, was his description of how he had spent nine hours preparing his seven- or eight-minute tribute to Churchill.

There was one aspect of the work on Wilson's memoirs that made me realize how lucky I was to be writing about Churchill. One afternoon Wilson broke off the work for a few moments to read a letter that was brought in to him, from one of his Shadow Cabinet, on a matter of some importance. He read it, pondered for a while, and then, satisfied that he had understood the matter, scrumpled up the letter and threw it into the wastepaper basket. I was astounded. If Churchill had done such things, his archive would simply not suffice to tell his story. Similarly, very few of the manuscript notes of Wilson's speeches had survived. In Churchill's case, it was possible to know not only what he said, but some of the things he had intended to say, and some of the modifications, or toughenings, that he had made at the last moment.

Churchill, like Wilson, was an avid reader of the newspapers. Shortly before he became Prime Minister in 1940, Churchill told the editor of the *Manchester Guardian*, who had come to see him at the Admiralty: 'I always read the MG you know. There it is, on the table.' I was intrigued, therefore, to find in Wilson's draft account of a Fleet Street crisis in 1967 the sentence 'Nearest to disaster was the *Guardian*; it was my view then, and would always be, that no government could stand aside and allow the *Guardian* to close.'

'Why not?' I asked him at one of our sessions. But rather than explain in the text, he cut out the sentence altogether. I never learned the reason.

It was fascinating to watch a former Prime Minister at work, out of office but determined to return. At one point I objected, on linguistic grounds, to his description of Birmingham Ladywood as 'that very small downtown constituency'. Was this not an Americanism? I asked. To which he replied: 'It was the slummy centre of a great city. I can't say that. We'd lose all their votes.'

Much of my work was editorially pedantic. But it derived from my experience with Churchill, where, for example, I was and still am often confronted by abbreviations which I cannot understand, and which I cannot find in the standard reference books. Each generation knows the meaning of its abbreviated institutions through daily usage. But for the next generation they can be inexplicable. Wilson was keen on abbreviations. In the draft of his memoirs there were more than a hundred. I pressed him to spell them out in full, though he expressed surprise, almost annoyance, when I told him there were several I did not know. Even readers who lived through the Wilson era may be hard pressed to recall some of the following random selection: AEA, AMC, COCOM, DEP, ECGD, GAB, ICRC, IDC, IRC, MHLG, NBPI, NEDC, NIBMAR, NRDC, ODM, OPD, PESC, PNQ, RPA, SET, WEU* and WMG. This last abbreviation,

---

* These were: the Atomic Energy Authority, the Association of Municipal Corporations, the Co-ordinating Committee for Multinational Export Controls, the Department of Employment and Productivity, the Export Credits Guarantee Department, the General Agreement to Borrow, the International Committee for the Red Cross, the Industrial Development Certificate, the Industrial Reorganization Corporation, the Ministry of Housing and Local Government, the National Board for Prices and Incomes, the National Economic Development Council, No Independence Before Majority Rule (for Rhodesia), the National Research and

which foxed me completely, appeared in the following Wilson sentence: 'The professional WMG group were at work.' It stood for 'Wilson Must Go.'

In 1974 Wilson became Prime Minister for the second time. My own researches having then reached the inter-war years, he offered to help me with one of the more knotty problems in Churchill's story, the negotiations with the coal miners in the summer of 1926. There are few misconceptions more deeply rooted than the belief that Churchill had some deep antipathy for British miners. In 1992, when his grandson, Winston Churchill MP, spoke publicly against the closure of thirty coal mines, a television commentator remarked: 'His grandfather was never the miners' friend.' Wilson was one of those who knew that this was a misconception. In the Second World War, as a young civil servant, he had made a study of the coal industry, and knew a great deal about the negotiations of 1926. He also prided himself on his tenacious memory.

I was invited to 10 Downing Street for a 'tutorial'. It was a day of economic crisis, with the pound in serious trouble. A crisis Cabinet had been called for that morning. I telephoned from Oxford, to ask if I should postpone my visit. Not at all, came the answer, the Prime Minister is expecting you. I took the train and arrived at Number Ten as asked, shortly after midday. As ministers hurried out of the Cabinet Room in search of their coats and cars, I was ushered in. For three hours Wilson spoke about coal. There were no interruptions of any sort, no telephone messages or hurried consultations with his staff. After two hours, tea and sandwiches were brought in. Even then there was no break from the work in hand.

The former Oxford don, now Prime Minister, had put the current economic problem aside as he recounted the events of almost half a century earlier. He had been impressed, he told me, when studying the coal negotiation files, by Churchill's determination to give the miners a fair deal. He wondered what the archives would reveal. I said I would make it a priority to find out. It had been a fascinating talk, a Labour Prime Minister expatiating with admiration about a

Development Council, the Overseas Development Ministry, the Ministerial Committee on Overseas Policy and Defence, the Public Expenditure Survey Committee, Private Notice Question, the Representation of the People Act, the Selective Employment Tax (in force from 1966 to 1973), and Western European Union.

Conservative Chancellor of the Exchequer. When I left the Cabinet Room, one of Wilson's staff hurried up and seemed to want to know what the discussion had been about. Had I, perhaps, been privy to some new development in the economic crisis?

Following this Downing Street 'tutorial', I spent many hours with Susie in the Public Record Office, studying the Cabinet and ministerial records, and at the Cambridge University Library, looking through Baldwin's papers. The story that we pieced together over several months was hitherto unknown. Eight days after the end of the General Strike in 1926, but with the coal strike continuing, the Prime Minister, Stanley Baldwin, had asked Churchill to take charge of the Government's negotiations with the miners. Churchill emerged at once as the miners' friend. When the owners insisted on a reduction in miners' wages, Churchill countered by proposing that any such reduction in wages should be paralleled by a reduction in owners' profits. There was also a limit to reduced wages, he insisted, 'below which on social grounds miners ought not to work'.

As the coal strike continued with increasing bitterness on both sides, and Baldwin set off for his annual holiday in France, Churchill had told the Cabinet that he approved the miners' desire for a national minimum wage. That same day, in talks with the miners' leaders, he told them, 'I sympathize with you in your task,' and asked them for some offer of terms which he could then press the owners to accept. To accelerate a solution, he invited the Labour leader, Ramsay MacDonald, to Chartwell. MacDonald offered to ask the miners' leaders to agree to negotiations on the basis of a comprehensive national settlement with a minimum wage. Two days later, in London, Churchill met secretly with the miners' leaders and worked out with them a formula, which the Government could then put to the owners in order to bring the strike to an end. The formula was based on the miners' demand for a minimum wage which could not be undercut by individual owners. Churchill then undertook to persuade the owners to accept the formula. He invited them to Chartwell, in the hope that the country-house atmosphere would induce conciliatory thoughts. But the owners would not yield.

Angered by the owners' attitude, Churchill wanted to incorporate the principle of a minimum wage in a government bill, the aim of which, he told the Cabinet on September 15, was 'to bring pressure to bear on the owners'. But the Cabinet objected to any such pressure being applied, and Baldwin, who returned that day from France, declined to support Churchill's efforts. Nor would the Cabinet endorse another proposal by Churchill, which was also acceptable to the miners, for a compulsory arbitration tribunal 'having the force of law'.

Churchill was out on a limb. But despite the political risk, he persevered. The owners' refusal to attend a tripartite meeting with Churchill and the miners was, he told the Cabinet, 'wholly wrong and unreasonable' and without precedent 'in recent times'. The Cabinet refused, however, to order the owners to a meeting, and to Churchill's chagrin decided that the Government should now dissociate itself from the dispute, leaving the owners and the miners to continue their strife until its conclusion.

Later, I reported back to Wilson about these discoveries, but by then he had left 10 Downing Street. I was not to see the inside of the building again for several years: its fascination for any biographer of a Prime Minister is enormous. Churchill had first entered the building in 1898, when the then Prime Minister, Lord Salisbury, had asked to see the twenty-seven-year-old Churchill to discuss *The River War*, his book on the Sudan campaign. In 1905, as a junior minister, he sat for the first time at the Cabinet table. In 1940, and again in 1951, he had lived and worked there as Prime Minister. On my coal strike visit, Wilson showed me the door off the Cabinet Room, leading to the room in which Neville Chamberlain's adviser, Sir Horace Wilson ('no relation, I'm pleased to say') had kept an eagle eye on all those seeking to disturb his master's equanimity, and had intercepted those who, he felt, might argue against appeasement. Between Wilson's defeat in 1970 and his return in 1974, that very room had been occupied by Michael Wolff, Randolph's former director of researches, who had become one of Edward Heath's closest advisers. In Wilson's day the room was occupied by Marcia Williams, later Baroness Falkender. As I write these words it is home to the head of John Major's political office, Jonathan Hill.

During the summer of 1974 Wilson invited me to Chequers, which I had never seen. Churchill had been one of the first people to stay there after it had become the Prime Minister's country residence in 1922. From 1940 to 1945 it had been his weekend retreat and power-house. 'We go into the sitting-room,' I noted in my diary later that day. 'Very comfortably furnished, but not much sign of life – no papers, no boxes. A view across the rose garden to Churchill's "Victory Drive".' This drive was a line of beech trees running from the house to the main gate, planted in honour of Churchill and the victory over Germany in 1945.

Wilson was proud of his capacity for work. When the telephone rang in a distant room he said: 'In Neville Chamberlain's time there was only a single telephone. Now there is a communications room which cost a million.' He went on to say how much he liked Chequers, 'except when the Irish were here last week. What a lot happens in a week in Ireland!' By chance, my own work had just reached the Irish Treaty of 1922, one of Churchill's most remarkable negotiating achievements, the creation of the Irish Free State and the retention of Northern Ireland, at least as an interim measure, as part of the United Kingdom. The Irish crisis was yet again bedevilling British politics. 'In the end', Wilson told me about the previous week's discussions, 'we decided that 16,000 troops simply could not do the work of 250,000 strikers. It couldn't be done. We had experts among the troops, but not enough of them.'

There was a moment during our talk when Wilson began to quizz me about Churchill's second premiership. Was Churchill 'gaga'? Had he gone senile while in office? Had he lost his grasp on events? I made a somewhat spirited defence of Churchill as a more active Prime Minister from 1951 to 1955 than many imagined. Wilson listened for a while, then remarked, almost to himself, 'I do not want to decline in office.'

Before I left Chequers that day, Wilson told me: 'Number Ten is a prison. You can't sleep, and you wander downstairs, and you look at the telegrams coming in. There's no escape. Mary would be going along the corridor to say goodnight to Giles' – their younger son – 'when burly messengers would push by carrying boxes.'

The life of a Prime Minister is dominated by the official boxes, to which Wilson had made several references during our talk. I knew that when Churchill retired, what he missed more than anything were these locked red boxes with their daily bundle of information to be absorbed and problems to be resolved. In 1955, Anthony Eden had no intention of letting his predecessor see anything official. But when Macmillan became Prime Minister two years later, understanding Churchill's sense of isolation, he at once arranged for him to be sent a selection of secret materials in a red box, so that he might feel wanted once more.*

In 1977, after James Callaghan had succeeded him as Prime Minister, Wilson had decided to write a book about some of his predecessors at Number Ten. He sent me the drafts of the twentieth-century chapters, telling me on the telephone that he would do one prime ministerial essay a week, and kept his target.

'Sorry to call you on Sunday night,' another telephone call began – it was Sunday, 20 March 1977. 'I've finished Churchill. It's very massive and rather long. It should be the longest chapter, shouldn't it?' I could hardly disagree. The next night there was another call: 'I posted Winston to you tonight,' and he went on, politics ever on his tongue: 'I lunched with Jim Callaghan today. He wanted me to see him. I told him, the main thing is, "Do not resign." He should have called a Vote of Confidence at once, as I did, not left it to Mrs Thatcher to take the initiative.' Then (back to the task in hand): 'Neville Chamberlain is still being done. I worked on it from eleven to seven yesterday.'

Indefatigable, I thought, and geared myself up for the work. It was good training, as the Churchill essay focused on the pre-war years, about which I was even then assembling material. Indeed, the outline chronology on Churchill and defence that I prepared for Wilson served a few years later as the basis for my own presentation of Churchill's efforts to ensure that Britain was strong enough to deter German aggression in Europe.

On one of Wilson's typescripts he had added in his own hand an account of a Churchill story that had much amused him about Churchill's 'post-midnight activities', as he called them. In the Great Hall of Chequers, he explained, is a large Rubens painting of the Aesop fable in which a lion, caught in the toils of a net, is rescued by a mouse nibbling at the rope which binds the net to the tree. As Wilson recounted it, 'Churchill, in the small hours, decided, "Can't

---

* The red boxes are not necessarily a welcome adjunct to power. In 1992 John Major told *The Times*: 'I think how tempting it is to leave affairs of State behind. Even the dreariest of nil-nil draws on a wet afternoon can seem attractive in comparison to those red boxes.'

see the moushe" and immediately demanded that his paints and brushes and a ladder be produced. He painted in the mouse – though later Prime Ministers telling the story to their visitors still had some difficulty "seeing the mouse".'

Wilson continued, not without a little envy: 'It takes a confident and authoritative Prime Minister to decide to touch up a Rubens.' But the sequel was 'a little unhappy'. The one-million pound fund-raising appeal for Churchill College, Cambridge asked the Chequers Trustees to loan the painting for three months to the Churchill exhibition in London. 'It was decided to clean the picture of its centuries of varnish and stains. This was successfully done, but of course Churchill's adornment had been over the varnish, and his artistic effort went with the varnish.'

This story, charming though it is, and often retold, may be typical of (dare I say it?) the wilder shores of oral evidence. Churchill was surely too great an art lover to 'touch up' a Rubens.

Four years after my last working sessions with him, I sent Wilson the Churchill document volume in which the 1926 coal negotiations appeared. In my covering letter I reminded him of the tutorial he had given me. He replied a few days later to say that the book had indeed arrived, but that the parcel was so bulky that Special Branch feared it might be a bomb. Several squad cars had arrived, followed by the bomb-disposal squad, and a posse of policemen. All was set to detonate the monster. In the end it proved only to be his Christmas reading.

XVI

'Dear Mr Gilbert'

From my first days as Churchill's biographer in 1968 I began to receive letters from people who wanted to tap my imagined expertise. Sometimes I get as many as a dozen such letters a week. Most people want me to confirm a Churchill story or to verify a quotation. This, though seemingly simple, can take hours, even if it can be done at all. Auction houses seek confirmation that a Churchill signature being offered for sale is genuine (it is surprising how often it is not). Many of those who write to me hope that I may be able to date a photograph, or to identify the people who appear on either side of Churchill. Some want to know if Churchill had stayed at their homes, or had some connection with their region or their professional work, with a view to putting up a plaque.

Every facet of Churchill's life, from the most profound to the most bizarre, has crossed my desk in the form of queries. The most frequent are about his cigars, his brandy and his cats. On two occasions I was asked if a Churchill oil-painting was a fake. One was genuine: amid the mass of the Churchill papers was the copy of a letter from Churchill's pre-war secretary, Violet Pearman, in which she wrote: 'I have despatched today by Carter Paterson to your address a picture which Mr Churchill has painted himself, and which he promised to give you some time ago. He hopes the picture reaches you safely and that you will like it.'

The second painting was neither Churchill's style, nor did it carry his genuine initials (WC rather than WSC). But when a First World War medal, the 1914 Star, engraved with the letters WSC (his normal signed initials) was sent to me for verification, I was able to say, having on my bookshelves a monograph on Churchill's decorations, that all Churchill's war medals had been engraved by the Army Council with his full initials, as used when he entered the army in

1895: WLSC. This was not one of them. It wasn't the 1914 Star, but the 1914–15 Star that he had received for his efforts to prolong the resistance of Antwerp in October 1914. Randolph's emphasis on the mastery of reference books had led me, usefully in this case, to amass the most abstruse and dry-as-dust books which might, even through a listing of old street addresses, hold the clue to one of the queries reaching me, or even one of my own.

Churchill's ancestry was, and still is, a frequent subject of enquiry. A former Hungarian diplomat writing a book about 'the mixing of the nations and the races' wanted to know if it was true that one of Churchill's American ancestors was an American Indian woman. This query reaches me annually. The answer seems to be a qualified 'yes'. Randolph was always proud of a possible Indian link, and I remember his pleasure when he received at Stour, in May 1963, a letter from the United States Secretary of the Interior, Stewart Udall, indicating two separate possible sources of Indian blood in Lady Randolph's veins, both of them Iroquois women (Mirabah, who died in 1768 and Anna Baker, whose daughter was born in 1796). If, as was believed, Anna Baker was a full-blood Iroquois, then, the Secretary of State wrote, 'Sir Winston is 1/16th degree Indian.'

Another letter that I received in my early days was from a lady who was linked by marriage both to the Churchills and the Roosevelts, thus establishing a genealogical link between the two war leaders. Another of Roosevelt's relations wrote: 'Is Sir Winston descended from English *royal* blood? We are, in the Delano line, from all the monarchs up to and including Edward I. If Sir Winston had royal blood as well, then he and FDR were *many times* related.' Alas, neither I, nor any of the members of the Churchill family whom I approached could find a royal link.

A few of those who wrote to me claimed to be Churchill's illegitimate children. Several others asked me to confirm that Brendan Bracken, his friend and wartime Minister of Information, was such a child. In no case did illegitimacy seem at all possible, despite the uncertainty of paternity. I was able to give a decisive reply to the woman who said that Churchill and her mother had had an illicit liaison (Churchill had then been a married man for seven years) on board a troopship in the eastern Mediterranean in the summer of 1915, nine months before her birth. Throughout that summer

Churchill had been in London and, at weekends, at Hoe Farm near Godalming, in Surrey.

The desire to have some link with Churchill in distant lands was a regular feature of enquiries. When I was in the Crimea in 1989, I was offered a trip to 'the grave of Churchill's father', killed in action, it seems, during the Battle of Balaclava in 1854, twenty years before Churchill's birth, and buried within sight of the Black Sea. In fact, Lord Randolph had died in London in 1895, and was buried at Bladon, within sight of the towers of Blenheim Palace. Also in 1989, as the Soviet Union turned from communism to glasnost, the Lvov Medical Institute, a branch of the Ukrainian Ministry of Health, asked the British Embassy in Moscow to confirm that Churchill had gone to the Carpathian spa town of Skole in the 1930s 'with the aim of restoring his health'. A new medical centre was being developed there; no doubt the institute hoped to put up a plaque: 'Britain's war leader took the waters here,' a good advertisement in the changing times. But there was no evidence that Churchill had gone anywhere in Europe east of Munich in the 1930s, let alone into deepest then-Polish Galicia.

Requests such as these would lead me to fantasize as to possible unknown tales of my subject: his visit to Skole, not to take the waters, of course, but to hold a secret meeting with Stalin, who was smuggled incognito across the Soviet-Polish border. A recent correspondent, Admiral Fisher's biographer, Jan Morris, wondered if there was any truth in Fisher's outburst to Clementine at the height of the Dardanelles crisis, when Churchill was in Paris negotiating an Anglo-Italian naval agreement: 'Your husband is not in Paris negotiating, he is there visiting his mistress.' Lady Churchill had told me at one of our lunches how it was this remark that made her realize that Fisher must have gone mad, and that her husband's career would indeed be in trouble if the Admiral were to persist, as he did, in his bizarre behaviour.

I hastened to assure Jan Morris that there had been no mistress. In all the millions of words that I have studied, the diaries, letters, reports of observers, including the most hostile, Churchill's total devotion to his Clemmie was yet another feature of Bishop Creighton's 'true history'.

In 1985 I was approached by the Attorney-General's office of

Alberta, Canada. The province was seeking to put on trial a teacher who, in denouncing the malign influence of the Jews, had quoted Churchill as an authority. The quotation that he used was well known to me, and as it was also taken out of context, I was able to provide the court with the full quotation, and an explanation of Churchill's views.

As cited by the teacher, Churchill had denounced the Bolshevik Jews controlling the Soviet regime in 1920, and had likened them to a worldwide 'sinister conspiracy' of Jews who worked to undermine democracy. Churchill's actual article, published in the *Illustrated Sunday Herald* of 8 February 1920, had set out his thoughts on three very different types of Jewish involvement in national life: the Bolshevik involvement, which he abhorred; the assimilationists, of whom he approved; and the Zionists, about whom he wrote with both fervour and prescience: 'If, as may happen, there should be created in our own lifetime, by the banks of the Jordan, a Jewish state under the protection of the British crown, which might comprise three or four millions of Jews, an event would have occurred in the history of the world which would, from every point of view, be beneficial.' This was written in 1930. In 1992 the Jewish population of the State of Israel reached four million.

Many queries have come from people who suffer from depression, or whose loved ones do, wanting to know about Churchill's much-publicized periods of what he described as his 'black dogs'. One of the founders of the Manic Depression Fellowship was among those who wrote, as did an American who hoped that Churchill's means of overcoming his depressions might be a means to helping his own wife.

One correspondent, a Freemason in the United States, asked me if Churchill had ever been a mason. I did not know, but was stimulated by his query to try to find out. The archivist at the United Grand Lodge of England invited me to look at their records, and, to my surprise, there was Winston Churchill admitted to the United Studholme Lodge, a few yards from where he was then living in London, in May 1901. He was then a young Conservative MP. He remained a member until July 1912, when, as First Lord in the Liberal administration, he resigned. Before I left the building, I was shown his ceremonial apron. When, in 1936, a friend warned

Churchill that French efficiency was being undermined by 'the Grand Orient masonry', he did not know that Churchill had once been a mason himself.

Sometimes the queries of others led me to discoveries of my own. When the Cunard Line asked me in 1985 if I could find out what Churchill had said, if anything, on the launching of the Queen Mary in 1935, I did not think that much of great interest would emerge. But, as a result of delving, I found an early version of one of Churchill's most famous remarks: 'Never in the history of human conflict has so much been owed by so many to so few.' Six years earlier he had sent the new ship his greetings: 'Never in the history of transatlantic travel has so much been done for those who travel tourist.'

Public personalities have always sought Churchill-related information, in particular for their speeches. A vigilant Margaret Thatcher, some years before she became Prime Minister, had been struck by a brief footnote in one of my document volumes, that Churchill, in the late 1920s, had prepared notes for a book called *Socialism, The Creed of Failure*. She asked me if I could send her copies of the notes. All that existed, however, were Churchill's proposed chapter headings. The book was never written.

In 1977 President Carter, on the eve of an address to the United Nations General Assembly, asked his speechwriter to telephone me for a Churchill quotation on atomic energy. It is not always easy, and in the majority of cases impossible, to locate quotations at the drop of a hat, or even with long searches – at least that is my experience. Sometimes the most familiar quotations elude discovery. But in this case I was able to help in the few hours allotted to me. The quotation read: 'This revelation of the secrets of nature, long mercifully withheld from man, should arouse the most solemn reflections in the mind and conscience of every human being capable of comprehension. We must indeed pray that these awful agencies will be made to conduce peace among the nations, and that instead of wreaking measureless havoc upon the entire globe they may become a perennial fountain of world prosperity.'

Carter duly used the quotation in his speech. I was less successful in finding a worthwhile answer when I received a query from one of President Bush's speechwriters: 'I need for the White House any references to WSC on shooting, particularly bird or duck shooting – information on rifles used, shooting estates frequented, etc.' Quite why that particular information was needed I never did find out.

On one occasion, when Margaret Thatcher was Prime Minister, about to leave for Moscow, she asked for a quotation that she could use in the same hall in which Stalin had entertained Churchill in 1942. I searched and searched, in vain, for any warm words or enthusiasm: that particular meeting had come at a very low ebb indeed in Anglo-Soviet relations. Finally I came across a reference by Churchill to the splendid deeds of the Red Army. I sent it to Downing Street but, a few hours later, there was a telephone call from someone in the Foreign Office who told me that it was not Britain's policy to praise the Soviet forces. The quotation was not used. With not much time to spare, and with difficulty, I found another.

One set of quotations that Mrs Thatcher did use caused me acute embarrassment. She had asked for something by Churchill on the Jewish National Home, and his support for Jewish aspirations in Palestine. I provided these and they were woven into the speech. I was sitting near the back of the hall and awaited her speech, knowing that I would feel a glow of pride as she read out my contribution. Imagine therefore my horror when Lord Wolfson, the speaker who introduced her, used the very same quotations. His speechwriter, and his own considerable grasp of history and its sources, had led him to my Churchill volume four. Mrs Thatcher did not bat an eyelid. When her turn came to speak, she commented on how remarkable it was that Churchill's views were so clear and forthright, so much so that Lord Wolfson had chosen some of the very ones that she herself considered so important, as to deserve repeating. One of the twice-chosen quotations was Churchill's remark to a Palestinian Arab delegation in Jerusalem in 1921: 'It is manifestly right that the Jews, who are scattered all over the world, should have a national centre and a National Home where some of them may be reunited. And where else could that be but in this land of Palestine, with which for more than three thousand years they have been intimately and profoundly associated?'

Another embarrassing moment with regard to Churchill's speech-making came in 1972, when I was invited to tea with Edward Heath in the garden of 10 Downing Street. It was the first and only time I sat in that garden. The Prime Minister was accompanied by his Political Secretary. At one point Heath asked me how Churchill prepared his speeches, how did his speechwriters work? I interrupted keenly to say that Churchill did not use speechwriters, but dictated all his own speeches, even on occasion writing them out in longhand. As I spoke, I noticed the young man go somewhat red, and Heath look a little put out. I realized at once that I was in the presence not only of a Prime Minister but of a speechwriter. Twenty years later the young man, Douglas Hurd, was Foreign Secretary.

In the very first days of January 1991, after the Iraqi invasion of Kuwait but before the Americans had committed themselves to direct intervention in the Gulf, I received a message from one of President Bush's staff, with regard to a Churchill speech in October 1939, less than two months after the start of the war, in which Churchill had given details of the already horrific Nazi atrocities against the Poles. It seems that the President was impressed that the evils of occupation had been so swiftly seen, and publicized. Later, as the Iraqi occupation of Kuwait intensified, he drew his Cabinet's attention to this early episode of the Second World War (and even produced my volume in which it appeared), to warn of what went on behind the cloak of tyranny even in the early days of a dictator's rule.

The publication of this source led to an odd episode. After the outbreak of the Gulf War, the *Boston Globe* telephoned me to ask if there was any documentation to show that Churchill had ever ordered the assassination of Hitler. I knew of none. I could not help wondering if Saddam Hussein would have suffered a different fate had there been a clear precedent. The assassination of Heydrich, ruler of Bohemia, in 1942, by Czech agents trained in Britain, had provoked such a violent upsurge of Nazi reprisals against Czechs and Jews, that no further assassinations were, as far as I knew, authorized again from London.

Churchill could be used emphatically by all sorts of determined publicists and politicians. While I was still working for Randolph, and having to listen in on the spare telephone to take notes of conversations, Robert Kennedy rang. He was then Attorney-General of the United States and was looking for a Churchill quotation, of which he had been told, with regard to penal reforms that he was hoping to institute. I was thrilled, even while he was still on the phone to Randolph, to be able to swivel in my chair and pick the book with the correct quotation off the bookshelf (it was the biography of Churchill by Peter de Mendelssohn). The quotation, which represented at the time, 1910, a most radical attitude towards crime and punishment, read:

> The mood and temper of the public in regard to the treatment of crime and criminals is one of the most unfailing tests of the civilization of any country.
>
> A calm and dispassionate recognition of the rights of the accused against the State, and even of convicted criminals against the State, a constant heart-searching by all charged with the duty of punishment, a desire and eagerness to rehabilitate in the world of industry all those who have paid their dues in the hard coinage of punishment, tireless efforts towards the discovery of curative and regenerative processes, and an unfaltering faith that there is a treasure, if you can only find it, in the heart of every man – these are the symbols which in the treatment of crime and criminals mark and measure the stored-up strength of a nation, and are the sign and proof of the living virtue in it.

A year after this telephone conversation, Randolph died. A few hours before his death, he was told that Robert Kennedy had been assassinated in Los Angeles.

For historians who wrote to me with specific queries, I tried to operate an informal and voluntary rule: I will send you what I can, for your purposes, from the Churchill papers, in return for you sending me, from time to time, anything that you come across in the other archives you are looking at, if it has a Churchill aspect. In twenty-five years, and having sent out at least a thousand photocopies of documents to other historians, I have only seldom received Churchill-related items in return. One Eden biographer, to whom over several months I had sent several dozen important handwritten letters from his subject to Churchill, sent me nothing in return. But Macmillan's biographer, Alistair Horne (who like myself had been despatched to Canada in 1940), reciprocated by letting me see previously unpublished diary entries of Macmillan's meetings with

Churchill in 1954 and 1955. These gave me vital clues for my own work on the last months of Churchill's second premiership, when he was so keen to stay on, and most of his Cabinet colleagues anxious to see him step down.

Despite the essentially open archive system that I operated, historians have continued to relay, and even to publish, accounts that the Churchill papers are a closed book. Once this caused me to blow my top, though the circumstances were unfortunate. A young Canadian army officer, asked to give the vote of thanks after I had spoken in Toronto about Churchill and Canada in the Second World War, said (his sole aim was to be flattering) that as he had read in a recent Canadian account of the Dieppe raid that the Churchill papers for the raid were open only to me, they were privileged to have heard what I had to say. I did something I have never done before or since, I interrupted the vote of thanks, and cried out to an astonished gathering that this was a lie, that not only did I not have exclusive access to Churchill's Dieppe raid files, but that as these were at the Public Record Office at Kew, anyone in the audience, for the cost of a transatlantic ticket, could go to see them and copy them to his heart's content. The poor young officer went a bright puce, and I have felt sorry for him ever since.

When the Churchill papers went back to Churchill College, Cambridge, those seeking to use them were informed by the college: 'Unfortunately all the papers of Sir Winston Churchill are closed and must remain so until ten years after the completion of the official biography.' Even then, the closure was not as significant as it seemed: I was able to reply to one correspondent, interested in Churchill's contacts with Vichy France at the end of 1940, who had received the above reply, that every single document relating to that episode was in the public domain at Kew, and was able to point him to the specific prime ministerial, Foreign Office and Cabinet Office files.

For many of those who write to me, their own field of research is such that they find some aspect of Churchill's life important. For me, however, that aspect may be both obscure, and extremely difficult to discover. There is not yet any comprehensive index of the Churchill papers, and although I pride myself on my own itemized indexes to each of the (now) sixteen volumes, they, by their very nature, do not cover some of the esoteric aspects. Thus I was at first unable to help the Harvard professor who was doing a paper, for the Third International Symposium on the History of Anaesthesia, on what he called Churchill's 'experiences of, and attitudes to, anaesthesia'. But all was not lost. As is often the case, Churchill himself had done some of the work for me in his published works. In this case I was able to send the professor the article Churchill had written in 1931 for the *Daily Mail*, in which he described his feelings after being knocked down by a car in New York, and his subsequent experiences in hospital.

I also had a story (almost certainly embellished) which I gave to the professor, which had been sent to me by a correspondent, of Churchill resisting the efforts of French doctors to operate on him after his fall in the South of France towards the end of his life, when he began to mutter at them, 'You bloody butchers! I won't allow you to cut me up. If you try, I will drag you through the law courts,' which a friend who was with him quickly translated: 'Mr Churchill thanks you for your consideration, but has decided that he will fly home for the operation.'

An American journalist working on the correlation between high achievers and short sleepers wanted to know if Churchill 'was among those who got by on less sleep than the rest of us'. I replied: 'Churchill was a good sleeper and a long sleeper. He tended to go to bed shortly after midnight and wake up between seven and eight in the morning, having slept soundly. He was also in the habit of taking a nap in the late afternoon. He himself recorded only one occasion when he was unable to sleep. This was at the time of the resignation of Anthony Eden in February 1938.' I concluded my reply: 'More than six hours a night for ninety years, seems quite a lot of sleep to me!' I assumed that my questioner knew that Margaret Thatcher, who was Prime Minister at the time of his letter, needed less sleep than Churchill.

Over the years, I learned that the archives held the answer to almost every query. The most frequent letters were those that repeated the commonest myths. A sixteen-year-old American schoolgirl, Mayrav Taylor, wrote from Washington: 'I am currently doing a term paper on the decision of Winston S. Churchill not to evacuate Coventry, when he knew that it would be bombed.' She had tried the Library of Congress and the British Embassy, but in vain. I hastened to send her the relevant passages of my volume six, in which I was able to show how Churchill had been led to believe, from the latest Intelligence reports available to him in the afternoon, that London would be the target that night. He therefore turned his car back from its journey to Oxfordshire in order to be in the capital while it was under attack. As soon as he reached Whitehall he ordered his secretaries into the shelter and told his Private Office staff to go home.

Later that evening, when the target was revealed as Coventry, every effort was made to send fire-fighting equipment and civil defence services to the threatened city. On no occasion was a city left to burn in order to confuse the Germans as to any British prior knowledge. The rule was clear: at the first accurate pointers, the target city was to get the maximum support from the widest possible area around it.

Another regular request was to confirm that an actor, Norman Shelley, had read Churchill's broadcast speech of 18 June 1940, pretending to be Churchill. Quite why Churchill had not done it himself was never explained; after all, broadcasting was his strength and a main method of maintaining national morale. So persistent was this particular belief, that Churchill's daughter Mary raised it, and approached his wartime Principal Private Secretary, Sir John Martin, for help. I was able to point out that, in a letter home three days after the speech, Martin himself had written: 'His halting delivery at the start seems to have struck people and we had e.g. a telegram from someone saying that he evidently had something wrong with his heart and ought to work in a recumbent position. The fact was, I gather, that he spoke with a cigar in his mouth.'

In 1978 I received a letter from a television producer, Tom Bower, then unknown to me except by reputation. He had recently been in Germany, where he heard the eminent West German politician, Franz Josef Strauss, say 'Even Winston Churchill spoke favourably about Adolf Hitler.' This was far from the first time that I had been taxed with this. Bower's must have been the twentieth letter on this theme. His offer to send my answer to Strauss, and to urge him to set the record straight, spurred my historian's quest.

Thanks to the sharp eye of a German researcher (whose name I am ashamed to say I cannot find in my own correspondence – which fills sixty box files) I had been sent a copy of a German diplomatic report of Churchill's comment, at the German Embassy in London in October 1930, that it was the Nazi party, under Hitler, that had 'contributed towards a considerable deterioration of Germany's external position', particularly towards France. In March 1931, in an article about the German Chancellor's proposed Austro-German union, Churchill had written for the Hearst Newspapers in the United States that the one reason for supporting such a union was that giving support to the Chancellor, Dr Bruning, would rob 'the much more dangerous Hitler movement of its main spring', and he had gone on to ask: 'Will not the mastery of Hitlerism by the constitutional forces in Germany be a real factor in the immediate peace of Europe?'

In September 1932 Churchill had been in Munich, on his way to the battlefield of Blenheim, to write up the battle for his biography of his ancestor John Churchill, first Duke of Marlborough. A German friend of Randolph's asked Churchill if he would be willing to meet Hitler. Churchill said yes, then questioned the intermediary about Hitler's anti-Semitic views. 'Tell your boss from me', Churchill said, 'that anti-Semitism may be a good starter, but it is a bad sticker. Why should you be against a man because of his birth? How can any man help how he is born?' When this was reported back, Hitler decided not to meet his future adversary.

Churchill had seen enough on his journey to take alarm about the rising tide of Nazism. Shortly after his return he told the House of Commons, with regard to a possible German threat to France, Belgium, Poland, Romania, Czechoslovakia and Yugoslavia: 'All these bands of sturdy Teutonic youths, marching through the streets and roads of Germany, with the light of desire in their eyes to suffer for their fatherland, are not looking for status. They are looking for weapons, and, when they have the weapons, believe me they will then ask for the return of lost territories and lost colonies, and when that demand is made, it cannot fail to shake, and possibly shatter to their foundations, every one of the countries I have mentioned, and some other countries I have not mentioned.'

In April 1933, in the first House of Commons debate about Nazism, Churchill emphasized that the nature of the 'most grim dictatorship', including militarism, appealed 'to every form of fighting spirit',

the reintroduction of duelling in the universities, and the persecution
of Jews. Seven months later he pointed out to the Commons that,
in each press report from Germany, 'we see that the philosophy of
blood lust is being inculcated into their youth in a manner unparal-
leled since the days of barbarism.'

These were clear, unambiguous views, sincerely held and publicly
expressed. It was equally so with an article in the *Strand* magazine
in October 1935, which was the basis of the remark by Franz Josef
Strauss, and others who thought Churchill had been 'soft' on Hitler.
In the article Churchill had written that the world still hoped that
'the worst' might be over and that 'we may yet live to see Hitler a
gentler figure in a happier age.' But, usually ignored by those who
quoted this phrase, Churchill had gone on to point out that, while
Hitler 'now spoke words of reassurance', the fact was that in Germany itself 'the great wheels revolve; the rifles, the cannon, the
tanks, the shot and shell, the air bombs, the poison-gas cylinders,
the aeroplanes, submarines, and now the beginnings of a fleet, flow
in ever-broadening streams from the already largely war-mobilized
arsenals and factories of Germany.'

Early in this same article, as I pointed out in my reply for Strauss,
Churchill had written, about Nazi internal policy:

The Jews, supposed to have contributed, by a loyal and
pacifist influence, to the collapse of Germany at the end
of the Great War, were also deemed to be the main prop
of communism and the authors of defeatist doctrines in
every form. Therefore, the Jews of Germany, a community
numbered by many hundreds of thousands, were to be
stripped of all power, driven from every position in public
and social life, expelled from the professions, silenced in
the Press, and declared a foul and odious race.

The twentieth century has witnessed with surprise, not
merely the promulgation of these ferocious doctrines, but
their enforcement with brutal vigour by the Government
and by the populace. No past services, no proved patriotism, even wounds sustained in war, could procure immun-
ity for persons whose only crime was that their parents
had brought them into the world. Every kind of per-

26. *Left:* Harold Macmillan and 'the case of the busy Premier', 1963 *(see page 235)*

27. *Below:* Gilbert Lushington, one of Churchill's pre-1914 flying instructors, in his cockpit. He was killed not long after this photograph was taken *(see pages 282-4)*

28. *Overleaf:* Churchill's below-ground bedroom at the Cabinet War Rooms. To accommodate today's visitors the bed area has been turned into a corridor and the bed moved inside the sitting area. On the left is a map showing 'vulnerable points' along the coast in 1940. When most visitors came, the curtain was closed

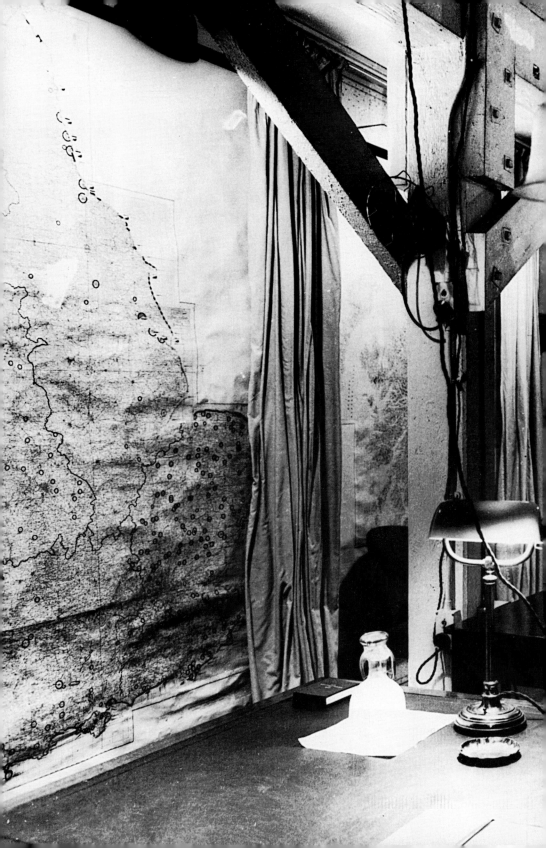

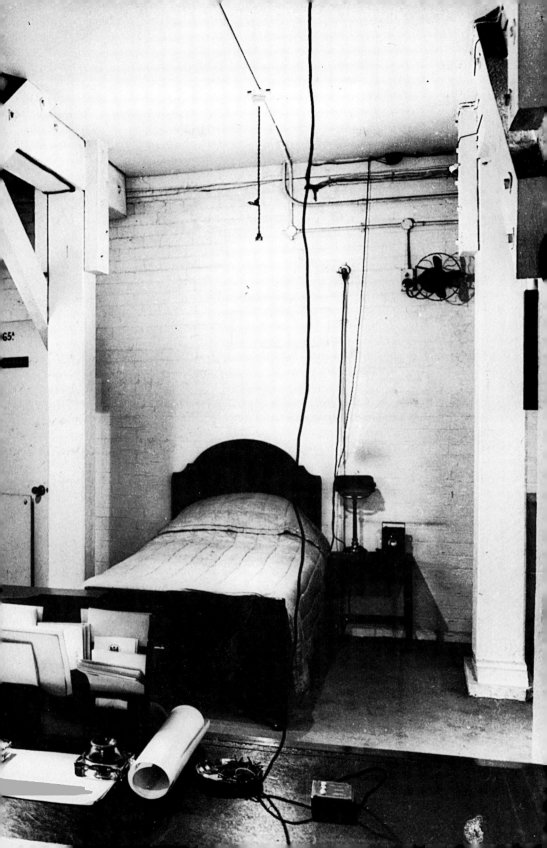

The "liberation" of CAEN!!

B. L. Montgomery
General

29. Churchill and General Montgomery (in beret) in Normandy, 22 July 1944. Montgomery has signed the photograph and written on it 'The "liberation" of CAEN!!'

30. Churchill and General Alexander on the Italian front, near Siena, 24 August 1944: one of Alexander's favourite photographs

31. Stefan Lorant and Churchill in the dining-room at Chartwell, 3 February 1939 *(see page 306)*. Before the photograph was taken, Churchill suggested putting the brandy glasses under the table and covering them with a napkin

32. 'Now they listen to Churchill', *Picture Post*, 25 February 1939

NOW THEY LISTEN TO CHURCHILL

Kept out of Conservative Cabinets for years, Winston Churchill comes back as a political power because his warnings proved true.

33. *Opposite above:* Churchill's bedroom at Chartwell, one of a sequence of five photographs taken by my son, David Gilbert, in 1993. To the left is the specially-designed ledge which swung out to become a table *(see pages 307-8)*; to its right, a photograph of Churchill's mother; above the bed, a photograph of his father. On the bedside table, a photograph of his racehorse Colonist II

34. *Opposite below:* The stone structure which housed the swimming-pool heating system at Chartwell. It was designed by Churchill to serve as an air-raid shelter *(see page 303)*

35. *Above:* The butterfly house at Chartwell, empty of its captives *(see page 316)*

36. The studio at Chartwell: Churchill's bust of the sculptor Oscar Nemon *(see page 314)*. Behind the bust is a picture by Churchill of Lake Louise in the Canadian Rockies, painted after his visit in 1929

37. The studio at Chartwell: the armchair, easel and portrait of Lord Randolph Churchill, scene of a conversation between Churchill and his father in 1947 *(see pages 314-6)*

secution, grave or petty, upon the world-famous scientists, writers and composers at the top down to the wretched little Jewish children in the national schools, was practised, was glorified, and is still being practised and glorified.

A similar proscription fell upon socialists and Communists of every hue. The trade unionists and liberal intelligentsia are equally smitten. The slightest criticism is an offence against the State.

Hitler, far from recognizing that Churchill had written 'favourably' (Strauss's charge) in this article, instructed the German Ambassador in London to lodge a strong protest against 'the personal attack on the head of the German state made in an article by Mr Winston Churchill'.

Two years later, when Churchill decided to reprint his Hitler article in book form, in *Great Contemporaries*, a Foreign Office official wrote to Churchill's secretary, Violet Pearman: 'It is hardly to be thought that this article would be at all palatable to the powers that be in Germany. In the present rather delicate state of our relations with that country, when one does not know which way the cat will jump, it might therefore be questioned whether republication just now was advisable.'

Words that Franz Josef Strauss and others had been told of as something supportive of Hitler were, at the time, regarded as exactly the opposite: words that were even in need of suppression, so as not to offend the Nazis. Churchill, needless to say, went ahead with publication.

The queries of readers, fellow historians, other writers and even schoolchildren stimulate the search and keep the focus sharp. Churchill will always be the object of curiosity and of controversy. To every enquiry there is an answer and to every controversy there is a truth. It is the search for truth that has made the quest so exhilarating. I suppose that letters will keep reaching me long after my Churchill pen is laid to rest. I shall certainly not complain if this is so.

XVII

Inkwells of Gold

At times the wealth of material in Churchill's papers was almost physically overwhelming. It took me twenty-five years to work my way from the first file to the last. I remember my elation when, late one morning in 1987, I reached the final file in the bottom drawer of the last filing cabinet. It was one of a dozen bulky files that contained the letters sent to Churchill by the general public on his ninetieth birthday.

Churchill had kept every letter that he ever received. From his first years in Parliament, he had also kept copies of many of the letters that he sent, but not all. There were certainly several thousand letters, some in his neat longhand, some of the greatest importance, of which he kept no copy. Where were they? It made sense that some of the most personal and revealing would have been hand-written.

My first realization of the size of the problem, and its extraordinary possibilities, came in New York in 1965. I was still working for Randolph, but was on my six months' sabbatical leave, teaching in the United States. He asked me to keep my eyes open for letters his father had written to people in America, but of which there were no copies in the Churchill papers. Churchill had first visited the United States in 1895. His last visit was in 1960. So there was a wide time-span to cover. Where better to start, I thought, than the New York Public Library.

It was a bitterly cold March day, two months after Churchill's death. Volume one of the biography was being prepared at Stour, where Randolph was busy on the Boer War narrative. Among the letters to Churchill at that time were several from a New York politician, Bourke Cockran, whose archive was at the Library. I entered the warm precincts of the building and with confident voice asked if I could see any letters in Cockran's papers that had been written by Winston Churchill. An assistant went away to look. When she returned she looked crestfallen. Alas, they had no letters at all from the great Winston Churchill, only a few from the American novelist of the same name, the author of many now forgotten works. This was the namesake whom Churchill had met in New York in 1900. They had some of his letters, but none written by 'my' Churchill.

I was very disappointed, thinking partly if not wholly of Randolph's disappointment. He had all Cockran's letters to his father but none of his father's replies. It was so cold outside, and I had been in the warm for so short a time in the library, that I decided to have another half hour of comfort, and asked the assistant if I could see the letters of the American novelist. She came back with a big package. I thought to myself, what a dull half hour I will have: an unknown novelist's letters from an almost equally unknown local politician. I opened the packet. There to my amazement were dozens of letters from 'my' Churchill. The assistant had been unable to believe that the Great Man's letters were in the archive of a long-ago figure with no known British connection. My first search had turned up trumps. Randolph was so pleased that he sent me a telegram (in reply to my telegram of triumph) urging me to find more such 'lovely grub', and announcing that he too was hard at work.

The letters from Churchill to Bourke Cockran filled many gaps. They revealed Churchill writing without inhibition to the man whose oratory and ebullience had so impressed him when they met in New York in 1895, while Churchill was on his way to Cuba (Cockran had arranged for a private railway car to take Churchill and his military companion from New York to Miami, to catch the boat for Cuba). The most remarkable of the letters had been written by Churchill on his twenty-fifth birthday, 30 November 1899, from the States School Prison, Pretoria, where Churchill was being held captive by the Boers, having been captured fifteen days earlier. The American Consul in Pretoria had informed the prisoner of a telegram of enquiry from Cockran, requesting news of him. 'I am alive,' Churchill replied, 'and have added another to the several vivid experiences which have crowded my last four years. I am also a prisoner, of which fact – as I am a correspondent and a non-combatant – I complain.'

Churchill's letter contained an extraordinary passage about the future financial struggles of the world:

> Capitalism in the form of Trusts has reached a pitch of power which the old economists never contemplated and which excites my most lively terror. Merchant princes are all very well, but if I have anything to say about it, their kingdom should not be of this world. The new century will witness the great war for the existence of the Individual.
>
> Up to a certain point combination has brought us nothing but good: but we seem to have reached a period when it threatens nothing but evil. I do not want to see men buy cheaper food & better clothes at the price of their manhood. Poor but independent is worth something as a motto.
>
> 'Then why', you will ask, 'with such views, do you sympathize with the Boers?' It is a pertinent question, but though I should not shrink from answering it I cannot do so at length in this letter, even though time hangs heavy on my hands – and to answer it briefly were impossible. Perhaps I do sympathize with their love of freedom and pride of race: but self-preservation seems to involve a bigger principle.

Later in this letter Churchill told his friend:

> I suppose you have never been in a prison. It is a dull occupation – even under the mildest circumstances, perhaps all the duller because the circumstances are mild. I could nurse a savage anger in a dungeon. This is damnably prosaic. My mind has become as stagnant as my body is penned up: and all the while great matters are being settled and history made – the history – mind you – I was to have recorded.

By 1899 Churchill had seen a great deal of war. He had been under fire in Cuba shortly after his twenty-first birthday. He had been nearly killed on several occasions on the North-West Frontier of

India in 1897, and again in the Sudan in 1898, when he had given a piece of his skin to help heal the wound of a fellow soldier, and had been repelled, and had publicly expressed his repulsion, by the cruel treatment of the defeated Dervishes. Now, in the solitude of captivity, he told Cockran: 'I think more experience of war would make me religious. The powerlessness of the atom is terribly brought home to me, and from the highest human court of appeals we feel a great desire to apply to yet a higher authority. Philosophy cannot convince the bullet.'

Churchill added a postscript: 'I am twenty-five today. It is terrible to think how little time remains!' At that moment, his life had sixty-four more years to run. Eleven days after writing this letter, he escaped from the prison, made his way to the Mozambique coast, and returned to the British lines a hero, and, this time, both as a journalist and a combatant. One of Randolph's most tenacious researchers, Martin Mauthner, had been to South Africa in search of exactly the type of material I had found in New York. He discovered the letter Churchill had left on his bed for the Boer Secretary of State in charge of prisoners-of-war, in which the about-to-escape journalist promised to set out in his writings 'a truthful and impartial account of my experiences in Pretoria'. Churchill's letter ended: 'Regretting that circumstances have not permitted me to bid you a personal farewell.' With that, he had clambered over the prison wall and made his way eastward.

There was a strange sequel to my discovery of Churchill's letters to Cockran. Six months later, on 17 July 1965, Randolph's cousin Anita Leslie came to Stour. Four days earlier she had been at a dinner where Adlai Stevenson, the American politician and twice democratic nominee for President, was present. Stevenson told the dinner guests the following story: he had at last met Churchill a decade earlier and asked, as he had always wanted to, 'on what mould he based his oratorical style'. Churchill replied: 'America – and Bourke Cockran, who taught me to use every note of the human voice as if playing an organ. He could play on every emotion and hold thousands of people riveted in great political rallies when he spoke.' Churchill then proceeded to quote many long passages from Cockran's speeches, astounding Stevenson at this feat of memory of sixty years earlier. Stevenson then said to Anita Leslie: 'Bourke

Cockran was an American politician you would never have heard of,' to which she replied, 'But actually he married my mother's sister and all the money he left came through my mother to my brother and myself. We each got £4,000 a year out of it.'

Adlai Stevenson told the assembled guests that he hoped he had managed to impress on them two things: 'Churchill's astounding memory, and the fact that he was always eager to attribute any of his own development or prowess or talent to America.' The next evening, while walking in a London street, Stevenson had a heart attack and died.

On my return from the United States, Randolph had put me in charge of reading the files relating to Churchill's efforts, between 1912 and 1914, when he was First Lord of the Admiralty, to learn to fly. I had found a document in Asquith's papers at the Bodleian in which Churchill, then President of the Board of Trade, had urged his colleagues to make contact with Orville Wright, the pioneer aviator. 'The problem of the use of aeroplanes is a most important one,' he told the Aerial Navigation sub-committee of the Committee of Imperial Defence, 'and we should place ourselves in communication with Mr Wright and avail ourselves of his knowledge.'

When I began work with Randolph, a fifty-year rule for all government archives was in force. This meant that in 1964 the archives for 1914, closed hitherto, were opened. I went to see the new files at the Public Record Office, then in a great Victorian building in Chancery Lane. My thrill at bringing back dozens of minutes by Churchill on aviation was matched by Randolph's pleasure at seeing what a pioneer his father had been. One set of the First Lord's minutes, of 3 March 1914, concerned the need to establish air routes and landing places. Having set up an inter-departmental committee to examine this, Churchill outlined its tasks:

> The object in the first instance is to establish certain well-marked flying routes along which at known intervals good landing places will be available. It ought to be possible, by removing hedges and filling up ditches, cutting down trees in the fences, &c, to secure a succession of good landing places at comparatively small cost.
>
> The Ordnance Survey should undertake the preparation

of a regular flying map in consultation with the above committee. This map, which must of course be made in sections, should study the country along these routes from a flying point of view.

The routes themselves should be studied in the same way as motor-car routes are studied, and descriptions and directions prepared.

A day later Churchill elaborated on the same theme:

Referring to my note about the provision of landing places, the committee should also consider how such landing places should be made visible to airmen from aloft. To this end metal signs, coloured and numbered, should be planted in the same way as motor-car guides are now fixed on all our roads.

Flags or other conspicuous aviation landmarks should be erected along the main aerial routes, like lighthouses at sea, so as to enable navigation to proceed with sureness. It ought to be possible for an airman flying along an aerial route to pick up a succession of points which would enable him to verify his position exactly in relation to each of which well-known landing places exist.

These Churchill minutes were part of his daily work at each of his ministries. The wealth of them staggered Randolph, who almost despaired at being able to make use of so much material. The original four volumes were clearly not going to be enough. When, a year later, the thirty-year rule for public documents was introduced, throwing open the archives at a stroke as far forward as 1935, it became clear that six and perhaps even seven or eight volumes would be needed to do justice to Churchill's ministerial work, and that they might have to be very long volumes indeed. Even to tell in reasonable outline the story of Churchill and the early days of air power would take at least a full chapter.

Churchill's own flying instruction had been a serious matter: many hours of practice, the enthusiastic quizzing of the young pilots who were teaching him, and a realization that flying held a vast potential. Tragically, one of his flying instructors, Captain Gilbert

Wildman-Lushington, Royal Marines, had been killed in December 1913 shortly after one of their practice flights. In the Churchill papers was a letter from Airlie Hynes, the dead pilot's fiancée, thanking the First Lord for the 'lovely wreath' he had sent to the funeral. She added: 'I want to thank you for sending me Gilbert Lushington's last letter, it was kind of you & I am so glad to have it. He was so pleased at having given you your first instruction and his last letters were all about it . . .'

'. . . his last letters . . .'

Could these letters possibly have survived? And if they had survived, how could they be found? Assuming that Miss Hynes had been twenty-one at the time of the fatal crash, she would be seventy by this time. Her letter to Churchill was written from Southsea, but unless she had never married her surname would be different. I was elated at the thought that there might just be some chance of finding her, and her fiancé's letters.

Without telling Randolph, and hoping to reverse some recent criticism of my work that he had made ('I don't know what you have done recently that merits the overly high salary I am paying you'), I telephoned Directory Enquiries and, asking them to start in Kent and work westward, then back to the East Coast and westward again, to give me all the numbers for Hynes. Kent, Surrey and Sussex revealed several Hyneses but with no connection with Airlie. I feared that when Randolph saw his phone bill even he, so lavish with calls, would be furious, and have his negative view of me confirmed, even enhanced. Perhaps I would be sacked.

After a break for half an hour, I was back on the quest. I reached Hampshire. At Emsworth, Captain W.B. Hynes RN seemed a possibility. I perked up even more when an obviously no-nonsense naval officer answered the telephone.

'Can't speak long. I'm just off. Have to get to London Airport fairly sharply.'

I quickly explained my purpose, truncating a little.

'Can't help you I'm afraid. Never heard of Airlie Hynes.'

Almost automatically, losing hope, I gave more of the background.

'Wait a minute. You must mean cousin Airlie. But she's not Hynes, she's Madden. Lives near Gosport. Why don't you give her a ring . . .'

The Captain left for the airport. Instead of writing, as I would normally have done, I went back to Directory Enquiries, who found Mrs Madden in the Gosport exchange. I made the call. Mrs Madden answered it. Yes, she was the former Airlie Hynes. Yes, Gilbert Lushington had been her fiancé. Letters? Why only the other day she had come across them while clearing out some cupboards. She had thought she had better throw them away, it was all so long ago, two wars ago. But no, she had not thrown them away. Would I like her to put them in the post?

I nearly fainted. Two days later the letters arrived at Stour. Randolph was overjoyed, coining a phrase which flattered my ego, 'tiger for research'. One of the instructor's letters, dated 30 November 1913, Churchill's thirty-ninth birthday, contained a gem: 'I started Winston off on his instruction at 12.15 & he got so bitten with it, I could hardly get him out of the machine, in fact except for about 3/4 of an hour for lunch we were in the machine till about 3.30. He showed great promise and is coming down again for further instruction & practice.' Later that day, when back at the Admiralty, Churchill had written to Lushington:

> Dear Captain Lushington,
> I wish you would clear up the question of the steering control and let me know what was the real difficulty I had in making the rudder act. Probably the explanation is that I was pushing against myself, though I am not quite sure about this. It may be that they are very stiff and hard to work. Certainly the feeling I had was that I was being repeatedly overridden, and I thought you were controlling the steering the whole time. Could you not go up with another officer and, sitting yourself in the back seat, see whether there is great stiffness and difficulty in steering, or whether it was all my clumsiness.

Lushington took the plane up again on December 2. In a letter to Churchill he reported that the difficulty did indeed probably arise from 'pushing against yourself', a very common error of beginners and 'even of experienced pilots'. He was sure that with practise the mistake would be rectified. Having sent off this letter, Lushington went up again. On coming in to land he side-slipped and was killed.

In the packet of letters which Mrs Madden sent me was one from Churchill:

> Dear Miss Hynes,
> This letter was written to me by Captain Wildman-Lushington on the morning of the second of December. Before it reached me he was dead. I think you ought to have it; and may I also ask you to accept my deepest sympathy in the blow which has befallen you. To be killed instantly without pain or fear in the necessary service of the country when one is quite happy and life is full of success & hope, cannot be reckoned the worst of fortune. But to some who are left behind the loss is terrible.

Mrs Madden had sent me a covering note. It remains to this day one of the treasures of my research:

> Dear Mr Gilbert,
> It seems very strange to resurrect the past in these letters. December 3rd 1963 will be 50 years since my beloved fiancé's death, though it seems no time at all. His vivid personality does not fade. I am sure some of those he instructed contributed to victory in 1918. I enclose the only letter I have describing Sir Winston's flight, also others I have kept all these years. You have taken great trouble to locate me!
> I married in 1918 Major J.G. Madden DSO. We lost two sons in the last war, one of whom gained the Military Cross. Excuse all this personal reminiscence, of no interest to you. Pride is a great help in old age. I can also boast of having flown several times with GWL in 1913. Return these at your leisure.
> Yours sincerely
> Airlie Madden
> What mercy for England that Sir W's flight was not the fatal one.

I read this letter to Randolph at the conclusion of my report. When I read out the postscript, he wept.

The search for letters was continuous. Lady Churchill had in her possession every single letter her husband had sent her. On a train journey from Stour to London she explained to me the choices that had been open to her: to destroy the letters, in view of how personal and revealing and intimate they were, lacking as they did any attempt to conceal his opinions, moods, fears and disappointments; to put them under lock and key for a hundred years, until the second half of the twenty-first century; or to make them available for the biography, but to avail herself of her undoubted right to refuse permission to publish things that she felt were too personal or too revealing. In fact she decided to make them available without any form of censorship whatsoever. Not one word would be cut out to protect her husband's reputation.

All this was while Randolph was biographer. When I was asked to succeed him Lady Churchill continued to maintain this absolutely unrestricted access policy, despite what I realized must have been the considerable difficulty of letting a non-family member, a virtual stranger, scrutinize without any restrictions the private life of a public man. After Lady Churchill's death her daughter Lady Soames continued this policy, very rare indeed in the history of biographies written by outsiders. Other family members did likewise. Jack Churchill's son Peregrine made available all the letters that Churchill had sent his father. The Duke of Marlborough, after a quarrel with Randolph that set things back for several months, agreed to open up the muniment room at Blenheim, in which were dozens of black tin boxes containing all Churchill's letters to his parents.

It was to Michael Woolf that Randolph had given the task of braving the Duke of Marlborough's anger once Randolph himself had been barred from his portals. The story behind the quarrel was this: about a year before I joined the team, Randolph and Michael had gone to Blenheim to get the duke's agreement to allow all the Lord Randolph, Lady Randolph and Winston Churchill letters in his archive to be used in the biography. During dinner in the main hall, the duke had asked a servant to wheel in the television set and turn it on: there was a programme he wished to see. Randolph asked the duke to have the set turned off: he, Randolph, did not watch television at dinner. The duke said that the set must stay on. An irate Randolph then announced that he would leave at once. Would the duke's servants be so kind as to pack his bags? 'You can pack your own bloody bags' was the duke's reply. Randolph left the table, packed his bags and left, spending the night at the Randolph Hotel in Oxford (where I had first seen him: perhaps it was the night of this very episode).

When, after Randolph's death, the duke invited me to Blenheim to see the archive, no reference was made to this incident, though during our conversation at lunch, in the same hall, he did describe Randolph as 'difficult'. My main problem had been entering Blenheim at all. It was a day on which the house was closed to the public. I walked forward under the ornamental arch towards the great courtyard, where I could see the duke standing. Assuming that I was a tourist he began waving his stick at me and shouting, in a stentorian voice 'Go away!'. I called back, 'I am your luncheon guest' but my words must have been blown by the wind in another direction and he heard nothing. 'Go away!' he bellowed even louder, as I drew nearer. I thought he would hit me with the stick before I could make my purpose and status known, but luckily I was just able to avoid that fate. 'DON STRUCK BY DUKE' might have been the local paper's headline.

Other archives willingly yielded up their treasures: the Royal Archives at Windsor provided copies of the long handwritten daily letters that Churchill sent to King George V, when he was Home Secretary, about the daily parliamentary scene. Other letters at Windsor included one that Churchill had written to the Prince of Wales (later King Edward VII) from Pretoria on the same day as his twenty-fifth birthday letter to Bourke Cockran, in which he revealed that he and his fellow prisoners-of-war had been allowed to become members of the State Library, 'so that now, although it is irritating to be out of everything while so much is going on, I have a secure refuge and I shall hope, philosophically, to improve my education'. Escape ten days later put an end to that.

The search for Churchill's letters not only took me to large numbers of archives outside Oxford, but made me realize how a biographer can only make a start using the papers of his subject. By themselves, these can form only a framework. Just as Churchill had searched in many archives while writing about his ancestor the 1st Duke of Marlborough, so I, in writing about the 8th Duke's grandson, had to range widely. In the course of my delving at Blenheim,

I found that there was a short period in 1895, only a few months, when Churchill's cousin the 9th Duke had no children, his own father was dead, and had the 9th Duke been killed, Winston Churchill would have succeeded to the dukedom.

I gave a shudder: not only would English history have been different, but whatever career Winston Leonard Spencer Churchill, 10th Duke of Marlborough, would have made for himself, he could not have become a twentieth-century Prime Minister. Whatever biography he deserved could have been finished in good time by his eldest son, Randolph Frederick Edward Spencer Churchill, Marquess of Blandford, either before or after he succeeded to the dukedom in his turn. Randolph as master of Blenheim; it was a pleasant fantasy.

After Lord Beaverbrook's death in 1964, Randolph was so impressed by the fortune that his widow had inherited that he mused, late one night when we were alone together, as to whether he should propose to her. He then proceeded to spend the Beaverbrook inheritance. It might be, he said, that the duke and all five or six Spencer-Churchills in line to the Marlborough dukedom before him would be killed together in a 'most unfortunate' car crash, whereupon he, Randolph, would succeed to the dukedom. His first use of the money would be to dismantle the ornamental flowers of Blenheim Palace, which he regarded as architectural excrescences. He also offered to buy me a new car, for the then princely sum of £800. In the event, he never proposed to the widow.

A member of Asquith's Cabinet once remarked that when the great Liberal Prime Minister was bored with the discussion he would look round at his colleagues with his 'obituary eye', amusing himself by preparing each of their obituaries. Churchill had no such eye, but on the death of colleagues and friends, was always moved to sombre reflections and words of particularly strong comfort. In the course of my search for letters of which he had kept no copy, such obituary letters were always striking. His power of expression was quite different to that of most such writers; he seemed to enter into an almost spiritual bond of affection and condolence. The historian John Grigg sent me a letter Churchill had written to his grandmother, Lady Islington, in early 1937, after the death of her husband, a Conservative MP before the First World War and one of Churchill's closest friends at the turn of the century. 'How lucky Jack was', Churchill wrote, 'to have you to look after him in all these long years of pain and illness.' Recalling the time they had spent together as young and rebellious Conservatives, Churchill wrote: 'What jolly times we had when our world was young! And then politics – so fierce and active. Do you remember the meeting outside the station when trains made such a noise – and that other meeting interrupted by the Tory trumpeter. Jack enjoyed it all . . .' Churchill ended his letter: 'As one gets old – the scene contracts, and the colours fade. Dear Anne, I hope & pray that there will be some mellow sunshine left for you, & that you will think kindly of your dear friend Winston.'

Churchill was then sixty-two. Inevitably, death was an increasing feature of his correspondence. One of the very first letters that I found, in 1963, when I was beginning my work for Randolph, was at Longleat, one of the letters Churchill had sent his Private Secretary Eddie Marsh. Writing in the spring of 1937 about his cousin Frederick Guest, who had died from cancer and was six months his junior, Churchill told Marsh: 'I have never seen anyone show such a complete contempt of death and make so little fuss about it.'

For every dozen discoveries there is nearly always one disappointment. Among the letters in Churchill's papers is one, dated 27 January 1924, handwritten, from the first Labour Prime Minister, Ramsay MacDonald, thanking Churchill for writing to him when he became Prime Minister. 'No letter received by me at this time has given me more pleasure than yours. I wish we did not disagree so much – but there it is. In any event I hope your feelings are like mine. I have always held you personally in much esteem, & I hope, whatever fortune may have in store for us, that personal relationship will never be broken. Perhaps I may come across you occasionally.'

What had Churchill written to the Labour Prime Minister, to elicit such a response? By good fortune Susie and I were allowed to see the MacDonald papers, then being worked on in Hampstead by his biographer David Marquand. We approached the task full of hope, expecting it to last a short while. But however long we searched the Churchill letter never turned up. I wonder where it can be, and whether someone reading these pages will chance upon it. Until it is found, we will never know what the special message was that Churchill wrote to the man who was not finally to leave Downing

Street until 1935, and who, when Churchill disapproved of his vacil-
lating position on trade union reform, was to receive the Churchillian
epithet, 'the Boneless Wonder'.*

The MacDonald papers had failed to yield up the special letter.
But for every disappointment there were certainly a dozen satisfying
searches and discoveries. One unexpected source of new material
was the transcript of a criminal trial. In the army I had been told by
one of my fellow recruits that Churchill had 'lined his pockets' during
the First World War. This seemed highly improbable, but every
allegation must be followed up, and its origin, if not its veracity,
ascertained.

As a result of my newspaper appeal in 1968 for information about
Churchill, a stranger (who later became a friend), Harford Montgomery Hyde, sent me the court transcript of a criminal libel action
brought by the Government in 1923 against Oscar Wilde's one-time
friend, the poet Lord Alfred Douglas. This action had been brought
because Douglas, in a series of lectures all over England, was accusing
Churchill of having been in the hands of Jewish financiers during
the First World War, when he had enabled them to make millions
by illegal speculation.

According to Douglas, Churchill had arranged for his successor
as First Lord of the Admiralty, A.J. Balfour, to issue a negative
communiqué after the Battle of Jutland in 1916, in which the battle
was clearly described as a defeat for the Royal Navy. As a result of
the communiqué the New York stock market was depressed. Churchill then went to the Admiralty and issued a second, much more
positive and optimistic communiqué. The New York stock market
rose. The Jewish financiers took their profit. Churchill was then
rewarded for his help, not only with money, but with the furnishing
of his London home.

There had indeed been two communiqués. After the first one,

---

* On 28 January 1928, during a debate on the Trade Disputes Bill, Churchill ended
his speech: 'I remember, when I was a child, being taken to the celebrated Barnum's
Circus, which contained an exhibition of freaks and monstrosities, but the exhibition
on the programme which I most desired to see was the one described as the "Boneless
Wonder." My parents judged that spectacle would be too revolting and demoralizing
for my young eyes, and I have waited fifty years to see the "Boneless Wonder" sitting
on the Treasury Bench.'

which was issued by the Admiralty, Balfour's advisers, surprised to find that Churchill viewed the battle in a more optimistic light, asked him – though he was then out of office and still under the shadow of the Dardanelles – to produce something more stimulating. This he had done, as he explained to the court.

At one point in the trial, the following altercation took place between Douglas and Patrick Hastings KC:

> HASTINGS: You say later on in reference to Mr Churchill: 'It is true that by most subtle means and by never allowing him more than a pony* ahead, this ambitious and brilliant man, short of money and eager for power, was trapped by the Jews. After the Jutland business his house was furnished for him by Sir Ernest Cassel.' Do you mean to say that Mr Churchill was financially indebted to the Jews?
>
> WITNESS: Yes, certainly.
>
> HASTINGS: Do you want to persist in that now?
>
> WITNESS: Of course I do.
>
> HASTINGS: Who were the Jews in whose clutches he was?
>
> WITNESS: Chiefly Cassel.
>
> HASTINGS: What justification had you in your own mind for making that charge against Mr Churchill?
>
> WITNESS: I had the evidence of what was told me by men at the Admiralty, and Sir Alfred Fripp† told me that Cassel had given Mr Churchill £40,000 in one cheque.
>
> HASTINGS: Do you realize that Mr Churchill is coming here and can be asked questions, financial and otherwise, which it is desired to ask him?
>
> WITNESS: Certainly.

When Churchill was asked about this payment from his father's friend Sir Ernest Cassel, a German Jew by origin, he stated emphatically that no such payment had been made. He pointed out that since his father's death in 1895 Cassel had been his financial adviser and friend. As for furnishing his home, that charge, he told the court, 'is the sole foundation of truth which exists for these libels; and, as

---

* A pony, in racing slang, is £25.
† Sir Alfred Dowling Fripp, Senior Surgeon at Guy's Hospital. He died in 1930.

I have stated, it occurred ten years before the battle of Jutland, and not after it'.

From the archives of the law court to the papers of Sir Ernest Cassel was my next step. These papers were in the possession of Lord Mountbatten, whose wife Edwina was Cassel's granddaughter. When I wrote to him, Mountbatten sent me the whole 'Churchill' file. In it was another of those exciting discoveries, a letter of which Churchill had kept no copy, written to Edwina after her grandfather's death in 1921. It was the year in which Churchill had lost his three-year-old daughter Marigold as well as his mother. 'This year has been very grievous to me,' he wrote, and of her grandfather: 'I had the knowledge that he was very fond of me & believed in me at all times – especially in bad times. I had a real & deep affection for him. I saw with sadness that he was approaching the end of his mortal span. The last talk we had – about six weeks ago – he told me that he hoped he would live to see me at the head of affairs. I could see how great his interest was in my doings and fortunes. I *did* hope he would live to see a few more years of sunshine.'

The Cassel papers also revealed the efforts that Churchill had made before the outbreak of war in 1914 to try to come to some amicable arrangement with the Kaiser, whom Cassel had visited on a secret mission, authorized by Churchill and Lloyd George, to bring a halt to the intensifying naval arms race.

Not all archives open their portals easily. Twenty-five years ago many more were closed than are closed today. One that was firmly closed was the archive of *The Times*. I had written repeatedly to the editor, Sir William Haley, who in graceful replies had upheld the permanent closure of the undoubted treasure trove at Printing House Square. The day came when Sir William was no longer editor. I wrote at once to his successor, William Rees-Mogg, whom I had met a short while earlier, suggesting that the archive be opened. What a good idea, he replied. He also had a suggestion of his own: why didn't I come down to London and be the first historian to see them. I did so, in February 1967. The editor and his secretary joined me for the historic moment. It was clear that the ancient archivist was not at all pleased that his wares were to be examined. Grumpily he handed each of us a duster. This was needed as the table on which I was to examine the documents was very dusty, as were the boxes in which he brought them in. I had asked to see the Churchill file. It came, and I began to pore over it, watched by the editor, his secretary and the still-disgruntled archivist. As we looked at the first page in front us, a large red spot appeared on it. Then another, and another. It took several seconds before anyone realized what had happened. The dust had brought on one of my not infrequent nose-bleeds.

In the archive of *The Times* was also a letter from Churchill to the paper's editor, sent from Khartoum to London two weeks after the battle of Omdurman. In it Churchill recounted that on the night after the battle, having learned that the newspaper's two correspondents had either been killed or wounded, he had decided to send *The Times* a despatch of his own, 'a long descriptive telegram' about the cavalry charge in which he had taken part. This had been duly passed by the military censor, but Lord Kitchener, 'having heard that I had written it refused to allow it to be sent and would doubtless have refused to allow any military officer to act as a newspaper correspondent – but no military officer with more satisfaction than myself'. Churchill's letter ended: 'I only regret for many reasons that for only one reason I was unable to serve you.'

Kitchener's dislike of Churchill gave way to friendship only in August 1914, when Churchill had been instrumental in persuading Asquith to make him Secretary of State for War, and delaying his return to Egypt on the eve of war. In 1915 Churchill was to feel that all hostility was redeemed by Kitchener coming to see him at the Admiralty, after the Dardanelles disaster, and telling him, with reference to the outbreak of the war: 'Well, there is one thing at any rate they cannot take from you. The Fleet was ready.'

One set of letters I badly wanted to see were those of Lord Thurso, who, as Sir Archibald Sinclair, had been Churchill's adjutant on the Western Front, and was his Secretary of State for Air throughout the Second World War. I set about finding these letters by writing to his family. I was told in reply that all Sinclair's private papers had been destroyed when a bomb hit their house during the Blitz. Something worried me about this answer, I cannot at this distance remember what, but about two years later I wrote again. This time I got an equally definite answer. The papers had been destroyed in a fire in the family's home in Scotland after the war. There was nothing I could do but wait: in due course a former secretary of mine (who had been involved in the original search for these very letters) wrote to me in some embarrassment that she was now working for the Sinclairs, and that all the letters from Churchill were safe and sound. This welcome news came too late for volume three, in which they would have been a jewel, but not too late for me to publish them in full in the document volume to volume four, a then unexplained touch of 1915 and 1916 for the readers of 1917!

Among the letters to Sinclair were several in which Churchill, at the lowest ebb of his political fortune, revealed his inner feelings. A month after he had been removed from the Admiralty, while he was Chancellor of the Duchy of Lancaster, he wrote:

> I have now much time on my hands and can feel thoroughly every twinge. It is a horrible experience remaining here in the midst of things knowing everything, caring passionately, conscious of capacity for service, yet paralysed nearly always. It is like being in a cataleptic trance while all you value is being hazarded. But I have managed to bear it so far.
>
> It will comfort my soul to come out for a few months and serve with my regiment, and my mind turns more and more in its malaise to that. But till victory is won at the Dardanelles my post is plainly here.

In one of his letters to Sinclair, written in 1916, after the two of them had served together in Flanders, Churchill contemplated a different world altogether. 'I am looking about to buy a country seat, and am just off to Sussex to examine one that has been offered. I wish to find a place to end my days amid trees and upon grass of my own! Freed from the penury of office these consolations become possible. Soon we shall correspond as between one landlord and another!'

It was to be another six years before Chartwell was to provide Churchill with the greenery he sought. This letter to Sinclair, hidden and then revealed, was an early clue to this Churchillian aspiration. The pleasures of the search had been restored.

Another area of satisfaction when the search went well was the discovery of photographs. Shortly after I took over from Randolph in 1968 I received a message from the daughter of George Rance, a man in his nineties, and a veteran of the Boer War. Throughout the Second World War he had been the custodian of the underground Cabinet War Rooms, and of Churchill's permanent quarters above ground. I went to see him, and saw for the first time (the rooms were not then open to the public) photographs of the wartime hideaway. Once the rooms were opened to the public, changes had to be made to accommodate the flow of visitors. Churchill's room was made smaller, and his wife's disappeared altogether. Rance also showed me photographs of the rooms that Churchill and his wife lived in above ground – small, uncomfortable, with iron girders to protect them against the blast of the bombs that fell nearby Whitehall and Horse Guards Parade.

Two Field Marshals, Alexander and Montgomery, also let me see their personal photograph albums. One of Alexander's favourite pictures showed him and Churchill near the front line in Italy in 1944, sitting on a grassy bank. Montgomery had annotated his photographs. He also wrote to me after my visit: 'You can count on me to back you 100% in your work, and to "see off" those who now work to denigrate a great national leader in a crisis. My view has always been that by standing firm when all seemed lost Winston saved not only Britain but also western civilization.' This view, unfashionable in 1969 when Monty wrote me this letter, has in several circles become even less fashionable with the passage of time. The very concept of leadership has become one for mockery. Yet my search for Churchill heightened my sense of the ability of a single person to influence events, and of the impact of leadership in both the foreign and domestic scene.

In the 1920s Churchill was known among journalists as the 'smiling' Chancellor, and photographs bore this out. Yet his puckish grin gradually disappeared from the characterization of him by historians. I remember, during the final stages of a BBC programme on Churchill, chancing upon an internal memo with the instruction, 'More gloomy pics needed.' Churchill had become the man of frowns and stern visage.

The grim-visaged Churchill was most borne out by the Karsh photograph taken in the Second World War. In one of our talks after lunch in her flat in 1969, Lady Churchill had mentioned how much she disliked this photograph, not because she did not like to see her husband frowning so severely, but because it was 'not real', as she put it. The 'real' Churchill on that occasion, she said, had been in happy mood. He had just made a successful speech to the Canadian Parliament in Ottawa. Two days earlier he had concluded very successful discussions in Washington with President Roosevelt. He had left the parliamentary chamber smiling. One Karsh photograph taken on that occasion, she told me, had shown him in happy mood; yet she had never seen it used.

I searched but failed to find the 'happy' photograph of Lady Churchill's recollection. Whenever I contacted Yusuf Karsh's office, they offered me the frown, and pointed out that thousands of authors and newspapers had used it. This was indeed so; the frown had become the standard representation of Churchill, severe and unyielding. It had been reproduced, and also distorted, on dozens of stamps and coins, in brochures and advertisements.

In 1988 I was staying in Ottawa for a lecture. Getting out of the hotel lift on my floor I saw, facing me before I turned into the corridor to my room, a modest plaque: Karsh's studio. I went in. The master was not there, but his assistant gave me the telephone number of his agent. I literally ran along the corridor to my room, telephoned the agent (in New York), ascertained that there was indeed a happy as well as a frowning photograph, and obtained permission to use it.

Four years later, when I was briefly back in Ottawa, I went to see Karsh, and to hear from him the story of the two pictures. On 30 December 1941, a few minutes after Churchill's 'some chicken, some neck' speech (making fun of the Vichy French belief a year earlier that Britain would soon have its neck rung like a chicken), he was led into the Speaker's Chamber where Karsh had set up his camera and lights. Churchill was in happy mood; Karsh had hoped for something stern and warlike. To secure the picture he wanted, he went up to Churchill and plucked the cigar out of his mouth. 'By the time I got back to my camera', Karsh recalled, 'he looked so belligerent he could have devoured me. It was at that instant I took the photograph.' Churchill's anger at losing his cigar was what 'made' the picture, but it was artificially induced: at no other point in the war did anyone see him look like that, for the simple reason that no one ever pulled a cigar out of his mouth again.

Typical of the man, Churchill's anger at Karsh's action quickly evaporated. Smiling benignly, he said to Karsh 'you may take another one.' The result was the smiler.

The first photograph was known by Karsh as 'The Roaring Lion.' It has been reproduced many thousands of times. But it is the smiling, unused photograph that represented the man I had heard so much about, who certainly could be stern and severe, but was also, and often, a smiler; the Churchill seen in good times, and even in bad, by his family, friends, and contemporaries; hence my choice of it for this jacket: the first time that it has ever appeared on the front of a British book.

XVIII

Chartwell

Churchill lived at Chartwell for forty years, from 1924 to 1964. He had found the house in 1922 during a series of drives through Kent, Sussex and Surrey in search of somewhere that could be his own residence in the country. In my search for Churchill I visited Chartwell many times, most recently while writing this book, when I was accompanied by Grace Hamblin, whose memory of the house, and of Churchill, went back sixty-four years. The atmosphere of Churchill's life and work, which pervades the house in a quite remarkable way, seemed to span the generations as we went from room to room, and walked through the garden down to the painting studio and towards the lakes.

Five years before buying Chartwell, Churchill had rented an Elizabethan haven, Lullenden, on the Surrey-Sussex-Kent border, where he had painted and awaited his return to office. 'The past is full of sadness and the future of anxiety,' he wrote from Lullenden to Admiral Fisher in May 1918. 'But today is Bank Holiday! In my sunlit garden I have the joy of the present.' He had been unable to afford to buy Lullenden when it came up for sale in 1919. A year later he inherited an estate in Northern Ireland from a distant cousin, Lord Herbert Vane-Tempest, who had been killed in a railway accident: the estate was to bring him £4,000 a year in rents and revenue. It was this windfall, the modern equivalent of more than £100,000, that stimulated his search for a country residence.

One of my first research successes when I began work on the 1917 to 1922 volume was to find the estate agent who had accompanied Churchill on several drives through the Kent and Sussex countryside to find a property. His name was H. Norman Harding, and he recalled the circumstances of their first drive with a precision born of its unusual nature. The IRA had just assassinated Field Marshal

Sir Henry Wilson, the Chief of the Imperial General Staff when Churchill was at the War Office, and there were fears that Wilson's murder (on the front steps of his London house) might be followed by more. As Harding told me:

> Having sat down, I looked around, and he asked me what I was looking at and I said, 'It is the darkest car I had ever been in,' and he replied, 'Well, you see, it is armoured, and the windows are bullet resisting and I have a loaded revolver,' and he produced it, and in front, sitting by the chauffeur, was a gentleman, who, he informed me was Detective Sergeant Thompson, and Mr Churchill said 'He also has a revolver.'
>
> He then turned round, slid back a small shutter, and said 'you see that car behind us' (as far as I remember there were three men in it) 'that car will accompany us 10 miles out of town, and on our return, will pick us up again and escort us back to the Colonial Office or to my home'.
>
> He then went on to say that 'I have a number of threatening letters each week, some telling me the actual time and method of my death, and I don't like it.

Harding remembered another episode during those summer drives. One day, when they were passing through Guildford, there was a loud retort. Churchill quickly put his hand over his face and said 'Drive on, driver, drive on.' When they pulled into a side street, they saw that it had been a burst tyre: the tyre had been cut to ribbons.

As soon as Churchill saw Chartwell he knew that it was the house he wanted. Randolph told me how his father took him and Diana for a drive into the country one day, then pulled into the driveway at Chartwell and said, 'This is where we are going to live.' The last to be told was Clementine, who would have preferred to stay in London, but deferred to her husband's enthusiasm.

Churchill made his offer to buy the house on 15 September 1922, the very day on which his daughter Mary was born. That offer, incidentally, was ten per cent less than the asking price. H. Norman

Harding was summoned to Churchill's room in the Colonial Office. There, he told me, Churchill 'strode up and down, using every argument he could think of to lower the price, but I repeated he could have it at the price my client had named, but if not he would have to go on searching. Eventually, with a very bad grace, he gave way. This was the only time during my various meetings that he was anything but courteous, kind and considerate.'

Five days later Churchill agreed to pay the asking the price, £5,000, scarcely more than one year's income from his new property. In the course of the following two years he made substantial additions and changes, keeping a constant and active watch on the architectural designs, and on the building works that followed. Chartwell became his home, the centre of his family life, his place of work and relaxation, a hub both of activity and tranquillity. He was forty-eight when he bought the house and was in his ninetieth year when, for the last time, he looked across its lakes and woodland. As with so much else at Chartwell, he had made the lakes to his own design, and with his own physical labour.

In search of Churchill, my visits to Chartwell were a source of constant revelations. On my first visit in 1970 I was shown the house by his and Lady Churchill's former secretary, Grace Hamblin, who, by a pleasing coincidence, also went round the house with me, and my fourteen-year-old son David, on my most recent visit in 1993. Chartwell is now a National Trust property, meticulously maintained to preserve the atmosphere of Churchill's day. In the summer months as many as 240 visitors go round it each hour. The administrator, Jean Broome, with her staff, ensures that each visitor will have a sense not only of rooms and artefacts but of the personality of Churchill himself.

A tour of Chartwell is a tour of Churchill's life. From the drawing-room, which he himself helped to design, are magnificent views over the Weald of Kent to the South Downs beyond. On a table in the drawing-room is the first issue of a literary magazine which his mother founded, the *Anglo-Saxon Review*. It was published in 1899, but the copy on display is a gift from his mother on his thirty-second birthday in 1906. He was then a bachelor living in London. In the front of the magazine his mother copied out a remark by Disraeli, made in 1870, four years before Churchill's birth: 'The author who speaks about his own books is almost as bad as a mother who talks about her own children.'

As a young man, Churchill had threatened legal action to prevent his mother spending money that he felt ought to have been held in trust for him. But she was the one who sent him, when he was a soldier in India between 1896 and 1898, the books he needed to complete his education. It was to her that he confided his thoughts, ambitions and fears in many hundreds of letters, up until the time of his marriage. Though he chided her in her later years for marrying a man younger than himself, the love between Churchill and his mother was deep. He was shattered when she died in 1921, as a result of a haemorrhage following a fall. On the window-ledge by his desk at Chartwell is a metal cast of her hand.

Just to the left of the entrance hall is a small library with a wall model of the Arromanches artificial harbour designed for the Normandy landings, a post-war gift: 'my beach' Churchill used to call it, when showing it to visitors. This room was for many years the research room in which his literary assistants worked: in the 1930s, Maurice Ashley, John Wheldon and Bill Deakin, and after the war, Denis Kelly and Alan Hodge. Miss Hamblin recalled on my latest visit 'the black tin boxes on the floor', 'papers all over the place', and Churchill in his study asking her, as he prepared to work, 'send me one of my young gentlemen.'

On the desk in this library, as in Churchill's study upstairs, is a hole puncher, used to prepare bundles of papers for the treasury tag that would hold them together. Churchill called the hole punchers 'clop', after the noise they made. On one occasion he asked Mrs Hill, then new to Chartwell, 'Fetch me clop.' He was working on his biography of the 1st Duke of Marlborough, and she, being knowledgeable about history, knew that there was a multi-volume work by the Dutch historian Klop on the fall of the House of Stuart. She located it at the very top of a bookshelf, took a ladder and brought the set down volume by volume, then proudly laid it on the floor by Churchill's feet. 'Christ Almighty!' was his response.

Also in the library were volumes of newspaper cuttings that had belonged to Churchill's father. 'If there's a fire', he would say, 'take my father's papers first.'

Just beyond the library, past Randolph's bathroom, was the secretaries' room, his 'factory'. One wall was covered in specially-made deep shelves, piled from floor to ceiling with tin boxes and box files. The filing scheme had been devised by Mrs Pearman in 1929 and survived to the completion of the first draft of Churchill's four-volume *A History of the English-speaking Peoples*, in 1939. The working of the filing system was regarded by those who had to operate it as little short of a miracle. 'He would send for you in the dining-room,' Miss Hamblin recalled. 'The room might be full of people. "Do find me that letter that I wrote to so-and-so five years ago." Then you'd go back to the factory and find it.'

The secretaries learned fairly quickly how the letters were arranged, in their personal, literary and political sections, and what particular letters he was likely to want. Most of the secretaries worked at Chartwell for five years and more, some for ten: they became adept at recognizing what he would want, and at interpreting his grunts and mumbles. 'Gimme . . .' was the call to action for them. They also loved their master's sense of fun and whimsy.

Chartwell was full of activity at all times, and costly to run: the house required a minimum of eight indoor staff up to the war. There were also at that time three gardeners, an estate bailiff, a chauffeur, and at least two secretaries.

Whenever Clementine was away from Chartwell, Churchill would send her long accounts of the goings-on there: he called them his 'Chartwell bulletins.' Many of them concerned the animals which he loved to watch and to write about. 'A minor catastrophe has occurred in the pig world,' he wrote to Clementine in 1927, when he was Chancellor of the Exchequer. 'Our best sow, irritated by the noise of a pick-axe breaking the ground near the pigsty, killed six of a new litter of eight little pigs. She was condemned to be fattened and die, but today she has received the remaining two and proposes to bring them up in a sensible manner. She is therefore reprieved on probation.'

Churchill had delighted in supervising the rebuilding and expansion of the house, preparing it for Clementine, who was reluctant to leave London. His first letter from Chartwell was written from what was to be her bedroom, with its vaulted roof and spectacular views across the wide countryside: he called the room her 'magnificent aerial bower'. Among ten helpers with whom he was working to restore the garden were Thompson, his Special Branch detective, Aley his chauffeur, and Waterhouse, the gardener who had worked for the previous owner:

> This is the first letter I have ever written from this place, & it is right that it sh'd be to you. I am in your bedroom (which I have annexed temporarily) & wh is sparsely but comfortably furnished with the pick of y'r two van loads.
>
> We have had two glorious days. The children have worked like blacks; & Sergeant Thompson, Aley, Water-house, one gardener & six men formed a powerful labour corps. The weather has been delicious & we are out all day toiling in dirty clothes & only bathing before dinner. I have just had my bath in your deluxe bathroom. I hope you have no *amour propre* about it!
>
> The household consists of the nursery party, reinforced by Lily – the kitchen maid.
>
> I drink champagne at all meals & buckets of claret & soda in between, & the cuisine tho' simple is excellent.
>
> In the evenings we play the gramophone (of which we have deprived Mary) & Mah Jongg with your gimcrack set.
>
> All yesterday and today we have been turfing & levelling the plateau. The motor mower acts as a roller . . .

Three months before he bought Chartwell, Churchill, then Secretary of State for the Colonies, had written what he called 'A dissertation on dining-room chairs.' This now became his guide in instructing Heals of Tottenham Court Road to make them for him. A dining-room chair, he wrote, should 'be comfortable and give support to the body when sitting up straight'. It should also have arms, 'which are an enormous comfort when sitting at meals'. It should also be compact. 'One does not want the dining-room chair spreading itself, or its legs, or its arms, as if it were a plant, but an essentially upright structure with the arms and the back almost perpendicularly over the legs. This enables the chairs to be put close together if need be, which is often more sociable, while at the same time the arms prevent undue crowding and elbowing.'

In the dining-room to this day are the chairs that were made according to these specifications. They are very comfortable indeed. For Churchill's staff, however, the effect of those chairs could sometimes be too comfortable. 'He would sit for hours after a meal,' Miss Hamblin told me, 'talking with his guests. He used to drive the staff mad, and Lady Churchill too. He would sit here after lunch until four in the afternoon. The staff couldn't clear things away.' Yet lunch could be a time of magnificent talk and loud, shared laughter. 'He made everybody enjoy everything' was Miss Hamblin's reflection.

Guests rejoiced in the weekend life at Chartwell. In 1934 Lady Diana Cooper noted in her diary a typical episode. It took place after Churchill had finished his late-afternoon sleep, from which he always rose refreshed. 'Then (unexpectedly) bathing at seven in pouring rain', she wrote, 'intensely cold with a grey half light of approaching night, yet curiously enough very enjoyable in its oddness.'

Everyone swam, including Clementine and Randolph; the secret on that cold evening was that the swimming-pool, at the top of the garden, which Churchill had designed himself with meticulous care, was heated. 'It is Winston's delightful toy.' Twenty-four hours after that first swim, Diana Cooper noted, 'He called for Inches the butler, and said: "Tell Allen to heave a lot more coal on. I want the thing at full blast." Inches returned to say that Allen was out for the day. "Then tell Arthur I want it full blast," but it was Arthur's day off as well, so the darling old schoolboy went surreptitiously and stoked himself for half an hour, coming in on the verge of apoplexy.'

What Diana Cooper may not have known was that, as Churchill's literary assistant of those days John Wheldon told me, in designing the boilerhouse for the swimming-pool Churchill had asked for specifications that would enable it also to serve as a bomb shelter. It was to be large enough, he insisted, that both family and staff could be protected. In the event the nearest bomb, a flying bomb, was to fall only a mile away at Crockham Hill, killing twenty-four babies and eight staff at a children's home: five of the babies were only a month old, the oldest, eleven months.

Not only had Churchill designed and supervised the making of the swimming-pool: he had taken infinite pains to lay the bricks for the large outer garden walls, and to join the bricklayers in building a cottage in the grounds for his chauffeur, as well as a miniature one for his youngest daughter Mary. His work on the lakes was of particular importance to him. 'The days have slipped by very quickly here,' he wrote to Stanley Baldwin in 1925. 'I have passed them almost entirely in the open air, making a dam, which largely extends my lake and finally, I hope, removes it from the category of ponds.'

In 1928, as a result of the press publicity given to his bricklaying work at Chartwell, Churchill, while Chancellor of the Exchequer, was invited to become a member of the Amalgamated Union of Building Trade Workers. 'None of my men are trade unionists,' he wrote to the Cabinet Secretary, 'and about here they rather mock at trade unions. Personally, as you know, I am strongly in favour of organizing workmen for trade purposes.' Churchill decided to join: he must have been the only Conservative Chancellor of the Exchequer to hold a trade union card. A visitor to Chartwell noted in his diary that year: 'Winston is building with his own hands a house for his butler, and also a new garden wall. He works at bricklaying four hours a day, and lays ninety bricks an hour, which is a very high output.' Dr Brand, who attended to Mrs Pearman when she became ill, wrote to me of a bricklayer who helped Churchill build the main garden wall: 'He liked Mr Churchill because he insisted on taking his turn with the unpopular chores as well as the bricklaying and this included going up to the house to collect the drinks for the tea breaks.'

When Churchill left the Exchequer in 1929 he took on the twenty-eight-year-old Patrick Buchan-Hepburn, a would-be Member of Parliament, as his Private Secretary. Shortly after I began work on my own, I made contact with Lord Hailes (as he had become: he had been an MP from 1931 and a minister in 1955) and visited him in his London home. He recalled his first visit to Chartwell. 'Winston treated me like a grown-up and an equal. He was full of humanity and kindness. I remember when we walked in the garden we found some rose bushes which were only receiving a trickle of water. Turning to the gardener, Winston said: "You must arrange for a more generous flow of water here." When I was ready to leave he said, "You must never call me Sir. We leave that for the barrack square," and then: "May I call you Patrick, if it's not too sudden."'

Lord Hailes was impressed by Churchill's attitude to his many guests. 'Winston was a meticulous host,' he told me. 'He would watch everyone all the time to see whether they wanted anything. He was a tremendous gent in his own house. He was very quick to see anything that might hurt someone. He got very upset if someone told a story that might be embarrassing to somebody else in the room. He had a delicacy about other people's feelings. In his house and to his guests he was the perfection of thoughtfulness.' On the wider aspect of Churchill's attitudes, Hailes told me: 'He had no class consciousness at all. He was the furthest a person could be from a snob. He admired brain and character; most of his friends were people who had made their own way.'

On the ever-controversial matter of Churchill's drinking habits, Hailes was an interesting witness. 'I never knew him to get drunk,' he told me. 'He sipped coloured water all day, from morning to night: there was hardly any whisky in it at all,' and he added: 'He had ox-like strength.'

I thought of Lord Hailes each time I passed the rose bushes at Chartwell, where every vista, every artefact and every room has a story behind it. In the room that served after the war as a dining-room are eight mounted porcelain horsemen, a gift from Brendan Bracken. One of them depicts Napoleon, with his arm outstretched. 'Turn him to point to me,' Churchill would say. It had been an early ambition of his to write a biography of Napoleon, though it was an ambition unfulfilled. Charlie Chaplin, for whom Churchill wanted to write a film script based on the young Napoleon, visited Chartwell in 1932: there is a photograph of Churchill welcoming him at the front door.

Another of those who went to see Churchill at Chartwell was Aircraftman T.E. Shaw, the erstwhile Lawrence of Arabia. Sarah Churchill, on a visit to Oxford, told me: 'Lawrence would arrive on his motor-bicycle from a nearby Air Force station on Sunday afternoons for tea. He never announced his arrival. He was a small, slight man, and his fine head looked almost out of proportion. He had a very soft voice and we noisy, extroverted Churchills were silenced by his quiet personality, and we would all listen in pin-drop silence to what he had to say. I remember my father sitting back, watching him with a half smile, and letting him run the conversation.'

Clementine Churchill's cousin, Sylvia Henley, a frequent guest at Chartwell, also gave me an account of a Lawrence visit. 'Rather out of the blue at luncheon', she told me, 'Winston asked Lawrence, "In the event of an air attack, what would be our best defence?" to which Lawrence replied, "Multiple air force defence stations to intercept."' Patrick Buchan-Hepburn also remembered Lawrence at Chartwell. When he first saw him, he told me, 'He was wearing his RAF uniform and looked quite undistinguished. He was handing bricks to Winston, who was building a wall. For dinner, Winston made Lawrence put on his Arab robes. It was Winston who had kept the robes, he had them at Chartwell. Lawrence looked quite different with them on.'

Buchan-Hepburn remembered another facet of Churchill's life at Chartwell. Even in his Exchequer years, he told me, 'He used to say to me, when he was depressed, "I must go down to Chartwell to assault a canvas."' Churchill's paintings are to be found throughout the house. But there are other paintings that also have their place. In Lady Churchill's bedroom are two watercolours by their daughter Sarah, showing her beach-house at Malibu in California, at night and in the morning. Sarah, or 'Mule' as she signed her letters to her parents, was a staunch supporter of her father, but was never afraid of speaking her mind.

It was during the wilderness years that Chartwell, the home of a man without political office, hummed most with activity. After Munich, the magazine *Picture Post* decided to support, and to enhance, the campaign for Churchill's return to office. In February 1939 its picture editor, the Hungarian-born Stefan Lorant, whose book *I Was Hitler's Prisoner* had told at first hand of the cruelties of life in the concentration camps in 1933, drove to Chartwell to prepare an article and photographs for a special 'bring back Churchill' edition. Then in his early seventies (he is now in his mid-nineties), Lorant told me how, when the time came for the cover photograph to be taken, Churchill put the brandy glasses under the table and covered them with a napkin, in case readers got the wrong impression. In the event, that particular photograph was not used. Lorant sent it to me: he is sitting in one of Churchill's special dining-room chairs. For the picture taken at table that was used, the curtain was closed to give a dark background. The cigar was the same.

Politics were part of the fabric of life in the Churchill household. But whenever I spoke to Sarah or Randolph or Mary about life at

Chartwell, they stressed the fun and laughter, the equality and sharing, the humour and electricity of life, even when politics were not going their father's way. Guests were always welcome, meals were always the scene of lively talk and favourite games. Gentle teasing and loud laughter abounded. On one occasion, Sarah told me, a cacophony of loud voices was suddenly silenced by their father's stentorian laughter: 'Randolph, do stop interrupting me while I'm interrupting you!'

Although the laughter is now stilled, many facets of Churchill's character remain for the visitor to catch a glimpse of. He was fascinated, for example, by medals and medallions, and his own personal medals are on display in a special cabinet. They start, chronologically, with his first campaign medal in 1897, won when he was twenty-two. His Queen's South Africa Medal for his service during the Boer War includes five clasps: one is for his action at the Battle of Diamond Hill, when he went forward to the crest of a ridge on a most dangerous reconnaissance mission, and was thought by his commanding officer to be worthy of a Victoria Cross. Another of the clasps was for an episode just before the capture of Johannesburg: while the city was not yet in British hands, Churchill had cycled through it with an urgent despatch for the Commander-in-Chief.

Among the medallions of which Churchill was most proud, and they too are on display, are his First Prize in the Public Schools Fencing Competition for 1892, when he was seventeen; his award in 1933 from the French Senate; his *Sunday Times* Literary Award given to him in 1938 for his four Marlborough volumes; and the medallion awarded to him in 1946 by the City of New York. His mother had been born in Brooklyn in 1854; he had first visited New York in 1895. Also on display is the large medallion that he gave to all those, of all political parties, who had served in his wartime government. It is inscribed: 'LET US SALUTE THE GREAT COALITION, 1940–1945.' In the Royal Archives is his comment when sending one of these medallions to the King: 'It would make an excellent paperweight.'

Churchill's bedroom was one of the smallest rooms in the house. When Miss Hamblin first took me into it in 1970 the aroma of cigar smoke still lingered. The room has a window overlooking the view that is most entrancing, across the Weald of Kent. Miss Hamblin recalled how Churchill liked to be told if a storm was on its way: 'When will it be here?' he would ask. He could then watch it as it approached. Also visible from his bedroom window, closer to, is the lake that he had helped dig out, hiring a mechanical digger, laying a rail track across the lawn, and standing knee-deep, in waders, supervising the work.

Everything in Churchill's bedroom is simple. A small wooden ledge on the wall alongside the bed could hold a cigar and matches, or be turned round so that he could use it as a work surface for the despatch boxes in which his correspondence and documents were brought to him. In the built-in cupboard next to the bed was a specially-designed wooden bed tray, with a semi-circle cut out in it 'for my tummy', as he used to say. Among the books at his bedside was one – typical of many – out of which his budgerigar Toby had taken many small nibbles; and inside the book, used a bookmark, was one of Toby's beautiful feathers, blue-green on one side, and reddish on the other. 'He would hand you the book,' Miss Hamblin told me, 'and say, "Put that away, Toby's read it."'

One of the most practical devices in the room was a table by the window, with a cord attached which pulled up a mirror. Nothing in the room was grandiose. There was a small bathroom leading off the bedroom, with a sunken bath. Sometimes Churchill would dictate while lying in the bath, much as he had once done when he was a schoolboy at Harrow. He also installed a special mirror in the bedroom cupboard so that, by clever use of the bathroom mirror, he could see his back and front at the same time: 'He could see himself all round.'

On the bedroom walls is a photograph of Lady Randolph in resplendent formal dress ('she shone for me like the evening star, brilliant, but at a distance' he wrote in his autobiography[*]) and two photographs of Lord Randolph Churchill. There was also, in his later years, a photograph of one of the horses that he owned, Colonist II. Lady Churchill had been somewhat sceptical of his racing enthusiasm, but in his later years he enjoyed the excitement of the turf. His

---

[*] In 1918 Lady Randolph married Montagu Porch, of the Northern Nigeria Civil Service. At the time of their marriage she was sixty-four, her husband forty-one. One diarist, Colonel Repington, noted: 'Winston says he hopes marriage won't become the vogue among women of his mother's age.'

earliest childhood 'den' had been built in the garden of a house that his parents had taken near Newmarket racecourse, and he had heard of the outbreak of war on the North-West Frontier of India in 1897 – a war to which he hurried, and in which he fought – when he was at the racecourse at Goodwood.

At Churchill's bedside was his favourite aid to sleep, especially when on a journey, a black satin eye-band. Also at the bedside today is his Cellar Account Book. He liked to look at it once a month; all his life he would carefully scrutinize his bills. Leaving the bedroom, through an opening that had no door, one enters the study, the centre of Churchill's thirty-year literary productivity at Chartwell. It too had some financial elements. On the wall facing his desk is one of his favourite documents, a photograph of the single page on which his father devised his Budget in 1886. The total expenditure for the year is £90,400,000. The Government's total income is £90,000,000. This miracle of budgeting, quite a distance from today's figures and concepts, was to be obtained by cuts in military and naval expenditure.

To ensure these cuts Lord Randolph had threatened resignation. The Prime Minister, Lord Salisbury, called his bluff and accepted. Lord Randolph was finished. He never presented a Budget and never held public office again. This terrible set-back, at the age of forty, was to cast a long shadow over the Churchill family, and to serve as a spur to Lord Randolph's elder son, who was eleven at the time of his father's humiliation, to thrust his way forward in the political arena. In 1924, Churchill's first year at Chartwell, he became Chancellor of the Exchequer: unlike his father, Churchill not only presented one Budget but five.

On Churchill's desk, as set out today, is a typed sheet of monthly accounts. Each month he would look through it, and, as with the cellar accounts, mark what should and should not be paid. A note with the accounts outstanding on 25 September 1956 states: 'Miss Hamblin, Please do not pay the accounts against which I have marked "details" until I have seen them.' There are three that he has queried: one for wines and spirits (£115), one for the wiring of special lighting for paintings in the first-floor corridor (£96), and one for clothes and repair of clothes by Turnbull and Asser of Jermyn Street (£105). Miss Hamblin told me: 'He would go through the list, "We will pay that one," "we will pay half of this one," and, with an electricity bill for example, "clearly £80 is impossible – look up the same quarter four years ago."'

For several consecutive years at Chartwell in the 1930s, Churchill's annual expenditure, for the house, for his helpers, and for his staff, including his car and chauffeur, was running at £10,000: he was forced to embark on many budgeting exercises, such as cutting out some of the daily newspapers (he liked to read every national newspaper every day) and, in 1938, following severe stock exchange losses, he was forced to put Chartwell on the market. The estate agent's brochure was printed and ready to be sent to would-be buyers: it included eighty acres of land, nineteen bed- and dressing-rooms, eight bathrooms, five reception rooms, 'central heating throughout', two lakes, and a hard tennis court. The cottage Churchill had built was 'one of three' also for sale. 'The floodlit swimming-pool of about 35,000 gallons is another special feature.' The sale price was £20,000. Fortunately for Churchill and his family, a friend came to his rescue and paid his losses. Chartwell was taken off the market. The estate agent's brochure did not say that the heating system for the swimming-pool, the room dug out of the side of the hill, had been specially designed by Churchill to have thick enough walls to serve as an air-raid shelter in the event of war. In his wilderness years he had to accept that, when war came, he might still be a private citizen, living at Chartwell for the duration of hostilities.

At Churchill's desk in the study, his chair faces the same panoramic view over the Weald of Kent that so many rooms look out over. When he dictated letters or books, the secretary would sit in the chair, and Churchill would pace up and down the room. The study is a long room, and when he reached the far end his voice was not always audible. 'Never mind,' he told one secretary, Joan Taylor, on her first day, 'I always remember what I've said.'

Most of the books in the study were in bookshelves. But there was one antique bookcase in the room, 'my snob bookcase' he called it. The books on the bookshelves were constantly being taken down and consulted, or laid on the special upright writing desk at which he would stand and write; only the books in the bookcase remained in any real semblance of order. If someone sent him an inscribed, or particularly fine or old book, he would say to his secretary: 'Yes, it's beautiful, do put it in my snob bookcase.' His collection of books included complete signed editions (signed for him, that is) of H.G. Wells, many books sent by George Bernard Shaw, and signed editions of the First World War poems of Siegfried Sassoon. One of Churchill's First World War pilots when he was Minister of Munitions, frequently visiting France, told me that when a general protested that Sassoon wrote anti-war poems and lampoons of generals, Churchill replied: 'I'm not a bit afraid of Siegfried Sassoon. That man can think. I am afraid only of people who cannot think.' This pilot, Gilbert Hall, also recalled Churchill's keenness in the summer of 1918 to open a regular air service between London and Paris: this was done.

On the desk in Churchill's study are photographs of his family, including one signed 'Clemmie, New Year 1943' and one of Randolph taken outside the Ritz in London by Lord Snowdon. There is also a small cameo photograph of his father, the ever-present influence in his life. On the window-ledge a large piece of jagged metal bears the inscription: 'This fragment of a 30lb shrapnel shell fell between us and might have separated us for ever but is now a token of union.' It was a gift from his cousin the 9th Duke of Marlborough, a souvenir of the South African war. There is also a First World War souvenir in the study, a sketch of Clementine by John Lavery, painted in 1916 while Churchill was in the trenches. In a corridor nearby is one of the paintings Churchill himself did at Ploegsteert, showing the village under German bombardment.

Diarists and visitors have recorded many episodes that took place in Churchill's study. Harold Macmillan, then a back-bench Conservative MP out of sympathy with the general policy of appeasement, recalled a visit immediately after Mussolini had invaded Albania in April 1939: 'Maps were brought out, secretaries were marshalled, telephones began to ring.

The secretaries who made this activity possible were headed first by Violet Pearman, from 1929, and then by Kathleen Hill, from 1936. Among the recent discoveries in the study was an old cigar box which, when opened, did not contain cigars, but secretarial knick-knacks. A note in the box by Miss Hamblin states: 'The writing on this box is Mrs Pearman's and it must be well over 50 years old! We always kept it filled – and at the ready – with tags, clop, clips, pencils, rubber, ribbons etc. in case of sudden travel!! And when the wanderer returned, it was immediately filled & put by for the next!!'

Miss Hamblin recalled a typical morning remark: 'I'm going to Paris this afternoon,' and commented: 'You had to be ready.' Mrs Pearman's cigar box was the emergency travel box. One of its most important contents was the key to Churchill's despatch box, in which he kept his most important correspondence, and sealing wax, to enable letters of particular secrecy to be sealed.

After the Second World War the downstairs dining-room was converted into a cinema. Churchill had always loved films and became something of an addict. His staff would choose a film for every other night of the week. 'He liked a big audience,' Miss Hamblin told me. 'All the outdoor staff and the indoor staff would be invited. We would all be seated. He would come in after dinner, like the Queen, and he would say, "Let her go." After each film the lights would go up, and the others would wait for Churchill to comment. Once, after watching *Wuthering Heights*, he was silent for quite a while, then piped up: 'What terrible weather they have in Yorkshire.' A favourite film was *Lady Hamilton*, with Vivien Leigh and Laurence Olivier. When it was first released in the United States in 1941, with the title *That Hamilton Woman*, Churchill advised Alexander Korda by telegram to change the title for the United Kingdom release, and Korda did so. The film would bring Churchill to tears: Nelson's patriotism in exile was portrayed in the very language of Churchill's wilderness years, the very years when Chartwell had hummed the most.

Chips Gemmell, who joined Churchill's secretarial team in 1958, recalled, when we met in New York in 1990, the evening film shows at Chartwell: 'He loved the films, any film. After it, tears down his face, then wiping them away, "The best film I've ever seen." '

As well as films, Churchill loved to sing the songs of his youth. On his seventy-fourth birthday his family arranged for the popular actress and singer, Audrey Cleaver, to sing some of his favourite songs to him. The list they prepared for her gives a vivid glimpse of his love of ballads and refrains. It included the Harrow School song 'Forty Years On,' 'Tipperary,' 'Land of Hope and Glory,' 'Lily of Laguna,' 'A Life on the Ocean Wave,' as well as 'any Ginger

Rogers, Fred Astaire and Noël Coward tunes'. The list emerged during my researches in a London saleroom.

As well as being a house, Chartwell was also a farm: over the years Churchill had bought several farmhouses and fields to add to it. In the 1950s his son-in-law Christopher Soames took charge of that aspect of Chartwell's activities. Churchill was delighted: although never a farmer he loved the rural aspects of Chartwell, the animals and the woodlands, and was proud of its productivity and produce. In Lord Beaverbrook's papers (when they were at the Beaverbrook Library in Fleet Street under the custodianship of my former tutor, A.J.P. Taylor) I found a letter from Sir Archibald Sinclair to Beaverbrook, describing a visit to Chartwell in 1949: 'He took me round the farms, showed me short-horns, and Jerseys and then a huge brick hen-house he had built himself – "Chickenham Palace". Alongside was a noisome & messy little piece of bare ground – "Chickenham Palace Gardens". "What kind of hens?" I asked. "Oh, I don't bother about the details," growled Winston.'

Being a painter, Churchill was fortunate that he could place his works alongside those by Sargent, Nicholson, Lavery and Monet to provide colours and associations of their own. The still life of a vast array of bottles was one Churchill had most enjoyed painting: he called it his 'bottlescape'. I was given two versions of how it came to be done, contradictory but equally charming. According to Miss Hamblin, the bottles had been brought from the wine cellar and laid out on the dining-room table while Clementine Churchill was abroad: 'He wanted to get it done before she came back. The whole place was upside down.' Churchill's nephew Peregrine recounted another version: it was Christmas, the whole family were there including Clementine, carol singers had been invited in to sing, and the bottles had been put out on the sideboard for them. I was lucky that the differing versions did not relate to some major matter of government policy. But they pointed up one of the hazards of oral history.

In search of his own painting haven, Churchill converted part of a cottage in the grounds to serve as a studio. Today the whole range of his paintings can be seen there: among them a picture of the pyramids painted in 1921, after Churchill had presided over eight days of intensive talks in Cairo, out of which emerged the British

Mandates for Palestine, Transjordan and Iraq. There are several scenes of Marrakech and the distant snow-capped Atlas mountains, which he had first seen when on holiday there in 1936, had returned to briefly in the war (when he painted the only canvas he had time for during the Second World War), and went back to in 1948 when he was writing his war memoirs. There are also paintings of the Canadian Rockies, and in particular of Lake Louise, where he had spent several entrancing days sightseeing on horseback in 1929. There is a painting that he did in Italy immediately after the war, his only picture of the effects of bombing on a building. As he painted, a group of Italians had gathered round, and began to boo and shake their fists. To Brigadier Harold Edwards, who was with him and who sent me an account of the incident, Churchill admitted that it was a 'tactless thing' to have done and that he would have been 'damned annoyed if Hitler had started to paint the bomb damage in London'.

Also in the studio at Chartwell is a small sculpted head, not of Churchill but of the sculptor Oscar Nemon. I once asked Nemon about it (when he was measuring my own head with a tape measure, intending to sculpt me). He told me that while he was sculpting Churchill, his sitter had said that he would do the same, and then produced his only known piece of sculpture. It is a striking work, conveying Nemon's intensity.*

Now on an easel in the studio is a portrait of Lord Randolph, painted during the 1880s. It was sent to Churchill in May 1945 by a well-wisher who had chanced upon it at an auction in Northern Ireland and had bought it for a pound. It had a tear in the canvas, and some of the paint had been damaged. One foggy afternoon in November 1947 Churchill set up his easel and decided to make a copy of it. He had been painting for about an hour and a half when he felt an odd sensation. Turning round, palette in hand, he saw, in his leather armchair, his father. They began to talk. Lord Randolph questioned his son about what had happened in Britain since his death in 1895. He was shocked to learn there was a socialist govern-ment in power, and amazed that there should still be a monarch in such circumstances. Had Churchill earned his money from painting?

---

* The bust of Winston Churchill that Nemon sculpted on this occasion is in the Queen's Guard Chamber at Windsor Castle.

Lord Randolph asked. 'No indeed,' Churchill replied, 'I write books and articles for the Press.'

Lord Randolph had then recalled his son's stupidity at school and the 'stilted letters' that he had written. 'I was not going to talk politics with a boy like you ever.' He supposed his son, with his love of toy soldiers, had made a career in the army. 'I was a Major in the Yeomanry,' Churchill replied. Lord Randolph was not impressed.

Father then questioned his son at length about the wars and regimes of the new century. Did Russia still have a tsar? Yes, his son replied, 'but he is not a Romanoff. It's another family. He is much more powerful, and much more despotic.' But as a result of the most recent war, Europe was a ruin. 'Many of her cities have been blown to pieces by bombs.' Thirty million people had been killed in battle and seven million in cold blood. 'They made human slaughter-pens like the Chicago stockyards.' Ten European capitals were now 'in Russian hands'. 'They are Communists now, you know, Karl Marx and all that. It may well be that an even worse war is drawing near. A war of East against West. A war of liberal civilization against the Mongol hordes.'

As his son recounted the story of the twentieth century, Lord Randolph expressed surprise at his grasp of events. 'Of course you are too old now to think about such things, but when I hear you talk I really wonder you didn't go into politics. You might have done a lot to help. You might even have made a name for yourself.' Then Lord Randolph tried to light a cigarette: as he struck the match, he vanished.

A few days later Randolph and Sarah were eating alone with their father at Chartwell when Sarah asked him, 'If you had the power to put someone in that chair to join us now, whom would you choose?' They expected him to say Julius Caesar or Napoleon. Instead he answered without hesitation, 'Oh, my father, of course.' He then told them about the episode in the studio. They urged him to set it down but he was at first reluctant to do so. Then, over the next few months, he dictated the whole conversation. Randolph was thrilled when he found the typescript (headed simply 'Private article') among his father's papers. He published it in the *Sunday Telegraph* a year after his father's death, and I had no hesitation in publishing it as a chapter of its own in volume eight of the biography.

At the time of his conversation with Lord Randolph in the studio, Churchill was seventy-two. Four years later he became Prime Minister for the second time, resigning when he was eighty. After that he spent most of his time at Chartwell and in the South of France, where he would look from time to time for what he called his 'dream villa'. But the real dream villa of his life was Chartwell. There, at the end of 1963, he reached his ninetieth year. The following October, three months before his death, Sir Leslie and Lady Rowan were his guests for dinner. Sir Leslie had been his Principal Private Secretary at the end of the Second World War. 'It was sad to see such a great man become so frail,' Lady Rowan wrote to me when I asked her about that visit.

A few days later, Churchill returned to London. He was never to see his beloved Chartwell again.

As I sat on the terrace at the spot overlooking the lakes where Churchill had sat in his last years, my search reached its final phase. 'Old age is intolerable,' he would say to those nearest to him, as he struggled bravely through increased physical infirmity and mental weariness. 'My life is over, but not yet ended,' he had told his daughter Diana some years before. A few guests were still invited, those whom his secretary Doreen Pugh thought he would like to see. Though he did not always speak to them, he was aware of their presence and would anticipate their arrival with obvious pleasure. Field Marshal Montgomery became a regular visitor, content to do the talking.

Once painting was no longer possible, Churchill sat for hours on the terrace in silence, looking at his favourite view across the lakes, and waiting for a heron, which came often, to appear. He would look up with pleasure when it was pointed out to him. He had always loved animals and felt an affinity with them. At Chartwell, Rufus the dog (and following him, Rufus II), birds, sheep, cows, goldfish, even butterflies had their place in his scheme of things. Miss Hamblin remembered the day on which, shortly after his retirement in 1955, he was walking slowly past the butterfly house by the garden wall, stopped, and then in silence opened the netting, giving the butterflies their freedom. He no longer wished to be their captor.

Maps

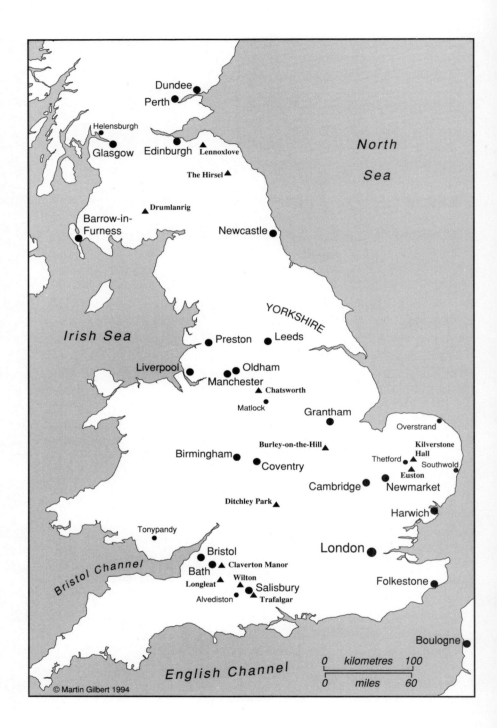

© Martin Gilbert 1994

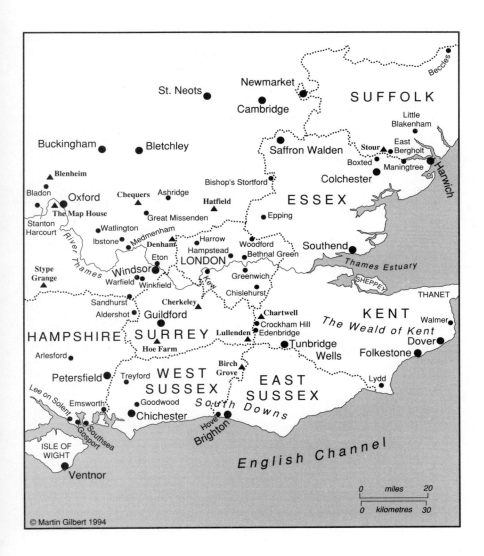

St. Neots

Newmarket

Cambridge

SUFFOLK

Beccles

Little
Blakenham

Buckingham

Bletchley

Saffron Walden

Stour
East
Bergholt

Blenheim

Bladon

Oxford

Chequers

Ashridge

Bishop's Stortford

Boxted

Maningtree

Harwich

The Map House

Hatfield

Colchester

Stanton
Harcourt

Great Missenden

ESSEX

Watlington

Epping

Ibstone

Medmenham

Denham

Harrow

Woodford

River Thames

Eton

Hampstead

Bethnal Green

Southend

Stype
Grange

Windsor

LONDON

Thames Estuary

Warfield

Winkfield

Kew

Greenwich

SHEPPEY

Sandhurst

Cherkeley

Chislehurst

THANET

Aldershot

Guildford

Chartwell

KENT

Walmer

HAMPSHIRE

SURREY

Lullenden

Crockham Hill

The Weald of Kent

Dover

Hoe Farm

Edenbridge

Arlesford

Tunbridge
Wells

Folkestone

Petersfield

Treyford

WEST
SUSSEX

Birch
Grove

EAST
SUSSEX

Lydd

Lee on Solent

Emsworth

Goodwood

South Downs

Chichester

Hove

Southsea

Brighton

Gosport

ISLE OF
WIGHT

English Channel

Ventnor

0   miles   20

0   kilometres   30

© Martin Gilbert 1994

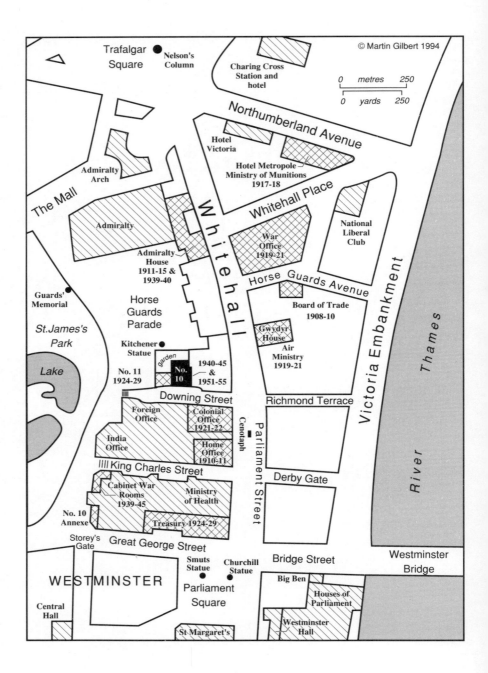

© Martin Gilbert 1994

Trafalgar Square — Nelson's Column

Charing Cross Station and hotel

Northumberland Avenue

Hotel Victoria

Hotel Metropole — Ministry of Munitions 1917-18

Whitehall Place

Admiralty Arch

The Mall

Admiralty

Admiralty House 1911-15 & 1939-40

Whitehall

War Office 1919-21

National Liberal Club

Horse Guards Avenue

Guards' Memorial

St.James's Park

Lake

Horse Guards Parade

Kitchener Statue

garden

No. 11 1924-29

No. 10

1940-45 & 1951-55

Gwydyr House

Board of Trade 1908-10

Air Ministry 1919-21

Victoria Embankment

River Thames

Downing Street

Foreign Office

Colonial Office 1921-22

India Office

Home Office 1910-11

Cenotaph

Richmond Terrace

King Charles Street

Cabinet War Rooms 1939-45

Ministry of Health

No. 10 Annexe

Treasury 1924-29

Parliament Street

Derby Gate

Storey's Gate

Great George Street

WESTMINSTER

Central Hall

Smuts Statue

Churchill Statue

Parliament Square

St Margaret's

Bridge Street

Big Ben

Houses of Parliament

Westminster Hall

Westminster Bridge

0   metres   250
0   yards   250

GREAT BRITAIN

North Sea

HOLLAND

GERMANY

Chequers

London

Chartwell

Dover

Folkestone

The Hague

Antwerp

Ypres

Brussels

Aachen

BELGIUM

Verchocq

Loos

LUX.

Notre Dame de Lorette

English Channel

Montreuil

Dieppe

Arromanches

St. Georges Motel

Paris

Metz

Strasbourg

Dreux

Tours

Briare

Zurich

Berne

SWITZERLAND

Geneva

Annecy

FRANCE

Bay of Biscay

Bordeaux

ITALY

Turin

Genoa

Mimizan

Roquebrune

Aix-en-Provence

Eze

Monte Carlo

Biarritz

Bordaberry

Pyrenees

Cannes

Marseille

Cassis

SPAIN

Mediterranean Sea

0   kilometres   150

0   miles   100

© Martin Gilbert 1994

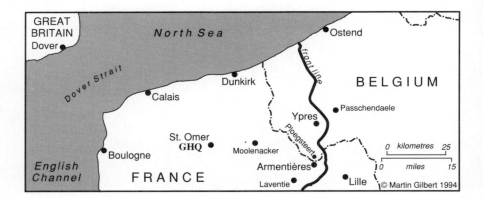

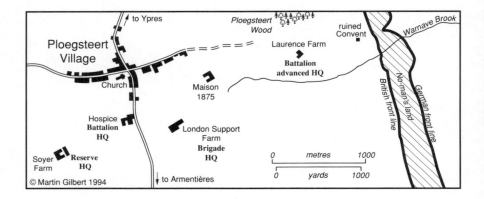

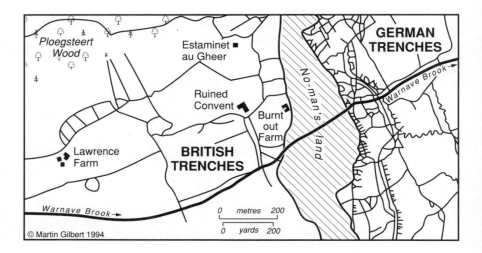

INDEX